INDIA AND
THE WTO

INDIA AND THE WTO

Aaditya Mattoo and Robert M. Stern,
Editors

**A copublication of the World Bank
and Oxford University Press**

Cover photo credit: AFP/CORBIS.

A textile worker puts a thread through an embroidery machine on display at Garmentech International 2000, a garment technology trade fair in New Delhi billed as Asia's largest-ever such fair.

CONTENTS

Figures

Tables

PREFACE

India's increasing engagement in the international economy has created a growing awareness that multilateral trade negotiations can and must be used to serve development goals. At the same time, India is a developing economy of key importance in the World Trade Organization, and it played a pivotal role in the negotiation and design of the Doha Development Agenda. The chapters in this volume are intended to provide new information and analysis to policymakers and other stakeholders in India, and to assist them in articulating their interests and in developing negotiating strategies. Because the issues raised in the context of the Doha Development Agenda are critical to both industrial and developing countries, we hope that this volume will be of much wider interest.

We would like to thank the United Kingdom government's Department for International Development, India's National Council of Applied Economic Research (NCAER), the University of Michigan, and the World Bank for their financial and administrative support. We are also grateful to Philip English, Bernard Hoekman, and Rakesh Mohan for their guidance on different aspects of the project; Tercan Baysan, Ezra Benethan, Garry Pursell, Maurice Schiff, and particularly Jayanta Roy for their valuable comments on the manuscript; Rajesh Chadha and his colleagues at the NCAER and Malina Savova for their help in organizing the New Delhi conference at which earlier versions of the articles were presented; Robb Sims for editorial assistance; Judith Jackson, Santiago Pombo-Bejarano, Melissa Edeburn, and Ilma Kramer for their assistance in producing the final manuscript, managing production of the book, and coordinating printing of the book.

Aaditya Mattoo
The World Bank
June 18, 2003

Robert M. Stern
University of Michigan

INTRODUCTION AND OVERVIEW

Aaditya Mattoo and Robert M. Stern

The chapters in this volume focus on the issues of central importance in the negotiation and design of the Doha Development Agenda, which was approved at the WTO Ministerial Meeting held in Doha, Qatar, in November 2001, and which launched a new round of multilateral trade negotiations.[1] India played a pivotal role in the Doha meeting on its own behalf and on behalf of other developing countries. This volume is intended especially to clarify India's interests in the Doha Development Agenda, which coincide in many respects with the interests of other developing countries, and to assist in the development of negotiating strategies.

The topics covered in this volume span the Doha Development Agenda and include calculations of the economic effects on India and the other major developing and the industrial countries of the Uruguay Round negotiations and the prospective Doha Agenda negotiations; the implications for India and other South Asian exporting countries of abolition of the Multifibre Arrangement (MFA); services trade liberalization; telecommunications policy reform; foreign direct investment; intellectual property rights; competition policy; government procurement; technical barriers to trade; trade and the environment; and an analysis of the issues coupled with concrete proposals to inform the participation of India in the Doha Development Agenda negotiations.

In this introduction we first provide brief summaries of the individual chapters and then highlight the menu of negotiating and domestic policy positions and the benefits of India's active involvement in the Doha Agenda negotiations.

Chapter Summaries

The chapter summaries that follow are designed to give the reader an indication of the coverage and main conclusions of the chapters, and they may help the reader decide which chapters to read in depth.

In Chapter 2, "Computational Analysis of the Impact on India of the Uruguay Round and the Doha Development Agenda Negotiations," Rajesh Chadha, Drusilla Brown, Alan Deardorff, and Robert Stern note that the Indian economy experienced a major transformation during the decade of the 1990s. Apart from the impact of various unilateral economic reforms undertaken since 1991, the economy had to reorient itself to the changing multilateral trade disciplines within the newly written framework of the General Agreement on Tariffs and Trade (GATT)/World Trade Organization (WTO). The unilateral policy measures encompassed the exchange rate regime, foreign investment, external borrowing, import licensing, import tariffs, and export subsidies. The multilateral aspect of India's trade policy included India's WTO commitments regarding trade in goods and services, trade-related investment measures, and intellectual property rights. This chapter analyzes the economic effects of the Uruguay Round trade liberalization and the liberalization that might be undertaken in the Doha Development Agenda negotiations on the major industrial and developing economies and regions, including India. India's welfare gain is expected to be 0.68 percent of its 2005 gross domestic product (GDP) (an additional US$2.8 billion) when the Uruguay Round scenarios are fully implemented. When the assumed liberalization under the Doha Development Agenda is implemented, the additional welfare gain for India is an estimated 1.7 percent ($7.0 billion). Resources there would be allocated to such labor-intensive sectors as textiles; apparel; leather and leather products; and food, beverages, and tobacco. These sectors would also experience growth in output and exports. Real returns to both labor and capital would increase in the economy, insofar as the scale effect (percent change in output per firm) is positive for all manufacturing sectors, indicating that Indian firms have become more efficient than they were before. Finally, even if India undertakes unilateral trade liberalization of the order indicated in the Doha Agenda multilateral scenarios, it would benefit, although less so than with multilateral liberalization. The computational results for the other economies and regions are presented in the chapter's detailed tables.

In Chapter 3, "Implications of Multifibre Arrangement Abolition for India and South Asia," Sanjay Kathuria, Will J. Martin, and Anjali Bhardwaj provide an introduction to the economics of the MFA and use available empirical evidence to examine the impact of the MFA on exports of textiles and clothing, focusing particularly on India. A review of the basic economics of the MFA shows the discriminatory character of the arrangement. Although exporting countries can gain from quota rents, much of the gain is likely to be offset by losses in exports to unrestricted markets and by efficiency losses resulting from inability to put resources to their best uses, or to be shared with industrial country importers. The chapter draws on empirical work by Kathuria and Bhardwaj (1998), which uses the concept of an export tax equivalent (ETE), to provide comprehensive estimates of the extent to which Indian textiles and clothing exports are restricted by the MFA. It provides new results on the magnitude of the ETEs, which suggest that they increased in 1999/00, after staying at lower levels for a couple of years.

Although the abolition of MFA quotas in 2005 will create opportunities for India and other developing economies, it will also expose them to additional competition from formerly restrained exporters. Countries that use the opportunity to streamline their policies and improve their competitiveness are likely to increase their gains from quota abolition, and the Indian context is used in particular to illustrate the need for a sound policy response. It is further shown that South Asia as a whole would gain from quota abolition, although experiences may differ depending on the nature of domestic reforms in individual countries.

In Chapter 4, "Services Issues and Liberalization in the Doha Development Agenda Negotiations: A Case Study of India," Rajesh Chadha notes that the General Agreement on Trade in Services (GATS) negotiated in the Uruguay Round is the first multilateral agreement to provide legally enforceable rights to trade in a wide range of services. Although very little liberalization was actually achieved in the Uruguay Round, GATS established the institutional structure for negotiating liberalization in the future. Chadha argues that GATS provides India and other developing countries with an opportunity to integrate into the global economy through adoption of more liberal policies with regard to trade in services. Both the developing and the industrial countries would gain through liberalization of various service sectors. Inefficiencies in the service sectors have a negative effect on the export competitiveness of agriculture and manufacturing sectors through forward linkages. Chadha examines salient features of India's commitments under GATS and a study of India's success in software services. Unilateral moves by the Indian Government toward liberalizing imports of computer software and hardware along with facilitating the inflow of foreign direct investment into these sectors during the 1990s have been the major contributors to this success.

In Chapter 5, "Telecommunications Policy Reform in India," Rajat Kathuria, Harsha Vardhana Singh, and Anita Soni note that telecommunications reform policies everywhere have recognized that exposing the incumbent firm to competition from new firms will positively influence the efficiency of service provision and enhance the process of telecommunications network expansion and service development. The question is no longer whether to have competition, but how quickly competition should be ushered in and under what conditions.

Following the announcement of the National Telecom Policy, which sought private-sector participation in the Indian telecommunications market, liberalization was initially riddled with uncertainty. This resulted especially from jurisdictional disputes between the Department of Telecom Service and the Telecom Regulatory Authority of India. This situation has now changed and more open competition has been allowed. Clear open access and interconnection guidelines among operators have created an enabling environment for an increase in tele-density and a quantum expansion in reach.

Telecom technologies and services and the market structure for India's telecommunications sector are changing rapidly. The authors stress that telecom policies should ensure that services provided are affordable and efficient, and should cater to both the demand for telephony by the general public and the demand for value-added and high-bandwidth services made possible by modern technologies. Furthermore, policies should ensure that the transition from the present regulatory regime be managed so that there is no conflict between the mandates of different regulatory bodies, such as the bodies for telecom and competition policy. It also must be recognized that the nature of policy planning has changed because of the introduction of increased competition in the market.

In Chapter 6, "Economic Impact of Foreign Direct Investment in South Asia," Pradeep Agrawal notes that India's policy toward foreign direct investment (FDI) has changed several times since the 1950s, thus showing a lack of clarity or consensus about its true economic impact on the national economy. He analyzes the effect of FDI inflows on investment by national investors and on GDP growth, using panel data from five South Asian countries: Bangladesh, India, Nepal, Pakistan, and Sri Lanka.

Agrawal finds that increases in the FDI inflows in South Asia were associated with a manifold increase in the investment by national investors, which suggests strong complementarity between foreign and domestic investment. Furthermore, the impact of FDI inflows on the GDP growth rate was found to be insignificant prior to 1990, but strongly positive over the 1990–96 period, which supports the view that FDI is more beneficial in more open economies. Agrawal also reports that, since 1980, FDI inflows contributed more to GDP growth in South Asia than did an equal amount of foreign borrowing.

In Chapter 7, "An Indian Perspective on WTO Rules on Foreign Direct Investment," Satya P. Das describes India's official stance at the WTO on the issue of FDI and examines what India's stance ought to be. He begins with provisions on FDI that are already encoded in existing WTO agreements, namely, in the GATS and in the Agreement on Trade-related Investment Measures (TRIMs). Das also summarizes the views of various member countries, including India, toward FDI provisions in the WTO, as expressed in documents submitted to the WTO December 1999 (Seattle) and November 2001 (Doha) meetings.

Das reviews India's FDI policies since its independence from British rule in 1947, with an emphasis on recent policy changes. He documents data on FDI flows into India relative to other Southeast Asian countries, noting that FDI into India entered a phase of absolute decline from 1997 to 2000. The only other country that witnessed a decline in FDI in his sample countries is Malaysia. Malaysia, however, was hit by currency crises whereas India was not. Thus this phase of India's inward FDI should worry policymakers. India's FDI reforms are obviously not sufficient to attract foreign firms in increasing numbers. Das outlines the welfare gains from FDI inflows as well as the gains from technology transfer gains from FDI and the possible losses in terms of adverse effects on domestic entrepreneurship, the environment, and so forth. He briefly reviews the empirical evidence on the effects of FDI on a host country and on India in particular. After weighing the benefits and costs of FDI and the history of policy discretion by Indian policymakers, Das concludes that India should be forthcoming toward multilateral rules on FDI. This is very different from—indeed opposite of—the official position of India toward the WTO and FDI.

In Chapter 8, "India as User and Creator of Intellectual Property: The Challenges Post-Doha," Arvind Subramanian notes that although external pressure to change intellectual property (IP) regimes has abated, India faces other challenges not only as a net user and importer but as a potential net creator of IP. He outlines the responses to five future challenges. First, India should consider revising its draft IP legislation so that Trade-Related Aspects of Intellectual Property Rights (TRIPS) obligations can serve as a mechanism for enforcing its market access rights in the WTO. Second, compulsory licensing and competition policy regimes need to be implemented expeditiously to mitigate some of the most egregious effects of TRIPS. Third, India should seek changes in the TRIPS agreement to enable it to contribute to significant public health crises, such as the AIDS crisis in Africa. Fourth, India needs to identify where its interests lie in relation to the new technologies (i.e., plants, biotechnology), and appropriately to adapt IP rights legislation as well as complementary institutions that would allow the benefits of these technologies to be harnessed while minimizing attendant risks. Finally, establishing workable domestic systems for protecting intellectual property and resources created in India would serve as a basis for seeking their replication internationally.

In Chapter 9, "Trade, Investment, and Competition Policy: An Indian Perspective," Aditya Bhattacharjea notes that the interaction among trade, investment, and competition policies is a relative newcomer on the WTO agenda. Two working groups were set up by the 1996 Singapore Ministerial Conference to study the issues, and the issues studied by the working groups may well be on the negotiating agenda after the next ministerial conference in September 2003. In a parallel development, the Indian Parliament recently passed a new competition law to replace the 1969 Monopolies and Restrictive Trade Practices (MRTP) Act. Bhattacharjea undertakes an integrated review of the international debate and India's new and old legislation, in light of the theoretical literature on trade policy under imperfect competition and recent empirical research in India. He surveys merger trends and the regulation of anticompetitive conduct and points out the ineffectiveness of many MRTP provisions, the long delays in rendering judgments, the existence of other government policies that encourage price-fixing, and the apparent absence of exclusionary vertical arrangements that would impede market access to imports. He also notes that some Indian industries have found MRTP injunctions against alleged predatory pricing by foreign producers easier to obtain and more effective than antidumping remedies.

Contesting the conventional wisdom that more competition is always better, Bhattacharjea reviews some theoretical results on welfare-decreasing domestic and foreign entry under oligopoly, and points to indirect Indian evidence that liberalization of entry barriers in conjunction with tardy trade liberalization might have caused fragmentation of industrial capacities and inefficient investment decisions. He shows that the Indian approach to predatory pricing has ignored some basic conceptual issues, allowing it to be used for protectionist purposes. Finally, he examines the provisions of the new Indian Competition Act and suggests a course of action for India both domestically and at the WTO. This course of action involves implementing the act in phases; building technical expertise; carefully scrutinizing cartels, entry, and mergers involving foreign firms; and taking a more relaxed attitude to domestic mergers. Consequently he makes a case for resisting the national treatment clause in possible multilateral agreements on investment and competition.

In Chapter 10, "India's Accession to the Government Procurement Agreement: Identifying Costs and Benefits," Vivek Srivastava notes that the Government Procurement Agreement (GPA) is a plurilateral agreement with 27 signatories, and that 18 WTO members have observer status. There are two potential sources of benefits for the signatories to the GPA. One is through better market access and gains from trade, and the second is through the cost savings and quality gains likely to result from the procurement disciplines imposed by the agreement. It appears that India is willing to negotiate an agreement on transparency in government procurement, but it is opposed to the extension of this to a market access agreement. Even with respect to this limited agenda, a major problem is the inclusion of state governments and public sector undertakings within the ambit of the agreement. Although this has not been documented (most likely, not calculated), implicit in this decision is the assumption that the costs of entering into an agreement like the existing GPA, and of including state governments and public enterprises in a transparency agreement, outweigh the possible benefits.

Srivastava describes the important features of the GPA, compares them with Indian procurement practices, and discusses the possible costs of switching to the GPA disciplines. He provides some estimates of benefit to India on the assumption that gains from market access are likely to be small and that the only significant source of gain is from the potential saving of government resources resulting from better procurement practices. Thus he focuses on the direct gains that could accrue exclusively as a result of reduced domestic procurement costs resulting from the disciplines imposed by the GPA. His estimates reveal that benefits could range from approximately Rs. 80 billion (US$1.7 billion) if only the central government is included, to approximately Rs. 105 billion (US$2.3 billion) if state governments are also included—a significant 0.4 percent to 0.5 percent of GDP. Although there may be some costs resulting from the possible misuse or overuse of the domestic review provision, the costs of switching over to the GPA disciplines are likely to be small. Srivastava concludes, therefore, that at the very least India should have no hesitation in negotiating a transparency agreement and would benefit from it.

In Chapter 11, "Technical Barriers to Trade and the Role of Indian Standard-Setting Institutions," Mohammed Saqib notes that the Sanitary and Phytosanitary (SPS) Agreement and the Technical Barriers to Trade (TBT) Agreement (which relate to the development or application of standards-related measures that affect trade) define the international rights and obligations of WTO member countries. These agreements are based on the principle that countries have a right to adopt and apply standards-related measures as long as they do not restrict international trade more than is necessary or unavoidable.

Despite growing concerns that certain technical or phytosanitary measures may be inconsistent with WTO provisions and may unfairly impede exports, the Indian Government is not well positioned to address these issues. Trade associations and key government officials face difficulty in defining the nature and scope of the problem that these measures could create for India's exports, partly because of the complex nature of the issues themselves. The preliminary evidence indicates that exports of a broad range of commodities could be affected, which could result in a variety of negative trade effects.

Although the Indian Government's approach to addressing the SPS and TBT measures has been improving, it still has many weaknesses. Even though a number of government, quasi-government, trade, regulatory, and research entities have some responsibility for addressing SPS and TBT measures, no single entity exists for providing direction and coordination to their overall efforts. As a result these entities find it difficult to coordinate their activities because their roles are not clearly defined. There is no composite evaluation process so the government entities lack comprehensive data on the measures being addressed and on the progress that has been made.

India's participation and coordination with international standard-setting systems (e.g., ISO/CODEX) apparently has been poor. Domestically there are multiple standards, laboratories are ill equipped, implementation authorities are understaffed, and the regulatory system is complex. There is a dire need to upgrade the whole system, and that will require financial and technical support at the international level.

In Chapter 12, "Trade and Environment: Doha and Beyond," Veena Jha notes that enhancing understanding and strengthening policy coordination in the areas of trade, environment, and development are of key interest to India and other developing countries. Doing so has become particularly relevant since the beginning of the 1990s for several domestic and external reasons, including the economic liberalization policy that India has followed since 1991, the increasing importance of the environment as a factor influencing market access and export competitiveness, and the inclusion of environment on the international trade agenda of the WTO. The Doha Declaration has brought trade and environment within the realm of negotiations in the WTO, so it is even more urgent to develop expertise on this issue to safeguard India's national interest.

India has followed a defensive agenda on trade and environment, strongly resisting calls for mainstreaming environment in WTO negotiations and for changes in WTO rules to make allowances for environmental standards. On the other hand, India has advocated changes in TRIPS to accommodate the environment and has advocated that safeguards in existing agreements be tightened further to ensure that measures taken for environmental reasons are not used against its trade interests. Although the Doha Declaration takes account of some of its interests, there are several issues (such as ecolabeling) on which India did not wish to see any negotiations.

Although the new negotiating agenda may not be entirely in India's interest, India has to build capacity and identify specific issues on which it can derive some benefit. In this process of give and take, capacity building and expertise building are of key importance. Jha concludes by providing some details of the specific issues on which India needs to build capacity.

In Chapter 13, "India and the Multilateral Trading System Post-Doha: Defensive or Proactive?" Aaditya Mattoo and Arvind Subramanian argue that India and other developing countries should engage more actively in the multilateral trading system. The argument is based on four reasons. First, engagement can facilitate domestic reform and enhance access for India's exports. India is now at a critical juncture. It is an increasingly willing reformer, but is confronted by domestic opposition to reform. At the same time, market access remains impeded in areas of major export interest. Multilateral engagement pits these two elements against each other constructively. On the one hand, domestic reform would be helped if the government could demonstrate that there were payoffs in terms of increased access abroad. The gainers from the increased access—whether exporters of textiles, software, professional services, or other products—could represent a countervailing voice to groups that resist reform. On the other hand, the need to demonstrate external payoffs to secure greater openness at home makes India a credible bargainer and could help induce trading partners to open their own markets.

Second, engagement can serve as a commitment to good policies. The experience of unconstrained choices in Indian trade policy has not been salutary. External commitments can foster good policies in two respects: providing guarantees against reversal of current policies and credibly promising future reform. For instance, in recent years India has reversed some of its tariff liberalization, which could have been prevented by more meaningful tariff bindings. India also failed in services sectors to take advantage of multilateral commitments to lend credibility to future reform programs. Such precommitment can help strike a balance between reluctance to unleash competition immediately and desire not to be constrained by the weakness of domestic industry or the influence of vested interests.

Third, engagement can serve as a means of securing market access rights that have been established. In a situation of asymmetric power, a rules-based system protects the weaker party, albeit imperfectly. The WTO dispute-settlement system thus far has enabled developing countries to enforce their rights. Although this experience affords some comfort, there is increasing concern that the required elimination of quotas on textiles and clothing may not happen on time and may be difficult to enforce. Mattoo and Subramanian argue that in such an eventuality India can enforce its rights by threatening to wield an effective retaliatory weapon: withdrawing its TRIPS obligations.

Fourth, multilateral engagement can serve as a bulwark against regionalism. The proliferation of regional agreements is having a serious if unrecognized impact on India's trade. A particularly stark example relates to the potential trade diversion consequences of the North American Free Trade Agreement. India has a strong interest in multilateral tariff reduction to neutralize this policy-induced disadvantage.

Overall, the value of multilateral engagement might be limited if prospects for securing increased market access are dim. But with the conclusion of the WTO Ministerial Meeting in Doha and the launching of a new round of multilateral trade negotiations in 2002, Mattoo and Subramanian conclude that the challenge for India is to open its markets in return for improved access. Success in this regard is not ensured, but its chances can be improved if India aligns itself with countries that press for sound open policies.

The Negotiating and Domestic Policy Positions of India

In Chapter 13 Mattoo and Subramanian review the major challenges that India faces in designing and implementing their domestic and external policies in the context of their engagement in the Doha Development Agenda negotiations. In their table 13.9, they recommend the following strategies:[2]

- *Industrial tariffs*—Reduce own bound and actual tariffs and seek to reduce tariffs in other countries, especially in textiles, clothing, and footwear.
- *Agriculture*—End domestic policies that discriminate against agriculture. Push for liberalization on a global basis and consider joining the Cairns group.
- *Services*—Further domestic liberalization, emphasizing competition more than a change of ownership, and greater use of the GATS to precommit to future liberalization. Create intermodal negotiating linkages to enhance the scope for export of services through greater mobility of labor and capital. Strengthen domestic regulations and push for stronger multilateral disciplines on regulatory barriers to trade.
- *Electronic commerce*—The current WTO decision on duty-free treatment has little meaning because quotas and discriminatory internal taxation are still permitted in many cases. Therefore, widen and deepen the scope of cross-border supply commitments under the GATS on market access (prohibiting quotas) and national treatment (prohibiting discriminatory taxation) to ensure that current openness continues in areas of export interest, such as software and business services.
- *TRIPS*—Change IP legislation to ensure that TRIPS benefits can be withdrawn in the event of noncompliance by partners with commitments that affect India's exports adversely. Institute workable systems for protecting traditional knowledge domestically to seek the replication of such systems internationally. Use new competition policy and judicious compulsory licensing to mitigate the egregious effects of the TRIPS agreement.
- *Preferential agreements*—Argue for the inclusion of a compensation provision for third countries adversely affected by trade diversion.
- *Competition policy*—Strengthen the implementation of new competition law and be open to the development of meaningful multilateral disciplines, which ideally also would cover antidumping and international cartels.

- *Standards*—Strengthen disciplines on mutual recognition agreements to ensure that they are nondiscriminatory. Push for multilateral disciplines on domestic regulations in goods and services based on the necessity test. Improve domestic standards. On labor standards, be proactive in the International Labour Organisation while resisting attempts to bring the issue into the WTO.
- *Government procurement*—Be open to creation of multilateral disciplines, but link them to the elimination of barriers to trade in goods and services so that foreign procurement contracts can be contested in areas of comparative advantage, such as labor services.
- *Investment*—Be willing to discuss multilateral disciplines, but examine the case for preserving discretion beyond that provided by a strengthened competition policy.
- *Antidumping*—Curtail domestic use of antidumping. Argue for drastic reform of multilateral antidumping rules to eliminate current protectionist use, ideally by subjecting the rules to competition policy.

In the final analysis, India's engagement in the Doha Development Agenda negotiations and the associated changes in domestic and external policies needed to achieve its objectives will require the strong and consistent backing of government and political parties and leaders. Many of the issues and requisite policies are fairly clear, whereas others require greater analysis and engagement by stakeholders and researchers. The main question, however, is whether the variegated domestic interests are able to coalesce and support a proactive rather than a defensive posture under the Doha Agenda.

Endnotes

1. The text of the Ministerial Declaration of the Doha Ministerial Conference is available at www.wto.org.
2. In this connection see also Srinivasan (2001) and Panagariya (2002).

References

Kathuria, Sanjay, and A. Bhardwaj. 1998. "Export Quotas and Policy Constraints in the Indian Textile and Garment Industries." Policy Research Working Paper 2012. World Bank, Policy Research Department, Washington, D.C.

Panagariya, Arvind. 2002. "India at Doha: Retrospect and Prospect." *Economic and Political Weekly* 37(January 26): 279–84.

Srinivasan, T. N. 2001. "India's Reform of External Sector Policies and Future Multilateral Trade Negotiations." Discussion Paper 830 (June). Yale University, Economic Growth Center, New Haven, Connecticut.

2

COMPUTATIONAL ANALYSIS OF THE IMPACT ON INDIA OF THE URUGUAY ROUND AND THE DOHA DEVELOPMENT AGENDA NEGOTIATIONS

*Rajesh Chadha, Drusilla K. Brown,
Alan V. Deardorff, and Robert M. Stern*

The Indian economy experienced a major transformation during the decade of the 1990s. Apart from the effects of various unilateral economic reforms undertaken since 1991, the economy has had to reorient itself to the changing multilateral trade discipline within the newly written framework of the General Agreement on Tariffs and Trade (GATT) and the World Trade Organization (WTO). The unilateral policy measures have encompassed exchange-rate policy, foreign investment, external borrowing, import licensing, import tariffs, and export subsidies. The multilateral aspect of India's trade policy pertains to India's WTO commitments with regard to trade in goods and services, trade-related investment measures, and intellectual property rights.

This chapter is an outgrowth of a collaborative program of computable general equilibrium modeling research that began in 1994 between the National Council of Applied Economic Research (NCAER), New Delhi, and the University of Michigan (UM), Ann Arbor. We would like to express our gratitude to S. L. Rao and Rakesh Mohan for active and sustained support of the NCAER-UM collaborative research effort. Special thanks are due to K. L. Krishna, Arvind Panagariya, V. N. Pandit, and T. N. Srinivasan for having provided valuable comments on our earlier work. Thanks are also due to Sanjib Pohit who participated in the earlier work. Devender Pratap, Bikram Prakas Ghosh, and Praveen Sachdeva of the NCAER and Alan Fox and Soraphol Tulayasathien of UM provided excellent research assistance.

Multilateral trade liberalization under the auspices of the Uruguay Round Agreement and the Doha Development Agenda is aimed at reducing tariff and nontariff barriers on international trade. The purpose of this chapter is to provide a computational analysis of the effect of such changes in trade barriers on the economic welfare, on trade, and on the intersectoral allocation of resources in India and its major trading partners.

A liberal international trade policy is now widely accepted as an important part of growth and development policy. Growth, in turn, is the key to permanently alleviating poverty (Winters 2001). It is expected that trade liberalization will stimulate production in labor-intensive sectors in India. Productive resources would then be allocated more efficiently than during the preliberalization period because India would specialize in the sectors where it has comparative advantage. Of course, there may be transitional costs resulting from the intersectoral movement of factors of production. Beyond such welfare gains, trade liberalization is also expected to have a procompetitive effect on domestic firms, which results in additional gains from the economies of large-scale production. When firms are protected from foreign competition through tariff and nontariff barriers, they may take advantage of their market power by raising their prices and reducing their domestic sales. The result is that the protected firms may produce below their minimum cost, efficient plant size. Trade liberalization then should bring about competitive pressures on the formerly protected firms and induce them to raise production and productivity and to achieve more efficient plant size and lower per-unit costs. Thus gains in economic welfare are expected to come from the improved allocation of resources and from the lower prices and greater variety available to consumers and firms. Realizing economies of scale in manufacturing also reinforces the welfare-enhancing effect.

This chapter is organized as follows. The next section deals with the experience of India during the 1990s with regard to its unilateral liberalization moves and to changes induced through multilateral trade negotiations. In the third section we present a computational analysis of the impact on India of the Uruguay Round negotiations and the current Doha Development Agenda negotiations. We used a specially designed version of the National Council of Applied Economic Research (NCAER)-University of Michigan (UM) computable general equilibrium (CGE) model of world production and trade for this purpose. Conclusions and policy implications are discussed in the final section.

India in the Changing Global Trade Scenario

Even though India's trade regime began to be liberalized in the late 1970s, 93 percent of its local production of internationally tradable goods were still protected by some type of quantitative restrictions (QRs) on imports as of 1990/91 (Pursell 1996).

The QR coverage was 94 percent for agricultural and 90 percent for manufactured intermediate and capital goods. Import licenses were granted subject to indigenous clearance—that is, a proof that there was no source of indigenous supply. India had one of the most restrictive import tariff structures among developing countries. The import-weighted tariff rate was 87 percent in 1989/90, accompanied by a collection rate of 51 percent. There was a rapid increase in import tariffs in the latter half of the 1980s. Such a protective regime led India into a sustained phase of allocating its resources inefficiently. Its share in world trade declined from 2 percent in 1950/51, to 1 percent in 1965/66, and to 0.5 percent by 1973/74. Its share continued to hover around that figure until 1990/91.

India's trade policy regime was quite complex until the beginning of the 1990s. There were various categories of importers, import licenses, and methods of importing. The regime's details were contained in 19 Appendixes and spanned more than 200 pages. The Import and Export Policy, introduced in 1990, was replaced by the Export and Import (EXIM) Policy, which took effect on April 1, 1992.[1] The content was reduced to 20 pages in the latter policy, thus making matters simpler for exporters and importers. The new EXIM Policy contained negative-list imports subject to licensing.[2] Almost all consumer goods remained subject to import licensing.

The first stage of India's reforms after 1991 continued to focus on manufacturing while largely ignoring agriculture. The share of value added in the manufacturing sector protected by QRs declined from 90 percent to 47 percent by May 1992 and to 36 percent by May 1995 (Pursell 1996, p. 5). The corresponding decline was much less in agriculture—from 94 percent to 93 percent by May 1992 and to 84 percent by May 1995.

It has been estimated that about one-third of the value of India's imports in 1998/99 were still subject to some type of nontariff barrier (Mehta 1998, pp. 35–36). In April 1998, about 30 percent of the 10-digit tariff lines (3,068 of 10,281) under the Harmonized System (HS) of India's trade classification were subject to nontariff barriers.[3] The 3,068 restricted tariff lines include 1,379 lines for consumer goods. The import value of these consumer goods is only 0.2 percent of India's total imports, which reflects the relatively high degree of restrictions. The import of 40 percent of agricultural products was still restricted because these were classified as consumer goods.

Prior to 1991 India's import tariff rates were among the highest in the world. The Tax Reforms Committee, chaired by Raja J. Chelliah, proposed that the import-weighted average duty rate should go down from 87 percent in 1989/90 to 45 percent in 1995/96 and further to 25 percent by 1998/99 (Government of India 1993). India has lowered its average (unweighted) applied tariff rate for the overall economy from 125 percent in 1990/91 to 71 percent in 1993/94, to 41 percent

TABLE 2.1   India: Tariff Structure, 1990–91 to 1997–98 (Percent)

	1990/91[a] Applied[e]	1993/94[b] Applied[e]	1995/96 Applied[e]	1996/97[c] Applied[e]	1997/98[d] Applied[e]
Average unweighted					
Agriculture	113	43	27	26	26
Mining	100	70	30	26	25
Manufacturing	126	73	42	40	36
Whole economy	125	71	41	39	35
Index of dispersion[f]	32	42	47	49	42
Maximum tariff rate[g]	355	85	50	52	45
Average weighted[h]	87	47	25	22	20

a. Prior to the reform package of July 1991. Includes auxiliary duty, mostly at 45 percent.

b. The auxiliary duty was merged with the basic customs duty in the 1993/94 budget.

c. Includes special rate of 2 percent.

d. Includes special rate of 5 percent.

e. Effective most-favored nation rate—that is, actual rates applied where basic rates have been reduced by exempt rates. However, many exempt rates cannot be incorporated, such as where the exempt rate applies to only a part of the HS six-digit tariff line. The effective rate also excludes specific exemptions.

f. Index of dispersion for the whole economy as measured by the coefficient of variation, percentage points.

g. Higher than the so-called maximum rate is applied to a few items; in 1997/98, to 0.4 percent of tariff lines.

h. Weighted by 1992/93 import values.

Notes: Tariff averages consider only those tariff lines with ad valorem rates. Year beginning April 1. Classification used is based on the International Standard Industrial Classifications (ISIC): agriculture = ISIC 1; mining = ISIC 2; manufacturing, including food processing = ISIC 3.

Source: WTO 1998, p. 46.

in 1995/96, and to 35 percent in 1997/98 (table 2.1). The corresponding reduction in the import-weighted average has been from 87 percent in 1990/91 to 47 percent in 1993/94, to 25 percent in 1995/96, and to 20 percent in 1997/98, thus exceeding the recommendations of the Chelliah Committee.[4] The maximum tariff rate has declined from 355 percent in 1990/91 to 45 percent in 1997/98 and was scheduled to fall to 40 percent in 1999/00.

The World Bank estimates of changes in tariffs on consumer, intermediate, and capital goods are given in table 2.2. Although the average import-weighted tariff rate on consumer goods was reduced from 153 percent in 1990/91 to 25 percent in 1997/98, a large portion of this category still remained protected by QRs.

The import of some restricted items was liberalized through freely transferable special import licenses (SILs). Apart from being used as a step toward liberalization, the SIL regime also provided incentives to large established exporters; exporters of

TABLE 2.2   India: Tariffs by Products, Average Import-Weighted Rates, 1990–98 (Percent)

	1990/91	1992/93	1993/94	1994/95	1995/96	1996/97	1997/98
Consumer goods	153	131	86	48	36	33	25
Intermediate goods	77	55	42	31	22	19	18
Capital goods	97	74	50	37	29	29	24

Note: Year beginning April 1.

Source: WTO 1998, p. 49.

electronic and telecommunications equipment, diamonds, gems, and jewelry; and manufacturers who have acquired the prescribed quality certification.

The coverage of tariff lines has gradually expanded since their introduction in 1992/93. Typically tariff lines have moved from the restricted list to the SIL list, and thereafter to the free list. SILs were concentrated in industrial products with nearly 56 percent of the HS eight-digit tariff lines under SIL as of April 1, 1997. The corresponding coverage was 30 percent for textile and clothing products and 15 percent for agricultural products, including fisheries (WTO 1998, p. 66). The SIL coverage has been extended systematically since April 1997, moving various items from the restricted list to the SIL list and from there to the open general license (OGL) list.

Various items also have been liberalized from two of the most restricted groups—namely, agricultural products and consumer goods. The recently freed agricultural products include dairy items, fish, and a variety of processed foods, and the consumer goods include toiletries, electronic items, and cooking ranges. In the WTO balance-of-payments committee India's unrestrained use of QRs was strongly challenged by the European Union, the United States, and other industrial countries in December 1995.[5]

India is a founding member of the 1947 General Agreement on Tariffs and Trade (GATT) and of the WTO, which came into effect January 1, 1995. By virtue of its WTO membership, India automatically receives most-favored-nation (MFN) treatment and national treatment from all WTO members for its exports, and vice versa. Its participation in this increasingly rule-based system is aimed toward ensuring more stability and predictability in its international trade.

The Uruguay Round resulted in increased tariff-binding commitments by developing countries. India bound 67 percent of its tariff lines compared with

6 percent of its lines prior to this round. All agricultural tariff lines and nearly 62 percent of the tariff lines for industrial goods are now bound. The unbound lines include some consumer goods and industrial items. Ceiling bindings for industrial goods are generally at 40 percent ad valorem for finished goods and 25 percent on intermediate goods, machinery, and equipment. The phased reduction to these bound levels is to be achieved during the 10-year period that began in 1995. Tariff rates on equipment covered under the Information Technology Agreement and on software are to be brought down to zero by 2005. The only exception is in textiles, for which India has kept the option of reverting to the 1990 tariff levels in case the Agreement on Textiles and Clothing does not fully materialize by 2005. It may be seen in table 2.3 that applied tariff rates in India are below the Uruguay Round bound levels. The differential is greatest in the cases of agriculture and unprocessed primary goods.

On balance-of-payment grounds, quantitative restrictions on imports were being maintained for 1,429 tariff lines at the eight-digit level. These include items relating to textiles, agriculture, consumer goods, and a variety of manufactured goods. With the improvement in India's balance of payments since 1991, India was asked to phase out its QRs. Based on presentations before the balance-of-payments

TABLE 2.3   India: Bound Tariff Rates and Applied Rates of Duty (Percent)

	Bound Rate of Duty[a] by Year 2005	Applied Rate of Duty[b] 1997/98
Average unweighted tariff *(percent)*		
Agriculture (ISIC 1)	94	26
Mining (ISIC 2)	36	25
Manufacturing (ISIC 3, includes food processing)	52	36
Whole economy	54	35
Average unweighted tariff by stage of processing *(percent)*		
Unprocessed	74	25
Semiprocessed	44	35
Processed	56	37

a. Includes only items bound during the Uruguay Round. The bound rates do not include the commitments under the Information Technology Agreement.

b. Effective most-favored nation rate—that is, actual rates applied where basic rates have been reduced by exempt rates. Many exempt rates cannot be incorporated, however, such as where the exempt rate applies to only a part of the HS six-digit tariff line. The effective rate also excludes specific exemptions.

Note: Tariff averages consider only those tariff lines with ad valorem rates, year beginning April 1.

Source: WTO 1998, p. 54.

committee and subsequent consultations with India's main trading partners, an agreement was reached to phase out QRs by 2001.

In line with the Agreement on Trade-related Investment Measures (TRIMs), India has reported to the WTO the TRIMs that it has maintained. These measures were to be eliminated by January 1, 2000. Under the Information Technology Agreement tariffs were to be brought down to zero on 95 HS six-digit tariff lines by the year 2000, on 4 more tariff lines by 2003, on another 2 tariff lines by 2004, and on the balance of 116 tariff lines in the year 2005. Under the Agreement on Technical Barriers to Trade and the Agreement on Sanitary and Phytosanitary Measures, India was also committed to establishing and administering national standards and technical regulations, keeping in view the basic precepts of MFN status, national treatment, and transparency.

With respect to services, the General Agreement on Trade in Services (GATS) has a "positive-list" approach that allows WTO members to take on obligations in the sector of their choice. India has made commitments in 33 activities, compared with an average of 23 activities for all developing countries. India's objective in the service negotiations was to offer entry to foreign service providers in cases considered to be most advantageous in terms of capital inflows, technology, and employment.

Notwithstanding the recent liberalization of the foreign direct investment regime, restrictions on these investments continue to impede market access in the service sectors. Foreign equity is limited to 49 percent in some of the major components of the telecommunications sector (including basic cellular, mobile, paging, and other wireless services). The corresponding limit is 20 percent in the banking sector. Other service areas, such as shipping, roads, ports, and air, are beginning to open up but foreign participation remains low. Railways remain one of the six areas reserved for the public sector, although some private sector participation is encouraged in some offline activities. The insurance sector remained closed to private investors until recently. Opening of the service sectors to international competition under the GATS is expected to make these sectors more efficient, which in turn would lead to gains in India's gross domestic product (GDP).[6]

It is evident from the preceding discussion that India has undertaken a relatively broad liberalization of its trade policy compared with that of the pre-1991 period. This is true for both its unilateral and multilateral reform commitments. But as Srinivasan (2001) has stressed, much more remains to be done, particularly because tariff barriers remain relatively high and some consumer goods imports remain constrained.

With the foregoing as background, we turn now to a computational analysis of the trade-liberalization provisions in the Uruguay Round and of some possible liberalization efforts in the Doha Development Agenda negotiations.

Computational Analysis of India's Trade Reforms in a Global Setting

The empirical evidence from a number of studies points to a strong and significant effect of openness to trade on growth performance (Srinivasan 1998). Thus, it is expected that the multilateral liberalization of trade should benefit countries of the world in general. In this section we will analyze the impact of trade liberalization provisions in the Uruguay Round and some possible liberalization efforts in the Doha Development Agenda negotiations. For comparative purposes, we shall also analyze hypothetical scenarios when only India undertakes unilateral liberalization. For this purpose we use simulation analysis to assess the potential economic effects of implementing various liberalization provisions. The simulations are based on a special version of the NCAER-UM computable general equilibrium patterned after the Michigan Model of World Production and Trade. The main features of the model are described by Brown and others (1993, 1996), Chadha and Pohit (1998), and Chadha and others (1998a,b, 1999), and the equations and other details are available on the University of Michigan Web site: www.umich.spp.edu/rsie/. The economy/region and sectoral coverage of the model are noted in tables 2.4 and 2.5.

Computational Scenarios

The main data source for the model is the Purdue University Center for Global Trade Analysis Project, "GTAP4 Data Base" (McDougall, Elbehri, and Truong 1998), which refers to 1995. For purposes of analysis we have projected this database from 1995 to 2005 to get an approximate picture of what the world will look like in 2005, assuming that the 1995 Uruguay Round (UR) Agreement had not existed. We analyzed the impact of the UR-induced changes that may occur during the 10-year implementation period after 1995 with respect to reduction/removal of tariff and nontariff barriers on trade.[7] Then we readjusted the scaled-up database of 2005 to mimic the world as it might look when the UR Agreement has been fully implemented. After that we devised some liberalization scenarios for Doha Round Development Agenda negotiations, which we refer to as the Doha Round (DR) and which involve possible reductions in tariffs on agriculture and manufacturing and reductions of barriers to services trade and to foreign direct investment.

The following are the computational scenarios:[8]

- *UR-1*—Agreement on Textiles and Clothing (ATC) is analyzed by simulating the effects of the Multifibre Arrangement (MFA) phase-out under the UR

TABLE 2.4   Economies and Regions of the Model

Economy or Region
Industrial
Australia and New Zealand
Canada
European Union and European Free Trade Association
Japan
United States
Developing
Asian
India
Sri Lanka
Rest of South Asia
China
Hong Kong, China
Republic of Korea
Singapore
Indonesia
Malaysia
Philippines
Thailand
Other
Mexico
Turkey
Central Europe
Central and South America

Agreement. This is done by reducing to zero the export tax equivalents of the MFA-affected developing economies/regions.[9]

- *UR-2*—All the economies/regions in the model reduce their bilateral import tariffs in accord with the UR Agreement on manufactures.[10]
- *UR-3*—This combines UR-1 and UR-2.

On the basis of those scenarios we adjusted the projected 2005 database for the changes brought about by the UR Agreement and ran the following scenarios for the Doha negotiating round.

- *DR-1*—All the economies/regions reduce by 33 percent their post-UR bilateral agricultural import tariffs, export subsidies, and production subsidies.
- *DR-2*—All the economies/regions reduce by 33 percent their post-UR bilateral import tariffs on minerals and manufactured products.

TABLE 2.5 Sectors of Production

Sector
Agriculture
Mining and quarrying
Food, beverages, and tobacco
Textiles
Wearing apparel
Leather products and footwear
Wood and wood products
Chemicals, rubber, plastic, and petroleum products
Nonmetallic mineral products
Metal and metal products
Transport equipment
Machinery and equipment
Other manufactures, including electronic equipment
Electricity, gas, and water
Construction
Trade and transport
Finance, business, and recreational services
Public administration, defense, education and health, and dwellings

- *DR-3*—All economies/regions reduce by 33 percent the import tariff equivalents of estimated post-UR services barriers.
- *DR-4*—This combines DR-1, DR-2, and DR-3.

Finally, for purposes of comparison with the multilateral DR scenarios, we have run the following unilateral liberalization scenarios for India alone (UNIDR):

- *UNIDR-1*—India reduces by 33 percent its post-UR agricultural import tariffs, export subsidies, and production subsidies.
- *UNIDR-2*—India reduces by 33 percent its post-UR tariffs on minerals and manufactured products.
- *UNIDR-3*—India reduces by 33 percent its tariff equivalents on services.
- *UNIDR-4*—All three scenarios (UNIDR1, UNIDR2, and UNIDR3) combined.

Uruguay Round Results

Table 2.6 provides aggregate, or economywide, results from the UR scenarios described above for the 20 economies and regions that have been modeled. The results reported include absolute changes in imports, exports, and equivalent variation (a measure of economic welfare); and percentage changes in the terms of trade, equivalent variation, real wage rate, and the real return to capital. (Disaggregated sectoral results for India for the UR-3 and DR-4 scenarios will be presented in tables 2.8 and 2.9 below.)

For help in interpreting the results, you may find it useful to review the features of the model that identify the various economic effects being captured in the different scenarios. Although the model includes the imperfect-competition features of the New Trade Theory,[11] it remains true that markets respond to trade liberalization in much the same way that they would with perfect competition. That is, when tariffs or other trade barriers are reduced in a sector, domestic buyers (both final and intermediate) switch toward imports, and the domestic competing industry contracts production while foreign exporters expand. With multilateral liberalization reducing tariffs and other trade barriers simultaneously in most sectors and countries, each country's industries share in both of these effects, expanding or contracting depending primarily on whether their protection is reduced more or less than in other sectors and countries. At the same time, countries with larger average tariff reductions than their trading partners tend to experience a real depreciation of their currencies in order to maintain a constant trade balance, so that all countries therefore experience mixtures of expanding and contracting sectors.

Worldwide these changes cause increased international demand for all sectors, with world prices rising most for those sectors where trade barriers fall the most. This in turn causes positive or negative changes in countries' terms of trade. Those countries that are net exporters of goods with the greatest degree of liberalization will experience increases in their terms of trade as the world prices of their exports rise relative to their imports. The reverse occurs for net exporters in industries where liberalization is slight (perhaps because it already happened in previous trade rounds).

The effects on the welfare of countries arise from a mixture of these terms-of-trade effects with the standard efficiency gains from trade and with additional benefits resulting from elements of the New Trade Theory. Thus we expect, on average, that the world will gain from multilateral liberalization as resources are reallocated to those sectors in each country where there is a comparative advantage. In the absence of terms-of-trade effects, these efficiency gains should raise national welfare (our "equivalent variation") for every country, although some

TABLE 2.6   Summary Results of the Uruguay Round: Change in Imports, Exports, Terms of Trade, Welfare, and the Real Return to Labor and Capital

Economy or Region	Imports (Millions)	Exports (Millions)	Terms of Trade (Percent)	Economic Welfare (Percent)	Economic Welfare (Millions)	Real Wage Rate (Percent)	Return to Capital (Percent)
Scenario UR-1: Removal of the Multi-fiber Agreement							
Industrial economies							
Australia and New Zealand	144.7	114.0	0.030	0.018	94.5	0.012	0.028
Canada	782.3	719.4	0.065	0.094	683.8	0.066	0.133
European Union and European Free Trade Association	2,517.7	2,275.1	0.055	0.058	6,320.8	0.051	0.071
Japan	−121.4	191.0	−0.050	0.004	257.1	−0.002	0.012
United States	6,497.4	4,482.0	0.148	0.095	8,608.2	0.084	0.114
Developing economies							
Asia							
India	1,517.9	1,992.1	−0.954	0.231	972.2	0.224	0.238
Sri Lanka	98.7	159.1	−1.101	0.143	23.8	0.032	0.251
Rest of South Asia	449.1	652.8	−1.088	0.263	307.4	0.207	0.319
China	1,849.7	2,760.4	−0.366	−0.161	−1,458.5	−0.120	−0.194
Hong Kong, China	1,544.3	1,364.5	0.187	−0.473	−609.2	0.121	−0.988
Republic of Korea	405.0	428.0	−0.015	0.025	142.7	0.045	0.006
Singapore	−510.4	−591.4	0.054	−0.001	−0.8	−0.025	0.020
Indonesia	147.5	207.8	−0.089	−0.005	−13.8	0.030	−0.032
Malaysia	223.0	354.0	−0.121	0.275	328.7	0.735	0.025
Philippines	2,080.9	2,513.8	−1.316	0.900	794.3	2.057	0.045
Thailand	140.3	259.0	−0.143	0.029	59.4	0.161	−0.019

TABLE 2.6   (Continued)

Economy or Region	Imports (Millions)	Exports (Millions)	Terms of Trade (Percent)	Economic Welfare (Percent)	Economic Welfare (Millions)	Real Wage Rate (Percent)	Return to Capital (Percent)
Other							
Mexico	−45.3	24.8	−0.030	−0.010	−36.6	−0.010	−0.010
Turkey	−157.3	−120.0	−0.094	−0.015	−31.6	−0.031	−0.006
Central Europe	−20.3	−0.6	−0.026	0.037	138.3	0.026	0.054
Central and South America	−162.9	−106.2	−0.050	−0.004	−73.9	−0.002	−0.006
Total	**17,380.9**	**17,679.5**			**16,506.8**		
Scenario UR-2: Tariff Reductions in Manufactures							
Industrial economies							
Australia and New Zealand	2,848.0	2,527.6	0.347	0.327	1,674.8	0.345	0.300
Canada	1,071.9	1,354.5	−0.086	0.127	926.3	0.137	0.114
European Union and European Free Trade Association	16,826.6	15,358.5	0.145	0.159	17,405.6	0.157	0.163
Japan	8,680.6	8,331.3	0.062	0.102	6,608.4	0.092	0.115
United States	12,426.0	13,459.3	−0.133	0.123	11,187.1	0.124	0.122
Developing economies							
Asia							
India	2,585.3	3,628.9	−2.099	0.446	1,875.4	0.316	0.577
Sri Lanka	98.8	106.3	−0.193	0.558	93.0	0.507	0.608
Rest of South Asia	3,454.8	4,820.1	−7.541	2.025	2,366.5	2.224	1.828
China	3,112.6	1,917.7	0.456	0.305	2,762.2	0.347	0.271
Hong Kong, China	763.5	480.1	0.254	0.360	464.1	0.346	0.373
Republic of Korea	2,858.6	2,733.2	0.068	0.422	2,403.3	0.409	0.435

TABLE 2.6   (Continued)

Economy or Region	Imports (Millions)	Exports (Millions)	Terms of Trade (Percent)	Economic Welfare (Percent)	Economic Welfare (Millions)	Real Wage Rate (Percent)	Return to Capital (Percent)
Singapore	3,539.8	3,647.5	−0.078	2.111	1,570.3	1.943	2.258
Indonesia	936.5	894.5	0.068	0.247	626.0	0.291	0.215
Malaysia	2,790.9	3,411.4	−0.563	1.919	2,293.9	1.816	1.974
Philippines	2,452.6	3,102.1	−1.989	1.917	1,691.7	1.853	1.964
Thailand	1,264.7	1,002.3	0.291	0.366	753.9	0.597	0.283
Other							
Mexico	−64.9	1.4	−0.026	0.019	66.3	0.038	0.010
Turkey	319.3	253.9	0.143	0.123	259.1	0.122	0.124
Central Europe	1,871.7	1,846.1	0.020	0.294	1,091.2	0.311	0.270
Central and South America	3,778.8	2,999.5	0.423	0.022	377.1	0.043	0.004
Total	71,616.2	71,876.4			56,496.0		
Scenario UR-3: Uruguay Round Combined Liberalization							
Industrial economies							
Australia and New Zealand	2,992.8	2,641.6	0.377	0.345	1,769.3	0.357	0.328
Canada	1,854.2	2,073.9	−0.021	0.221	1,610.1	0.202	0.247
European Union and European Free Trade Association	19,344.2	17,633.6	0.200	0.216	23,726.4	0.208	0.234
Japan	8,559.2	8,522.3	0.011	0.106	6,865.5	0.090	0.127
United States	18,923.4	17,941.3	0.014	0.218	19,795.3	0.208	0.236
Developing economies							
Asia							
India	4,103.2	5,620.9	−3.053	0.677	2,847.5	0.540	0.815

TABLE 2.6 *(Continued)*

Economy or Region	Imports (Millions)	Exports (Millions)	Terms of Trade (Percent)	Economic Welfare (Percent)	Economic Welfare (Millions)	Real Wage Rate (Percent)	Return to Capital (Percent)
Sri Lanka	197.5	265.4	−1.293	0.701	116.8	0.539	0.859
Rest of South Asia	3,903.9	5,473.0	−8.629	2.288	2,673.9	2.430	2.147
China	4,962.4	4,678.2	0.089	0.144	1,303.8	0.227	0.077
Hong Kong, China	2,307.9	1,844.7	0.442	−0.113	−145.1	0.467	−0.615
Republic of Korea	3,263.6	3,161.2	0.053	0.447	2,546.1	0.454	0.441
Singapore	3,029.4	3,056.1	−0.024	2.110	1,569.4	1.917	2.278
Indonesia	1,084.0	1,102.4	−0.021	0.242	612.2	0.321	0.183
Malaysia	3,013.9	3,765.4	−0.684	2.194	2,622.6	2.552	1.999
Philippines	4,533.4	5,615.9	−3.305	2.817	2,486.0	3.910	2.009
Thailand	1,405.0	1,261.3	0.148	0.395	813.3	0.758	0.264
Other							
Mexico	−110.2	26.1	−0.056	0.008	29.6	0.027	0.000
Turkey	162.0	133.9	0.049	0.108	227.6	0.091	0.117
Central Europe	1,851.4	1,845.5	−0.006	0.331	1,229.4	0.336	0.324
Central and South America	3,615.9	2,893.3	0.373	0.017	303.2	0.041	−0.002
Total	**88,997.2**	**89,555.9**			**73,002.8**		

factor owners within a country may lose. It is possible, however, for a particular country whose net imports are concentrated in sectors with the greatest liberalization to lose overall if the worsening of its terms of trade swamps these efficiency gains.

On the other hand, although the New Trade Theory is perhaps best known for introducing new reasons why countries may lose from trade, its greatest contribution is to expand the list of reasons for gains from trade. These gains are the dominant contribution of the New Trade Theory in our model. That is, trade liberalization permits all countries to expand their export sectors at the same time that all sectors compete more closely with a larger number of competing varieties from abroad. As a result, countries as a whole gain from lower costs due to increasing returns to scale, lower monopoly distortions as a result of greater competition, and reduced costs and increased utility prompted by greater product variety. All of these effects make it more likely that countries will gain from liberalization in ways that are shared across the entire population.

In perfectly competitive trade models such as the Heckscher-Ohlin model, one expects countries as a whole to gain from trade, but the owners of one factor—the "scarce factor"—to lose through the mechanism known as the Stolper-Samuelson theorem. The additional sources of gain from trade as a result of increasing returns to scale, competition, and product variety, however, are shared across factors, and we routinely find in our CGE modeling that both labor and capital gain from liberalization (for details, see Brown and others [1993]). That is often the case here.

A final point concerns the modeling and role of nontariff barriers, such as are included here, especially in textiles and apparel. These are quantitative restrictions captured in the model by endogenous tariff equivalents that rise and fall with changing supplies and demands for trade. The tariff equivalents generate quota rents that accrue to whatever group is granted the rights to trade under the restriction. In the case of the MFA these are the textiles and apparel–exporting countries. Liberalizing these nontariff barriers reduces or eliminates the quota rents—an action that can be costly to those who possessed them disproportionately beforehand. Therefore, it is not the case that exporting countries necessarily benefit from relaxing these trade barriers because their loss of quota rents can more than outweigh their gains from increased exports. Indeed, their exports can actually decline, along with their national welfare, if increased exports from other countries displace them in world markets.

In the real world, all of these effects occur over time, some of them more quickly than others. Our model is static, however, based on a single set of equilibrium conditions rather than on relationships that vary over time. Our results refer to a time horizon that is somewhat uncertain, depending on the assumptions that have been made about which variables do and which do not adjust to changing market conditions, and on the short- or long-run nature of these adjustments. Because our elasticities of supply and demand reflect relatively long-run adjustments and because we assume that the demand and supply in markets for both labor and capital equilibrate within countries, our results are appropriate for a relatively long time horizon of several years—perhaps two or three at a minimum.

On the other hand, our model does not allow for the very long-run adjustments that could occur through capital accumulation, population growth, and technological change. Our results should therefore be thought of as superimposed on longer-run growth paths of the economies involved. To the extent that these growth paths themselves may be influenced by trade liberalization, therefore, our model does not capture that.

Let us turn now to the Uruguay Round results. As mentioned, table 2.6 reports various economywide changes for each of the economies/regions of the model. These include changes in exports and imports in millions of dollars; the changes in terms of trade, real wage rate, and real return to capital in percentages; and changes in economic welfare measured by equivalent variation, both in millions of dollars and as a percentage of country GDP. The terms of trade is the world price of a country's exports relative to its imports. The equivalent variation is the amount of money that, if given to the country's consumers at initial prices, would be equivalent in terms of their level of welfare to the effects of the assumed liberalization. In general, as discussed above, a worsening (fall) in a country's terms of trade has an adverse effect on its consumers' welfare. But this can be outweighed by the other gains from trade resulting from economic efficiency and the other benefits modeled by the New Trade theory.

UR-1: Elimination of the MFA Quota Constraints.   The results for the Uruguay Round elimination of the MFA quota and of other bilateral constraints on developing country exports of textiles and apparel, shown in scenario UR-1 of table 2.6, indicate an increase in global welfare of US$16.5 billion. When interpreting the results note that, with increased exports of these goods to world markets, their prices will fall and both the terms of trade of the MFA exporting countries and their economic welfare may deteriorate. The decline in terms of trade is experienced as a loss of quota rents from the MFA and can be seen in the terms-of-trade column in table 2.6 for most of the developing economies. Although several of those economies also experience reductions in welfare, India's welfare increases by $972 million. The industrial countries all gain from MFA elimination. Changes in returns to labor and capital are mostly small.

UR-2: Liberalization of Manufactures.   Scenario UR-2 in table 2.6 covers the reductions in import tariffs on manufactures that were negotiated in the Uruguay Round. Global economic welfare increases by US$56.5 billion and the gains are positive for all economies and regions. The largest welfare increases noted are for European Union/European Free Trade Association (EU/EFTA, $17.4 billion), the United States ($11.2 billion), and Japan ($6.6 billion). India's welfare increases by $1.9 billion. The effects on returns to labor and capital are uniformly positive.

UR-3: Combined Liberalization Effects (UR-1 + UR-2).   The combined effects of the Uruguay Round liberalization are indicated in Scenario UR-3 of table 2.6. As noted, this table is the linear combination of UR-1 and UR-2. Global welfare is increased by US$73.0 billion. It is noteworthy that the industrial countries all gain, with an increase in welfare of $23.7 billion for the EU/EFTA, $19.8 billion for the United States, and $6.9 billion for Japan. All of the developing economies, except Hong Kong (China), show an increase in welfare from the combined UR liberalization. India's welfare increases by $2.8 billion. Changes in the real wage and the return to capital are positive but relatively small for the industrial countries, and relatively sizable in several of the Asian developing economies.

As mentioned earlier, we used scenario UR-3 as the basis for updating our database to the year 2005, which is the base for our subsequent scenarios for the Doha Round of liberalization. We first scaled up the GTAP data for 1995 by constant growth rates for labor and output to get estimates of output, employment, and trade for the year 2005 in the absence of the Uruguay Round liberalization. We then used the detailed results of scenario UR-3 to adjust these data further to include the changes that the Uruguay Round can be expected to bring about. Thus, for example, the trade data for each economy in the model were expanded by the percentages implicit in the terms-of-trade and economic welfare (percent) columns of table 2.6. Of course this was actually done using the disaggregated results for percentage changes in output, trade, and employment that are applied to the scaled levels from the GTAP data.

We turn now to the Doha Round scenarios.

Doha Round Results

DR-1: Agricultural Liberalization.   The results for assumed 33 percent reductions in post-UR agricultural import tariffs, export subsidies, and production subsidies (taken here as a proxy for the aggregate measure of support) are shown in table 2.7. (More detailed results are available from the authors on request.) In the

TABLE 2.7 Summary Results of the Doha Development Agenda Negotiations: Change in Imports, Exports, Terms of Trade, Welfare, and the Real Return to Capital and Labor

Economy or Region	Imports (Millions)	Exports (Millions)	Terms of Trade (Percent)	Economic Welfare (Percent)	Economic Welfare (Millions)	Real Wage Rate (Percent)	Return to Capital (Percent)
Scenario DR-1: 33 Percent Reduction in Agricultural Protection							
Industrial economies							
Australia and New Zealand	566.2	−168.1	0.798	−0.063	−320.7	−0.182	−0.224
Canada	−248.6	−768.3	0.168	−0.051	−368.4	−0.218	−0.209
European Union and European Free Trade Association	157.1	416.2	−0.041	0.258	28,328.0	−0.045	0.023
Japan	564.3	3,199.9	−0.470	−0.044	−2,826.4	−0.039	−0.003
United States	2,690.9	928.3	0.219	−0.122	−11,081.1	−0.190	−0.193
Developing economies							
Asia							
India	324.2	285.3	0.066	0.384	1,617.4	−0.109	−0.030
Sri Lanka	−93.9	−67.5	−0.240	−2.734	−455.7	−0.307	−0.480
Rest of South Asia	106.6	157.2	−0.118	0.310	362.1	−0.078	−0.119
China	−522.8	−652.7	−0.013	−0.434	−3,932.0	−0.163	−0.320
Hong Kong, China	−380.7	−256.9	−0.026	−0.294	−379.0	−0.186	−0.180
Republic of Korea	285.4	912.9	−0.333	−0.230	−1,311.4	0.132	0.134
Singapore	−153.9	−39.5	−0.067	−0.244	−181.4	−0.038	−0.068
Indonesia	−436.5	−466.7	−0.006	−1.259	−3,185.5	−0.113	−0.462
Malaysia	−10.8	49.0	−0.076	−0.264	−315.8	0.189	0.104
Philippines	−344.8	−241.8	−0.199	−1.336	−1,179.1	−0.062	−0.076
Thailand	−621.2	−1,119.3	0.613	0.045	92.4	−0.703	0.054
Other							
Mexico	−200.7	−193.6	−0.089	−0.121	−425.6	−0.354	−0.185

TABLE 2.7   (Continued)

Economy or Region	Imports (Millions)	Exports (Millions)	Terms of Trade (Percent)	Economic Welfare (Percent)	Economic Welfare (Millions)	Real Wage Rate (Percent)	Return to Capital (Percent)
Turkey	−189.1	−119.0	−0.087	−0.414	−871.4	−0.327	−0.347
Central Europe	−432.7	−428.6	0.025	−0.457	−1,695.6	−0.363	−0.391
Central and South America	1,500.6	870.3	0.377	−0.285	−4,988.0	−0.252	−0.358
Total	**2,559.5**	**2,297.3**			**−3,117.2**		
Scenario DR-2: 33 Percent Reduction in Manufactures Tariffs							
Industrial economies							
Australia and New Zealand	3,720.7	3,457.2	0.267	0.545	2,790.6	0.508	0.515
Canada	1,996.0	2,097.3	−0.013	0.347	2,526.2	0.216	0.251
European Union and European Free Trade Association	23,184.8	22,840.3	0.050	0.358	39,273.0	0.190	0.199
Japan	19,071.4	15,817.0	0.548	0.696	45,190.9	0.234	0.304
United States	20,454.2	18,337.3	0.167	0.260	23,634.2	0.198	0.224
Developing economies							
Asia							
India	3,280.4	4,054.2	−1.384	0.733	3,084.4	0.439	0.592
Sri Lanka	536.8	592.1	−1.025	3.207	534.5	1.565	2.010
Rest of South Asia	1,892.0	2,018.4	−0.604	1.895	2,214.7	0.889	1.025
China	16,080.3	19,416.3	−1.221	1.199	10,859.3	1.470	1.323
Hong Kong, China	3,182.8	1,840.3	1.246	1.444	1,859.1	0.947	0.647
Republic of Korea	8,023.4	8,440.7	−0.233	1.515	8,622.9	1.158	1.003
Singapore	4,382.9	4,161.8	0.131	2.276	1,692.5	2.481	2.611
Indonesia	2,362.7	2,336.0	0.053	0.835	2,113.3	0.645	0.447

TABLE 2.7 *(Continued)*

Economy or Region	Imports (Millions)	Exports (Millions)	Terms of Trade (Percent)	Economic Welfare (Percent)	Economic Welfare (Millions)	Real Wage Rate (Percent)	Return to Capital (Percent)
Malaysia	4,242.8	4,805.2	-0.488	2.555	3,055.1	2.896	2.812
Philippines	3,984.0	4,535.1	-1.192	5.478	4,834.4	3.310	2.461
Thailand	3,406.1	3,970.1	-0.675	0.873	1,798.6	1.664	0.972
Other							
Mexico	916.3	1,132.6	-0.166	0.364	1,283.1	0.195	0.204
Turkey	1,421.0	1,558.6	-0.335	0.827	1,740.3	0.349	0.272
Central Europe	3,866.3	4,366.4	-0.428	0.734	2,724.2	0.816	0.722
Central and South America	5,038.9	6,103.2	-0.612	0.206	3,610.0	0.159	0.108
Total	131,043.7	131,880.0			163,441.4		
Scenario DR-3: 33 Percent Reduction in Services Barriers							
Industrial economies							
Australia and New Zealand	2,354.4	1,962.3	0.385	1.050	5,379.6	0.694	0.657
Canada	2,244.0	2,136.3	0.083	0.811	5,910.4	0.317	0.316
European Union and European Free Trade Association	35,478.1	35,336.8	0.032	1.295	142,003.2	0.553	0.546
Japan	14,797.7	15,501.6	-0.067	0.891	57,875.1	0.247	0.277
United States	32,467.7	32,231.5	-0.033	1.448	131,426.8	0.524	0.534
Developing economies							
Asia							
India	919.2	803.9	0.212	0.552	2,321.6	0.170	0.204
Sri Lanka	121.7	99.1	0.335	1.202	200.4	0.881	0.507
Rest of South Asia	374.3	286.7	0.286	0.689	804.9	0.293	0.453

TABLE 2.7   *(Continued)*

Economy or Region	Imports (Millions)	Exports (Millions)	Terms of Trade (Percent)	Economic Welfare		Real Wage Rate (Percent)	Return to Capital (Percent)
				(Percent)	(Millions)		
China	5,660.3	6,210.9	-0.128	1.320	11,959.1	0.840	0.603
Hong Kong, China	7,587.2	8,058.4	-0.611	4.382	5,643.1	5.638	5.927
Republic of Korea	4,842.2	5,002.5	-0.102	1.339	7,619.5	0.913	0.956
Singapore	3,325.1	3,776.2	-0.297	3.322	2,470.8	4.821	3.972
Indonesia	1,401.3	1,469.4	-0.072	1.256	3,177.0	0.327	0.307
Malaysia	1,487.6	1,466.8	0.049	1.267	1,514.5	1.026	0.928
Philippines	1,986.7	2,195.0	-0.462	2.342	2,067.1	1.739	1.622
Thailand	3,324.2	3,625.3	-0.413	1.401	2,886.4	1.088	0.904
Other							
Mexico	863.1	809.1	0.110	0.878	3,099.3	0.204	0.195
Turkey	1,733.3	1,462.9	0.589	1.781	3,745.9	0.695	0.884
Central Europe	3,841.7	3,744.5	0.061	1.409	5,227.2	1.067	0.996
Central and South America	4,199.9	4,442.8	-0.179	1.050	18,363.5	0.256	0.272
Total	**129,009.6**	**130,621.8**			**413,695.4**		
Scenario DR-4: 33 Percent Reduction in All Trade Barriers							
Industrial economies							
Australia and New Zealand	6,641.2	5,251.4	1.449	1.532	7,849.3	1.020	0.947
Canada	3,991.3	3,465.3	0.238	1.107	8,068.2	0.315	0.359
European Union and European Free Trade Association	58,819.3	58,592.5	0.041	1.911	209,609.8	0.697	0.768
Japan	34,433.4	34,518.5	0.012	1.544	100,239.5	0.442	0.579
United States	55,612.4	51,496.8	0.353	1.586	143,980.5	0.533	0.565

TABLE 2.7   (*Continued*)

Economy or Region	Imports (Millions)	Exports (Millions)	Terms of Trade (Percent)	Economic Welfare (Percent)	Economic Welfare (Millions)	Real Wage Rate (Percent)	Return to Capital (Percent)
Developing economies							
Asia							
India	4,523.7	5,143.3	−1.106	1.669	7,023.4	0.500	0.766
Sri Lanka	564.6	623.7	−0.930	1.675	279.2	2.139	2.037
Rest of South Asia	2,372.9	2,462.3	−0.436	2.894	3,381.8	1.104	1.360
China	21,217.8	24,974.6	−1.361	2.085	18,886.9	2.148	1.606
Hong Kong, China	10,389.2	9,641.7	0.609	5.532	7,123.1	6.399	6.394
Republic of Korea	13,151.0	14,356.1	−0.668	2.624	14,930.8	2.203	2.094
Singapore	7,554.0	7,898.6	−0.233	5.354	3,982.0	7.264	6.516
Indonesia	3,327.5	3,338.6	−0.025	0.832	2,104.8	0.858	0.292
Malaysia	5,719.6	6,321.0	−0.515	3.558	4,253.8	4.111	3.845
Philippines	5,625.9	6,488.3	−1.854	6.485	5,722.5	4.987	4.007
Thailand	6,109.1	6,476.1	−0.475	2.319	4,777.4	2.050	1.930
Other							
Mexico	1,578.6	1,748.0	−0.145	1.122	3,957.0	0.045	0.214
Turkey	2,965.1	2,902.4	0.167	2.194	4,614.5	0.718	0.809
Central Europe	7,275.2	7,682.1	−0.342	1.686	6,255.3	1.521	1.327
Central and South America	10,739.4	11,416.1	−0.414	0.971	16,985.8	0.163	0.021
Total	262,611.2	264,797.6			574,025.4		

model, the reductions in agricultural import tariffs will have the effects of tariff reductions already described. In the case of export subsidies, their effects will be to reduce world prices and raise domestic prices. When export subsidies are reduced, world prices rise and domestic prices in the subsidizing countries fall, with the possible consequences that economic welfare may rise in the countries reducing their export subsidies and fall in net-importing countries now facing higher world prices. Similarly, production subsidies will have the effect of reducing prices both domestically and abroad. When production subsidies are reduced, the cost of agricultural products will rise with consequent terms-of-trade effects similar to those just discussed. In addition, depending on the input–output structure, a rise in the cost of agricultural inputs will push up marginal cost relative to average total cost in some sectors. To return to the optimal markup of price relative to marginal cost, firm output in these sectors has to fall, and economic welfare may then decline as a result of reduced economies of scale.

In the underlying results, the reductions in agricultural import tariffs alone increase global economic welfare by US$9.5 billion. Welfare increases in the Asian developing countries, the EU/EFTA, Japan, Mexico, and Turkey as resources are shifted away from agriculture. Correspondingly, welfare declines in Australia/New Zealand, Canada, and the United States as resources are shifted to agriculture and away from nonagricultural increasing-returns industries. As noted above, when export subsidies are reduced, world prices rise and domestic prices fall. This is borne out in the underlying results of welfare increases in the EU/EFTA and welfare declines in all of the economies in the model, except Thailand. Global welfare falls by an estimated $23.2 billion. When production subsidies are reduced, domestic and foreign prices rise and, depending on input–output structures, the increased cost of agricultural inputs may cause firm output in some sectors to decline for the reasons discussed above. In the underlying results, it turns out that the EU/EFTA region benefits the most when its agricultural production subsidies are reduced, whereas welfare declines for most developing economies. Global welfare rises by $10.6 billion.[12] Agricultural liberalization thus involves a complex of differential changes because both tariffs and subsidies are being reduced. The net effect indicated in table 2.7 is a reduction in global welfare of $3.1 billion. The net effect on India is a welfare increase of $1.6 billion.

DR-2: Liberalization of Manufactures.   The assumed 33 percent reduction of post-UR manufactures tariffs results in an increase in global welfare of US$163.4 billion, which is considerably greater than the $56.5 billion welfare gain from the Uruguay Round manufactures liberalization. As was the case in the Uruguay Round results, the assumed liberalization of manufactures in the Doha Round would increase welfare in all of the economies and regions listed and would have positive effects as well on real wages and the return to capital. The largest welfare gains are for Japan ($45.2 billion), the EU/EFTA ($39.3 billion), and the United States ($23.6 billion). Although the welfare gains for the developing economies and regions are much smaller in absolute terms, the percentage gains are mostly larger, ranging from 0.2 percent for Central and South America to 5.5 percent for the Philippines.[13] India's welfare increases by $3.1 billion, which is 0.7 percent of its GDP. There are also sizable percentage increases in the real factor returns in the Asian developing economies.

DR-3: Services Liberalization.   As noted above, the Uruguay Round negotiations on services resulted in the creation of the GATS, but there was no significant liberalization of barriers to services. Following the Uruguay Round there have been successful multilateral negotiations to liberalize telecommunications and financial services. Although it would be desirable to assess the economic effects of these sectoral agreements, lack of data prevents us from doing so. What we have done then is to use the estimates of services barriers based on the calculations of gross operating margins for services firms in the economies and regions in our model. These estimates of services barriers are intended to be indirect approximations of the actual barriers. Assuming that the ad valorem equivalents of these barriers are reduced by 33 percent, it can be seen in table 2.7 that global economic welfare rises by US$413.7 billion, which exceeds the $163.4 billion in welfare increase for manufactures liberalization. All of the economies listed experience positive welfare gains and increases in real wages and returns to capital. The EU/EFTA region has the largest welfare gain ($142.0 billion) in the group of industrial countries, compared with $131.4 billion for the United States and $57.9 billion for Japan. For the smaller industrial and developing countries, the percentage increases in welfare and factor returns are especially noteworthy. India's welfare increases by $2.3 billion, which is 0.6 of its GDP. It should be borne in mind that the foregoing results of services liberalization depend on the size of the services barriers that have been calculated indirectly from financial data and they may be overstated. Nonetheless, it seems fair to say that services barriers tend to be considerably greater than the tariffs on manufactures.

DR-4: Combined Liberalization Effects (DR-1 + DR-2 + DR-3).   The results for DR-4 are a linear combination of the other three scenarios. As can be seen in table 2.7, global welfare overall rises by US$574.0 billion. Among the industrial countries, the EU/EFTA region has a welfare gain of $209.6 billion, the United States a gain of $144.0 billion, and Japan a gain of $100.2 billion. The percentage welfare gains and increases in returns to factors are sizable in most of the smaller industrial countries and in the developing economies. India's welfare increase is $7.0 billion, which is 1.7 percent of GDP.

Sectoral Impact of Trade Liberalization on India

A major contribution that this sort of CGE modeling can make is to identify those sectors that will expand and those that will contract as a result of various patterns of trade liberalization and the sizes of these changes. Given our assumption that expenditure adjusts within each country to maintain a constant level of total employment, each country must experience a mixture of expansions and contractions at the industry level. This must be true of employment, and it is likely to be true for industry output. (Detailed sectoral results are available for all the economies and regions included in the model from the authors on request.) We will concentrate here on the sectoral results for India that are given in tables 2.8 and 2.9.

We expect that trade liberalization will stimulate production of labor-intensive sectors in India. Productive resources would then be allocated more efficiently than they would in the preliberalization situation because India would specialize in the sectors where it has comparative advantage. There may, of course, be transitional costs resulting from intersectoral movement of production factors. In addition to such welfare gains, trade liberalization is expected to have a procompetitive effect on domestic firms, resulting in additional gains from the realization of economies of large-scale production. When firms are protected from foreign competition through tariff and nontariff barriers, they may take advantage of their market power by raising their prices and reducing their domestic sales. The result is that the protected firms may produce below their minimum-cost, efficient plant size. Trade liberalization should then bring about competitive pressures on the formerly protected firms and induce them to raise production and productivity and to achieve more efficient plant size and lower per-unit costs. Thus gains in economic welfare are expected to come from improved allocation of resources, lower prices to consumers and business firms, and availability of more varieties to consumers and firms. Realizing economies of scale in manufacturing also reinforces the welfare-enhancing effect.

The sectoral results for UR-3 for India presented in table 2.8 indicate that the largest employment increases are in textiles (388,154), wearing apparel (231,338), trade and transport (124,360), mining (46,546), and leather products and footwear (42,892). India's largest employment declines are in wood and wood products (–226,363), agriculture (–143,922), and the combined categories of industrial products and machinery. The sectoral results for DR-4 in India presented in table 2.9 show employment increases in government services (340,109);

TABLE 2.8   Sectoral Results of the Uruguay Round Negotiations (UR-3): Change in Exports, Imports, Output, Scale, and Employment in India

Sector	Exports (Percent)	Imports (Percent)	Output (Percent)	Scale (Percent)	Employment (Percent)	Employment (000s)
Agriculture	0.70	-2.04	-0.09	0.00	-0.05	-143,922.3
Mining	3.73	-2.07	1.79	0.67	1.41	46,546.0
Food, beverages, and tobacco	5.18	10.66	0.06	0.35	-0.07	-7,841.8
Textiles	18.86	7.43	4.34	1.25	3.34	388,153.9
Wearing apparel	54.34	-9.57	29.23	1.33	28.26	231,337.8
Leather products and footwear	7.97	34.60	4.61	1.21	3.70	42,892.0
Wood and wood products	4.81	31.29	-2.68	0.60	-3.09	-226,363.1
Chemicals	4.44	12.54	-1.02	0.70	-1.46	-21,998.1
Nonmetallic mineral products	6.55	22.26	-0.45	0.66	-0.94	-32,502.0
Metal products	4.37	7.23	-2.34	0.65	-2.76	-96,777.2
Transportation equipment	7.09	25.24	-1.62	0.79	-2.23	-30,912.3
Machinery and equipment	2.65	16.36	-5.65	1.10	-6.56	-156,588.3
Other manufactures	2.60	19.31	-1.55	0.76	-1.98	-106,883.9
Electricity, gas, and water	4.37	-2.27	1.21	1.11	0.36	6,171.9
Construction	2.86	-2.68	-0.27	-0.03	-0.08	-11,520.2
Trade and transport	2.49	-2.99	0.33	0.28	0.26	124,360.2
Other private services	2.05	-2.39	-0.24	-0.06	-0.03	-962.6
Government services	1.57	-2.12	-0.18	-0.03	-0.01	-3,189.9
Average	11.31	8.22	0.43	0.00	0.00	0.0

TABLE 2.9 Sectoral Results of the Doha Development Agenda Negotiations (DR-4): Change in Exports, Imports, Output, Scale, and Employment in India

Sector	Exports (Percent)	Imports (Percent)	Output (Percent)	Scale (Percent)	Employment (Percent)	Employment (000s)
Agriculture	11.50	0.71	-0.19	0.00	-0.15	-449,827.9
Mining	5.43	-1.84	2.68	1.03	2.07	69,399.1
Food, beverages, and tobacco	7.75	17.83	0.40	0.06	0.52	60,679.6
Textiles	8.69	21.56	1.82	0.78	1.23	148,188.9
Wearing apparel	14.06	24.77	9.30	0.86	8.75	95,004.0
Leather products and footwear	9.30	9.13	6.63	1.10	5.82	69,966.9
Wood and wood products	5.40	5.53	0.03	0.46	-0.27	-18,859.3
Chemicals	5.75	10.53	-0.65	0.92	-1.29	-19,167.5
Nonmetallic mineral products	7.61	15.32	0.55	0.92	-0.20	-6,811.1
Metal products	5.23	11.70	-2.15	1.13	-3.01	-102,891.1
Transportation equipment	7.33	12.93	-0.03	1.23	-1.05	-14,198.4
Machinery and equipment	4.53	10.83	-3.04	1.58	-4.44	-99,199.1
Other manufactures	4.93	15.52	-0.51	1.21	-1.32	-70,109.0
Electricity, gas, and water	6.33	-4.53	0.71	0.75	0.17	2,982.9
Construction	15.90	2.99	0.63	0.72	0.14	20,273.2
Trade and transport	15.06	14.66	0.26	0.64	-0.07	-35,549.3
Other private services	16.86	10.16	0.58	0.58	0.35	10,009.5
Government services	15.45	-2.91	1.22	0.86	0.81	340,108.6
Average	9.22	8.30	0.50		0.00	0.0

textiles (148,189); wearing apparel (95,004); leather products and footwear (69,967); mining (69,399); food, beverages, and tobacco (60,680); and construction (20,273). There are employment declines in agriculture (−449,828), the combined categories of industrial products and durable manufactures; and trade and transport (−35,549).

Although the employment changes for several sectors appear fairly large in percentage terms in tables 2.8 and 2.9, it should be noted that the Uruguay Round liberalization was to be phased in over a period of 10 years and presumably the Doha Round will be phased in over several years. As a consequence, being spread over time would mitigate possible sectoral employment dislocations.

Unilateral Liberalization by India

In earlier work by Chadha and others (1998a,b), the effects of India's unilateral, post-1991 economic reforms were analyzed using a standalone model of the Indian economy in which the rest of the world was assumed not to undertake any liberalization. It is interesting in this light to consider how India would be affected by multilateral liberalization in the Doha Round negotiations compared with what it might undertake unilaterally. For this purpose, we repeated the DR-1 to DR-4 scenarios for India on a unilateral basis. The results are reported in table 2.10. It is interesting that India would appear to gain more from unilateral liberalization in agriculture, whereas multilateral liberalization of manufactures and services produces greater welfare effects. In any case there is reason to believe that India stands to gain by pursuing trade liberalization.

We should also note that India may gain even more if it were to undertake measures to improve trade facilitation, which is an important but often neglected area in discussions of international trade. According to one estimate, the global costs to business of unnecessary red tape and procedures could be as high as US$70 billion a year and such costs often fall disproportionately on small and medium enterprises, which ultimately pass it on to consumers in developing countries (Mehta 2002). Trade facilitation covers a wide range of noneconomic measures aimed at promoting the expansion of international trade by smoothing its flow. Such facilitation is expected to benefit trades and consumers by lowering transaction costs and to benefit governments by enabling them to realize higher revenue collection as a result of simplified procedures.[14] The central budget (2003/04) presented by the Finance Minister of India on February 28, 2003, has proposed new measures toward trade facilitation (Government of India 2003, paras. 184–86).

TABLE 2.10   Impact of Multilateral and Unilateral Trade Liberalization for India

	DR-1	DR-2	DR-3	DR-4
Multilateral				
Equivalent Variation				
Percent	0.4	0.7	0.6	1.7
Million US dollars	1,617	3,084	2,322	7,023
Returns to Factors, % change				
Wage Rate	−0.1	0.4	0.2	0.5
Returns to Capital	−0.3	0.6	0.2	0.8
Trade				
Imports (million US dollars)	324	3,280	919	4,524
Exports (million US dollars)	285	4,054	804	5,143
Unilateral				
Equivalent Variation				
Percent	0.9	0.3	0.3	1.4
Million US dollars	3,658	1,370	1,074	6,103
Returns to Factors, % change				
Wage Rate	−0.1	0.2	0.0	0.2
Returns to Capital	0.2	0.5	0.1	0.8
Trade				
Imports (million US dollars)	215	2,182	296	2,694
Exports (million US dollars)	279	3,364	437	4,080

Multilateral

DR-1: 33 percent bilateral reduction in post-Uruguay Round agricultural import tariffs, export subsidies, and production subsidies

DR-2: 33 percent bilateral reduction in post-Uruguay Round tariffs on minerals and manufactures

DR-3: 33 percent bilateral reduction in tariff equivalents of barriers to trade in services

DR-4: 33 percent bilateral tariffs reduction in all sectors combined (**DR1, DR2,** and **DR3**)

Unilateral

India's unilateral:

UNIDR-1: 33 percent reduction in post-Uruguay Round agricultural import tariffs, export subsidies, and production subsidies

UNIDR-2: 33 percent reduction in post-Uruguay Round tariffs on minerals and manufactures

UNIDR-3: 33 percent reduction in tariff equivalent of barriers to trade in services

UNIDR-4: 33 percent tariff reduction in all sectors combined (**UNIDR-1, UNIDR-2,** and **UNIDR-3**)

Conclusions and Implications for Policy

The failure of the Third WTO Ministerial Conference in Seattle led to a temporary setback to the launch of a new round of multilateral trade negotiations. Despite the consequent uncertainties, the built-in agenda from the Uruguay Round was mandated for negotiations on agricultural and services liberalization to begin in the year 2000. In November 2001 the agenda for a new negotiating round was approved at Doha, Qatar. In this chapter, we have provided computational estimates of the economic effects that might be realized from UR and DR trade liberalization for India and other major trading economies.

An important message that emerges is that multilateral liberalization enhances the economic welfare of all of the major trading economies. India's welfare gain is 0.68 percent (US$2.8 billion over its 2005 GDP) when the UR scenarios are fully implemented. The country's additional welfare gain amounts to 1.67 percent ($7.0 billion) when the assumed DR multilateral trade liberalization is completed. Resources in India are allocated toward labor-intensive sectors, such as textiles; wearing apparel; leather and leather products; and food, beverages, and tobacco. Real returns to both labor and capital increase. Finally, India benefits even if it were to undertake unilateral trade liberalization of the order indicated in the multilateral scenarios.

The gains from the liberalization scenarios that have been noted, of course, should be interpreted in the light of the assumptions of our modeling structure. In particular, our computational model abstracts from the effects of macroeconomic changes and policies. Also, we do not capture the effects of dynamic changes in efficiency and economic growth. Furthermore, we have not analyzed the effects of possible changes in inflows of foreign direct investment. Finally, the analysis of intersectoral employment shifts makes no allowance for the constraining effects of India's sectoral exit barriers and its domestic labor laws.

Endnotes

1. Before the announcement of India's EXIM policy, all imports unless specifically exempted required a license or a customs-clearance permit. All imports were classified under one of four main licensing types: restricted items, banned items, limited permissible items, and open general licenses (OGL). The items falling under OGL were only nominally unrestricted. In practice many OGL imports required government approval and most remained subject to actual user conditions. The system was complicated further by applying different import and approval procedures among license types and frequently shifting products across licensing categories.

2. The goods under licensing included precious, semiprecious, and other stones; safety, security, and related items; seeds, plants, and animals; insecticides and pesticides; drugs and pharmaceuticals; chemicals and allied items; items relating to small-scale sector; and miscellaneous and special categories.

3. India implemented the Harmonized Commodity Description and Coding System (HS) for classifying imports and exports in February 1986. Although the Indian Customs Tariff Schedule is subdivided into 5,134 standard HS 6-digit codes (as of April 1, 1997), India uses a 10-digit HS classification for import licensing purposes.

4. The Chelliah Committee recommended seven different rates of customs tariff, namely, 5, 10, 15, 20, 25, 30, and 50 percent, to be achieved by 1997/98 (Government of India 1993). It was further suggested that additional or special protection might be given for a limited period to new industries, new products, or new technologies. The 5 percent rate was to apply to inputs for fertilizer and newsprint, 10 and 15 percent to other basic inputs, 20 percent to capital goods, and 25 percent to chemicals and intermediates. Other final products (excluding nonessential consumer goods) would be charged 30 percent duty. Nonessential consumer goods, if permitted for import, would have a duty rate of 50 percent. Although the multiple suggested tariff rates can be used to achieve the Committee's philosophy of systematic escalation according to the degree of processing, the result may be effective rates of protection that are much higher than the nominal tariffs on finished goods. Thus, for example, when QRs on consumer goods are removed, a 50 percent duty on imports of consumer goods combined with a duty of 25 percent or less on tradable inputs would lead to an effective rate of protection close to 100 percent (Joshi and Little 1994, p. 76). This tariff escalation was prevalent in India's economy throughout the 1990s. Whereas the simple average tariff on processed goods was 37 percent in 1997/98, unprocessed goods (primary products) had an average tariff of 25 percent. Significant tariff escalation is further evident in paper and paper products; printing and publishing; wood and wood products; and food, beverages, and tobacco (WTO 1998, p. 19).

5. India obtained the right to use QRs from the General Agreement on Tariffs and Trade in 1949 for balance of payments reasons and retained it thereafter. This right was reasserted in its Uruguay Round submissions. As noted below, however, QRs were to be phased out by 2001.

6. See Chadha (2001 and Chapter 4 of this volume) for a more detailed analysis of India's services commitments and policies.

7. It should be noted that we are not considering the effects of the Agreement on Trade-related Aspects of Intellectual Property Rights and the other agreements on rules and procedures that the Uruguay Round negotiations encompassed.

8. Agricultural liberalization in the Uruguay Round negotiations presumably was to be as follows: agricultural import tariffs were to be reduced by 20 percent for the industrial countries and by 13 percent for the developing economies; agricultural export subsidies were to be reduced by 36 percent for the industrial countries and by 24 percent for the developing economies; and agricultural production subsidies were to be reduced by 20 percent for the industrial countries and by 14 percent for the developing economies. However, as noted in Francois (2001), "Basically, in agriculture, we are in a world that allows scope for great policy discretion and uncertainty as a result of the loose commitments made." This means that many countries introduced quantitative restrictions on imports in the form of tariff rate quotas. There is also evidence of considerable leeway in the choice of the reference period from which to measure reductions in export subsidies. Furthermore, the disciplines on domestic subsidies were weakened by changes in the definition of the aggregate measure of support. As a consequence, relatively little agricultural liberalization was accomplished in the Uruguay Round negotiations. In the absence of detailed information on the various agricultural policy changes that have been made, we have chosen not to include agricultural liberalization in the Uruguay Round computational scenarios.

9. Under the ATC agreement, quota growth rates will increase in stages over the decade from 1995 to 2005. We assumed in our computations that the MFA quota constraints are eliminated all at once.

10. The post-UR tariff data were adapted from Francois and Strutt (1999).

11. The agricultural sector in the model is assumed to be perfectly competitive, and the manufacturing and services sectors are assumed to be monopolistically competitive with free entry.

12. All we can capture with our model is this aggregate change. Were we able to distinguish the incomes of the rural and urban populations, we would presumably find a rise in the incomes of the mostly poor rural population.

13. Our results differ from those obtained by Hertel, Hoekman, and Martin (2002, p. 121), who concluded that "... the bulk of the gains go to developing countries, which are estimated to receive three quarters of the total gains from liberalizing manufacturing trade." The differences in our results compared with those of Hertel and colleagues most likely stem from the assumptions made in projecting the database for the model to 2005. That is, Hertel, Hoekman, and Martin projected significantly greater expansions of the output and trade of the developing economies than in our simpler extrapolations noted above.

14. See Wilson and others (2002) for an analysis of the potential benefits in the Asia Pacific region of improvements in port facilities, regulatory systems, technical and health standards, and electronic commerce.

References

The word "processed" describes informally produced works that may not be available commonly through libraries.

Brown, Drusilla K., Alan V. Deardorff, Alan Fox, and Robert M. Stern. 1996. "The Liberalization of Services Trade: Potential Impacts of the Aftermath of the Uruguay Round." In Will Martin and L. Alan Winters, eds., *The Uruguay Round and the Developing Countries.* Cambridge, U.K.: Cambridge University Press.

Brown, Drusilla, Alan V. Deardorff, and Robert M. Stern. 1993. "Protection and Real Wages: Old and New Trade Theories and Their Empirical Counterparts." Discussion Paper 331. Research Seminar in International Economics, University of Michigan, Ann Arbor.

Chadha, Rajesh, 2001. "GATS and Developing Countries: A Case Study of India." In Robert M. Stern, ed., *Services in the International Economy.* Ann Arbor: University of Michigan Press.

Chadha, Rajesh, and Sanjib Pohit. 1998. "Rationalising Tariff and Non-Tariff Barriers on Trade: Sectoral Impact on Indian Economy." Paper prepared for the Tariff Commission, Government of India.

Chadha, Rajesh, Sanjib Pohit, Alan V. Deardorff, and Robert M. Stern. 1998a. "Analysis of India's Policy Reforms." *World Economy* 21: 235–59.

———. 1998b. *The Impact of Trade and Domestic Policy Reforms in India: A CGE Modeling Approach.* Ann Arbor: University of Michigan Press.

———. 1999. "Phasing Out the Multi-Fibre Arrangement: Implications for India." Paper presented at the Second Annual Conference on Global Economic Analysis, June, Copenhagen.

Francois, Joseph. 2001. "The Next WTO Round: North-South Stakes in New Market Access Negotiations." Centre for International Economic Studies, Adelaide, and Tinbergen Institute, Amsterdam and Rotterdam.

Francois, Joseph, and Anna Strutt. 1999. "Post-Uruguay Round Tariff Vectors for GTAP Version 4." Faculty of Economics, Erasmus University, Rotterdam, Netherlands. Processed.

Government of India. 1993. *Tax Reforms Committee: Final Report Part II.* Ministry of Finance.

———. 2003. *Budget 2003–2004.* Ministry of Finance.

Hertel, Thomas W., Bernard M. Hoekman, and Will Martin. 2002. "Developing Countries and a New Round of WTO Negotiations." *World Bank Research Observer* 17: 113–40.

Joshi, Vijay, and I. M. D. Little. 1994. *India: Macroeconomics and Political Economy 1964–1991.* Washington, D.C.: World Bank.

McDougall, Robert A., Aziz Elbehri, and Truong P. Truong. 1998. *Global Trade, Assistance and Protection: The GTAP4 Data Base.* Center for Global Trade Analysis, Purdue University, West Lafayette, Ind.

Mehta, Pradeep. 2002. "WTO and India: An Agenda for Actions in Post-Doha Scenario." Jaipur, India: Consumer Unity and Trust Society.

Mehta, Rajesh. 1998. "Tariff and Non-Tariff Barriers of the Indian Economy: A Profile." Study report submitted to the Tariff Commission, Government of India.

Pursell, Gary. 1996. "Indian Trade Policies Since the 1991/92 Reforms." World Bank, Washington, D.C. Processed.

Srinivasan, T. N. 1998. *Developing Countries and the Multilateral Trading System*. Boulder, Colo.: Westview Press.

————. 2001. "India's Reform of External Sector Policies and Future Multilateral Trade Negotiations." Discussion Paper 830. Economic Growth Center, Yale University, New Haven, Conn.

Wilson, John S., Catherine Mann, Yuen Pau Woo, Nizar Assanie, and Inbom Choi. 2002. "Trade Facilitation: A Development Perspective in the Asia Pacific Region." Singapore: Asia Pacific Economic Cooperation.

Winters, L. A. 2001. "Harnessing Trade for Development." Issue Paper prepared for the Conference on Making Globalisation Work for the Poor—The European Contribution, June 20–21, Kramsfors, Sweden.

WTO (World Trade Organization). 1998. *Trade Policy Review: India*. Lanham, Md.: Bernan Associates.

3

IMPLICATIONS OF MULTIFIBRE ARRANGEMENT ABOLITION FOR INDIA AND SOUTH ASIA

Sanjay Kathuria, Will J. Martin, and Anjali Bhardwaj

An important feature of the Uruguay Round negotiations was the agreement by members of the World Trade Organization (WTO) to abolish the Multifibre Arrangement (MFA) quotas[1] that (with their predecessors) have restricted exports of textile and clothing products from developing countries for close to 40 years. This iniquitous system of quotas has violated all of the fundamental principles of the multilateral trading system and has discriminated against the poorest countries and those seeking to move up from reliance on commodity trade toward an emphasis on manufactures.

Developing countries had to invest a large amount of their negotiating capital into securing the developed countries' agreement to abolish these quotas. As Mattoo and Subramanian argue in Chapter 13 of this volume, those countries may need to press hard to ensure that the abolition of the quotas goes according to plan.

Although enormously welcome, the prospective abolition of these quotas will not necessarily generate automatic benefits to all developing countries. Quota abolition will create opportunities for developing countries, but also will expose them to additional competition from other, formerly restrained exporters. The outcome for any individual country will depend heavily on its policy response.

The views expressed in this chapter are entirely those of the authors and should not be attributed in any manner to the World Bank (Kathuria and Martin are at The World Bank, and Bhardwaj works as a freelance consultant). We are grateful to D. K. Nair, Secretary General of the Indian Cotton Mills Federation, for numerous discussions on the subject of this chapter that have contributed greatly to our understanding of the Indian textiles industry. We also thank Garry Pursell for useful comments and suggestions.

Countries that take the opportunity to streamline their policies and improve their competitiveness are likely to increase their gains from quota abolition.

In the following section we introduce the economics of the MFA, using a simple diagrammatic treatment of the effects of MFA-type quotas. In the second section we examine some of the empirical evidence, focusing particularly on India. Kathuria and Bhardwaj (1998) recently have provided some new results on the magnitude of the effective taxes imposed by the MFA on India's exports of textiles and clothing. This chapter further updates those results, and in the third section we discuss the likely effect of quota abolition on South Asia, with a focus on India. In the fourth section we examine the domestic distortions that affect this industry and then discuss policy options in the fifth section. The final section summarizes the chapter.

The Basic Economics of the MFA

A key feature of the MFA quotas is that they are imposed only by a subset of countries and only on exports from a subset of exporters (Hamilton 1990). For an individual exporter, these quotas restrict access to the MFA importer markets and encourage the exporter to divert its exports from those restricted markets to other, unrestricted markets. An important feature of this policy regime is that the importers allow exporters to allocate the quotas and hence to benefit from the higher prices in the restricted markets. This complication may thus be considered a kind of payoff, given that the system of quotas was of such doubtful legality under the General Agreement on Tariffs and Trade (GATT).

The basic economic implications of the MFA for an individual exporter can be summarized in the simple diagram drawn from Martin and Suphachalasai (1990) and presented as figure 3.1. To keep the diagram simple we base it on the widely used Armington assumption that the products produced by the exporter of interest are differentiated from those produced by other countries. This assumption allows us to draw well-defined import demand curves for the country's products in the restricted markets (D_R) and in the unrestricted markets (D_U). The horizontal summation of these two demand curves gives the global demand (D_T) for the exports from the exporter under consideration. In the absence of any quota restrictions, as in figure 3.1, the intersection of this total demand curve and the export supply curve from the country in question will yield the uniform price at which exports are sold.

In the undistorted equilibrium represented in figure 3.1 the same price applies in both the "restricted" (the restriction, of course, comes about in figure 3.2) and unrestricted markets, and the allocation of exports between the two markets depends only on the magnitude of demand in those markets. When quotas are introduced in the restricted market as shown in figure 3.2, the quantity exported to that market declines. Because of the restrictions, the price received for exports

FIGURE 3.1   Market Equilibrium in the Absence of Quotas

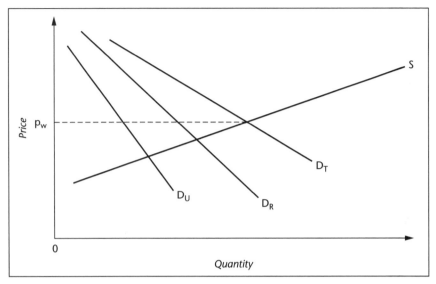

Source: Adapted from Martin and Suphachalasai (1990).

FIGURE 3.2   Market Equilibrium in the Presence of Quotas

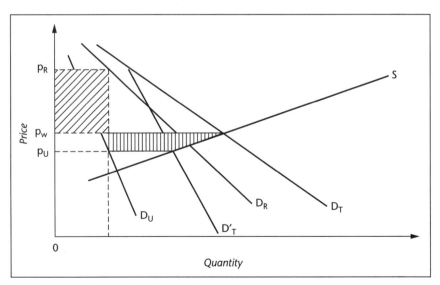

Source: Adapted from Martin and Suphachalasai (1990).

to the restricted market increases from p_w to p_R. The price received for exports to the unrestricted market, however, declines from p_w to p_U (which is the new world price/marginal price). Note also that the overall demand curve facing the country (D_T') becomes steeper, and hence less elastic, because of the zero elasticity of demand in the restricted market. Because the marginal price of output falls, the volume of output in the industry unambiguously declines. Whether static welfare increases or decreases depends on whether the net gain from quota rents in the restricted export market compared with the situation in figure 3.1 (represented by the crosshatched area in figure 3.2) outweighs the losses in the unrestricted markets (represented by the vertically shaded area in figure 3.2).[2]

The overall effect of the MFA on a country's welfare cannot, of course, be determined simply by the static welfare effects depicted in figure 3.2. A major problem with gains that accrue in the form of rents is that they create incentives for what Bhagwati (1988) has termed Directly Unproductive (DUP) activities in which enterprises and individuals use real resources in pursuit of the quota rents. Krishna and Tan (1998) pointed out that the systems of quota allocation used in the South Asian countries encourage such activities. Quota allocations frequently are based on historic export performance, which creates an incentive for firms to increase their exports to unrestricted third markets even when those markets are not directly profitable, thus increasing the losses accruing in unrestricted markets. A further source of loss with quota rents is loss to exporters through rent sharing. According to Krishna and Tan (1998), when export quotas are sufficiently narrowly defined, some major importers appear to acquire sufficient market power to appropriate some of the quota rents.

Although figure 3.2 provides a basis for evaluating the partial effect of quotas on a single country's exports, it is inadequate as a basis for evaluating the *overall* impact of the MFA on a country because it does not take into account the effect of restrictions on other countries' exports. Restrictions on those exports tend to increase the demand for exports from the country of interest. It is clearly possible that some exporters might benefit in the short term from these arrangements if they are less restricted than other countries. Traditionally, small suppliers have had an advantage in being less likely to trigger quotas than were such major suppliers as India or China. It should be mentioned, however, that in recent years the key gainers in terms of restricted market access have been relatively large suppliers, such as Mexico, Turkey, and the Central European countries that have benefited from regional preferences granted by the major importers.

One very crude indicator of the restrictiveness of quotas for a particular country is the share of its exports directed to quota markets. If all countries were broadly similar, one might expect the share of exports directed to quota and nonquota markets to be roughly the same.[3] Because each country's MFA quota levels are based on more or less arbitrary historical factors there are good reasons to anticipate that they will result in barriers whose export-tax equivalents vary considerably between exporter-importer pairs. Under such circumstances the shares of export revenues from restricted and unrestricted markets will vary. The more competitive a country is relative to its quota allocation, the greater is likely to be the share of its export revenues received from sales outside the restricted markets. A better indicator, where this is available, is the export-tax equivalent of the MFA quotas that restrict exports from one supplier to a particular market.

All of the analysis to this point has been based on comparatively static methodology. When we take a dynamic perspective on the problem, the costs of the MFA are potentially more serious. A key feature of an outward-oriented development process seems to be identifying industries where relatively high levels of productivity can be achieved. Bernard and Jensen (1999) found that the expansion of such industries, rather than learning by doing within industries, appears to account for the bulk of the potentially formidable gains associated with export growth. Where superior technology in one sector can be introduced into an economy with low productivity in other sectors, and hence low factor prices, such a sector is extremely profitable at first. When the policy environment is sufficiently accommodating and the infrastructure is adequate, such a leading sector can grow *extremely* rapidly. The extraordinary growth rates achieved by the clothing-export industry in Bangladesh, where exports are said to have grown at close to 30 percent a year since 1985, manifest this phenomenon.

The presence or continuing threat of export quotas reduces the opportunity for developing countries to use the relative ease of adopting new technology in the clothing sector as a first step on the ladder of economic development. At the other end of the product life cycle, it encourages economies like Hong Kong (China), whose natural comparative advantage in this labor-intensive industry has largely dissipated, to continue producing because of the quota rents that are available to incumbent exporters.

Export Tax Equivalents[4]

One of the major problems associated with nontariff barriers (NTBs) such as quotas is their lack of transparency. The presence of a quota of a certain size does not indicate clearly whether exports are being restricted by a large or a small amount. Because MFA quotas are administered by exporting governments, these valuable quotas could be used to generate government revenues. More commonly, they are allocated to individual firms, which usually choose to use them or to sell them to another exporter. To export apparel or textile goods subject to quotas, exporters must either buy quotas for these goods or pass up the opportunity to sell quotas they already hold. From the point of view of the exporter, the quotas have an effect akin to an export tax. The price of a quota per unit of exports is equivalent in its effect to an export tax of the same magnitude. If we divide the quota price by the value of the good in the absence of quotas, we obtain a measure of the quota rent in proportion to the value of the export. This is potentially a very useful indicator of restrictiveness, which enables the impact of the quota regime to be evaluated.

The quota price corresponds to the difference between p_R and p_U in figure 3.2. Export tax equivalents (ETEs) are calculated here on the basis of unit values of exports, as $[QP/(UV - QP)] \cdot 100$, where QP is the quota price and UV is the unit value of exports.[5] The ETE indicates the quota premium as a percentage of the unit value of exports excluding the quota premium.[6] Kathuria and Bhardwaj (1998) gave details of individual ETEs calculated for each quota category. Here we report only the quotas aggregated by country or region and by fiber. In this exercise we focused on the two largest markets for Indian textiles and garments, the United States and the European Union (EU), which accounted for 73 percent of total textile and garments exports in 1995/96 (66 percent of garment exports in 1998/99). As a proportion of quota-restricted (MFA) markets, their share is even larger, accounting for 94 percent of total garment exports in 1998/99. For the United States as a whole, table 3.1 shows that overall ETE (weighted by value of exports), which was 38.8 percent of the unit value of exports in 1993, and 36–37 percent in 1994 and 1995, declined over the next three years before picking up in 1999 to over 40 percent. Exports to the EU appear less restricted, with aggregate weighted ETEs being about 14 percent between 1993 and 1995, increasing to about 19 percent in 1996, and returning to that level in 1999 after declining in 1997 and 1998.

The table also displays the simple averages that show the same trend over time as the weighted averages. One difference worth pointing out is that the simple and weighted averages are much more disparate in the U.S. case than in the EU, which implies that the dispersion of individual product ETEs is much lower in the EU. Also, for 1995–98, the simple average ETE is larger for the EU than for the United States. Finally, table 3.1 shows ETEs for synthetics and cottons until 1996. For the United States, the ETEs for cotton products are higher than for synthetics. This tendency is not evident in the EU.

Exports to the United States are divided into two categories, Groups I and II. Group I products have quotas defined for individual products, such as men's shirts, ladies' blouses, and so forth. For Group II the quotas are administered for all of the products in the group as a whole (for example, gloves, handkerchiefs, knit shirts, and so forth)—and so the quota premium is the same for all products within the group, and the variations in ETE arise only from differences in unit values

TABLE 3.1   Export-Tax Equivalents for Indian Garment Exports to the United States and the European Union (Percentage)

Category	1993	1994	1995	1996	1997	1998	1999
United States:							
Group I							
Weighted average	44.1	37.8	41.2	31.3	26.5	29.1	41.7
Simple average	32.8	24.7	25.9	23.4	23.1	24.0	32.2
Group II							
Weighted average	5.8	9.7	0.8	0.6	5.1	5.2	31.4
Simple average	13.8	14.6	1.5	1.3	5.2	4.8	35.6
Total							
Weighted average	38.8	35.7	36.9	28.0	23.9	25.9	40.2
Simple average	18.5	17.1	7.2	6.4	9.7	9.2	34.8
Cotton							
Weighted average	48.2	50.9	51.0	38.9	n.a.	n.a.	n.a.
Simple average	28.1	23.7	15.8	14.2	n.a.	n.a.	n.a.
Synthetics							
Weighted average	4.7	13.0	16.4	16.4	n.a.	n.a.	n.a.
Simple average	11.8	19.0	13.1	10.4	n.a.	n.a.	n.a.
European Union:							
Total							
Weighted average	14.0	13.9	14.4	18.6	15.5	14.8	18.8
Simple average	12.5	12.9	11.9	14.8	13.4	12.1	17.1
Cotton							
Weighted average	13.7	14.1	13.3	17.4	n.a.	n.a.	n.a.
Simple average	14.3	14.3	12.7	16.2	n.a.	n.a.	n.a.
Synthetics							
Weighted average	14.5	9.0	16.8	22.9	n.a.	n.a.	n.a.
Simple average	10.8	11.4	10.6	12.6	n.a.	n.a.	n.a.

n.a. Not applicable.

Source: Field work, updating analysis in Kathuria and Bhardwaj (1998).

(see Kathuria and Bhardwaj [1998] for product-wise ETEs). In 1995 Group II garment ETEs in the United States declined sharply, but because of the low weight of Group II in the total, the weighted average did not decline. It was only in 1996, when the ETE of some of the important Group I garments (338—knit shirts and blouses) fell sharply, that the weighted ETE fell for Group I and for the United States as a whole. The recovery in 1999, on the other hand, related to increases in ETEs for both Group I as well as Group II products.

It also should be noted that ETEs in the range of 28–40 percent for the United States are *higher than the actual tariffs* levied by the United States on imports of textiles and apparel, and (partially) indicate the hidden cost of the MFA, for both the exporting and the importing countries.

The presence of substantial ETEs in the Indian garment and textiles industry is indicative of excess demand, given quota allocations. After what appears to have been a temporary decline in 1997 and 1998, the ETEs for Indian garments recovered strongly in 1999. These high ETEs mean that there may be static welfare gains (see figure 3.2) for India from the quota rents—but those gains need to be set off against possible declines in prices in unrestricted markets. A more fundamental loss, however, would seem to be the loss of potential output and all its associated welfare effects in terms of employment growth, productivity growth, and potentially high profits.

There is little doubt that the ETEs could have been even higher had there been lesser domestic policy constraints on the operation and productivity of Indian firms. To put it another way, India has the potential to benefit substantially from the abolition of quotas in terms of increased market access, employment and output growth, and productivity gains. Policy constraints must be eased for another reason—the increased import competition resulting from the removal of India's own import restrictions since April 2001.[7] Such constraints, which are well known in India, are discussed in the fourth section below.

Implications of MFA Abolition

Recent studies using general equilibrium modeling techniques have examined the implications of MFA abolition for South Asia. Another relevant series of studies has assessed the implications of domestic reforms in India before and after such abolition. In these various studies a key input is the availability of export-tax equivalents such as those just discussed for India.

Evaluating the implications of MFA abolition requires a model comprehensive enough to take into account the interactions between suppliers and their markets, as well as the interactions between the textile and clothing sectors and other sectors of each economy. This requirement favors the use of computable general equilibrium models, which can incorporate these different features. Several such studies were conducted as part of the evaluation of the Uruguay Round, including those of Hertel and others (1996) and Harrison, Rutherford, and Tarr (1996).

Both studies concluded that South Asia in total would benefit significantly from abolition of the MFA. Hertel and others concluded that the gains to the region would be about US$2 billion per year. These results point to substantial overall gains that are likely to be even greater today than they were estimated to be in 1996 because of the increases in export-tax equivalents reported above and because of the completion of regional arrangements (that is, the North American

Free Trade Agreement [NAFTA] and agreements between Europe, Central Europe, Turkey, and other Mediterranean countries) that have diverted export opportunities away from South Asia.

Quota abolition will greatly increase the return from reforms in the domestic industry, and increase the defensive need for South Asian countries to improve productivity in these sectors because countries that do not reform to increase their efficiency will face greatly increased competitive pressure as other exporters currently repressed by the quotas will also be liberalized.

Elbehri, Hertel, and Martin (1997) examined the implications of a number of policy reforms that could increase productivity in the textile and clothing industries in India. One experiment considered a series of reforms that would raise labor productivity in the clothing sector by 67 percent—to roughly the level enjoyed by China. This increase in productivity would seem a realistic goal for such policy reforms as reductions in disincentives for operating in factory mode (see Kathuria and Bhardwaj [1998]) and allowing foreign direct investment (FDI) in the industry. The experiment was conducted both before and after abolition of the quotas to assess the importance of prior abolition of the MFA. The welfare results were then decomposed to allocate them to their sources. The results of the experiment are shown in table 3.2.

The total welfare gains in table 3.2 are divided into direct effects of productivity growth, increases in allocative efficiency, and terms-of-trade gains. The welfare gains resulting from productivity increases depend on the size of the sector in which the gain occurs. The gains in allocative efficiency depend on the induced changes in the quantities of exports and imports passing over trade barriers—the higher the barriers over which additional imports pass, the larger the difference between the value of imports in the country and their external cost, and the larger the gains from additional imports.[8] The terms-of-trade changes depend on the effects of the reform on the average prices for India's exports.

TABLE 3.2   India: Welfare Effects of Reforms That Raise Labor Productivity in Clothing Sectors, 1992 (US$ millions)

	Total Welfare	Terms of Trade	Allocative Efficiency	Productivity
Before MFA abolition	577	62	74	442
After MFA abolition	1,700	476	255	970

Source: Adapted from Elbehri, Hertel, and Martin (1997).

Somewhat surprisingly, the terms-of-trade effects reported in table 3.2 were positive in both of the experiments considered. Two main factors contributed to this result.[9] The first is that the boost to productivity in the clothing industry caused it to draw resources from other sectors. As a consequence, exports of all goods other than clothing fell and that led to an increase in the export prices received for those goods. A second important factor was that the elasticity of substitution[10] for clothing in the Global Trade Analysis Project (GTAP) database is twice as high as for most other products (Huff and others 1997, p. 125), thereby making the elasticity of export demand for clothing higher than for other products. This difference in elasticities means that the terms-of-trade losses resulting from falls in the export price for clothing are less than the gains for other goods. In the first case in table 3.2, that is, before abolition of quotas, an additional factor comes into play. In this situation the rent-inclusive price received for exports to quota markets does not decline even after an increase in clothing exports—rather, the quota rents received by India increase in these markets. Clearly there is some uncertainty about whether the terms-of-trade effects will be positive in all cases. What is important for our purposes is whether the gains from reform rise or fall as a result of quota abolition.

From table 3.2 it is very apparent that the gains from reforms are much higher after the quotas are abolished. Part of this increase merely reflects the greater size of the industry when quotas have been removed. For that larger industry a given increase in productivity has a greater positive effect on income. Another substantial source of welfare gains is the improved terms-of-trade effect resulting from abolition of the quotas. Prior to abolition an outward shift in the supply curve must confront a relatively inelastic demand curve. After abolition the overall demand curve facing the country becomes more elastic and hence the favorable terms-of-trade effect becomes much larger, which more than makes up for the loss of the quota-induced positive price effects mentioned in the previous paragraph. The allocative efficiency effect is also larger because the increase in productivity after the reform permits a much greater increase in imports over India's high tariff barriers. The overall effect is roughly to triple the gains from domestic reform.

This experiment considered only the effect of improving productivity in the Indian textile and clothing sectors. The abolition of the MFA quotas agreed to in the Uruguay Round will not be confined to India, of course, but will cover all members of the WTO.[11] Although model-based research has suggested that South Asia will gain from this process (Yang, Martin, and Yanagishima 1997), South Asia will face greatly increased competition in the industrial country markets. Unless the pace of reforms is maintained, South Asia is likely to suffer severely from this increase in competition.

Domestic Policy Constraints in India

Having considered the implications of the abolition of the MFA, we now consider the domestic policy constraints that have long affected the textile and clothing industries in India and elsewhere in South Asia. These constraints are particularly severe in India, which has perhaps a stronger tradition of intervention in industry policies than do other South Asian countries. Many of the distortions that reduce the efficiency of the sector are quite complex and assessments of their impact require detailed studies.

Disincentives to Operating in the Factory Mode

The garment industry is based on a system of decentralized production. This decentralization results at least partly from the existence of labor legislation and the lack of an effective exit policy, as well as the reservation of garment (until recently) and hosiery production for the small-scale sector.[12] Decentralized production, however, also has natural advantages, such as cheap labor in the subcontracted firms and production flexibility. The tax regime that grants exemptions and concessions in tax payments to small-scale producers also favors the decentralized mode. The question that now needs to be addressed is whether the decentralized system of production is becoming a constraint to investment and therefore to increased productivity and growth in the apparel industry.

Indian garment exports have been niche-based, focusing on low volume and high variety of outputs, within the broad area of fashion clothing and especially ladies' outerwear. The flexibility in the Indian production system is eminently suited to meeting this demand. In fact, the nature of demand and the characteristics of the production system are mutually reinforcing. The downside of relying on fabricators is that variations are likely among different lots of output. This effectively *prevents India from becoming a major player in the mass market for clothing*, which demands good and consistent quality across huge volumes of a single item of clothing.[13] Moreover, the average quality of output, although much improved, still has not allowed the price to go beyond the middle range.

All of the countries with very successful garment exports have a much lower level of subcontracting than does India. As Khanna (1993, p. 285) pointed out, in the early 1990s apparel firms in India subcontracted 74 percent of their output, compared with only 11 percent for Hong Kong (China), 18 percent for China, 20 percent for Thailand, 28 percent for South Korea, and 36 percent for Taiwan (China). All of these countries have a broader base of exports and have done very well in the market for large volumes of uniform products. Khanna also presented evidence that apparel firms are more productive in East Asian countries than in

India because of far larger investments in machinery, even in low-wage China. Indian firms tend to invest more in sewing machines and less in processing and special machinery.[14] For Indian exports to grow substantially beyond present levels the current overwhelming reliance on fabricators will have to change.

Much of the garment industry is aware that factory investment is needed but the industry has been unwilling to commit itself to larger investments. This hesitancy is to some extent a response to the failures of some high-profile garment factories, caused at least partly by labor problems. It is not as though there are no large organized-sector firms in India—quite the contrary. So what makes the garment industry so different or unable to handle the labor issue? Perhaps it is the high export orientation of the industry and its focus on fashion goods, wherein even a short strike can cripple the firm.[15] A second reason for the lack of investment in factories is that the domestic fabric base is not fully compatible with the demands of factory production. The large lengths of uniform lots of fabric that are needed for factories are not being produced in the domestic sector because fabrics are sourced largely from (small) powerlooms and because there are few high-quality fabric dyeing and printing facilities.

Our own judgment on this is that subcontracting is a low-risk, low-capital strategy. In subcontracting, the bulk of the labor force is "outsourced," which results in a major decline in fixed costs. Investments in equipment and factory space are also minimized. Exporters are unwilling to trade this off against an unproven and high-risk strategy, unless they are pushed to the wall because demand for the present kind of products starts to decline—and that has not happened so far. Risks are high for the following reasons. First, labor is a fixed cost in India because of the grave difficulty of shedding labor in an industry where demand can be cyclical. Second, while investing in a large factory for garments, exporters had to make a commitment to export 50 percent of their output in perpetuity (until de-reservation of garments in 2000). Although actual exports may exceed the commitments, the obligation and the *attendant monitoring* of the obligation (the "Inspector Raj syndrome") by the authorities enhance the investor's perception of inherent risk. Third (and this is more speculative), the factory mode may make the final product more expensive (albeit of higher quality), whereas the additional return from the domestic market is uncertain because it is still highly sensitive to price. This may make the exporter more export-oriented than he would like to be or than the government requires him to be.

Fiber Bias, Product Reservation, and the Hank Yarn Obligation

Perhaps the most critical aspect is the policy bias against synthetic fibers. This bias arose from the view that "... cotton is for the masses and synthetics for the classes!"[16] as well as from a concern for cotton producers. Manmade fibers (MMF) have always been subject to higher rates of indirect taxation vis-à-vis similar cotton-based products. Moreover, domestic costs of manufacturing synthetic fibers and polyester-filament yarn are high because of uneconomic plant size in an industry where economies of scale are very important. This situation arose from the industrial-licensing policy that licensed relatively small plants for production of specified outputs with little interfiber flexibility. The latter policy changed with the coming of the Textile Policy of 1985, which adopted a distinct multifiber approach. The gap has narrowed, although tax policies still discriminate against MMF vis-à-vis cottons, and this discrimination at the fiber stage continues into the yarn and fabric stages. For example, whereas the excise duty on cotton yarn in 1997/98 was 5.75 percent, it was 20.7 percent on blended yarn and 34.5 percent on PFY (polyester filament yarn).[17] Moreover, imported inputs for production of PSF (polyester staple fiber) and PFY are still subject to high duties. In 1998, for example, the duty was 25 percent on dimethylene terephthalate (DMT), purified terephthalic acid (PTA), and monoethylene glycol (MEG), and 30 percent on caprolactum.[18]

Although the policy bias has narrowed since 1997/98, the differential still prevails in the following ways: (a) controls on the export of cotton and cotton yarn mean that prices of raw cotton are typically below international prices, which provides an implicit subsidy to consumers of cotton; (b) the still high import duties raise the cost of synthetic yarn and intermediates; and (c) the domestic duties such as excise are lower for cotton fabrics. This combines with a trade regime that, despite improvements, remains cumbersome and imposes high transaction costs, for example, when exporters claim duty drawback on exports or want duty-free imports for exports. The combination of the cotton bias and the high transaction costs imposed by the trade regime has meant that India's production, consumption, and export of textiles and garments are still heavily *weighted in favor of cotton-based products*. For example, cotton exports were 83 percent by volume and 75 percent by value of all apparel exports from India in 1993, and this fell only slowly to 81 percent and 71 percent, respectively, in 1998. By comparison, world exports and consumption are predominantly in the synthetic blends.

The potential gains from promoting a true multifiber policy cannot be precisely estimated but the possibilities are very promising. One could think of an increase in India's overall exports based on the world-demand pattern of noncotton to cotton consumption, using as a base the current value of cotton-based exports. In 1998/99, 71 percent of US$5.3 billion in garment exports and 70 percent of $8.4 billion in all textiles exports (including garments) were cotton based. If cotton-based exports had been only 50 and 40 percent of total exports, respectively, and assuming no decrease in cotton exports, total exports of textiles in

1998/99 would have been $11.7 billion and $14.7 billion, respectively, and garments would have been $7.5 billion and $9.4 billion, respectively. Thus, *had India's policies not been cotton biased, its textile and garments exports could have been as much as 75 percent higher than they are on this count alone.* Of course the domestic bias could have been substantially mitigated had the import-duty drawback and the duty-free import-for-export system worked more efficiently.

Promotion of the handloom sector has been a central feature of the textile policy in India. According to the Ministry of Textiles Annual Report of 1998/99, handlooms provided direct and indirect employment to over 12.4 million weavers. This and a desire to preserve culture and heritage have meant that the government has used several instruments to prop up the handloom sector. One of these instruments is the reservation of 11 textile articles (such as cotton and silk sarees, dhotis, towels, lungis, bedsheets, shawls, blankets, and so forth) for exclusive production in the handloom sector, under the 1996 policy on this issue. The implementation of this policy got a boost when in 1994 the Indian Supreme Court dismissed the petitions challenging the Handlooms (Reservations of Articles for Production) Act of 1985.

The futility of this policy can be gauged from the fact that there were, according to government estimates, as many as 1.4 million powerlooms in India at the end of 1995. As Misra (1993) pointed out, the policy ignores the dismal past record of enforcement measures and the huge administrative machinery required to enforce this policy. Besides requiring this totally unproductive administration, the policy is also a breeding ground for corruption. It is no surprise that Misra concluded that the Handlooms Act has made little material difference to the state of the handloom sector. On the other hand, it has penalized the domestic industry as a whole. As in the case of small-scale industry (SSI), foreign-made products in the form of imports can compete on these items even while domestic industry is kept out.

The Hank Yarn Obligation stipulates that spinning mills should supply not less than 50 percent of the yarn marketed by them in the form of hanks for use by the handloom sector (reduced to 40 percent under an order of the Textile Commissioner dated January 2003). Hank yarn is exempted from excise and sales tax and opens up possibilities for corruption, misdeclaration, and the like. There have been direct costs to this policy and longer-term effects on investment decisions. Misra (1993) advocated doing away with the obligation and, if necessary, having handloom-development agencies set up independent hank-reeling centers close to areas where handlooms are concentrated.[19]

All these policy restrictions impair the efficiency of the industry and result in an upward shift in its supply curve. This in turn results in lower measured ETEs than would have prevailed in a less constraining policy environment (a downward shift in the supply curve results in an increase in the quota price—intuitively, it can be thought of as an increase in competition for the same quota). Removing these restrictions will be vital in the post-quota world where competitiveness will be the key.

Key Policy Imperatives

To summarize the policy discussion, India's textile industry will benefit from policy action along the following lines:

- *Reduction of disincentives for factory-mode production.* The recent repeal of the reservation of garments production for small-scale units has removed a major disincentive for factory-mode production.[20] Such policies have allowed China, with factor endowments very similar to those of India, to march well ahead of India in the export business. Second, and accompanying SSI de-reservation, is the introduction of a labor policy wherein labor can be retrenched if necessary, with appropriate safeguards.[21] Part of the pressure for these changes is already appearing from international buyers who are demanding to see factory-type production in conditions where they can be confident about production systems, quality control, and working conditions.
- *Removal of the policy bias (high taxation) against synthetic fibers* (which is admittedly lower than in the past), thereby increasing the domestic base of synthetic fibers and providing the factories with an additional source of demand and an avenue to increase exports in a major way. Cheaper domestic sourcing may also reduce the need for exporters to import synthetic fibers and would thereby reduce their transaction costs.
- *Eliminations of the reservation for exclusive handlooms production* will enable large and small Indian firms to compete equally with large foreign firms (which cannot be barred from exporting these products to India), and eliminate the large administrative apparatus that polices compliance, thereby reducing the bureaucratic (Inspector Raj) cost imposed on firms. In a similar vein, *elimination of the hank-yarn obligation* will help. Neither policy has been successful at propping up the noncompetitive segments within handlooms. The 2000 National Textile Policy promises to review these policies, "keeping in mind the needs of the handloom industry."
- Other policies of a more generic nature will also help—for example, making imported fabrics available for export production in an effective manner. Currently, there are *long delays in shipments and clearance,* and there are many problems in the operation of the duty-free input-for-exports schemes (see Nair and Kaul 1996). In general, the transaction costs of trading remain very high

and contribute in a substantial way to the antiexport bias that still persists in the Indian economy. Finally, continued easing of trade constraints including a reduction in the high rates of customs tariffs will also promote exports.[22]

Conclusion

This chapter has set out the basic economics of the MFA applicable to the South Asian countries and examined the implications for domestic reform. The key to assessing the implications of this discriminatory regime is to recognize the price discrimination among markets. This discrimination means that the benefits of any quota gains in the restricted industrial markets must be weighed against losses in the unrestricted markets where prices are depressed by the regime.

A key set of parameters for any evaluation of the MFA is the magnitude of the implicit export taxes that are imposed on a country's exports of textiles and clothing. These taxes were found to be substantial in an earlier study by Kathuria and Bhardwaj (1998). Updates of these estimates suggest that the ETEs of these quotas may well have declined in 1996, but they appear to have increased in 1999 to an average of 40 percent in the United States and 20 percent in the EU—thereby imposing substantial barriers to Indian exports and highlighting the strong competitiveness of India's producers of textiles and apparel even despite the regulatory and cost burdens they face.

The limited available evidence about effects on India and other countries in South Asia suggests that the gains from domestic reform to raise productivity in these industries will greatly increase following abolition of the quotas. Part of the increase in the gains comes from increases in the scale of the industry experiencing the productivity gain, but another important source of gains is a reduction in the terms-of-trade losses associated with increased textile and clothing exports. Following removal of the quotas, important parts of the world textile and clothing markets will be much more price responsive. Overall, there are substantial terms-of-trade gains when productivity rises after the abolition of the quotas because resources are attracted into clothing and out of sectors where export-demand curves are relatively inelastic. Overall gains of about US\$2 billion a year were found for India alone by increasing productivity by 67 percent in the clothing sector to bring it roughly into line with China.

The substantially improved gains after quota abolition provide an analytical foundation to the demands of India and its South Asian neighbors for "...an immediate need for a more meaningful integration of the textile and clothing sector...Measures in this regard should include, *inter alia*, accelerated removal of quota restrictions...and implementation of increased growth rates for the remaining years of the Agreement on Textiles and Clothing...."[23]

Within India, policymakers may have been prepared to accept a slow pace of reform in the textile and clothing sectors in the past, when opportunities were restricted and threats in the domestic market were limited. But to do so in the future will mean missing out on potentially far greater direct gains from productivity improvements. In addition, it will expose these industries to much greater risk of losing ground in a fiercely competitive world market. Finally, as trade barriers start coming down following World Trade Organization negotiations in India and elsewhere, the industries also will face substantially increased competition in their home markets—a fact that lends an urgency to domestic policy reform. Urgent action is therefore required to address the disincentives for factory-based operations, including labor laws, removing the policy bias against synthetic fibers, and reducing the still high transaction costs of trading.

Endnotes

1. Formally, the MFA was replaced by the Agreement on Textiles and Clothing but the basic architecture of these quotas is the same as those under the MFA and so we use the same terminology.

2. Producer welfare in figure 3.1 is represented by the area between p_W and the supply curve S. The gain in welfare in figure 3.2 is the area above p_W (the cross-hatched area), and the area below p_W is the loss in welfare (the vertically hatched area).

3. Of course countries are not the same, and there may be reasons, such as proximity or historical performance, for some countries to have much higher shares of exports to quota markets. However, the export share still provides a useful benchmark.

4. This section is based on an update of Kathuria and Bhardwaj (1998).

5. We define the export-tax equivalent as the value of the quota divided by the price received by a producer who does *not* own quota for this product.

6. In figure 3.2, the ETE is $[(PR - PU)/PU] \cdot 100$.

7. A surge of imports is unlikely, however, given that Indian garments and textiles are largely quite cost competitive.

8. Fukase and Martin (2000) showed that this source of welfare gains can be substantial. Vietnam's gaining most-favored-nation access to the U.S. market accounted for 40 percent of its welfare gain.

9. Another factor contributing to this outcome is the Armington specification used in the GTAP model. Because exports and products sold on the domestic market are the same, the increased demand for imports by India can be met without large increases in import prices.

10. This is the key parameter in determining the export-demand elasticities facing India's exports.

11. The timing of the abolition of restrictions on countries such as China that were not WTO members when the Agreement on Textiles and Clothing came into effect depends on the provisions of their accession to the WTO, or on bilateral agreements that they reach with the importing countries.

12. Alam (1991), in a study of small industrial firms, found that firms deliberately minimize the size of the labor force to reduce the bargaining power of employees and to avoid legal obligations toward them. The most common way to do this is to separate the most labor-intensive production process (for example, fabrication in the case of garments) and have that work done by outside contractors. As part of the National Textile Policy 2000, garments production was de-reserved and the production of garments by large firms in India was no longer barred.

13. In Khanna's (1993) study of 149 apparel manufacturers in five countries of Southeast Asia, manufacturers in Hong Kong (China) and Thailand observed that Indian garments lacked consistency and uniformity in quality.

14.

Typewise Average Number of Machines Installed by Each Apparel Export Firm

Economy	Precutting Machines	Cutting Machines	Sewing Machines	Special Machines	Processing Machines
Republic of Korea	2.9	12.3	134.3	77.5	31.0
Taiwan (China)	2.6	7.5	185.1	49.5	12.8
Hong Kong (China)	2.3	13.2	455.4	112.7	27.9
China	2.3	13.2	450.5	104.8	34.4
Thailand	2.0	12.8	460.8	72.4	21.9
India	0.0	2.3	103.7	8.6	4.6

Source: Kathuria and Bhardwaj (1998, p. 17), drawn from Khanna (1993).

15. In the case of non-fashion goods, because the demand for any good may last longer than for fashion goods, firms may be able to ride out a short strike even if by selling at a discount to another buyer.

16. Ramakrishna (1995, p. 5), in a discussion paper on restructuring the textile industry.

17. For details, see World Bank (1997), volume II, annex 1.

18. The decline in the policy bias can be seen from the gradual decline over the years in the rates of customs duty on synthetic fibers and inputs into the production of synthetic fibers. Customs duties on the most important fibers have declined: for VSF (viscose staple fiber) from 60 percent in 1987 to 25 percent in 1996; for PSF and ASF (acetate staple fiber) from more than 150 percent in 1987 to 45 percent in 1996 and 32 percent in 1997. Duties on inputs such as DMT, PTA, MEG, caprolactum and acrylonitrile have declined from 90–195 percent in 1987 to 20–45 percent in 1996. Along with this, the domestic industry has become more competitive, both at the input stage and at the output of fibers. This can be seen in declining NPCs (nominal protection coefficients) for fibers (that is, basic ex-factory prices relative to landed prices for imports of the same fiber). Declining NPCs signify that domestic production is becoming more competitive, and an NPC less than one means that domestic production is cheaper than the international benchmark. VSF was already close to international prices by 1987 (NPC of 1.05) and has consistently had an NPC less than one thereafter. PSF and ASF, the fibers that were less competitive to begin with, have also seen a steady decline in their NPCs, from 2.5–3.0 in 1984 to 1.3–1.5 by 1993 (helped by the devaluation of the rupee in 1991 and a depreciation thereafter), and by 1996 all three fibers were competitive. The inputs that go into fiber production have also witnessed declining NPCs in all cases, and for at least two of the most important (DMT and PTA) domestic prices were competitive by 1996. See Kathuria and Bhardwaj (1998, tables 10 and 11).

19. For details, see annex 3, World Bank, volume 2 (1997, pp. 10–12); and Misra (1993, pp. 223–26).

20. Hosiery products, however, are still reserved. According to the 2000 National Textile Policy the reservation will be reviewed. See Hussain Committee (1997), World Bank (1998), and Chatterjee and Mohan (1993) for more details on how the small-industry policy affected production, output, quality, and so forth. The Hussain Committee on small-scale industry recommended complete abolition of small-scale reservation in all sectors.

21. The Finance Minister's 2001/02 budget speech announced that the Industrial Disputes Act and the Contract Labor Act will be amended. Implementation of this announcement would allow easier layoffs for firms with less than 1,000 workers and facilitate contractual hiring and outsourcing of jobs.

22. See World Bank (2000, Chapter 6) for details relating to India's tariffs and other trade-related policies. The study also documents the increasing use of antidumping practices, and argues that improving India's domestic policies will be more beneficial in the long run, as opposed to practices that increase protection and thereby increase the antiexport bias.

23. Joint Statement by the SAARC (South Asian Association for Regional Cooperation) Commerce Ministers on the forthcoming Fourth WTO Ministerial Conference at Doha. New Delhi, August 23, 2001.

References

The word "processed" describes informally produced works that may not be available commonly through libraries.

Alam, Ghayur. 1991. "Impact of Non-Economic Factors on Choice of Technology and Organization of Production: A Study of Small Industrial Firms in India." New Delhi: International Labor Organization. Processed.

Bernard, Andrew, and J. B. Jensen. 1999. "Exporting and Productivity." Working Paper 7135. National Bureau of Economic Research, Cambridge, Mass.

Bhagwati, J. 1988. *Protectionism.* Cambridge, Mass.: MIT Press.

Chatterjee, S., and R. Mohan. 1993. "India's Garment Exports." *Economic and Political Weekly,* August 28, pp. M-95–119.

Elbehri, A., T. Hertel, and W. Martin. 1997. "Estimating the Impact of Trade Reforms on the Indian Cotton and Textile Sectors: A General Equilibrium Approach." Washington, D.C.: World Bank. Processed.

Fukase, E., and W. Martin. 2000. "The Effects of the United States Granting MFN Status to Vietnam." *Weltwirtschaftliches Archiv* 136: 539–59.

Hamilton, Carl B., ed. 1990. *Textiles Trade and the Developing Countries: Eliminating the Multi-Fiber Arrangement in the 1990s.* Washington, D.C.: World Bank.

Harrison, Glenn, T. Rutherford, and D. Tarr. 1996. "Quantifying the Uruguay Round." In W. Martin and L. A. Winters, eds., *The Uruguay Round and the Developing Countries.* Cambridge, U.K.: Cambridge University Press.

Hertel, Thomas, W. Martin, K. Yanagishima, and B. Dimaranan. 1996. "Liberalizing Manufactures Trade in a Changing World Economy." In W. Martin and L. A. Winters, eds., *The Uruguay Round and the Developing Countries.* Cambridge, U.K.: Cambridge University Press.

Huff, K., K. Hanslow, T. Hertel, and M. Tsigas. 1997. "GTAP Behavioral Parameters." In T. Hertel, ed., *Global Trade Analysis: Modeling and Applications.* New York: Cambridge University Press.

Hussain Committee. 1997. "Report of the Expert Committee on Small Enterprises." Abid Hussain, chairman. New Delhi.

Kathuria, Sanjay, and A. Bhardwaj. 1998. "Export Quotas and Policy Constraints in the Indian Textile and Garment Industries." Policy Research Working Paper 2012. World Bank, Policy Research Department, Washington, D.C.

Khanna, S. R. 1993. "The Challenge of Global Competition in the 1990s: An Agenda for Enhancing the Competitive Position of the Indian Textiles and Clothing Industry." New Delhi: Indian Council for Research on International Economic Relations. Processed.

Krishna, Kala, and L. Tan. 1998. *Rags and Riches: Implementing Apparel Quotas under the Multi-Fiber Arrangement.* Ann Arbor: University of Michigan Press.

Martin, Will, and S. Suphachalasai. 1990. "Effects of the Multi-Fiber Arrangements on Developing Country Exporters: A Simple Theoretical Framework." In Carl B. Hamilton, ed., *Textiles Trade and the Developing Countries: Eliminating the Multi-Fiber Arrangement in the 1990s.* Washington, D.C.: World Bank.

Misra, Sanjeev. 1993. *India's Textile Sector: A Policy Analysis.* New Delhi: Saga Publications.

Nair, R. M., and P. Kaul. 1996. "Exporting Garments from India." Policy Paper 4. New Delhi: Project LARGE.

Ramakrishna, R. 1995. "Workshop on Restructuring of Textile Industry." Background paper. New Delhi: Federation of Indian Chambers of Commerce and Industry.

World Bank. 1997. *India: Cotton and Textile Industries—Maximizing the Potential for Growth in a More Competitive Environment,* Volumes I and II. Washington, D.C.

———. 1998. *India Macroeconomic Update: Reforming for Growth and Poverty Reduction.* Washington, D.C.

———. 2000. *India: Reducing Poverty, Accelerating Development.* Delhi: Oxford University Press.

Yang, Y., W. Martin, and K. Yanagishima. 1997. "Evaluating the Benefits of Abolishing the MFA in the Uruguay Round Package." In T. Hertel, ed., *Global Trade Analysis: Modeling and Applications.* Cambridge, U.K.: Cambridge University Press.

4

SERVICES ISSUES AND LIBERALIZATION IN THE DOHA DEVELOPMENT AGENDA NEGOTIATIONS: A CASE STUDY OF INDIA

Rajesh Chadha

The preamble to the General Agreement on Trade in Services (GATS) states that the general goal of participants is to establish a multilateral framework of principles and rules for trade in services with a view to expanding such trade under conditions of transparency and progressive liberalization. This would promote the economic growth and development of all trading partners. The agreement expresses the desire "to facilitate the increasing participation of developing countries in trade in services and the expansion of their service exports including, *inter alia*, through the strengthening of their domestic services capacity and its efficiency and competitiveness." The preamble clearly recognizes the right of all parties to regulate the supply of services within their territories. It takes "particular account of the serious difficulty of the least-developed countries in view of their special economic situation and their development, trade and financial needs."

The objective of this chapter is to analyze the importance of the service sectors in India. In the first section, I present a discussion of what constitutes trade in services. In the second section, I highlight India's commitments in the GATS. In the third section, I present a discussion of how protected and inefficient service sectors

I am sincerely grateful to Alan V. Deardorff and Robert M. Stern for continued guidance and support on issues relating to trade and computable general equilibrium (CGE) modeling. Special thanks to Rakesh Mohan for providing enduring encouragement and useful comments during the course of this study. Thanks also are due to Sanjib Pohit, who worked with me on the National Council of Applied Economic Research initiative on CGE trade models. Devender Pratap, Bikram Prakas Ghosh, and Praveen Sachdeva provided excellent research support.

reduce the competitiveness of India's manufacturing sectors, and the success story of the software sector in India's economy and trade. In the fourth section, I discuss the potential gains that are expected to accrue for India and other countries and regions of the world as a result of an assumed reduction of 33 percent in the barriers to trade in goods and service sectors in the ongoing Doha Development Agenda negotiations. This is done using a multicountry, multisector computable general equilibrium (CGE) model of world production and trade.

What Constitutes Trade in Services

The International Monetary Fund's (IMF's) balance of payments statistics is the main source of information on international trade in services (IMF 1993). Those statistics, however, have some notable weaknesses. For example, some economies—such as the former Soviet Union—only recently began reporting data on trade in services. Disaggregation of important components is limited and varies across countries. There are inconsistencies in the methods used to report items, and those inconsistencies contribute to a downward bias in the value of the service trade reported in the balance of payments (see World Bank [2002] for details).

Commercial service exports are total service exports minus exports of government services not included elsewhere. International transactions in services are defined in the IMF's *Balance of Payments Manual (BPM5)* (1993) as the economic output of intangible commodities that may be produced, transferred, and consumed at the same time. Definitions may vary among reporting economies.

- **Transport** covers all transport services (sea, air, land, internal waterway, space, and pipeline) performed by residents of one economy for those of another and involving the carriage of passengers, movement of goods (freight), rental of carriers with crew, and related support and auxiliary services. Certain services are excluded from the transport service category: freight insurance, which is included in insurance services; goods procured in ports by nonresident carriers; and repairs of transport equipment are included in goods. Repairs of railway facilities, harbors, and airline facilities, which are included in construction services. Rental of carriers without crew is included in other services.
- **Travel** covers goods and services acquired from an economy by travelers in that economy for their own use during visits of less than one year for business and personal purposes. Travel services include the goods and services consumed by travelers, such as meals, lodging, and transport including car rental (within the economy visited).
- **Other commercial services** include such activities as insurance and financial services, international telecommunications, and postal and courier services; computer data; news-related service transactions between residents and nonresidents;

construction services; royalties and license fees; miscellaneous business, professional, and technical services; and personal, cultural, and recreational services.

The GATS encompasses all that is traded under the four modes of service transactions carried out among different countries of the world: cross-border trade (mode 1); consumption abroad (mode 2); commercial presence (mode 3); and movement of natural persons (mode 4). The traditional IMF definition of trade in commercial services is stated in the *BPM5*. The balance of payments statistics there are based on the concept of residency, and all transactions are recorded between residents and nonresident transactors.[1] The scope of service transactions is widened under the GATS through the introduction of additional concepts like nationality, territorial location, and ownership or control. The data on trade in commercial services as provided in the *BPM5* relate only to the first two modes of service transactions. In fact there is no mention of supply of services through commercial presence, and the trade in services based on the movement of natural persons is, at best, estimated as a proxy.

The *Manual of Statistics of International Trade in Services* (*MSITS;* UN 2002)[2] has been a major effort to resolve the divergence between the GATS legal framework and the traditional statistical framework of the *BPM5*. The *MSITS* sets out an internationally agreed, GATS-coherent framework for compiling and reporting statistics of international trade in services, but the *MSITS* conforms with and explicitly relates to the *BPM5*.

International transactions under mode 3 are based on the commercial presence of foreign affiliates and are referred to as *foreign affiliate trade in services* (FATS). The statistical concept of FATS is similar to the commercial presence notion under the GATS (Karsenty 2000), with two major differences. First, whereas the GATS refers to majority ownership and control, FATS data are based on majority ownership alone. Second, whereas the GATS covers services whether produced by a service company or a company classified under the manufacturing sector, FATS aims at measuring the output of companies classified according to their primary activity.

For our purposes, trade in *commercial services* refers to the first two modes of trade in services, and trade in *all services* (in line with the GATS definition) includes international service transactions under modes 3 and 4 and commercial services. The values of the four modes for 1997 and 2000 are indicated in table 4.1.

India's GATS Commitments

In the Uruguay Round, India's schedule under the GATS provided for specific commitments covering business services, communications, construction work for civil engineering, financial services, health-related and social services, and tourism services (WTO 1998, p. 152; see also Chadha 2002). The extent of commitments varied

TABLE 4.1   Trade in Services by Mode of Supply

Mode	Proxy Used[a]	Value (US$ Billions) 1997	Share (Percent)	Value (US$ Billions) 2000	Share (Percent)
1	BPM5 commercial services minus travel	890	40.9	972	
2	BPM5 travel	424	19.5	463	19.5
3	FATS gross output in services	820	37.7	896[b]	37.8
4	BPM5 compensation of employees	41	1.9	41	1.7
Total		2,175	100.0	2,372	100.0

a. Proxy refers to the closest possible estimates of four modes of trade in services.
b. Our estimate assuming growth in FATS is equal to that in BPM5 commercial services.

Sources: Karsenty (2000); author's estimates; IMF Statistical Yearbook (various issues).

across sectors, with certain restrictions on market access and national treatment under the four modes of supply. India has not made any commitments on services relating to distribution; education; environment; recreation, culture, and sporting; transport; and other services not included elsewhere. In all, India made commitments in 33 activities, compared with an average of 23 for developing countries (GATT 1994). These commitments generally bind India's existing policy framework, although in some cases the applied policy may be more liberal than the binding commitments.[3] India has listed some most-favored-nation exemptions under GATS Article II and reserves the right to offer more favorable treatment to some World Trade Organization (WTO) members in communication, recreational, and transport services.[4] India further liberalized its commitments in basic telecommunication services in early 1998. It is among 43 countries participating in the Information Technology Agreement that covers computers, telecommunication equipment, semiconductors, manufacturing equipment for semiconductors, software, and scientific instruments. India has offered zero duty on 217 information technology–related tariff lines at the Harmonized Commodity Description and Coding System (HS) six-digit level by 2005.[5]

Trade in Services: An Indian Case Study

Efficient services are crucial to an economy's global competitiveness. We have seen in the computational analysis presented in Chapter 2 that considerable benefits accrue when service sectors are liberalized. Another way to explore the inefficiencies in the service sectors is to calculate how protection in services affects effective rates of protection (ERPs).[6] It has been pointed out that the actual effective protection to manufacturing sectors may turn out to be lower if adjustment for high protection to service sectors, arising from regulatory policies, is also taken into account (Hoekman and Djankov 1997).[7] I have computed such ERPs for the manufacturing sectors of India for the year 1997/98, using Hoekman's (1995, 1996) "guesstimates" of tariff equivalents of implicit protection on India's service sectors. The results for the 30 input–output sectors, which account for more than 20 percent share of services in total intermediate inputs, are reported in table 4.2. Note that in 25 of 30 sectors, the inefficient services–adjusted ERP is less than the normal ERP, with the difference becoming large in some sectors. In the case of electrical machinery, the adjusted ERP is negative at −6.6 percent compared with an original value of 26.2 percent. The difference is substantial also for coal tar products, steel and ferrous alloys, fertilizers, and woolen textiles. The upshot is that the inefficient service sectors may act as a tax on manufacturing and thereby reduce effective protection.

The Indian Government is aware of the need to improve the provision of services, and it understands that the investment required is beyond the means available to it. Hence, the Government has been urged to seek private support (Mohan 1996). India liberalized its foreign direct investment (FDI) regime during the 1990s.[8] Foreign equity up to 51 percent is now automatically allowed in restaurants and hotels; support services for land and water transport; parts of renting and leasing; business services, including software; and health and medical services. The automatic approval provision for foreign equity is 74 percent in the case of mining services, nonconventional energy generation and distribution, land and water transport, and storage and warehousing. The limit is 100 percent in the case of electricity generation, transmission, and distribution. Foreign equity, however, is limited to 49 percent in telecommunications, 40 percent in domestic airlines, and 20 percent in banking services. Railway transport remains among the four industries reserved for the public sector. Only recently has the insurance sector been opened to the private sector.

India's Success Story: Software

The GATS Services Sectoral Classification List (GNS) includes "computer and related services" as a component of "business services" (GNS code 1B). Computer and related services include (a) consultancy services related to the installation of computer hardware; (b) software implementation services; (c) data processing services; (d) database services; and (e) others.[9] But it is not clear where to draw the line between computer "software" and "services."[10] In the case of India's commitments under "computer and related services," cross-border supply (mode 1) and consumption

TABLE 4.2   Protection in India, 1997–98 (Percent)

Sector	Nominal Rate of Protection	Share of Services in Total Inputs	Effective Rate of Protection	Adjusted Effective Rate of Protection[a]
1 Cement	43.7	35.1	57.9	36.0
2 Coal tar products	30.6	31.5	43.4	7.1
3 Inorganic heavy chemicals	34.3	29.3	36.0	16.4
4 Other nonmetallic mineral products	42.1	28.5	48.3	37.9
5 Nonferrous basic metals	31.6	28.3	34.4	17.6
6 Electrical industrial machinery	29.1	27.8	26.2	−6.6
7 Organic heavy chemicals	33.8	26.6	34.8	17.7
8 Other transport equipment	45.0	26.4	49.5	51.9
9 Iron, steel, and ferroalloys	28.4	25.8	28.4	6.0
10 Paper, paper products, and newsprint	33.4	25.6	35.3	22.2
11 Structural clay products	39.4	24.8	47.9	39.5
12 Iron and steel casting and forging	35.0	24.3	43.1	29.8
13 Cotton textiles and khadi	41.1	23.9	59.0	59.1
14 Watches and clocks	39.2	23.7	39.6	39.8
15 Ships and boats	32.9	23.3	32.7	28.6
16 Communication equipment	36.3	23.3	36.7	31.1
17 Jute, hemp, mesta, textiles	45.0	22.9	52.9	49.3
18 Industrial machinery (others)	26.6	22.7	23.1	13.8
19 Paints, varnishes, and lacquers	35.0	22.6	35.1	26.7
20 Fertilizers	25.7	22.5	19.9	2.6
21 Iron and steel foundries	35.0	22.2	41.0	27.6
22 Electronic equipment (including TV)	29.7	22.1	27.3	18.2
23 Leather footwear	45.0	21.8	52.3	53.6
24 Leather and leather products	32.1	21.7	32.2	27.1
25 Art silk, synthetic fiber textiles	43.3	21.3	50.0	47.9
26 Industrial machinery	31.7	20.9	24.3	16.2
27 Readymade garments	45.0	20.6	48.1	49.2
28 Motor cycles and scooters	45.0	20.5	51.1	51.0
29 Synthetic fibers, resins	40.0	20.4	44.7	39.3
30 Woolen textiles	23.2	20.3	12.8	3.9

a. Adjustment made for tariff equivalents for services.

Sources: Hoekman 1995; Chadha and Pohit 1998; and NCAER 1998.

abroad (mode 2) are unbound under both market access and national treatment. Commercial presence (mode 3) gets national treatment, but market access is possible only through incorporation with foreign equity. The presence of natural persons (mode 4) is unbound except as indicated in the horizontal section.

India has the world's second largest pool of English-speaking, scientific manpower. Moreover, Indian software is of high quality and relatively low cost. The software industry emerged as one of the fastest growing and most vibrant segments of India's economy during the 1990s. The domestic software market increased from US$160 million in 1992/93 to $944 million in 1997/98, thus registering an average annual growth rate of 43 percent (NASSCOM 1999). The exports of software increased from $225 million in 1992/93 to $1.75 billion in 1997/98, which is an average annual growth rate of 51 percent.[11] In May 1998 the National Task Force on Information Technology and Software Development was set up, consisting of ministers, bureaucrats, scientists, academicians, and industry representatives.[12]

India has already acquired a substantial market share in the global cross-country, customized software–development market. Recognized as an important base for software development, its share in the global market has increased from 11.9 percent in 1991 to 18.5 percent in 1998. In 1997/98, more than 158 of the *Fortune 500* companies outsourced their software requirements to India. Quality has become the hallmark of the industry with more than 109 Indian software companies having acquired international quality certification. Two out of six companies in the world that have acquired SEI CMM (Level 5) (the highest maturity level for a software process) are located in India, namely, Motorola and Wipro. After a major success in addressing the Y2K (year 2000) issue in the international market, India has set its sights on servicing Euro currency solutions, with 82 Indian software companies already participating in that effort. The strategic 12-hour time difference with the United States enables India to facilitate a 24-hour workday for many of the U.S. companies who prefer to "follow the sun."

The cost competitiveness of India will remain for at least another decade. The expansion of U.S. H1-B visa numbers that occurred between 1998 and 2000 (65,000 in 1998; 115,000 in 1999 and 2000) may be reversed, but U.S. companies are increasingly likely to outsource their work to India because of the continued shortage of software-skilled workers in the United States. I do not see the continued H1-B visa restrictions as a major disadvantage to the software-trained Indian workforce, however, because work will come to India as a result of its outsourcing reputation. The often-quoted lower wages paid to Indian software development and support personnel compared with the wages of their U.S. counterparts should not discourage the Indian workforce because the real difference may not be as large as it appears. To understand this, assume that Indian wages are about 10 percent of the corresponding U.S. wages (Mattoo 1999). For an Indian, this figure should be read as 40 percent instead of 10 percent under the "purchasing power parity'" paradigm (World Bank 1998). That figure grows to about 60 percent if one accounts for an "implicit" 30 percent wage discrimination against the "alien"

H1-B visaholders.[13] This wedge may further increase over the next 10 years as the United States and some other developed countries outsource their software-related work to India.

Liberalization of the Service Sector

Brown and others (1996) have analyzed the potential effects of the liberalization of trade in services. Because there was no such liberalization during the Uruguay Round negotiations, those authors examined what might happen when liberalization finally occurs. Using Hoekman's (1995) "guesstimates" of the size of trade barriers in services, they calculated the effects of an assumed 25 percent reduction in those barriers, which they assumed to be plausible.[14] To provide a benchmark for comparison, Brown and others also calculated the effects of the negotiated liberalization of tariffs on industrial products that were actually negotiated. They concluded that the world's major trading countries/regions, including India, could expect to gain from liberalization of trade in services, with gains increasing further when tariffs on industrial goods are reduced simultaneously.

In Chapter 2 of this volume, Chadha and others have estimated some potential results of the liberalization of trade in services as well as in agricultural and industrial products for the major industrial and developing countries, including India. For that purpose they used a specially constructed version of the University of Michigan Brown-Deardorff-Stern computable general equilibrium (CGE) model of world production and trade. The estimated results of 33 percent reductions in barriers to trade in agricultural products, manufactures, services, and all sectors combined are presented in table 2.7 of Chapter 2. Comparison of the scenario results shows substantial gains under both services liberalization and goods liberalization. Thus India's liberalization of services results in an estimated welfare increase of 0.55 percent of gross domestic product (GDP) and goods liberalization produces an estimated welfare increase of 0.73 percent of GDP.

The Indian sectoral employment effects of the assumed Doha Development Agenda liberalization of services barriers are shown in table 4.3. It is interesting that this liberalization results in employment increases in Indian agriculture and especially government services, and declines in most manufacturing sectors and in trade and transport services related to manufactures. It should be noted, however, that these sectoral employment changes would be altered when account is taken of the combined effects of the Doha Development Agenda liberalization of agriculture, manufactures, and services (shown in table 2.9). By themselves, however, the employment effects of the services liberalization presented in table 4.3 are all relatively small.

TABLE 4.3 Sectoral Effects for India of Doha Development Agenda Services Liberalization (Percent Change)

Product	Exports (Percent)	Imports (Percent)	Output (Percent)	Scale (Percent)	Employment	
					(Percent)	(000s)
Agriculture	0.38	−0.09	0.01	0.00	0.02	44,396.3
Mining	−0.07	0.38	−0.14	0.09	−0.19	−6,360.7
Food, beverages, and tobacco	−0.15	0.72	0.01	0.12	−0.08	−9,148.6
Textiles	−0.08	0.88	0.07	0.16	−0.06	−7,508.6
Wearing apparel	−0.11	1.17	−0.03	0.17	−0.16	−1,709.5
Leather products, and footwear	−0.24	0.78	−0.17	0.17	−0.30	−3,617.4
Wood and wood products	0.09	0.69	0.11	0.16	−0.03	−1,789.8
Chemicals	−0.01	0.60	−0.01	0.17	−0.14	−2,108.9
Nonmetallic mining products	0.24	0.63	0.11	0.20	−0.06	−2,136.0
Metal products	−0.18	0.44	0.02	0.18	−0.12	−4,132.0
Transportation equipment	0.27	0.72	−0.02	0.18	−0.17	−2,300.2
Machinery and equipment	0.04	0.43	0.02	0.22	−0.17	−3,808.4
Other manufactures	0.06	−0.12	0.19	0.18	0.06	3,310.8
Electricity, gas, and water	−0.05	−0.16	0.06	0.08	0.00	83.8
Construction	11.20	5.93	0.12	0.14	0.02	2,557.7
Trade and transport	11.16	18.59	−0.34	0.18	−0.46	−215,971.0
Other private services	13.58	12.94	0.29	0.32	0.09	2,603.7
Government services	12.76	−0.22	0.84	0.57	0.49	207,638.8
Average	1.44	1.69	0.10	0.19	0.00	0.00

Source: Author's calculations.

Conclusion

The main objectives of the GATS are the expansion of trade in services, progressive liberalization of such trade through negotiations, transparency of rules and regulations, and increasing participation of developing countries. Efficient services are crucial to an economy's global competitiveness. High levels of protection granted to the service sectors by an economy through its regulatory policies create inefficient service sectors and thereby reduce the effective protection to various sectors of production in the economy.

India's schedule under the GATS provides for specific commitments covering business services, communications, construction work for civil engineering, financial services, health-related and social services, and tourism services. The extent of commitments varies across sectors with certain restrictions on market access and national treatment under the four modes of supply of services. India has not made any commitments on services relating to distribution; education; environment; recreation, culture, and sporting; transport; and other services not included elsewhere. India has made commitments in 33 activities, compared with an average of 23 for developing countries. It has demonstrated success in the export of software services. The CGE model results noted here clearly demonstrate the additional benefits that services liberalization can bring about for India as well as for other major developing and industrial countries/regions, depending on their respective degrees of comparative advantage in different service sectors in a liberalized world economy.

In the ongoing Doha Development Agenda negotiations, services liberalization requires a change in negotiating strategies (Mattoo 2000). India especially needs to push for liberalization of domestic service markets, laying more emphasis on competition than on change of ownership. It is imperative to undertake domestic deregulation to encourage economic efficiency in remedying market failures and pushing social goals. Furthermore, external service markets need to be liberalized effectively by the elimination of both explicit restrictions and implicit regulatory barriers. Those efforts would lead GATS negotiations into a "virtuous cycle of mutually beneficial liberalization." India's dynamic and growing software sector would transform the country into a global software powerhouse even if the industrial countries continue to impose restrictions on the movement of foreign workers.

India should look forward to more active participation in the Doha Development Agenda negotiations and particularly to furthering the cause of the GATS. There is a compelling need to take great initiative in the process of GATS negotiations to put forward developing country points of view lest these countries have to accept sectoral agreements in which they did not fully participate. The industrial countries must listen to the needs and aspirations of the developing countries and adhere to the basic lessons of comparative advantage. The gains are going to be shared by the industrial as well as the developing economies, and both groups should participate actively to ensure more equitable distribution of the resulting gains. Keeping in view specific provisions for freer movement of capital under GATS commitments, similar provisions must also address the freer movement of labor. In the Doha Development Agenda, GATS negotiations must focus on a comprehensive approach rather than a case-by-case approach to discussions. Negotiations since the conclusion of the Uruguay Round Agreements have focused on financial services, insurance, and maritime transport. Simultaneous negotiations on all services must proceed so as to keep the interests of India and other developing countries fully involved.

An important single factor that can help India improve the efficiency of its service sectors and compete with international service providers lies in the certainty with which the country commits itself to future liberalization while binding the status quo. Serious analysis of strengths, weaknesses, and opportunities for services liberalization should be undertaken with a liberal view toward future commitments. Strengths and opportunities should be fully exploited in the future negotiations, and perceived weaknesses should not hinder the process of further liberalization The optimum solution lies in dealing with existing weaknesses and avoiding the closing of the economy to forces of international competition.[15]

Endnotes

1. People residing abroad for more than one year.

2. The *MSITS* is a United Nations publication in collaboration with the European Union, the International Monetary Fund, the United Nations Conference on Trade and Development, and the World Trade Organization.

3. India's commitments under GATS can be downloaded from the World Trade Organization Web site (http://www.wto.org). These commitments are summarized in tables AIV.3 and AIV.4 in WTO (1998).

4. India originally had declared some most-favored-nation exemptions in financial services (banking and insurance), which were later withdrawn during negotiations on financial services. India also increased the annual limit on foreign bank branches from 8 to 12.

5. A detailed and very informative discussion of India's existing regulatory policies and commitments under the GATS in financial, transportation, telecommunication, tourism, and software services is provided in WTO (1998).

6. The ERP is a measure of the extent to which trade barriers protect domestic value added in production. The effective protection coefficient (EPC) is computed by dividing the value added at domestic prices by value added at world prices. The ERP = EPC − 1.

7. Analogous to tariffs on traded inputs, the higher the tariff equivalent of regulatory policies for services, the lower the effective protection for industries that use the service inputs involved (Hoekman and Braga 1997).

8. See the *Handbook of Industrial Policy and Statistics* published by the Government of India (1999). For the latest version, see www.eaindustry.nic.in.

9. Telecommunication services under the GATS constitute a sector that is very closely related to computer services. Telecommunication services constitute a component of "communication services" (GNS code 2C). With regard to telecommunications, there appears to be considerable overlap, particularly for the activities such as database and data processing services to be performed and/or supplied online. Given the interplay between the two sectors' listed activities, it may not be clear when telecommunication services, computer services, or both are supplied. Whereas GATS directly addresses the progressive liberalization of computer and telecommunication services, the WTO agreements to eliminate tariffs and nontariff barriers on information and communication technology products are of great importance to both of those services (GNS 1B and 2C).

10. "Software" appears not to be covered under the existing GATS classification (GNS 1B). The provisional United Nations Central Product Classification (UNCPC) code 842 refers only to "consultancy" services related to "development and implementation" of software. The packaged or standardized software may be treated as a good, but consultants or other professionals hired by a firm producing packaged software may be covered by GATS mode 4 commitments. It is not clear whether the online supply of packaged or even customized software should be classified as a good or a service.

11. According to the National Association of Software and Service Companies (NASSCOM 1999), the share of on-site development, which was about 90 percent in 1998/99, was 59 percent in 1997/98. Offshore project development has been increasing since 1995 as a result of the proliferation of software technology parks, service of high-speed data transfer provided by the telecommunications company VSNL, liberalized economic policy, and visa restrictions by the United States and some Western European countries. Although the share of products and packages in the domestic market was 52 percent in 1997/98, it was only 8.8 percent in the export market. Major components of software export activity include professional services (48.4 percent) and projects (31.5 percent). The United States accounted for 58 percent of India's software exports and Europe accounted for 21 percent.

12. The Government of India (1998) supported the development of the software and hardware sectors during the 1990s. Since 1992 Electronic hardware technology parks (EHTPs) and software technology parks (STPs) have been attracting foreign investment. Compulsory industrial licensing for electronics-related industries was abolished in 1996. Investment in the electronics industry is unrestricted in terms of foreign shareholdings or repatriation of profits. For export industries there have been additional incentives, such as a five-year tax holiday, tax exemption for income from exports, duty-free imports of inputs, and access to some imports through special import licenses (SILs). There is no ceiling on the amount of foreign equity participation in EHTPs, STPs, and export-processing zones (EPZs), or in 100 percent export-oriented units. There is almost a computer revolution in the country, and both government and industry are growing more determined to strengthen the brand equity of the Indian software industry and make the country an information technology superpower.

13. According to Batuk Vora in 1999 (in an article previously available at <www.indiatimes.com>, an Indian H1-B visaholder may receive only $70 instead of the $100 paid to a native for similar work.

14. It is more difficult to provide quantitative measures of commitments to the liberalization of trade in services than for liberalization of trade in goods because there are no comprehensive international data for trade in services by the four modes of supply. Furthermore, there is no equivalent of customs duties in services. The barriers to trade in services are camouflaged under quantitative restrictions, prohibitions, and the framework of government regulation with regard to the supply of services. Analyzing the economic impact of such measures or the effect of their removal does not lend itself readily to quantitative measurement. Hoekman (1996) provided "guesstimates" of the size of trade barriers in services, and more recently, Dee and Hanslow (2001) estimated services barriers based on sectoral studies of the banking and telecommunications industries. Brown and Stern (2001) have used estimates of services barriers derived from measures of price-cost margins, and these have been used in the Doha Development Agenda computational scenarios in Chapter 2 of this volume.

15. See Chanda (2002) for an assessment of India's opportunities and constraints. Stiglitz (2000) has asked the WTO members to have well-balanced trade negotiations to reflect the interests and concerns of the developing world. The two key principles should be "fairness," especially to the developing

countries, and "comprehensiveness" such that sectors of interest to the developing economies (e.g., construction and maritime services) receive greater attention.

References

The word "processed" describes informally produced works that may not be available commonly through libraries.

Brown, Drusilla K., Alan V. Deardorff, Alan Fox, and Robert M. Stern. 1996. "The Liberalization of Services Trade: Potential Impacts in the Aftermath of the Uruguay Round." In Will Martin and L. Alan Winters, eds., *The Uruguay Round and the Developing Countries*. Cambridge, U.K.: Cambridge University Press.

Brown, Drusilla K., and Robert M. Stern. 2001. "Measurement and Modeling of the Economic Effects of Trade and Investment Barriers in Services." *Review of International Economics* 9: 262–86.

Chadha, Rajesh. 2002. "Competitiveness of Service Sectors in South Asia: Role and Implications of GATS." Draft Report. NCAER (National Council of Applied Economic Research), New Delhi, and CUTS (Consumer Unity & Trust Society), Jaipur.

Chadha, Rajesh, and Sanjib Pohit. 1998. "Rationalising Tariff and Non-Tariff Barriers on Trade: Sectoral Impact on Indian Economy." Paper prepared for the Tariff Commission, Government of India.

Chanda, Rupa. 2002. *Globalization of Services: India's Opportunities and Constraints*. New Delhi: Oxford University Press.

Dee, Philippa, and Kevin Hanslow. 2001. "Multilateral Liberalization of Services Trade." In Robert M. Stern, ed., *Services in the International Economy*. Ann Arbor: University of Michigan Press.

GATT. 1994. *Schedule of Specific Commitments Submitted by Member Countries under GATS*. Geneva.

Government of India. 1998. *National Task Force on Information Technology and Software Development*. New Delhi.

Government of India, Ministry of Commerce and Industry. 1999. *Handbook of Industrial Policy and Statistics*. New Delhi.

Hoekman, Bernard. 1995. "Tentative First Steps: An Assessment of the Uruguay Round Agreement on Services." Working Paper. Centre for Economic Policy Research, London.

———. 1996. "Assessing the General Agreement on Trade in Services." in Will Martin and L. Alan Winters, eds., *The Uruguay Round and the Developing Countries*. Cambridge, U.K.: Cambridge University Press.

Hoekman, Bernard, and Carlos A. Primo Braga. 1997. "Protection and Trade in Services: A Survey." *Open Economies Review* 8: 285–308.

Hoekman, Bernard, and Simeon Djankov. 1997. "Towards a Free Trade Agreement with the European Union: Issues and Policy Options for Egypt." In A. Galal and Bernard Hoekman, eds., *Regional Partners in Global Markets*. London: Centre for Economic Policy Research.

IMF (International Monetary Fund). 1993. *Balance of Payments Manual*, 5th ed. Washington, D.C.

———. 1998. *Balance of Payments Statistics Yearbook*. Washington, D.C.

Karsenty, G. 2000. "Assessing Trade in Services by Mode of Supply." In Pierre Sauvé and Robert M. Stern, eds., *GATS 2000: New Directions in Services Trade Liberalization*. Washington, D.C.: Brookings Institution Press.

Mattoo, Aaditya. 1999. "Developing Countries in the New Round of GATS Negotiations: From a Defensive to a Pro-Active Role." Paper presented at the WTO/World Bank Conference on Developing Countries and the Millennium Round, September, Geneva.

———. 2000. "Developing Countries in the New Round of GATS Negotiations: From a Defensive to a Pro-Active Role." *World Economy* 23: 471–89.

Mohan, Rakesh. 1996. *India Infrastructure Report*. New Delhi: National Council of Applied Economic Research.

NASSCOM (National Association of Software and Service Companies). 1999. *The Software Industry in India: A Strategic Review*. New Delhi. <www.nasscom.org>

NCAER (National Council of Applied Economic Research). 1998. *Protection in Indian Industry*. New Delhi. Processed.

Stiglitz, E. Joseph. 2000. "Two Principles for the Next Round: How to Bring Developing Countries in from the Cold." *World Economy* 23: 437–54.

World Bank. 1998. *World Development Report, 1998/99*. Washington, D.C.

———. 2002. *World Development Indicators*. Washington, D.C.

WTO (World Trade Organization). 1998. *Trade Policy Review: India*. Lanham, Md.: Bernan Associates.

5

TELECOMMUNICATIONS POLICY REFORM IN INDIA

Rajat Kathuria, Harsha Vardhana Singh,
and Anita Soni

The Indian economy is currently undergoing a structural shift. Agricultural and manufactured products are contributing a smaller share of economic output, whereas the service sector contribution is growing. The service sector in India today accounts for more than 48 percent of economic activity and is likely to grow at the rate of 8 percent per year (Reserve Bank of India 1998). A majority of service workers are engaged in creating, processing, and distributing information. The telecommunications sector therefore has assumed major importance as an enabling infrastructure. Accordingly, it is vital for the country that there be a comprehensive and forward-looking telecommunications policy that creates a suitable framework for development of this service industry. The availability of infrastructure for electronically transferring and accessing information is perceived as critical for hastening the realization of economic, social, and cultural benefits as well as for conferring competitive advantage.

In the last five years there have been rapid changes in India's telecom sector: far-reaching developments in information technology (IT), consumer electronics, and media industries around the globe. Convergence of both markets and technologies is a reality that is forcing an industry realignment. At one level, telephone and broadcasting industries are entering each other's markets, and at another level, technology is blurring the difference between such conduit systems as wireline and wireless. As in most countries, separate licenses have been issued in India for basic, cellular, and Internet service providers, and for satellite and cable television operators, each with a distinct industry structure, terms of entry, and varying requirement to create infrastructure. This convergence, however, which now enables operators to use their facilities to deliver some services reserved for other operators, requires a reexamination of the existing policy framework.

The Government of India has recognized that providing world-class telecommunications infrastructure and information is the key to the country's rapid economic and social development. This will not only help in developing the IT industry; it will also provide for widespread spillover benefits to other sectors of the economy.

The first step in this direction was the National Telecom Policy announced in 1994 (NTP 94). This policy opened up the telecommunications sector to competition in basic services as well as value-added offerings like cellular-mobile services, radio paging, very small aperture terminals (V-SAT) services, and so forth. It also set targets for providing telephone on demand and for opening long-distance telephony. These liberalizations were followed by a New Telecom Policy declaration in March 1999 (NTP 99) that removed some of the bottlenecks and moved the liberalization process forward.

This chapter is organized as follows. The next section details the existing structure of the Indian telecommunications sector. That discussion is followed by a comparison of the policy documents of 1994 and 1999. The third section analyzes crucial policy issues and addresses questions likely to arise in their implementation. The final section offers concluding observations.

Existing Structure of the Telecommunications Sector

Telecommunications was not perceived as one of the key infrastructure sectors for rapid economic development during the formative years of the Indian economy. The relatively low levels of investment in this sector affected the quality, quantity, and range of services available. In 1998 Indian telephone density per 100 people was 2.2, whereas the world average was 14.26 (ITU 1999b). The evolution of the subscriber base for basic services in India since 1997 is shown in table 5.1.

For the provision of basic services the entire country is divided into 21 telecom circles, excluding Delhi and Mumbai. Bharat Sanchar Nigam Limited (BSNL) (formerly the service provision arm of the Department of Telecommunications [DoT]) provides basic services in those 21 telecom circles, and Mahanagar Telephone Nigam Limited (MTNL) serves Delhi and Mumbai, two metropolitan license areas. Table 5.1 presents the subscriber numbers for basic services since 1996. BSNL's market share increased from 79 percent to 86 percent between March 1997 and June 2001, whereas the share for MTNL dropped from 21 percent to less than 13 percent of the total connections. In the early years after liberalization, India restricted the number of licenses awarded for basic services. The market was divided into separate circles and the policy admitted one private operator

TABLE 5.1   Subscriber Base, Basic Services

Service Provider	1996–97	1997–98	1998–99	1999–00	2000–01	2001–02	December 2002
BSNL	11,530,276	14,394,956	17,927,526	22,479,721	28,108,976	33,218,498	34,450,897
MTNL	3,012,324	3,406,740	3,653,913	4,031,624	4,327,158	4,629,709	4,561,714
Bharti Telenet Ltd.	Nil	Nil	13,980	91,967	115,212	180,989	317,220
Hughes Ispat Ltd.	Nil	Nil	6,070	22,110	69,599	160,672	202,967
Tata Teleservices Pvt. Ltd.	Nil	Nil	Nil	26,713	58,736	150,400	244,801
Reliance Telecom Pvt. Ltd., Gujarat	Nil	Nil	Nil	Nil	109	140	160
Shyam Telelink Ltd., Rajasthan	Nil	Nil	Nil	Nil	8,998	27,150	57,371
HFCL, Punjab	Nil	Nil	Nil	Nil	13,441	64,926	112,677
Total	14,542,600	17,801,696	21,601,489	26,652,135	32,702,229	38,432,484	39,947,807

Nil indicates that service has not yet begun.

Source: Data from service providers.

in each circle to compete with the incumbent DoT (now with BSNL) and MTNL. New entrants were allowed to offer intracircle long-distance services, but DoT maintained its monopoly on intercircle long-distance telephony. The bidding process led to six new entrants in basic services. In 2001 the policy was changed to allow unlimited entry into each circle for basic services and subsequently 22 license agreements have been signed. As opposed to the fixed-license-fee regime based on which licenses were awarded earlier, fresh licenses have been issued on the bases of a one-time entry fee and a percentage of revenue share that is linked to the area of operation.[1] Six privately owned service providers have begun services and newly licensed service providers are expected to start operations soon (see table 5.2).

Private participation in the cellular-mobile market, on the other hand, has been comparatively more successful. Eight cellular licenses, two in each of the four metropolitan areas, were awarded in October 1994. Subsequently, bidding resulted in the award of licenses in 18 Circles.[2] No bids were received for two circles—Jammu and Kashmir, and Andaman and Nicobar Island—and only one bid each was made for West Bengal and Assam. In the past year, cellular services have grown at an annual rate of more than 89 percent. The subscriber base exceeded 3.5 million by the final quarter of 2001 and at the end of December 2002 it was approximately 10.5[3] million (see table 5.3). As a percentage of basic

TABLE 5.2   List of Basic Service Providers and Their Areas of Operation

Area of Operation	Name of Service Provider
All over India	BSNL (formerly Department of Telecommunications)
Delhi and Mumbai	MTNL
Delhi, Haryana, Karnataka, Madhya Pradesh, Tamilnadu	Bharti Telenet Ltd.
Maharashtra	Hughes Ispat Ltd.
Andhra Pradesh, Delhi, Gujarat, Karnataka, Tamilnadu	Tata Teleservices Pvt. Ltd.
Gujarat	Reliance Telecom Pvt. Ltd.
Punjab	HFCL
Rajasthan	Shyam Telelink Ltd.

Note: Apart from the areas listed above, Reliance has yet to launch its services in 17 more circles (Andaman and Nicobar Island, Andhra Pradesh, Bihar, Delhi, Haryana, Himachal Pradesh, Karnataka, Kerala, Madhya Pradesh, Maharashtra, Orissa, Punjab, Rajasthan, Tamilnadu, Uttar Pradesh-West, Uttar Pradesh-East, and West Bengal)

Source: Data available at www.dotindia.com and from reports by service providers.

TABLE 5.3 Subscriber Base, Cellular Services

Category	March 1997	March 1998	March 1999	March 2000	March 2001	March 2002	December 2002
All metros	325,967	551,757	519,543	795,931	1,362,592	2,567,757	4,054,434
A Circle	9,698	176,954	354,799	585,653	1,165,778	2,134,333	3,515,333
B Circle	3,000	138,309	284,189	460,094	932,685	1,501,151	2,550,223
C Circle	366	15,296	36,915	42,633	116,040	227,573	360,440
All India	339,031	882,316	1,195,446	1,884,311	3,577,095	6,430,814	10,480,430

Source: Cellular Operators Association of India (www.coai.com).

subscribers, cellular subscribers make up approximately 26 percent. This number is expected to increase following significant changes in the Indian telecommunications industry that are likely to occur shortly, that is, another tariff review, competition in the national long-distance market, and entry of third and fourth operators in certain service areas. NTP 99 provided for the public-sector entities BSNL and MTNL to be the third cellular mobile operators in their respective service areas, and recent bidding for the fourth license has resulted in the award of licenses to 17 more operators. A list of existing cellular operators and their areas of operation is provided in table 5.4.

As many as 137 licenses (93 of which actually were operational by December 1998) have been issued to provide radio-paging services. The bids for those licenses were invited in two stages, first for 27 large cities (i.e., with a population of greater than 1 million) and second for 19 telecom circles. Two to four licensees were selected for each area. The radio-paging market in India, however, has been declining in the last few years, and some licensees have withdrawn services. The price differential between radio paging and cellular service is low enough to make the former unattractive.

Among other value-added services being offered, V-SAT–based data services to closed user groups are available from 9 of 14 licensed operators. Online services (i.e., email, fax on demand, Web page hosting, and electronic data interchange) have been operational in India since 1995. Although there is open entry into this segment, growth has been slow, chiefly because of exclusive dependence on DoT/MTNL for lines and access.

The growth of Internet services has also been retarded in India by the policy of retaining the monopoly of public sector entities, such as VSNL (Videsh Sanchar Nigam Limited) and MTNL. The current number of subscribers nationwide is 250,000. That policy was relaxed in a major way in 1998, and there has been a surge of interest since that time, boosted especially by a significant reduction in leased circuit charges through the Telecom Regulatory Authority of India (TRAI) Telecommunications Tariff Order (TTO) of March 1999, which is discussed below. At the time of this writing, 440 licenses have been issued to private Internet service providers (ISPs)—84 for category A (all India), 175 for category B (territorial circle and the four metropolitan telephone districts of Delhi, Mumbai, Calcutta, and Chennai), and 181 for category C (city). The liberal ISP policy (see appendix 5.1) is expected to promote rapid proliferation of the Internet within India and increase applications like electronic commerce, Web hosting, virtual private network, and so forth. On current estimations of demand, Internet subscriber numbers are expected to grow even faster in the next two years. One provisional license has been issued for offering global mobile personal communications by satellite (GMPCS). The issue of licenses to other prospective GMPCS

TABLE 5.4   List of Cellular Service Providers and Their Areas of Operation

Category	City/Circle	Operator 1	Operator 2	Operator 3	Operator 4
Metros	Calcutta	Bharti	UMTL	BSNL	Reliance
	Chennai	RPG	Bharti	BSNL	B.S. & Services
	Delhi	Bharti	Essar	MTNL	BATATA
	Mumbai	BPL	HMTL	MTNL	Bharti
A Circle	Andhra Pradesh	BATATA	Bharti	BSNL	B.S. & Services
	Gujarat	Fascel	BATATA	BSNL	Bharti
	Karnatka	Bharti	Spice Comm	BSNL	B.S. & Services
	Maharashtra	BPL	BATATA	BSNL	Bharti
	Tamilnadu	BPL	Aircel	BSNL	Bharti
B Circle	Haryana	Escotel	ADL	BSNL	Bharti
	Kerala	Escotel	BPL	BSNL	Bharti
	Madhya Pradesh	RPG	Reliance	BSNL	Bharti
	Punjab	Spice Comm	n.a.	BSNL	Escotel
	Rajasthan	ADL	Hexacom	BSNL	Escotel
	Uttar Pradesh-East	ADL	Koshika	BSNL	Escotel
	Uttar Pradesh-West	Escotel	n.a.	BSNL	Bharti
	West Bengal	Reliance	n.a.	BSNL	n.a.
C Circle	Assam	n.a.	n.a.	BSNL	n.a.
	Bihar	Bharti	Reliance	BSNL	n.a.
	Himachal Pradesh	Reliance	Reliance	BSNL	Escotel
	North East	Reliance	n.a.	BSNL	n.a.
	Orissa	n.a.	Reliance	BSNL	n.a.

n.a. = not available.

Source: Cellular Operators Association of India (www.coai.com).

TABLE 5.5 Telecommunications Market Structure

Segment	Market Structure	Number of Operators	Service Areas	Period of License (Years)
Fixed telephone services	Open competition	Unlimited	Circles	20
Domestic long distance	Open competition	Unlimited	All India	20
International	Open competition	Unlimited	All India	20
Cellular	Limited competition	4	Metros and circles	20
Radio paging	Limited competition	4	Cities and circles	10

Source: Authors' compilation of data from www.dotindia.com.

operators is reportedly under consideration. A summary of the telecom market structure emerging from the policy outlined above is presented in table 5.5.

The Policy Documents of 1994 and 1999

NTP 94 spelled out five basic objectives and two of them (availability of telephone on demand and universal service that connects all villages)—were to be realized by 1997. Both of those objectives remain unrealized. With regard to quality of service, matching the "world standard" and providing the "widest possible range of services at reasonable prices" were stated aims. Two other objectives were to make India a major manufacturing base and an exporter of telecom equipment and to ensure the country's defense and security needs. (The powers of licensing and spectrum management were retained by the government on the ground that both need to be strictly monitored to protect the strategic interests and security of the country.)

There were serious gaps in the policy document relative to provision of a suitable environment for the entry of private-service providers and the issue of regulation. Under the 1994 policy, a need for private sector contribution to the effort was clearly recognized, but various implementation problems, including incomplete reforms, mitigated the efforts to achieve the targets. Meanwhile, the nature of convergence had changed as a result of changes in technology and in the overall market structure for service provision, and there was a need to provide fresh directions through another policy.

The opening up of the Internet sector set the background to NTP 99, which was a major attempt to plug the loopholes in the 1994 policy. Its enunciation of policy objectives was a marked improvement. Provision of universal service (including service to unconnected and rural areas, retargeted for 2002) was sought to be balanced by provision of sophisticated telecom services capable of meeting the needs of India's economy. The latter objective was further amplified to include Internet access to all district headquarters by 2000 and high-speed data and multimedia capabilities in all towns with populations of 200,000 and more by 2002. Apart from a target-average penetration of 7 percent by the year 2005 (and 15 percent by 2010), targets for rural teledensity have been set to increase from the current level of 0.4 percent to 4.0 percent during the same period.

Recognizing the role of private investment, NTP 99 envisaged multiple operators in the market for various services. Another major change has been a shift from the existing license-fee-bid system to one based on a one-time entry fee combined with revenue-share payments. To meet the teledensity targets of NTP 99, it was earlier estimated that a capital expenditure of Rs. 4 trillion for installing about 130 million lines would be required. With a decline in equipment price and changes in technology, the current estimate is almost 25 percent lower and is expected to decline further.

Whereas NTP 94 only acknowledged the need to induce significant private participation into value-added as well as basic services and to "ensure fair competition," NTP 99 went further in targeting an enhanced competitive environment and a level playing field. Over time, the government has made attempts to remove restrictions that adversely affect performance of the licensee. For instance, there was a condition that the last mile of linkage should be made only with copper wire, but this condition has been relaxed. NTP 99 allowed DoT/MTNL to enter as the third cellular-mobile operators in their service areas if they wished to provide those services. To ensure a level playing field, DoT and MTNL would have to pay a license fee, but DoT's license fee would be refunded because it had to meet the universal service obligations (USO). It is worth noting that to the extent that the fee would be refunded specifically to counter the cost of USO, this aspect should be accounted for when the USO levy is calculated and the revenues from that levy are apportioned.

Some of the other notable advances marked by the NTP 99 are the following:

- Speeding up of competition in long distance, including usage of the existing backbone network of public and private entities in the rail transport, power, and energy sectors for data (immediately) and for domestic, long-distance voice communication when the latter opened to competition in January 2000. This increases the scope for entry of a new category of infrastructure providers or "carrier's carrier."

- Permission for fixed service providers (FSPs) to freely establish "last-mile" linkages to provide fixed services and carry long-distance traffic within their service areas without seeking an additional license. Direct interconnectivity between FSPs and any other type of service provider (including another FSP) in their areas of operation and the sharing of infrastructure with any other type of service provider was also permitted.
- Conversion of public call offices, wherever justified, into public teleinfo centers with such multimedia capability as integrated services digital network services, remote database access, government and community information systems, and the like.
- Transformation, in a time-bound manner, of the telecommunications sector into a greater competitive environment in both urban and rural areas, thereby providing equal opportunities and a level playing field for all participants.
- Strengthened research and development efforts in India and provision of an impetus to build world-class manufacturing capabilities.
- Efficiency and transparency in spectrum management.
- Commitment to restructuring DoT.
- Interconnection between private-service providers in the same circle and between a service provider and VSNL, along with introduction of competition in domestic long distance.
- Undertaking to review interconnectivity between private-service providers of different service areas, in consultation with TRAI.
- Permission for resale of domestic telephony.
- Clarity regarding the number of licenses that each operator may be granted. (This could lead to consolidation of industry operators over the long term.)
- Emphasis on certain other issues, including standardization, human resource development and training, disaster management, and legislative change.

According to NTP 99, the number of basic service providers in each circle and their mode of selection would be decided on the basis of recommendations from TRAI. As opposed to the bidding-based license fee regime in place earlier, licenses would be issued on the basis of a one-time entry fee and a percentage of revenue share to be determined by DoT on the basis of recommendations made by TRAI. In 2001 the license policy was changed to allow open entry into each circle for basic services, and 22 license agreements have been signed. As was noted above, the new licenses have been issued for a one-time entry fee and a percentage of revenue share that is linked to the area of operation.

In total, India's basic service comprised only 9.5 million users in 1991. The number of users had increased by almost 3.5 times as of June 2001 (to 33 million) and presently there are about 40 million users. By all measures, the growth of basic telecommunications services in India has been phenomenal over the last five years. Policymakers have provided further opportunities, including, for example, open competition and permission for cable operators to provide last-mile linkages and switched services within their service areas of operation. Subject to obtaining a basic service license, those operators also are permitted to provide two-way communication, including voice, data, and information services.

NTP 99 proposed that the long-term policy have uniform 20-year licenses for both basic and cellular-mobile services. Extending license periods initially by 5 years and subsequently by 10 years was also envisaged. Internet telephony has now been permitted, and this will bring major changes in the telecom industry in India as the entry costs for such telephony decline and quality of service improves. NTP 99 is a welcome effort to address key issues relating to telecom reforms and to lay down policies that could transform the sector into a competitive and efficient infrastructure within a reasonable time frame. The policy aims at providing a modern and efficient telecom infrastructure and takes account of the convergence of IT, media, telecommunications, and consumer electronics. The emphasis is on making India an IT superpower. As mentioned above, the regulatory scenario for telecommunications is changing rapidly, and many issues require further analysis and perhaps a change in policy framework in the next few years.

Key Policy Issues

As stated above, the new policy provided the framework within which India's telecom sector would function and focused on creating an environment to enable continued attraction of investment in the sector and to allow creation of a world-class telecommunications infrastructure. This section analyzes and provides details of the issues relevant in the implementation of the new policy; for example, the nature of the interconnection regime that will most likely result in attaining the objectives of the new policy, the achievement of USO, the license conditions to encourage more investment in the sector, and regulatory principles that are important for achieving the ambitious objectives of NTP 99. The significant issues are detailed below.

Interconnection

In a multi-operator environment, interconnection is a crucial regulatory issue for telecommunications policy. No new entrant into the market will be able to compete effectively unless it is able to interconnect its network with the facilities of the incumbent operator either directly or indirectly via the network of another competitive entrant. In the course of transition to competition, a pivotal issue is how best to meet the requirements of interconnection of each of the service providers. For most telephone users, the services offered by the new entrant will be almost useless unless the entrant can enable its subscribers to communicate with the large number of subscribers of the incumbent operator. Consequently, competition in the market can flourish only if entrants are able to interconnect their facilities with those of the incumbent and to do so at terms that allow the entrant to provide the service at competitive levels of price and quality. A "fair and reasonable" interconnection policy is a critical factor in fostering competition in telecommunications markets.

Prior to NTP 99, direct interconnection between service providers was not a policy; instead, two networks had to be connected via the incumbent operator, that is, DoT. This arrangement was combined with certain charges for interconnection that were, in several instances, above cost-based interconnection charges. For interconnection the following principles have been emphasized by TRAI:

- Principles of pricing, timeliness, point of interconnection, and quality of interconnection should be based on a "no less favorable standard" in comparison with another operator (including the conditions implicitly or explicitly provided to one's own operations).
- Interconnection charges should be cost based.
- Those costs should be those caused by constructing the link with, and through the use of, the network of the interconnecting service provider (these costs are directly attributable "incremental" or "additional" costs resulting from interconnection).
- The interconnecting service provider must be allowed access to unbundled elements of the network that it requires, and must not be charged for facilities that it does not require.
- For any particular interconnection service, the same interconnection charge should apply to any service provider.
- All interconnection service providers should be allowed to charge an interconnection price.

NTP 99 stated that direct interconnection between service providers in the same service area would be permitted. This implies, for instance, that a cellular-service provider can directly link its network to that of the other service provider in the same service area without having to interconnect via BSNL. Not only is this likely to reduce the price to the end user, but it may result in more efficient use of the networks. Although direct interconnection between private networks has been slow to take off following removal of policy restrictions, increased traffic and penetration are likely to provide private operators the necessary impetus to take advantage of direct interconnection.

The necessity of providing a level playing field for public and private operators is another key policy issue. In this context, for instance, an incumbent operator who deters entry to a new operator can keep efficiency from being maximized. To achieve the possible economies of scale and scope and network externalities, the role of regulation should be to reduce or eliminate market power and mimic the outcomes of the competitive process (ITU 1999a). In a press statement, the government has reiterated its commitment that, in terms of NTP 99, "there is going to be the same licensing regime for all operators, i.e., interconnect revenue-sharing arrangements for cellular services for payment of access charges between DoT and MTNL for STD and ISD traffic will be the same as applicable to the other private operators." With the opening up of the domestic long-distance (DLD) market to private competition to compete with BSNL, new opportunities and challenges are likely to emerge with regard to interconnection. A private operator granted a license to offer DLD services has proposed interconnection rates that are approximately 50 percent lower than the rates offered by the incumbent BSNL. BSNL has responded in an aggressive manner to these proposals. Although these offers are subject to regulatory approval based on the principles cited above, it is clear that increasing competition for DLD traffic is bound to put pressure on the cross-subsidy prevalent in the tariff regime, as will be noted below in more detail.

On December 14, 2001, TRAI issued a consultation paper on "Issues Relating to Interconnection between Access Providers and National Long Distance Operators." This process has led to TRAI's specifying a model reference interconnect offer (RIO) that covers various regulatory aspects relating to interconnection. The TRAI has also recently published in the official gazette notice of a regime of interconnect usage charges to facilitate commercial interconnection in a multi-operator environment.

Tariffs

Linked to interconnection and competitive efficiency are the issues of tariffs and tariff policy. It is now widely recognized that enhancing efficiency and investment in telecommunications requires the introduction of competition, which in turn needs a regulatory mechanism to facilitate competition. An essential ingredient of transition from a protected market to competition is the alignment of prices with costs (i.e., cost-oriented or cost-based prices), so that prices better reflect their likely levels in a competitive environment. In basic telecommunications, for example, a major departure from cost-based pricing—such as that under the prevailing price structure in several countries, including India—involves cross-subsidization. This introduces inefficient decisionmaking by both consumers and service providers. Cost-based prices also provide a basis for making subsidies more transparent and for more accurately targeting them on specific social objectives, for example, achieving the USO. For consumers, cost-based prices reflect economic costs and provide efficiency-oriented incentives for consumption. For service providers, cost-based prices better prepare the conditions for competition among different operators.

Cost-based prices restrict the possibility of cream skimming by operators, facilitate the smooth interflow of traffic, and reduce the dependency of operators on narrow market segments for maintaining their financial viability. This in turn promotes greater concern among operators for a wider set of their subscriber base and prompts them to focus on quality of service, improved technology, and service options. If tariffs for services that incorporate a high level of cross-subsidies (e.g., basic service) are not made cost oriented, major adjustments would be required in the pricing structure when competition takes place in the telecom market.

Traditionally, BSNL tariffs cross-subsidized the cost of access (as reflected by rentals) by domestic and international long-distance usage charges. To promote desired efficiencies, rebalancing tariffs is a necessity and therefore an important policy issue. Rebalancing tariffs involves reducing tariffs that are above costs and increasing those below costs. Thus rebalancing implies a reduction in the extent of cross-subsidization in the fixed-services sector. Such a rationalization is a required precondition for converting a single operator system to a multi-operator one.

Regarding tariff determination, as in other policy considerations, TRAI is obliged to ensure transparency in exercising its powers (for which TRAI has adopted a systematic procedure of consultation with all interest groups). After going through a comprehensive consultation procedure covering service providers, consumers, policymakers, and parliamentarians, TRAI issued its Telecommunications Tariff Order on March 9, 1999. The order represents a landmark for infrastructure regulatory agencies in India in terms of attempting to rebalance tariffs to reflect costs more closely and to usher in an era of competitive service provision. The chief features of the tariff order were substantial reductions in long-distance and international call charges, an increase in rentals and local charges, and steep reductions (an average of about 70 percent) in the charge for leased circuits.

For basic services, TRAI demonstrated that tariff rebalancing was necessary to prepare the market for competition. A small proportion of the subscribers account for a major share of call revenue, and these subscribers would be exposed to competition when private-sector operators enter the market (see table 5.6). Loss of such customers will have a significant effect on the revenue situation of the incumbent, making it difficult to meet the objectives of USO and network expansion. Thus, although tariffs have to be reduced for the services that are priced

TABLE 5.6   Revenue Contribution by Different Subscriber Groups

Share of Total Subscribers (%)	Contribution of These Subscribers to Call Revenue (%)
2.7 (those making more than 10,000 calls bimonthly)	46.1
2.5 (those making between 5001 and 10,000 calls bimonthly)	9.8
7.9 (those making between 2,001 and 5,000 calls bimonthly)	13.4
14.0 (those making between 1,001 and 2,000 calls bimonthly)	11.6
21.3 (those making between 501 and 1,000 calls bimonthly)	10.0
51.7 (those making 0 to 500 calls bimonthly)	8.1

Source: TRAI 1999b.

much above cost (e.g., long-distance and international calls), tariffs for below-cost items need to be increased. Such a rebalancing exercise is common when preparing the situation for competition. Otherwise, competition will result in a decline in above-cost prices without any compensating change in the below-cost prices.

The methodology of specifying tariffs included the following feature to impart flexibility. For certain services, TRAI specified particular tariff levels whereas for several others it showed forbearance. Even for those services for which tariff levels are specified, the framework includes the possibility of providing alternative tariffs. The tariffs specified by TRAI form a package that is termed the "standard tariff package." This package must always be provided to the customer. In addition, the service provider is left free to provide any "alternative tariff package." Because the standard tariff package is always available, any alternative tariff package must be better in order to attract any customer. Therefore, the standard tariff package provides a minimum guarantee to the customer. In one sense, it specifies the peak expenditure level for the customer, with the alternative tariff packages being attractive only if the expenditure involved in them is lower than that for the standard tariff package. This method of flexibility was adopted because of the growing tendency in telecom markets to provide different tariff combinations for various baskets of services.

In the case of basic telecom tariffs, changes in certain tariffs (e.g., rental, domestic long-distance, and international call tariffs) were to be phased in over a period of three years. Traditionally, rental charges in India have been linked to the size of the exchange providing the connection. The revised tariffs involved an increase in the price of local calls for low-calling subscribers and a decline in such call charges for high-calling subscribers. Domestic long-distance calls on average witnessed a reduction of up to 35 percent with further reductions of 15 percent anticipated over the period to 2002. Likewise, charges for international calls to areas outside of the South Asian Association for Regional Co-operation and neighboring countries decreased by over 30 percent, with further reduction of about 10 percent. With the entry of competition in the long-distance market, further reduction in the corresponding tariffs has taken place. Certain tariffs have declined by 60 percent. The TRAI has further addressed the basic tariff situation, taking into account the structural change in the telecom market occasioned by the introduction of competition in the domestic long-distance market. A revised tariff order has been issued, extending the process of tariff rebalancing, and a linked interconnect usage charge regime has been specified with origination, carriage, and termination charges in a multi-operator, multiservice environment.

For cellular-mobile service, tariffs were restructured because the prevailing rentals were low and call charges were high. This resulted in a tariff structure that dissuaded usage and loaded the subscriber base. Thus, call charges were reduced and rentals increased. The methodology clearly included license fee as a cost and showed that a high license fee translates into higher tariffs.

The standard monthly rental for cellular-mobile service was increased from Rs. 156 to Rs. 600, but the maximum call charge was reduced from a peak of Rs. 16.80 per minute to Rs. 6 per minute. The service providers were allowed to give alternative tariff packages that resulted in lower tariffs. Leased circuit tariffs were decreased in order to encourage the use of telecom by business and bulk users, and to provide a competitive stimulus to such users through the use of leased circuits. Because there was a major systemic change encompassed in the tariff changes, it was not possible to be definite about any eventuality. Thus the framework included an annual review of the situation.

TTO 1999 evoked considerable protest from a number of quarters. The tariff package was an attempt to balance several objectives. The explanatory memorandum to the order provided a detailed reasoning on this matter, including the affordability of tariffs. The possibility of giving alternative tariffs provided a means of addressing several concerns. Over time, with greater competition in the market, tariffs for long-distance calls and for cellular-mobile service have seen dramatic declines within such a framework. The reduction in tariffs has also been spurred by the introduction of wireless in local loop with limited mobility, and a major cost reduction due to technological change. With the new service providers relying on more recent, cost-efficient technologies, the Indian telecom market is emerging with very strong competitive pressure.

Convergence

Private sector participation in the Indian telecommunications sector will provide a fillip to technology upgrading and help bridge the gap in adoption of new technology. There have been far-reaching developments in the recent past in telecommunications, IT, consumer electronics, and media industries. According to NTP 99, convergence of both markets and technology is a reality that is forcing realignment of the telecom industry. Telephone and broadcasting industries are entering each other's markets, and technology is blurring the difference between conduit systems, such as wireless and wireline. These rapid changes in technology have largely diluted the monopoly characteristic of telecom-service provision, thereby opening up avenues for improved efficiency. Competition is now viable in a range of services, including long-distance transmission of voice and data. Facilitating effective competition among the various players is therefore a key policy issue. This fact was also acknowledged in NTP 99.

Convergence of technologies implies a need not only to consider the appropriate method of charging a license fee, but also to consider whether to regulate and the nature and extent of regulation. The goal of all the policy initiatives is to promote flexibility of technology choice and service provision. Thus neutrality of policies toward the technology platform is seen as desirable because it enhances opportunities, and because the policymaker is not in a position to anticipate the likely developments and to finetune policy.

The basic driving force of growing competition in what was once thought to be a natural monopoly is the increasing versatility with which services can be provided, based on the digitization of all signal-transfer technology. As the manner in which signals are transferred from one location to another becomes standardized, it is possible for a service provider in one segment of telecommunications (say, network television services) to perform the functions of another (perhaps the local phone company). Efforts to maintain barriers across such segments will eventually be overwhelmed by technology. Regulation will follow convergence rather than the other way around.

The nature of telecommunications and broadcasting transactions, the technology used, and the methods of funding the infrastructure are becoming more and more similar. Some of these diversification activities are on account of technical convergence of the medium (the fiberoptic cable) used to distribute services. The high and versatile data-carrying capacity of optic–optic networks means that those networks will also be ideal resources to be resold to multiple service providers, such as cable operators, broadcasters, telephone operators, ISPs, or any other company that needs to send digital signals into the connected units.

In several developed systems, broadcasting is increasingly exploiting the traditional telecommunications medium of cables rather than radio waves. Conversely, entertainment and advertising are among the areas turning to the ordinary telephone network. The use of telecommunications infrastructure to supply entertainment will make it possible to deliver a potentially unlimited number of television channels, and the need to limit the number of channels to preserve radio frequencies will disappear.

As is true elsewhere, the telecom sector in India has witnessed rapid changes in the last six years; and convergence that now allows operators to use their facilities to deliver some services reserved for other operators demands a reconsideration of the existing policy framework.

A proper regulatory framework is the first step toward effective regulation in a converged environment. A draft Communications Convergence Bill (available at http://communicationbill.dot.nic.in), introduced in India, aims to provide a regulatory framework for telecommunications companies confronted with the convergence of telecom, Internet, and broadcasting services. This draft legislation has been prepared along the lines of an amendment to the U.S. Telecommunications Act of 1996 and the Malaysian Communications and Multimedia Commission Act of 1998 (the latter available at http://www.cmc.gov.my/legisframe.htm). If the bill is passed, India will become one of the few countries in the world to adopt legislation covering the convergence of high-technology media. Under the proposed legislation, a commission will be established as the regulatory authority in convergence of IT, communications, and broadcasting, and will be responsible for managing spectrum, granting of licenses, enforcing license conditions, determining tariff rates, and ensuring a competitive marketplace. The proposal comes at a time when several countries have introduced or are in the process of introducing changes in their regulatory environments. Some countries with established regulators have chosen to build on current structures rather than set up new entities.

The proposed bill provides the framework within which convergence in the communications sector can start and be sustained. A major proposed change from the current legislation is that licensing powers would be transferred to the Communications Commission of India (CCI). The proposed commission is also intended to be independent and autonomous. Its independence is necessary for several reasons, not least the need to gain domestic and international credibility. Because one of the main objectives of the commission will be promoting the principles of a level playing field for all operators, even the slightest reservation about its independence and autonomy could adversely affect the competitive climate and constrain its regulatory efforts.

As stated above, convergence will eliminate the existing barriers between different types of services—for example, between basic and cellular services—and will enable service providers and thus consumers to benefit from scale and scope economies. Naturally, competition policy issues will need to be addressed more frequently in the converged environment, and the growing consolidation of the telecom industry will engage the regulatory resources more than in the current environment. Thus convergence often may result in issues falling within the competence of more than one regulator. Issues relating to competition and competition policy could fall under the jurisdiction of either the proposed Competition Commission of India or the Communications Commission of India.

It would be appropriate if the CCI is given adequate power to resolve all issues in the telecom sector, including issues relating to competition and observance of a level playing field. This aggregated power, in fact, should be applicable to all industry-specific regulators because in practice it would be extremely difficult to segregate competition issues from issues specific to a given industry. In case there is overlapping jurisdiction on competition policy and related issues between the CCI and the industry-specific regulatory body, the time required to resolve issues would increase, thereby decreasing the effectiveness of the process. Furthermore, a hybrid structure will allow the possibility of "forum shopping," which could increase the resources and time expended toward resolving issues. To achieve consistent and clear handling of sector-specific problems, including those relating to anticompetitive action, it is better that such problems be handled by the sector-specific regulator.

Regulatory uncertainty is an important factor that could stifle convergence before its benefits could be felt by the economy and society at large. Consistency in regulation is truly a challenge. For instance, delivery of different services over a single network does not make all services the same. And regulating different services similarly may result in discriminatory treatment, which may hold back competition, investment, and innovation. The nature of restrictions on market entry and licensing ultimately would affect the consumer and one of the most crucial decisions in this regard would relate to the licensing of existing and new players in the converged environment.

Technology

To become globally competitive, India has to keep pace with developments in telecommunication services and technology worldwide. Accessing related technologies and promoting needed investments in a competitive environment raise important policy concerns. With the huge reserve of highly qualified manpower, research and development is one area that should be given high priority. NTP 99 holds out the objective of India's emergence as an IT superpower and of Indian telecom companies becoming truly global players. It envisages government measures to ensure that industry invests adequately in research and development for service provision as well as manufacturing. Increased integration with global markets will provide the thrust (as evidenced by the software industry); this needs to be supplemented by targeted investment to realize the aims spelled out in NTP 99.

Quality of Service

A major objective and one around which important policies are designed is world-class quality of service. In India, as in many other developing countries, low tele-density has put great emphasis on rapid expansion. With the effort focused on expansion, issues relating to quality of service (QOS) have sometimes not received full attention, even though QOS has steadily improved over the years. One of the benefits expected from private sector entry is an improvement of QOS to international standards. QOS standards have been built into license conditions and have been identified as one of the major areas of concern on the regulatory agenda. In fact the regulator, TRAI, has developed QOS norms to apply across the board to all operators who offer basic and cellular mobile service. Not only are the QOS norms declared; they are also being monitored. This is a major consumer welfare strategy.

Consumer Welfare

Consumer welfare is the prime objective of the telecommunications revolution in India. Telecom as infrastructure is a necessity not only for businesses but for all consumers. The policy objective here is to extend the service to more new consumers by making access easier and to improve the service available to existing consumers. Providing greater choice through competition also is expected to benefit the consumer through better services and lower tariffs. Therefore, although liberalization policy is geared to improve consumer welfare, there is a need for specific policies to achieve this objective. The regulatory framework is an important means of ensuring consumer welfare. Customer satisfaction and the monitoring of operator performance are high on the regulatory agenda. Interconnection policy is also focused on achieving a nearly seamless architecture so that consumer access is unrestricted. Another policy initiative intended to improve consumer welfare is adopting a tariff structure suitable to social requirements to ensure that the tariff is affordable for all users.

Competition

Almost four years after the implementation of TTO 1999, BSNL and MTNL have approximately 98 percent of the total market in basic services. Thus private entry in basic services has had negligible impact on the market in the intervening years. There are several reasons for the slow growth of private provision of basic services. One reason involves the slow and delayed entry of basic service providers in the Indian market consequent to troubles with the licensing process. Another reason for the slow growth could be that most private operators have focused on the lucrative business segment of the market, without much concern for increasing market share. At the same time, the market for cellular services has shown high growth rates and comparatively more frequent tariff changes.

Two of the main tasks of a regulator are to control prices and the quality of service and to ensure that any service provider with monopoly power does not overcharge users for the service they offer—that is, regulation should result in outcomes that mimic those of a competitive environment. Furthermore, as the market for a service becomes increasingly competitive, the level or scope of regulation in that market should be reduced proportionately. The level of price regulation should be inversely related to the level of price competition. Thus the basic prescription is that weaker price regulation should prevail when competition is incipient but be withdrawn altogether when competition is stronger or effective.

In the telecom sector, one of the major barriers to entry is the capital needs of the entrant. If unbundling of the incumbent's network enables the new entrants to combine their own resources with those of the incumbent through fair interconnection terms, however, successful entry may occur. Thus market share indicators must be treated with caution. The industry's structural conditions, such as unbundling, must be factored in when one determines whether competition is effective. The goals of reforms are to open the sector to competition and to deregulate prices when competition is effective.

With the emergence of competition for the provision of basic services in certain circles and the continued increase in numbers of cellular services subscribers, signs of competition are emerging in the provision of local services. Although the circles where private basic services have been launched (Andhra Pradesh, Gujarat, Madhya Pradesh, Maharashtra including Mumbai, Punjab, and Rajasthan) account for a very small share of the total direct exchange lines (DELs) provided by BSNL, cellular services have shown considerable growth in the last year. As stated elsewhere in this chapter, the market for basic and cellular services has been opened to more players. More competition, therefore, will exist in the future, and developments in the cellular market will affect basic sources, and vice versa.

The market for domestic long-distance services also has been opened to new competition, and there has been a substantial decline in domestic long-distance tariffs. Where domestic long-distance tariffs have provided a cushion for the service providers, the decline in long-distance tariffs must be addressed in a way that ensures investment opportunities in basic services. The recent notification in the official gazette of the reference interconnection offer and the interconnection usage charge (IUC) regime are the relevant policy initiatives to address this situation.

Furthermore, international long distance was opened to competition in April 2002, and international tariffs have been reduced substantially as a result of competition. A decline in international tariffs will imply a decline in revenues, mitigated to some extent by the volume response. Making up for the revenue loss requires an increase in certain other tariffs (that is, those tariffs that are either below costs or not high enough to attract competition) or development of additional supplementary services. The problem is mitigated to some extent by the fact that costs in the telecom sector are consistently decreasing. The regulatory response to this is the specification of the IUC regime.

Regulatory Issues

One characteristic of India's telecom reforms—and the cause of many of the problems involved—is that major reform measures like private entry into services were attempted without the establishment of a regulatory body. The Telecom Regulatory Authority of India was constituted in March 1997. To achieve the objectives of the TRAI Act, TRAI was given power to issue directions to service providers, make regulations, notify tariffs by order in the official gazette, and adjudicate disputes between service providers. Among all its powers and duties, TRAI's authority and jurisdiction to settle disputes among the service providers have been important. Overall, TRAI was designed to provide an effective regulatory framework and adequate safeguards to ensure fair competition and consumer protection. There was a ruling, however, by the Delhi High Court against the TRAI in July 1998. The High Court ruled that it was not mandatory for the Indian government to seek the TRAI's recommendations before issuing licenses for telecommunications services in the country. The judgment affirmed the powers of the DoT—that is, the government—to issue licenses without recommendations from TRAI. It also clarified that TRAI did not have the power to over-ride the license conditions. This was reiterated by another High Court judgment in January 2000 which found that the calling-party-pays regime for cellular mobile as specified by TRAI could not be implemented. In January 2000 the TRAI Act was amended. More details are provided below.

World Trade Organization Issues

The World Trade Organization (WTO) rules and disciplines for telecoms comprise the General Agreement on Trade in Services (GATS), the schedules of commitments made under the GATS, and the Annex on Telecommunications. To get an indication of the basic thrust of major regulatory disciplines that are emphasized in the context of telecommunications, it is necessary to consider the Telecommunications Reference Paper. In the WTO India has made certain commitments for liberalizing the telecom sector. Comparing those commitments with the actual policy steps that India has taken shows that the extent of telecom liberalization there is significantly more than the commitments made. Moreover, the process of telecom liberalization is continuing, and this will further augment the telecom market that is available to investors in India and abroad, as can be seen in table 5.5 and appendixes 5.2 and 5.3. Likewise, the extent of foreign investment in Indian companies that provide telecom services is much more than the maximum of 25 percent that has been committed in the WTO. For instance, with the approval of the Foreign Investment Promotion Board, the maximum foreign equity permitted in the telecom services sector is as follows:

49 percent	Basic, cellular mobile, paging, V-SAT, mobile radio trunking, Internet; investment companies set up for investments in telecom services companies (investment by these companies in a telecom services company is treated as part of domestic equity and is not set off against the foreign equity cap)
51 percent	Email, voice mail, online information and data retrieval, online information and/or data processing; enhanced/value-added facsimile service, including store and forward, store and retrieve

Also, dividend income and capital invested are fully repatriable although telecom services companies are not permitted to make royalty payments.

Other incentives for the telecom sector include the following:

- License fee paid by telecom service providers is eligible for amortization for tax purposes.
- Licenses to provide telecom services can be assigned.
- Limit of external commercial borrowings (foreign currency debt) by telecom services companies has been raised to 50 percent of the project cost (including license fee).
- Investments in equity shares and debentures of telecom services companies qualify for tax rebate.
- Telecom services companies enjoy a 100 percent tax holiday for a period of 5 years and a 30 percent tax holiday for an additional 5 years during their first 15 years in business.

- Import of specified telecom equipment is permitted at concessional customs duty rates.
- Import of all capital goods for manufacturing telecom equipment does not require any license.

For the Internet sector, which is likely to provide a basis for much of the dynamic telecom-based activity in the future, India has a very permissive regime. The main features of the policy, announced in 1998, are provided in appendix 5.1.

Similarly, certain regulatory disciplines committed to by India (in terms of the Telecommunications Reference Paper) are less onerous than the disciplines actually applied in practice. For example, under the WTO India has not agreed to apply a nondiscriminatory interconnection regime, but nondiscrimination is one of the principles of the interconnection regime that has been specified by TRAI. Likewise, TRAI has specified that interconnection should be provided at any technically feasible point in the network. Furthermore, India is embarking on liberalization in a number of telecom sectors, and the actual extent of liberalization is likely to increase in the future. Such changes have already occurred with respect to Internet telephony and the long-distance call market.

Regulatory Overview

The policymaker for India's telecommunications sector is the Ministry of Communications and Information Technology, which operates through two government bodies—the Telecom Commission and the Department of Telecommunications. The Telecom Regulatory Authority of India is an independent regulator that reports to parliament through the minister of communications and IT. The Telecom Commission performs the executive and policymaking function. The DoT is the executive and policy-implementing body and the TRAI performs the function of an independent regulator. The secretary of the DoT is the ex-officio chair of the Telecom Commission.

Department of Telecommunications, Ministry of Communications and Information Technology   The DoT, Ministry of Communications, is the authority that looks after the licensing and overall policymaking in India. Until recently the DoT combined the roles of policymaker and main service provider. The service provider section has been separated from DoT and is now functioning as a corporate body, BSNL. One other government corporation is an important service provider—MTNL—which operates in Mumbai and Delhi as a service provider with license to provide basic, cellular-mobile, and Internet service, among other things. At an earlier point VSNL, which had a monopoly in the international call segment, was also a public sector enterprise. The government is a major shareholder in MTNL and is now a less-than-majority shareholder in VSNL. These firms now compete with each other for the same market—a situation that began happening earlier in such cases as MTNL and VSNL vying for the Internet market. The competitive situation would require greater autonomy for MTNL and VSNL.

Telecom Regulatory Authority of India   On January 24, 2000, an ordinance amended the 1997 TRAI Act and altered a number of its aspects. For example, the adjudicatory role of the TRAI was separated and assigned to a Telecom Dispute Settlement and Appellate Tribunal (TDSAT).[4] That tribunal has been given the powers to adjudicate any dispute, such as:

a. That between a licensor and a licensee
b. That between two or more service providers
c. That between a service provider and a group of consumers.

TDSAT has been granted additional powers compared with those previously exercised by TRAI. For example, it can settle disputes between licensor and licensee, and its decisions may be challenged only in the Supreme Court of India.

TRAI's remaining functions have been better defined and have increased, for instance, with respect to powers relating specifically to interconnection conditions. TRAI now has the power to "fix the terms and conditions of inter-connectivity between the service providers" (TRAI [Amendment] Act 2000, p. 5), instead of "regulating arrangements between service providers of sharing revenue from interconnection" (TRAI Act 1997). The new legalization signaled an attempt to reestablish a credible regulator. The government would be required to seek a recommendation from TRAI when issuing new licenses. The adjudication of licensor–licensee disputes would be undertaken by an independent tribunal specializing in telecommunications. In terms of interconnection arrangements, TRAI was given the powers to override the provisions of license agreements signed with the DoT. However, although there has been an increase in TRAI's powers (other than in the area of dispute settlement), the act has led to a weakening of the guarantee that was provided in the previous act with respect to the five-year working period for the TRAI chair and members. This statutory guarantee was done away with, and the revised act provides for less stringent conditions for removal of any authority member or chair.

Assessment of Regulatory Reform

Regulatory reform in the Indian telecommunications sector can be seen as a two-step process: (1) establishment of an independent regulator, and (2) the regulatory authority implementing reform on the basis of its policy initiatives. A crucial concomitant element of this process is the separation of the incumbent service provider from the policymaker. Since its establishment, the telecom regulator in India has taken a number of initiatives pertaining to tariffs, interconnection charges, and revenue sharing, and has provided its recommendations on license conditions/license fees for certain service segments. The regulator also has addressed a number of disputes under Section 14 of the act.

An important feature of the 1997 TRAI Act 1997 (amended in 2000) is that the authority has to ensure transparency while exercising its powers and discharging its functions. Hence, TRAI has adopted a procedure of consultations under which it prepares consultation papers on the issues under consideration; seeks comments from the general public and experts in the area; and provides an explanatory memorandum with its tariff orders, interconnection charges, or revenue-sharing regulation and its recommendations. TRAI was a pioneer in adopting such a process, which is being performed for the first time by policymakers in India.

TRAI has also been vested with powers to frame regulations necessary for its functioning, including the levy of fees and charges for services. The TRAI Act provides for a separate TRAI General Fund, which will be credited with all grants, fees, and charges received by TRAI and with funds from other approved sources. Provision has also been made for central government grants to help meet the expenses of the regulatory authority.

In several countries that have significantly liberalized the telecommunications sector, the focus now is on convergence of policies as well as on regulation that addresses "unfair competition." Furthermore, rapid developments in the area of the Internet are posing particular problems for the regulator. It is now evident that ISPs will be increasingly able to use their technologies to provide services that are competitive with those provided by the main telecom service providers. The changes are also raising new regulatory issues, which may even lead to a recasting of the established principles in certain cases. There is now a tendency for service providers to bundle different services, thus creating difficulties in regulating them as separate entities. In a number of instances, convergence of services and technologies is prompting a convergence of regulatory authorities or greater cooperation among the separate regulatory authorities handling the policy issues.

In this regard it is useful to consider the view expressed by the International Telecommunication Union:

> Licensing frameworks around the world are facing pressures for dramatic change, however. The future is uncertain by the voice-telephony paradigm that defines the telecommunication industry being overtaken and will inevitably disappear. It will be replaced with an IT paradigm that accommodates the multimedia characteristics, global seamlessness and virtuality that will characterize a pervasively IT-based global economy operating over converged technologies and services in cyberspace.
>
> Regulatory regimes of the future will have to reflect different public-interest concerns. Countries that embrace rather than resist the IT paradigm will shift their focus away from a concern for the assured availability of reasonably priced, basic voice services provided over traditional public networks. Instead, they will focus more on promoting multiple outlets for voice telephony and ensuring that a reliable and universal virtual-public network is maintained across a crazy quilt of interconnected technologies and applications.
>
> Overall, this will likely mean decreased reliance on individual licensing of particular services and facilities and increased reliance on general rules. It will also involve greater coordination among authorities in different industry sectors. Telecommunications regulation will be less concerned with licensing and pricing and more concerned with continuous efforts to adapt standards of reliability and interoperability to unrelenting technology changes, as well as with frequency allocation and assignment, dispute resolution and consumer protection. Much more of the telecommunication industry will probably end up being regulated by the market. (ITU 1999a, p. 129)

Recommendatory Role   In line with standard practice with regard to such legislation, the Government of India has reserved the right to give policy directions to TRAI and to seek its recommendations on matters connected with technology, service provision, and so forth. Both of these provisions have figured in the recent past in reported disagreements between TRAI and the government. NTP 99 has recognized the role of TRAI recommendations in a number of areas. To help implement NTP 99, the government has sought TRAI's recommendations on several important issues (mentioned in appendix 5.3).

Government Retention of Licensing Powers   Apart from the policymaking function, the government has retained the licensing function. Among countries of the world there is no common pattern for whether licensing powers reside with the regulator or with the government. According to ITU sources, countries in which the regulator has the licensing power include the following:

- In Africa: Botswana, Ghana, Mauritius, Namibia, Nigeria, South Africa, Tanzania, and Zambia.
- In the Americas: Paraguay, the United States, and República Bolivariana de Venezuela.
- In the Asia Pacific region: Australia, Hong Kong (China), Pakistan, the Philippines, and Sri Lanka (licensing spectrum).

In India the main issue with respect to licensing has not been whether the power should be with the regulator but that, under the 1997 TRAI Act, the terms and conditions of the license should involve a consideration of recommendations from TRAI. In the Communications Commission of India proposed under the Communications Convergence Bill it is expected that licensing powers will be transferred to the regulator.

Some Concluding Observations

Telecommunications reform policies everywhere have recognize̶ eed to have many more participants than the incumbent operator in the proces. ᵗelecommunications network expansion and service development. It is generalı, ᵓepted that these new participants will stimulate sector development and proᵥ ᵉ a degree of competition to the incumbent public telephone operator, thus positively influencing the efficiency of service provision. The question is no longer whether to have competition—the traditional arguments for exclusivity no longer hold. Instead, the question is how fast competition should be ushered in and under what conditions.

Nine years since the announcement of NTP 94, which sought private sector participation in the Indian telecommunications market, there is much to show by way of competition in the sector. The liberalization of the Indian telecom sector initially was riddled with uncertainty. The first bidding process for basic services resulted in only 6 out of 22 licenses being awarded, of which only 3 licensees commenced operations in 2000. In the early phase of regulation by an independent regulator, there were numerous disputes between the incumbent DoT and TRAI over the jurisdiction of the latter. This was one of the troubling issues. In recent years, this situation has changed, and the policy has allowed open competition in basic services, national long distance, and international long distance sectors. For cellular-mobile, only four service providers are allowed because of the limited availability of frequency spectrum. Nonetheless, this number is significant enough to generate effective competition. One indicator of competition is the sharp reduction in prices that has occurred in recent years. There were quite a few circles for basic services that private-service providers did not find attractive enough to enter. This situation has now changed, however, so that an effective communication infrastructure could contribute to the economic growth of these areas. There are still some 275,000 villages that remain to be connected by phone. Setting up a funding mechanism through the proposed universal service access levy has now been done.

In addition, clearer policy enunciation by the TRAI through its reference interconnect offer and interconnect usage charge regimes to establish open access and interconnection guidelines among operators will also create an environment in which teledensity can increase. The presence of many operators and a technological and regulatory environment that permits the interconnection of one network with another also would lead to a quantum expansion of reach.

In India's case, license fees were earlier identified as a source for government revenue. Given India's fiscal situation and the revenue-raising possibilities of telecom licenses, it is difficult to abjure the revenue-maximizing option. Focusing only on revenue maximization, however, does not lead to satisfactory results even from the view of this limited objective. Furthermore, if revenue has to be earned from a sector, it is more efficient to glean it from the actual earnings rather than to seek it from projected earnings in an uncertain environment. There is considerable evidence to suggest that the initial bids for high license fees were largely responsible for rendering telecom projects nonbankable and for the slow takeoff of sector liberalization. This situation has been addressed by moving to a regime of revenue-share-license fees, part of which would contribute to funding the universal service obligation.

In India there is a major emphasis on expanding teledensity in the next seven years, and the government has explicitly recognized the role of the private sector in meeting such targets. Delay in implementing the operations will create problems in meeting the stated objectives. The needs of the hour are to begin operations in as many places as possible, and to infuse competition so that another objective of the government policy can be met with success through the market itself—namely, to provide the services at affordable prices. To that extent, any license fees charged should be low, covering, for example, contributions to the proposed universal service access levy, the cost of regulation, and some additional amount to meet such other objectives as the creation of a telecom fund.

Telecommunications technologies and services and the market structure for India's telecom sector are changing rapidly. New converged services are emerging and the policymaker has allowed open entry in several segments of the market. Basic telecom is facing competition not only from new entrants but also from cellular-mobile service, which is growing rapidly. The consistent decline in costs will also put further downward pressure on prices and provide a basis for achieving the teledensity targets with lower investment levels than those indicated by present cost estimates.

With this background, the policymaker has to ensure that the telecom services provided in India are affordable and efficient, and cater both to the demand for telephony by the general public and to the demand for value-added and high bandwidth services provided by modern technologies (including the provision of adequate frequency spectrum). In time, with an increase of teledensity to more than 20 to 30 percent for the urban areas, the growth of telecom there will become self-sustaining. This demand base will be enhanced also with the growth of IT services, as well as the specific efforts by the Government to spread the use of data services through teleservices and e-governance. The market will then provide a minimum critical mass required for sustaining broadband and value-added services on a general scale. This would require a stable and consistent regulatory regime that encourages competition through a level playing field, the government's easing financial constraints on provision of interconnection, and through the achievement of social objectives. This would prepare the ground for the likely rapid growth of cellular-mobile, which may become the preferred technology for rural telecommunications. It would facilitate investment by creating time-bound, single-window procedures, promoting specific efforts to develop content for teleservices that will meet social objectives, and developing the software component of the telecom equipment sector. Frameworks should be developed for industry self-regulation and for interaction of the regulator with the consumer bodies. Furthermore, the policymaker will have to ensure that the transition from the present regulatory regime to a new one is managed smoothly, and that there is no conflict between the mandates of different regulatory bodies, such as those for telecommunications and for competition policy. And all this has to be managed in an environment in which the nature of policy planning has been changed by the introduction of competition in the market. The policy initiatives mentioned in this chapter are aimed at managing affordable, large-scale provision of telecom services and providing adequate opportunities for developing the market for modern services so that India is in a good position to provide its citizens telecom opportunities similar to those in the industrial world.

One final comment: it is in the fitness of things that policy statements for the telecom sector have been periodically reviewed with the changing telecom scenario. The reform process under way for more than eight years has introduced major competition in the sector, and there is awareness of the additional crucial issues that need to be addressed. Given the acknowledged importance of telecommunications to overall national interests, governments tend to get involved in the management of the sector's progress. It is unfortunate in terms of development that the interests of the government and the private sector are not always easily reconciled. This fact has resulted in telecom stagnation in many countries, including India. Evidence shows that governments that most "competently" foster private sector advancement of their telecommunications industries are best placed to gain world-class telecommunications services and the attendant benefits. Arguably, early liberalization could give any country a first-mover advantage in attaining high telecommunications performance, but hasty adoption by developing economies of liberal frameworks adopted by industrial economies could easily fail and in the process discredit the idea of liberalization.

Enthusiasm for liberalization and its possibilities must be juxtaposed with a realistic transformation program that takes into account the country's economic and political dynamics. The efforts of the regulator to build an appropriate framework for fostering fair competition are crucial in this regard. The steps being taken in India indicate that such an effort is under way, and the frameworks to address issues relating to interconnection, tariffs, and quality of service are either already established or will be established soon. Combined with open competition in general, this suggests low prices and dynamic evolution of the telecom sector in India.

Appendix 5.1: Salient Features of ISP Policy, 1999

Following are the main features of the policy for Internet service providers:

- There is no restriction on the number of service providers.
- Operation can be on a national, regional, or district basis.
- Service provider has the option of building or leasing capacity from infrastructure owners (railways, energy utilities).
- Foreign equity participation is capped at 49 percent.
- No prior experience in IT and telecommunications is required.
- Licenses will be issued for a period of 15 years, extendable by 5 years.
- There is no license fee for the first 5 years; token fee of Re 1 per annum thereafter.
- Service providers are allowed to set up international gateways after obtaining security clearance.
- Telephony on the Internet is not permitted.
- TRAI has the freedom to fix tariffs; that is, tariffs for Internet services have been forborne by TRAI, but TRAI may review and fix tariff at any time during the validity of the license.

Appendix 5.2: Chronology of Indian Telecommunications Deregulation

Year	Event
1992	Bids are invited for radio-paging services in 27 cities.
	Bids are invited for cellular-mobile services in 4 metro cities.
1994	National Telecom Policy is announced.
	Radio paging, V-SAT data services, email services, voicemail, and video-text services are opened to private providers.
	DoT issues guidelines for private sector entry into basic telecom services in the country.
	Eight cellular licensees for four metros are finalized after more than two years of litigation.
1995	DoT calls for proposal to operate basic services, cellular telecom services, and public mobile radio trunked (PMRT) services.
	DoT receives bids for basic, cellular, and PMRT services.
	Most cellular operators in the circles sign license agreements.
	DoT announces a cap on the number of circles in which basic operators can roll out services. Licensees are selected for 5 circles.
1996	After setting reserve prices for circles, DoT invites fresh bids for basic services in 13 circles.
	Five successful bidders are short-listed as providers of basic services.
	There is poor response to the third round of basic telecom bidding. Only one company bids (for Madhya Pradesh).
	The selected bidder from the first round refuses to extend bank guarantees for its 4 circles. In court the bidder challenges DoT's move to encash guarantees.
	Three more companies challenge DoT's move to encash guarantees in court.
1997	The Telecom Regulatory Authority of India is formed.
	The first basic telecom service company signs its license and interconnect agreements with DoT (for Madhya Pradesh).
	The second basic service provider signs its basic telecom license pact (for Gujarat).
	TRAI quashes DoT's move to increase tariffs for calls from fixed-line telephones to cellular phones.
	VSNL calls for global tenders to find a partner for its South Asian regional hub project.
	The Internet policy is cleared; license agreement for basic services in Maharashtra becomes operational.
	Basic service licensees for Andhra Pradesh and Punjab sign basic telecom agreements with DoT.
1999	TRAI issues its first tariff order.
	New Telecom Policy is announced.

J: what ›es that ean here?

Appendix 5.2: *(Continued)*

Year	Event
	TRAI issues the first regulation on interconnection and usage charge. Conditions for migration to revenue sharing from fixed license fee regime are issued. Cellular operators are allowed the use of any digital technology; MTNL is given a license to provide cellular-mobile service under those flexible technology conditions.
2000	Ordinance divesting TRAI of adjudicatory role is promulgated. TDSAT is created to settle disputes between licensors and licensees. Appeals against TRAI decisions are to be heard by TDSAT. TRAI implements the second phase of tariff rebalancing. Policies are announced to ease the entry and operation of new service providers in the various sectors (e.g., V-SAT, PMRT service, radio paging, unified messaging, and voicemail). The government allows private Internet operators to set up international gateways. Guidelines for issue of license for national long-distance service are released. Guidelines for issue of license for cellular mobile telephone service are released.
2001	Guidelines for issue of license for basic telephone are released. Convergence Commission Bill is introduced in parliament. Open competition policy is announced for international telephony service. Usage of voice-over Internet protocol is permitted for international telephony service. First license for national long-distance service is signed. Launch of WLL(M) (Wireless in Local Loop with Limited Mobility) services by basic service providers in the market.
2002	Guidelines for issue of international long-distance license are released. First license for international long-distance service is signed. First private operator begins international long-distance service. TRAI revises tariffs for WLL(M). TRAI leaves cellular tariffs to market forces; service providers to notify their reference tariff plans. TRAI introduces the reference interconnect offer regulation. TRAI introduces regulation on quality of service for voice-over Internet protocol–based international long-distance service.
2003	TRAI introduces the telecommunication interconnection usage charges regulation. TRAI leaves the domestic long-distance sector under forbearance, subject to a ceiling tariff (i.e., service providers can decide on tariff levels). TRAI leaves the international long-distance sector under forbearance.

Appendix 5.3: Recommendations Sought by the Government from TRAI to Help Implement NTP 1999

- Recommendations on the issue of the fifth license to cellular-mobile service providers
- Recommendations on issues concerning public mobile radio trunked (PMRT) service, namely, an increase in quantum of public switched telephone network (PSTN) connectivity, separate numbering scheme for PMRT service, and extension of the service area to cover the local charging area
- Recommendations to facilitate V-SAT operations, namely, permitting higher data rate, reducing license fees for captive V-SAT network, and reducing the minimum antennae size
- Recommendations on growth of the Internet by establishing a national internet exchange in the country
- The government has sought recommendations from TRAI regarding the opening up of internet telephony in the country.
- Policy regarding introduction of competition in international long-distance services, including recommendations on the number of international long-distance operators, license fee structure, selection criteria for service providers, and terms and conditions of the license
- Policy regarding introduction of competition in domestic long-distance services, including recommendations on the scope of service, service area, number of long-distance operators, license fee structure, selection criteria for service providers, and interconnection between service providers in different service areas
- Issue of fresh licenses for radio-paging service providers, including entry of more operators in the service area on the basis of review after two years, level of entry fee, percentage of revenue share as license fee, definition of revenue, basis for selection, and migration of existing licensees to revenue-sharing arrangement
- Issue of fresh licenses for V-SAT service providers, including level of entry fee, percentage of revenue share as license fee, and other license conditions
- Issue of fresh licenses for the fixed service providers, including a circle's number of private service providers in addition to DoT, selection criteria, migration from fixed license fee to revenue-sharing arrangement for existing licensees, and other license conditions
- Issue of fresh licenses to cellular-mobile service providers in the six vacant circles/slots (one slot each in West Bengal and Assam circles; two slots each in Jammu and Kashmir, and Andaman and Nicobar Island), including level of entry fee and percentage of revenue share from the licensor, definition of revenue for the purpose of revenue sharing, migration of existing cellular-mobile

service providers to revenue-sharing arrangement, and any other issue considered relevant

- Issue of fresh license for PMRT services, including issue of fresh licenses throughout the country, level of entry fee, percentage of revenue share as license fee, and definition of revenue for the purpose of revenue sharing
- Recommendations on terms and conditions of license agreement for global mobile personal communications by satellite, including an examination of the provisional license, terms and conditions of the license, and quantum and structure of the license fee
- Terms and conditions of usage of backbone network of utility service providers, including the class of operators to fund universal access levy, various cost models or approaches to determine the percentage contribution from the revenue for the operators, and the mechanisms for computing it; per-unit subsidy for village public telephones (VPTs) and rural DELs separately to cover capital and recurring expenditure, and whether per-unit subsidy will be the same or different in different geographical area/tribal and nontribal areas of the country.

Endnotes

1. License fees are fixed at 12, 10, and 8 percent of adjusted gross revenues for circles A, B, and C, respectively. Metros have a license fee equal to that of circle A.

2. Circles have been classified as category A, B, and C based on market characteristics and telephony potential in diminishing order of attractiveness.

3. At the end of February 2003, the cellular subscriber base stood at 11.7 million connections.

4. In its present form the CCI Bill also envisages the dispute-settlement function to be performed by the Communications Dispute Settlement Appellate Tribunal (CAT).

Bibliography

Athreya, M. B. 1991. *Report of the High Level Committee on Reorganisation of Telecom Department* (Athreya Committee). March. New Delhi.

DoT (Department of Telecommunications). 1994. *National Telecom Policy*. New Delhi: Government of India.

———. 1999. *New Telecom Policy*. New Delhi: Government of India.

———. 2000a. *Guidelines for Issue of Licence for Cellular Mobile Telephone Service*. New Delhi: Government of India.

———. 2000b. *Guidelines for Issue of Licence for National Long Distance Service*. New Delhi: Government of India.

———. 2001a. *Annual Report 2000-01*. New Delhi: Government of India.

———. 2001b. *Guidelines for Issue of Licence for Basic Telephone Service*. January. New Delhi: Government of India.

———. Various years. *Annual Telecom Statistics*. New Delhi: Government of India.

ICICI. 1992. *International Experiences in Telecommunications Reforms and Its Relevance to India*. Background Papers to Seminar, November.

India Infrastructure Report Expert Group. 1996. *Policy Imperatives for Growth and Welfare.* New Delhi: National Council of Applied Economic Research.

ITU (International Telecommunication Union). 1999a, "Trends in Telecommunication Reform 1999." Geneva.

———. 1999b. *World Telecommunication Development Report.* Geneva.

Melody, William H., ed. 2001. *Telecom Reform—Principles, Policies and Regulatory Practices.* Lyngby: Technical University of Denmark.

Planning Commission, India. 1999. *Ninth Five-Year Plan.* New Delhi: Government of India.

Reserve Bank of India. 1998. *Handbook of Statistics on the Indian Economy.* Mumbai, India.

TRAI (Telecom Regulatory Authority of India). 1998. "Consultation Paper on Framework and Proposals for Telecom Pricing." New Delhi.

———. 1999a. "Consultation Paper on Introduction of Competition in Domestic Long Distance Communications." New Delhi.

———. 1999b. "Telecommunication Tariff Order." New Delhi.

———. 2001. "Issues Relating to Interconnection between Access Providers and National Long Distance Operators." New Delhi.

Utton, M. A. 1986. *The Economics of Regulating Industry.* Oxford, U.K.: Basil Blackwell.

World Bank. 1997. *Telecommunications and Economic Development.* Baltimore: Johns Hopkins University Press.

6

ECONOMIC IMPACT OF FOREIGN DIRECT INVESTMENT IN SOUTH ASIA

Pradeep Agrawal

One of the important and contentious issues in the forthcoming World Trade Organization (WTO) multilateral trade negotiations is whether to establish a multilateral framework for investment. The industrial countries are seeking an agreement that would grant foreign investors virtually unfettered rights to invest in all sectors of the host country's economy and to obtain for those investors the same treatment as is received by investors from the host nation. Many developing countries, including India, however, are wary of such demands. They are concerned that the multinational firms might adversely affect the development of domestic firms and otherwise exploit them economically.

To negotiate effectively, it is important to understand the economic role of foreign direct investment (FDI) in developing countries in general, and particularly in India. Two of the important issues of contention are the following:

- Does FDI crowd out domestic private investment or does it increase it by fostering various backward and forward linkages with domestic firms?
- Does FDI increase the growth of gross domestic product (GDP) by creating jobs, increasing exports, and bringing new management and production techniques, or does it lower GDP growth in the long run by taking excessive profits out of the developing country?

These issues can be analyzed econometrically. A few earlier cross-country studies have suggested that, generally, FDI is economically beneficial to developing countries (see, for example, Balasubramanyam, Salisu, and Sapsford 1996; and Fry 1993).

Additional work is needed, however, to carry out more careful and country/region-specific studies to eliminate doubts that the cross-country results may be driven by a few extreme cases and may not apply to the specific country or region in question.

In this chapter, I analyze the above-mentioned issues econometrically. Because FDI inflows to India have been very small, averaging less than 0.1 percent of the GDP until 1991 and about 0.5 percent of GDP over the period 1992–96, for enhanced reliability I undertake time-series/cross-section (panel) analysis of data for five South Asian countries: Bangladesh, India, Pakistan, Nepal, and Sri Lanka. This is reasonable because the South Asian countries generally have similar economic structures and have followed similar policies toward FDI. The analysis here uses 25–32 years of data over the period 1965–96 from each of the five countries. My hope is to provide a better understanding of the economic impact of FDI in South Asia.

The chapter proceeds as follows. The first section provides a brief overview of India's policies toward foreign direct investment and presents data on FDI inflows to India. The second section analyzes the effect of FDI on investment by the citizens of the country. The third section analyzes the effect of FDI on GDP growth in South Asia. Some concluding remarks are provided in the final section.

Foreign Direct Investment in India: Policies and Inflows

This brief overview of India's policies toward FDI covers the period since independence and presents data on the amount of foreign direct investment flowing into India and other selected countries. It also provides a breakdown of the FDI into India by country of origin and by industry.

A Brief History of India's Policies Regarding FDI

India's policy regarding FDI can be classified into four phases: phase I (1957–67) was a cautiously welcoming approach; phase II (1967–79) can be characterized as a restrictive regime; phase III (1980–90) was marked by the progressive attenuation of regulations brought about in the 1970s; and phase IV (1991–2001) was a liberal and welcoming approach to FDI (Gopinath 1997). These phases are briefly discussed below.

Following independence in 1947, India initially had an ambivalent attitude toward FDI, alternating between the nationalist distrust of colonial firms and the hope that new foreign investment could provide the technology and capital essential for rapid industrialization. The positive view had the upper hand during the second and the third five-year plans, spanning the period 1957–67. Thus, the cautiously welcoming approach adopted during this period included features such as nondiscriminatory treatment of foreign investment, easy repatriability of profits by foreign firms, and emphasis on exports by foreign-controlled firms.

When an acute foreign exchange crisis began to develop in the late 1960s, it was felt that foreign firms were contributing to the problem through the import of inputs and repatriation of profits. The government nationalized some major oil-producing and retailing multinational companies in the early 1970s. The Foreign Exchange Regulation Act (FERA), passed in 1973, marked the tightening of the regulatory regime regarding the management of foreign capital. A process of indigenization and dilution of foreign equity was carried out whereby foreign companies were required within two years to dilute nonresident shareholding to the level prescribed by the Reserve Bank of India—generally to 40 percent. A restrictive approach was adopted for noncash inflows and use of foreign brand names for sales within India. Domestic firms requiring foreign technology were encouraged to acquire it through licensing rather than through joint ventures. Companies in high-technology and skills areas, however, were allowed foreign shareholdings up to 74 percent (see Kumar 1994).

In the 1980s, growing concern about stagnation and technological obsolescence in Indian industry drew attention to the restrictive licensing procedures. Poor quality and the high cost of Indian manufactured products contributed to the poor export performance, and created balance-of-payments problems in the wake of the second oil shock. The need was felt for foreign collaborations to increase exports and improve the quality of Indian manufacturing, so there was an easing of restrictions on FDI that was further strengthened after Rajiv Gandhi became prime minister in 1985. FERA restrictions were relaxed for FDI in areas of high technology and for 100 percent export–oriented units. Foreign investment equity up to 74 percent and 100 percent was allowed in the priority sectors and export-oriented units, respectively, with full repatriation of profits. Four export-processing zones were set up. During 1984 and 1985, many capital goods were moved to the open general license list, thus making them easier to import. In 1986 the tax rate on royalty payments was brought down from 40 percent to 30 percent. Bureaucratic bottlenecks remained, however, and foreign firms probably continued to distrust the Indian government. As a result, foreign equity inflows remained meager, and Indian industry continued to rely largely on foreign debt capital to meet its foreign exchange needs over this period.

A major change in regime came in 1991 when India introduced trade and investment liberalization policies. Tariffs were sharply reduced on most products, bringing down the average weighted tariff rate on imports from 87 percent in 1990/91 to 25 percent by 1994/95 and to 20 percent by 1997/98. The foreign technology requirement for allowing inward FDI was discontinued, and a large number of additional sectors, including many consumer goods sectors, were opened to foreign investment. The repatriation of profits by foreign-controlled firms was eased, and the earlier requirement that the export earnings balance the dividend payment over the first seven years from the date of commercial production by the foreign venture was dropped, except for 24 consumer goods industries. In 1994 India became a member of the Multilateral Investment Guarantee Agency. As a result all investments approved by the Government of India are now insured against expropriation or nationalization. Up to 100 percent equity was allowed in a number of industries (especially those in export-oriented and high-technology industries). The Reserve Bank of India was authorized to give automatic approvals (usually within two weeks) to proposals in the high-priority areas where foreign equity did not exceed 51 percent and in the mining sector where the foreign equity did not exceed 50 percent. A Foreign Investment Promotion Board (FIPB) was set up to act as a single-window clearance entity. It deals with large investment proposals and such other proposals as those in which foreign equity exceeds 51 percent, or the industry is not on the list of high-priority sectors, or foreign equity does not cover the import of capital goods. Proposals are usually cleared in four to six weeks. Unlike the Reserve Bank of India, the FIPB can initiate and carry on detailed negotiations with foreign firms. Overall it appears that during the 1990s the government adopted a much more welcoming attitude toward foreign investors—a stance exemplified by the common minimum program of the present government, which is aimed at nearly tripling the FDI inflows to US$10 billion a year.

This brief overview of the history of India's policies regarding FDI makes it quite clear that there has existed considerable confusion about the true economic impact of such investment on the national economy. My hope is that the analysis to be undertaken here will help resolve some of that confusion.

FDI Flows into India

Figure 6.1 shows FDI inflows into India and other South Asian countries as a percent of GDP over the period 1965–1996. Inflows in India have increased sharply since 1992, following the policy changes. Figure 6.1 also presents a comparison of the inflows into China and an average for the East Asian countries (simple average of Indonesia, Malaysia, Singapore, South Korea, and Thailand) over the same period. Evidently despite the sharp increase since 1992, India has had a much lower level of FDI inflows than have China, the East Asian countries, and even such South Asian countries as Sri Lanka and Pakistan.

Next let us consider the country and industry breakdown of FDI in India approved from 1991 to 2000, the period during which the bulk of FDI came into India.

FIGURE 6.1   Inflows of FDI as Percent of GDP

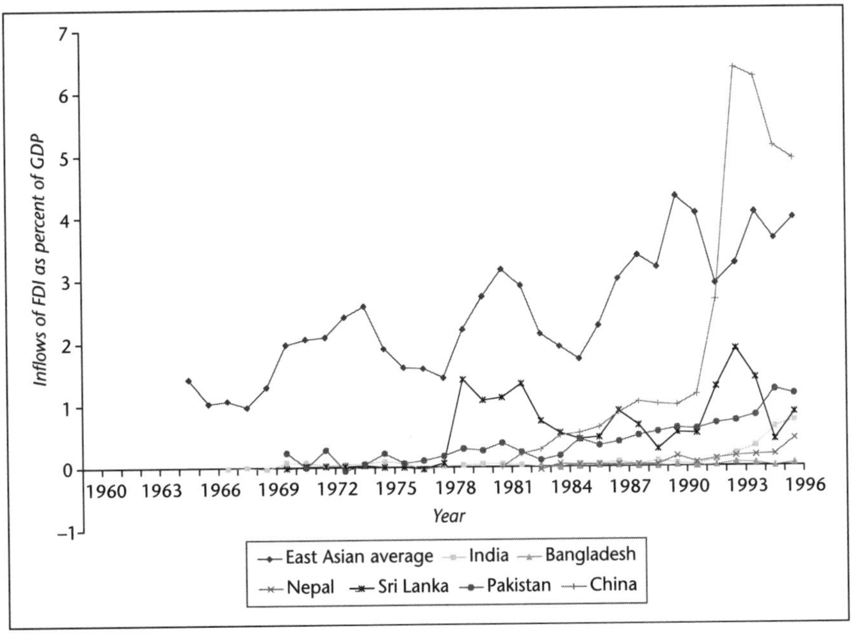

Note: East Asian average refers to simple average across five East Asian countries: Indonesia, the Republic of Korea, Malaysia, Singapore, and Thailand.

Source: Based on data from World Bank (1998).

Table 6.1 shows that the United States is the largest investor in India, accounting for over 20 percent of total FDI inflows over the period. Mauritius follows, but it is really a conduit for investors from various countries, including the United States, because of a special tax treaty with India that grants exemption from Indian taxes for Mauritius-based companies. The United Kingdom is the next largest investor in India followed by the Republic of Korea, Japan, and nonresident (or overseas) Indians. Korea has emerged as a major investor in India since 1996, especially in passenger cars and consumer durables such as refrigerators, televisions, and washing machines. Other significant investors in India include Germany, Australia, Malaysia, France, and the Netherlands. Malaysia especially has emerged as a significant investor in India since 1995.

The industry breakdown of FDI and technical collaborations approved from August 1991 to March 2000 is shown in table 6.2. The main sectors receiving inflows of foreign investment were power generation; oil refining; cellular-mobile and basic telephone services; telecommunications; and the transportation industry,

TABLE 6.1 Foreign Direct Investment Approvals, 1991–2000: Share of Major Investing Economies

Economy[a]	1991	1992	1993	1994	1995	1996	1997	1998	1999	2000[b]	Total/Average (1991–2000[c])
United States	34.80	31.68	39.08	24.59	22.00	27.82	24.72	11.56	12.60	14.63	21.26
Mauritius	0.00	0.00	1.40	3.77	5.64	6.46	19.00	10.27	13.41	20.19	11.57
United Kingdom	6.01	3.03	7.03	9.16	5.38	4.22	8.18	10.39	10.45	1.35	6.98
Korea, Rep. of	1.15	1.01	0.33	0.75	0.98	8.91	3.56	1.20	12.86	0.17	4.16
Japan	9.87	15.70	2.91	2.83	4.72	4.12	3.47	4.16	5.62	3.19	4.22
Nonresident Indians	3.69	11.30	11.78	3.46	2.21	6.06	3.31	2.44	1.60	3.03	3.70
Germany	7.83	2.22	1.99	4.01	4.18	4.25	3.93	2.77	4.03	1.48	3.53
Australia	0.49	2.00	0.33	2.74	4.69	2.31	0.79	8.56	2.29	0.18	2.82
Malaysia	0.03	1.91	0.10	0.18	4.32	0.12	3.83	5.85	0.41	0.03	2.38
France	3.62	0.76	1.46	0.63	1.31	4.62	1.30	1.67	5.11	0.31	2.19
Netherlands	10.47	2.49	3.63	1.46	3.01	2.90	1.59	1.61	2.23	0.91	2.10
Israel	0.00	0.03	0.02	0.06	12.90	0.04	0.09	0.04	0.03	0.00	1.81
Italy	3.33	2.30	1.32	2.76	1.44	0.38	2.18	0.90	6.20	0.41	1.95
Singapore	0.26	1.55	0.75	1.87	3.09	0.88	1.57	2.49	2.91	0.61	1.84
Belgium	0.30	0.61	0.07	0.05	0.52	0.54	0.39	10.67	0.05	0.10	1.69
Cayman Islands	0.00	0.00	0.04	0.02	0.00	0.02	6.57	0.00	0.04	0.34	1.59
Switzerland	6.65	17.74	4.82	0.34	0.96	0.44	0.90	0.93	1.03	0.27	1.20
Thailand	0.00	0.06	4.16	0.07	6.14	0.21	0.05	0.00	0.02	0.00	1.05
Canada	0.91	0.02	0.31	0.30	4.28	0.54	0.70	1.02	0.13	0.37	1.06
Hong Kong, China	3.96	1.47	0.99	1.16	1.27	1.41	0.47	0.77	0.16	1.56	0.92
Sweden	1.31	1.25	0.01	0.08	1.57	1.47	0.20	0.70	0.97	0.40	0.77
South Africa	0.00	0.00	0.00	0.00	0.05	0.16	0.17	5.54	0.09	0.02	0.81
Russia	1.61	0.30	0.02	0.74	0.36	0.00	0.00	0.05	0.03	0.00	0.11

TABLE 6.1 *(Continued)*

Economy[a]	1991	1992	1993	1994	1995	1996	1997	1998	1999	2000[b]	Total/Average (1991–2000[a])
Taiwan, China	0.08	0.46	0.11	0.07	0.01	0.22	0.00	0.01	0.03	0.02	0.06
Total of all countries (in US$ millions)	**206.78**	**1,483.79**	**2,823.24**	**4,521.09**	**9,116.46**	**10,060.34**	**13,974.38**	**7,253.65**	**6,522.54**	**5,431.50**	**53,103.79**
GDR/FCCB[c]	0.00	0.00	0.00	36.87	3.71	14.56	8.20	10.46	11.37	47.96	14.59

GDR = global depository receipt; FCCB = foreign currency convertible bond.

a. Ranking of all countries is according to cumulative total of approvals for the period 1991 to 2000.
b. Represents projected figures for 2000 based on data up to August 31, 2000.
c. Represents proposals for GDRs and FCCBs.

Source: Data from Secretariat for Industrial Assistance, Ministry of Commerce and Industry, Government of India, available at http://siadipp.nic.in/publicat/newsttr/sep2000/news4.htm.

TABLE 6.2 Foreign Direct Investment Approvals, August 1991 to March 2000: Share by Industry

Serial Number	Name of Industry	Share of Industry
1	Fuels	29.72
	Power generation	14.83
	Oil refinery	8.91
2	Telecommunications	17.32
	Cellular mobile and basic telephone services	11.61
	Telecommunications	4.24
3	Transportation industry	8.27
	Passenger cars	3.36
	Automobile industry	1.88
	Air/sea transport	1.12
4	Service sector	6.91
	Financial	4.7
	Nonfinancial services	1.44
	Electronics	1.27
5	Metallurgical	5.87
	Ferrous	3.44
	Mining service	1.13
6	Chemicals	5.63
7	Food processing industry	4.04
	Food products	3.99
8	Hotel and tourism	2.01
	Hotel and restaurants	1.65
9	Textiles (including dyed, printed)	1.51
10	Paper and pulp (including paper products)	1.45
11	Industrial machinery	1.05
	Total of all industries	Rs. 2,142 billion (US$53.1 billion)

Source: Data from the Secretariat for Industrial Assistance, Ministry of Commerce and Industry, Government of India, available at http://siadipp.nic.in/publicat/newslttr/apr2000/news5.htm.

especially the production of passenger cars. There were also significant inflows in financial services (e.g., banking and insurance), metallurgy, chemical production, and food processing industries.

Impact of FDI on Investment by National Investors

To study the effect of FDI on domestic investment, we need to estimate an investment function and then analyze the impact of FDI. In this section I will briefly discuss the variables that affect investment and specify a functional form for its determinants. Then we will consider the econometric procedures used and thereafter the results of the econometric estimations.

The Investment Function

Blejer and Khan (1984) described some of the difficulties of estimating neoclassical investment functions for developing countries, such as the lack of readily available measures of the capital stock or its rate of return. Thus the investment function estimated here is based on the flexible accelerator model developed by Fry (1998). The accelerator model has the desired real capital stock k^* proportional to real output, y:

$$k^* = \alpha y.$$

This can be expressed in terms of a desired investment rate $(\text{INV}/Y)^*$:

$$(\text{INV}/Y)^* = \alpha G$$

where INV denotes gross domestic fixed investment in current prices, Y denotes GDP in current prices, and G is the rate of growth of real GDP, y. A partial adjustment mechanism allows the actual investment rate to adjust to the difference between the desired investment rate and the investment rate in the previous period:

$$\Delta(\text{INV}/Y)_t = \lambda\left[(\text{INV}/Y)^* - (\text{INV}/Y)_{t-1}\right]$$

or

(1) $$(\text{INV}/Y)_t = \lambda(\text{INV}/Y)^* + (1 - \lambda)(\text{INV}/Y)_{t-1}$$

where λ is the coefficient of adjustment. The flexible accelerator model allows economic conditions to influence the adjustment coefficient, λ. That is:

(2) $$\lambda = \beta_0 + (\beta_1 X_1 + \beta_2 X_2 + \beta_3 X_3 + \cdots)/[(\text{INV}/Y)^* - (\text{INV}/Y)_{t-1}]$$

where X_i are the variables (including an intercept term for a constant depreciation rate) that affect λ, and β_i are their respective coefficients.

The explanatory variables used are GDP growth rate (G) over the previous year, domestic credit availability as share of GDP (CRDT/Y), net FDI inflows as share of GDP (FDI/Y), terms of trade (TOT)—an index with base-year (1990) value set to 100, real exchange rate (RER), net total foreign borrowing as share of GDP (ΔTEDtot/Y), and the real lending rate (RL). These variables are explained below.

FDI inflows constitute a source of investment funds. The use of this source of funds depends on the various policies regarding FDI, such as the maximum share of foreign equity allowed in joint ventures, regulations relating to repatriation of profits, various other policies and regulations pertaining to industry and labor, and the overall attractiveness of the country. FDI also can promote domestic investment through backward and forward linkages with domestic industries. Similarly, foreign borrowing can be used as a source of funds for investment, although public foreign borrowing does have a tendency to go (partially) into meeting urgent government budgetary requirements as well. Thus we also include as an explanatory variable the net total foreign borrowings as a share of GDP. This variable will enable us to compare the relative effectiveness of foreign borrowing and FDI inflows in promoting investment.

An improvement in the terms of trade (the unit price of exports divided by the unit price of imports) can increase investment by increasing real income, making capital goods (mostly importables in developing countries) less expensive than domestic goods. In some situations it could also decrease investment by decreasing the demand for domestic goods compared with importables (see, for example, Cardoso 1993).

Now consider the impact of an increase in the RER. It is defined as:

$$RER = E \cdot P^f/P$$

where E is the exchange rate (number of domestic currency units per U.S. dollar), P is the domestic price level (the GDP deflator), and P^f is the foreign price level (proxied here by the U.S. GDP deflator, given that the United States is the most important trading partner of the countries being studied). An increase in RER would increase the price of imported capital and intermediate goods and would result in a contraction of investment (Servén and Solimano 1992; Fry 1995). Van Wijnbergen (1982) developed a two-sector model showing that the net effect of a real depreciation is ambiguous: investment in tradable goods increases but investment in domestic goods declines.

True domestic costs of capital are very difficult to measure in the South Asian developing countries examined here because of selective credit policies, disequilibrium institutional interest rates, and the lack of data on tax rates. Therefore I use the real lending rate of banks as a proxy for the cost of capital. The real lending rate is obtained by subtracting the average of the current and next year's inflation rates from the nominal prime lending rate of the banks.

The availability of institutional credit is one of the most important determinants of the investment rate in developing countries (see Blinder and

Stiglitz 1983; Fry 1995). The quantity of credit is likely to be significant in a credit market where the interest rates are controlled at below market-clearing levels and/or directed credit programs exist for selected industrial sectors. The latter have continued in most of the countries under consideration even after they liberalized their financial systems during the 1980s. Furthermore, banks specialize in acquiring information on default risk. This information is highly specific to each client. Hence, the market for bank loans is a customer market in which borrowers and lenders are imperfect substitutes. A credit squeeze culls some bank borrowers who may be unable to find loans elsewhere and so will be unable to finance their investment projects (Blinder and Stiglitz 1983). Here, therefore, the investment rate INV/Y is influenced by the ratio of domestic credit to GDP, CRDT/Y.

Finally, note that the gross fixed domestic investment includes FDI. However, my interest is in studying the effect of FDI inflows on the investment made by host-country investors. Thus I consider the nationally owned gross fixed investment defined as gross fixed domestic investment minus the net FDI inflows, denoted as INVnf). Then I define the dependent variable as the ratio of nationally owned gross fixed investment to GDP (INVnf/Y). Given the above explanatory variables, equations (1) and (2) suggest estimating a long-run relation of the type:

$$\text{INVnf}/Y_t = b_0 + b_1 G + b_2 \text{CRDT}/Y_t + b_3\, \text{FDI}/Y_t + b_4 \text{TOT}_t$$
$$+ \, b_5\, \text{RER} + b_6\, \Delta\text{TEDtot}/Y + \text{RL}.$$

For our purposes, the crucial variable here is FDI/Y. The coefficient, b_3, of FDI/Y should be zero if FDI has no impact on investment by local or national sources. If FDI is associated with a decline in investment from host-country investors, b_3 should be negative; and if FDI inflows are associated with an increase in investment by local investors, b_3 should be positive.

Econometric Procedure Used

The above relation is estimated using pooled time-series/cross-section data for 25 to 32 annual observations of the five South Asian countries under consideration between 1965 and 1996. A dynamic version of the linear model was estimated by including the lagged dependent variable because the explanatory variables can be expected to determine the change in the investment rate rather than its absolute level. I used a fixed-effects model, which is usually appropriate when one has a relatively small number of countries and a large number of observations for each country. In this model, dummy variables were included for all but one country, although for brevity their coefficients are not reported.

The Results

The results of the estimation are presented in table 6.3. Most of the variables have the expected sign: higher GDP growth and additional credit availability are associated with increased investment. The impact of net total foreign borrowing as a share of GDP (ΔTEDtot/Y) is positive, and the impact of the real lending rate on investment is negative (column C). The coefficients of these variables have the correct signs but their magnitudes are not significant, so they were dropped from the estimation. Similarly, the changes in the terms of trade and the real exchange rate have an insignificant effect on investment (see columns C and B), and they too were dropped from the estimated relation.

The resulting relation is reported in column A. The crucial variable, the ratio of net FDI inflows to GDP (FDI/Y), has a strongly positive effect with a coefficient in the range of 1.7 to 2.9 in columns A to C. Note that when the lagged dependent variable is included in the regression, as is the case here, the long-run coefficient is obtained by dividing the coefficient of FDI/Y by 1 minus the coefficient of the lagged dependent variable.[1] Using this result, the long run coefficient of FDI/Y is found to be in the range of 4 to 5. This implies that a 1 percent increase in FDI is associated in the long run with a 4 to 5 percent *increase* in nationally owned investment. This suggests that there exists complementarity between FDI and the nationally owned investment, possibly through various backward and forward linkages.

There is a possibility, however, that this result could be driven by the requirement of less than 100 percent equity ownership by foreign direct investors. Such a requirement is common in most South Asian countries, except in some selected sectors (e.g., export-oriented units and those in certain high-technology areas). For example, India did not allow more than 40 percent foreign ownership of a firm until 1992. Given that such foreign equity restrictions in South Asia were gradually relaxed over the 1980s and loosened even further during the 1990s, one would expect this coefficient to decrease over time. To test this hypothesis, I repeated the regression in column A of table 6.3 over (a) all available observations during the period 1965–96, (b) all observations during 1980–96, (c) all observations during 1985–96, and (d) all observations during 1990–96. The results are shown in table 6.4, columns A to D, respectively, using the same explanatory variables as in table 6.3. The coefficient of FDI/Y does indeed decrease from 1.92 for the 1965–96 period to only 0.48 for the 1990–96 period. This decrease implies that the long-term coefficient of FDI/Y declined from 4.42 over the 1965–96 period to 1.98 for the 1990–96 period. This decline corroborates the hypothesis that the complementarity between FDI and national investment was at least partly policy driven. It is noteworthy, however, that the coefficient of FDI/Y remains positive

TABLE 6.3   Impact of FDI Inflows on Investment Rate (Net of FDI) for South Asia, 1965–96, Ordinary Least Squares Panel Estimation (Fixed-Effects Model)

Explanatory Variable	A Final Version with All Significant Variables Deleted	B Some Variables Deleted	C Initial Version with All Explanatory Variables
Constant	4.263 (4.366)**	5.191 (3.396)**	5.348 (3.031)**
GDP growth rate	0.0399 (0.759)	0.1034 (1.650)	0.0977 (1.232)
Total domestic credit as share of GDP	0.0929 (3.770)**	0.0913 (3.078)**	0.129 (3.770)**
FDI (net) inflow as share of GDP	1.917 (4.005)**	1.705 (2.809)**	2.853 (3.847)**
Terms of trade	Not included	−0.01003 (−1.260)	−0.617 (−0.680)
Real exchange rate	Not included	−0.0115 (−0.216)	−0.263 (−0.041)
Net foreign borrowing as share of GDP	Not included	Not included	0.0312 (0.561)
Real lending rate	Not included	Not included	−0.0119 (−0.246)
Lagged dependent variable	0.566 (8.204)**	0.570 (7.252)**	0.447 (4.656)**
Long-term coefficient for FDI/Y	4.417	3.965	5.159
R^2	0.873	0.890	0.906
Standard error of regression	1.468	1.506	1.569
Durbin-Watson statistic	1.91	1.87	2.13
Number of observations	127	98	69

** Significant at the 1 percent confidence level.

Note: The t-ratios of regression coefficients are given in parentheses.

Source: Author's calculations.

TABLE 6.4   Impact of FDI Inflows on Investment Rate (Net of FDI) for South Asia, Four Different Time Periods, Ordinary Least Squares Panel Estimation (Fixed-Effects Model)

Explanatory Variable	A All Observations	B 1980–96	C 1985–96	D 1990–96
Constant	4.263	4.535	4.956	2.623
	(4.366)**	(1.940)*	(1.440)	(0.565)
GDP growth rate	0.0399	0.054	0.0897	0.154
	(0.759)	(0.722)	(1.050)	(1.181)
Total domestic credit as share of GDP	0.0929	0.107	0.0413	0.0415
	(3.770)**	(2.521)**	(0.767)	(0.518)
FDI (net) inflow as share of GDP	1.917	1.461	0.934	0.476
	(4.005)**	(2.402)**	(1.605)	(0.630)
Lagged dependent variable	0.566	0.519	0.660	0.759
	(8.204)**	(5.498)**	(5.977)**	(5.095)**
Long-term coefficient for FDI/Y	4.417	3.037	2.747	1.975
R^2	0.873	0.893	0.929	0.930
Standard error of regression	1.468	1.453	1.090	1.175
Durbin-Watson statistic	1.91	2.263	2.099	2.007
Number of observations	127	84	60	35

* Significant at the 5 percent confidence level.
** Significant at the 1 percent confidence level.

Note: The *t*-ratios of regression coefficients are given in parentheses.

Source: Author's calculations.

even over the 1990–96 period, so that FDI inflows have a positive effect on the nationally owned investment during all periods of our analysis.

Furthermore, the long-run coefficient for gross fixed investment net of FDI when foreign equity is 40 percent, as in pre-1992 India, would be 1.5, which would decline to 0.33 when foreign equity increases to about 75 percent. This is a reasonable estimate for India for the 1992–96 period because foreign equity limits varied from 51 to 100 percent, depending on the sector of operation. Because the estimated long-run coefficients for the South Asian countries during the two periods are 4.42 and 1.98, respectively, they suggest that the FDI inflows had a positive effect on nationally owned investment beyond that necessitated by the policy restrictions on foreign equity share. Thus the complementarity between FDI and nationally owned investment can be expected to continue even if the restrictions on foreign equity share are further liberalized or removed. Doing so, however, would dilute the complementarity. That is, increases in domestic investment accompanying a given amount of FDI would be lower. Further liberalizing equity restrictions on foreign firms is especially desirable when doing so attracts considerably larger inflows of FDI (as was the case in India following the 1992 liberalization of restrictions on foreign equity share) *and* when the impact of FDI inflows on economic growth is positive. That last aspect is considered in the next section.

Impact of FDI on GDP Growth

In the previous section, FDI was shown to have had a strong complementary effect on investment, leading to additional investment by host-country investors that was several times the FDI inflow. But the more important question is how FDI inflows may affect GDP growth. The inflows could promote growth by providing additional employment in a labor-surplus economy and by improving technological know-how and human capital. On the other hand, as the analysis of Brecher and Diaz-Alejandro (1977) suggested, foreign capital inflows could lead to immiserizing growth when such inflows can earn excessive profits in the host country, which may be particularly likely in economies subject to various trade and financial distortions. India and most other South Asian economies suffered from severe trade distortions while they were following protectionist policies in the 1960s and 1970s. Those policies have eased slowly as liberalization gradually occurred during the 1980s and 1990s. Thus the issue assumes added significance in the context of South Asia.

To test the impact of FDI on growth, I use the conventional neoclassical production function, but add foreign capital as a variable.[2] Following a large number of empirical studies that have supported the export-led growth hypothesis (Ram 1985, Salvatore and Hatcher 1991, Greenaway and Sapsford 1994, and Edwards 1996), I also introduce exports as a variable in the production function. This is done because exports, like FDI, can result in a higher rate of technological innovation and dynamic learning from abroad. Exports also impose a certain market discipline, thus reducing the rent-seeking ability of special-interest groups and so minimizing distortions in the economy (Agrawal and others 2000). The production function can be written as follows:

$$y = F(L, k_d, k_f, x, t)$$

where y = gross domestic product in real terms, L = labor input, k_d = stock of domestic capital in real terms, k_f = stock of foreign capital in real terms, x = exports in real terms, and $t =$ a time trend that captures the improvement in productivity resulting from technical progress.

Assuming the production function to be log-linear, taking logs and differentiating with respect to time, we obtain:

$$G = a + b\hat{k}_d + c\hat{k}_f + d\hat{x} + e\hat{L} + u$$

where a caret on a variable denotes its growth rate, G denotes the growth rate of real GDP (y), and u denotes a random-error term. In the context of the labor-surplus economies of South Asia, growth of the labor force is not likely to be a significant determinant of GDP growth (this was also confirmed by empirical estimations) so this variable was dropped as an explanatory variable. Furthermore, in view of serious difficulties associated with measuring capital stocks (especially in the context of developing countries), I follow the precedent set in numerous previous studies and approximate the rate of growth of domestic and foreign capital by the ratio of domestic fixed investment (net of FDI) to GDP (INVnf/Y) and the ratio of net FDI inflows to GDP (FDI/Y). Thus the equation to be estimated is:

(3) $G = a + b\,\text{INVnf}/Y + c\,\text{FDI}/Y + d\hat{x} + u.$

For our purposes the crucial variable here is again FDI/Y. Note that the coefficient, c, of this variable should be equal to the coefficient, b, of INVnf/Y if FDI is just as efficient in promoting GDP growth as is nationally owned investment. If the greater technological know-how, human capital, or exporting capabilities of FDI make it more efficient in promoting growth, coefficient c can be expected to be greater than coefficient b. On the other hand, if FDI takes excessive profits out of the country without contributing much in terms of technology, and so forth, coefficient c should be smaller than coefficient, b. Finally, if the coefficient, c, of FDI/Y were negative, it would imply a net negative impact on GDP growth, that is, immiserizing growth resulting from FDI inflows. For the five countries considered, the above estimate uses pooled time-series/cross-section data for 25 to 32 annual observations between 1965 and 1996. Again I used a fixed-effects model. The results of the estimation are shown in table 6.5, column A. Both a higher rate of growth of exports $(\hat{x})$ and a higher investment rate (INV/Y) are associated with a higher rate of GDP growth. The crucial coefficient of FDI/Y is negative, although not statistically significant. This result suggests that, in the case of South Asia, FDI is neither significantly harmful nor beneficial. Brecher and Diaz-Alejandro suggested that FDI could result in immiserizing growth primarily in the presence of trade and financial market distortions that present FDI with an opportunity to earn excessive profits. In the case of most South Asian countries, there were considerable trade and financial market distortions during the 1960s and 1970s, but

TABLE 6.5 Impact of FDI Inflows on GDP Growth in South Asia, 1965–96, Ordinary Least Squares Panel Estimation (Fixed-Effects Model)

Explanatory Variable	A All Observations	B 1980–96	C 1985–96	D 1990–96
Constant	1.043	2.627	2.998	2.301
	(0.617)	(0.993)	(0.804)	(0.526)
Growth rate of real exports	0.0452	0.0873	0.0337	0.0376
	(2.837)**	(4.042)**	(1.403)	(1.289)
Fixed investment (net of FDI) as share of GDP	0.170	0.107	0.106	0.102
	(1.961)*	(0.872)	(0.625)	(0.541)
FDI (net) inflow as share of GDP	−0.302	0.179	0.595	1.378
	(−0.361)	(0.200)	(0.703)	(1.401)#
R^2	0.121	0.261	0.179	0.161
Standard error of regression	2.485	2.063	1.745	1.682
Durbin-Watson statistic	2.31	2.385	2.17	2.29
Number of observations	132	85	60	35

Significant at the 10 percent confidence level.
* Significant at the 5 percent confidence level.
** Significant at the 1 percent confidence level.
Note: The t-ratios of regression coefficients are given in parentheses.
Source: Author's calculations.

during the 1980s and 1990s there has been gradual movement toward economic liberalization and a reduction in trade and financial market distortions. Thus it would be interesting to examine whether the economic impact of FDI has changed over time.

Accordingly I reestimated the above relation with observations only for the periods 1980–96, 1985–96, and 1990–96. The results of these three additional regressions are also shown in table 6.5, columns B, C, and D. The sign of the coefficient of FDI/Y variable becomes positive over the period 1980–96 and gradually increases in magnitude as we move to later periods. Over the period 1990–96, it is positive and statistically significant. In fact it is as much as 1.38, almost 13 times the coefficient of total national investment, INVnf/Y. Thus, we can conclude that over the period 1990–96, foreign direct investment was associated with higher economic growth and had a much greater impact on economic growth than did domestic investment.

In this context it is also worth comparing the relative merits of FDI inflows and foreign borrowing (an alternative form of foreign capital). For this purpose I reestimated relation (3) after adding another variable, namely, net total (private and public) additional foreign borrowing as a share of GDP, ΔTEDtot/Y. This variable was obtained by calculating the change in total external debt in U.S. dollars, converting it to current local units, and dividing by nominal GDP. That is, I estimated the following relation:

$$G = a + b\ \text{INVnf}/Y + c\ \text{FDI}/Y + d\ \Delta\text{TEDtot}/Y + e\hat{x} + u.$$

This relation was estimated over the same four periods as shown in table 6.5. The estimation results are presented in table 6.6. Throughout the periods since

TABLE 6.6   Impact of FDI Inflows on GDP Growth in South Asia: Comparison of FDI Inflows and Foreign Borrowing, 1965–96, Ordinary Least Squares Panel Estimation (Fixed-Effects Model)

Explanatory Variable	A All Observations	B 1980–96	C 1985–96	D 1990–96
Constant	1.0033 (0.596)	2.498 (0.939)	1.676 (0.430)	−0.473 (−0.109)
Growth rate of real exports	0.0471 (2.956)**	0.08520 (4.080)**	0.0352 (1.468)#	0.0348 (1.271)
Fixed investment (net of FDI) as share of GDP	0.1647 (1.897)#	0.1075 (0.872)	0.153 (0.892)	0.212 (1.146)
FDI (net) inflow as share of GDP	−0.288 (−0.345)	0.225 (0.252)	0.7668 (0.895)	1.840 (1.940)#
Net foreign debt inflow as share of GDP	0.077 (1.418)	0.0547 (0.663)	0.0906 (1.146)	0.2066 (2.148)**
R^2	0.135	0.261	0.199	0.287
Standard error of regression	2.476	2.063	1.740	1.580
Durbin-Watson statistic	2.28	2.385	2.12	2.16
Number of observations	132	85	60	35

Significant at the 10 percent confidence level.
** Significant at the 1 percent confidence level.

Note: The *t*-ratios of regression coefficients are given in parentheses.

Source: Author's calculations.

1980, the coefficient of $\Delta TEDtot/Y$ is positive and statistically significant. However, it is small ($d = 0.21$ over 1990–96) compared with the coefficient of FDI/Y ($c = 1.84$ over 1990–96). This suggests that FDI inflows are more beneficial than is foreign borrowing.

There still remains the question about the direction of causation in the positive association between FDI/Y and GDP growth. Thus if higher GDP growth attracted larger FDI inflows, this positive association might not be meaningful for FDI-related policies. But if higher FDI/Y caused higher GDP growth, South Asian countries would be well advised to attract more FDI. Therefore, I next consider the direction of causality between FDI/Y and GDP growth using the Granger causality analysis. The vector autoregression (VAR) framework used for testing the Granger causality is explained briefly in the appendix. The lag length for the VAR was chosen by minimizing the Schwartz Bayesian criterion, which selected a lag length of one. The results of the test are shown in table 6.7. The causality test was undertaken for 1990–96 given the above finding that the impact of FDI inflows on GDP growth was significant only over this period. The null hypothesis that GDP growth did not cause FDI/Y is not rejected whereas the null hypothesis that FDI/Y did not cause GDP growth is rejected, albeit mildly at about 18 percent significance level. This evidence suggests that the larger inflows of FDI as a share of GDP did help cause higher GDP growth in South Asia during the period 1990–96.

The above results suggest therefore that FDI inflows helped achieve faster economic growth in South Asia in the liberalized environment, beginning in the 1980s and especially during the 1990s. This finding may be the result of a reduction in excessive profits brought about by reduced distortions and a greater contribution to technological know-how in the more competitive environment during the 1980s and 1990s. Additional FDI inflows appear to be desirable in the liberalized economic policy framework that now prevails and should be encouraged.

TABLE 6.7 Granger Causality Test between GDP Growth and FDI Inflows as a Share of GDP in South Asia, 1990–96

Null Hypothesis	Number of Lags[a]	Test Results for Rejection of Null,[b] F Statistic (p-Value)
GDP growth does not cause FDI/Y	1	0.0318 (0.860)
FDI/Y does not cause GDP growth	1	1.892 (0.180)

a. Number of lags was chosen to minimize the Schwartz Bayesian criterion.
b. See the appendix for a brief explanation of the Granger causality test procedure used.

It may be worth noting that during the 1990s FDI inflows averaged about 5 percent of GDP in China and about 3 percent of GDP in the rapidly growing East Asian economies, although they averaged only 0.5 percent in South Asia (see figure 6.1). Thus there is considerable scope for increasing FDI inflows in South Asia and doing so could increase the South Asian GDP growth rates by a few percentage points.

Conclusion

In this study I have tried to assess the economic impact of FDI in India and South Asia by using panel data from five South Asian countries (Bangladesh, India, Nepal, Pakistan, and Sri Lanka) to estimate the impact of FDI inflows on nationally owned investment and on GDP growth. I found that an increase in FDI in South Asia was associated with a manifold increase in the investment by domestic investors. The analysis suggests that this association may in part result from foreign direct investors having to hold less than 100 percent equity ownership, a requirement in most South Asian countries. Because the long-run positive impact of FDI on national investors was considerably more than the equity-ownership effect alone would imply, however, my analysis suggests that there exist complementarity and linkage effects between foreign and nationally owned investment beyond the effects of the restrictions on foreign equity ownership.

The impact of FDI inflows on the GDP growth rate was found to be insignificant over the 1970s and 1980s, but positive and statistically significant over 1990–96, which is when the bulk of FDI came into India and South Asia. It is noteworthy that most South Asian countries followed import-substitution policies and had high import tariffs in the 1960s and 1970s. These policies gradually changed during the 1980s, and by the early 1990s most countries had largely abandoned that strategy in favor of more open international trade and generally market-oriented policies. These results can be understood in terms of the analysis of Brecher and Diaz-Alejandro (1977), who showed that foreign capital would be less beneficial (or even harmful) in the presence of trade and financial market distortions than otherwise. Thus my analysis suggests that FDI inflows have a positive impact on economic growth under the economic conditions now prevailing in South Asia.[3]

I also found that FDI inflows since 1980 have contributed more to investment and to GDP growth in South Asia than has an equal amount of foreign borrowing. This finding suggests that to the extent that some foreign capital is needed in the economy, FDI is preferable to foreign borrowing. Finally, Granger causality tests showed that the larger FDI inflows as a share of GDP during the 1990–96 period caused greater economic growth in South Asia, rather than having merely been induced through increased economic growth.

These results support more liberal policies toward FDI. We have seen that China and the East Asian countries that have grown much more rapidly over the 1990–96 period attracted much larger inflows of FDI as a share of GDP. The factors behind the larger inflows in China and East Asia include generally foreign investor–friendly policies and government attitudes (including easy repatriation of profits and dividends in international currencies, liberal laws on equity share that foreign firms can have in local enterprises, and so forth). Those governments also have provided good infrastructure and a well-trained, efficient, and cost-effective workforce.

Since the 1991 economic reform policies, India has removed most restrictions on foreign investors relating to profit or dividend repatriation and equity share in local enterprises and thus has now generally foreign investor–friendly policies. India now needs to improve its infrastructure further through appropriate policies (e.g., significant improvements have been achieved in the telecommunications sector via the entry of private enterprises in the sector) and to make labor more efficient through appropriate reforms of labor laws that might apply only in export-processing zones where the bulk of FDI is concentrated. And many foreign investors should be vigorously encouraged to come into each sector that is opened to FDI so that the possibility of excessive profits is minimized.

Appendix: Determining the Direction of Granger Causality

Following Granger (1969), an economic time series Y_t is said to be "Granger caused" by another series X_t if the information in the past and present values of X_t helps to improve the forecasts of the Y_t variable; that is, if $\mathrm{MSE}(Y_t \mid \Omega_t < \mathrm{MSE}(Y_t \mid \Omega_t')$, where MSE is the conditional mean square error of the forecast of Y_t, Ω_t denotes the set of all (relevant) information up to time t, and Ω_t' excludes the information in the past and present X_t. The conventional Granger causality test involves specifying a bivariate p^{th}-order VAR as follows:

$$Y_t = \mu + \sum_{i=1}^{p} a_i Y_{t-i} + \sum_{j=1}^{p} b_j X_{t-j} + U_t$$

$$X_t = \mu' + \sum_{i=1}^{p-1} C_i Y_{t-i} + \sum_{j=1}^{p-1} d_t X_{t-j} + U_t'$$

where μ and μ' are constant drifts; U_t and U'_t are error terms; and, more generally, the equation may include any number of additional relevant variables. Then the null hypothesis that X_t does not cause Y_t amounts to testing

$$b_1 = b_2 = \cdots = b_n = 0.$$

This can be tested by standard methods, such as an F test. Similarly, the null hypothesis that Y_t does not cause X_t amounts to testing

$$c_1 = c_2 = \cdots = c_n = 0.$$

Endnotes

1. To see the logic behind this, note that if $Y_t = aX_t + bY_{t-1}$, then in the long-run equilibrium, where $Y_t = Y_{t-1} = Y$ and $X_t = X$, we have $Y = aX + bY$, so that $Y = [a/(1-b)]X$.
2. This approach has been used by Balasubramanyam, Salisu, and Sapsford (1996).
3. Das reviews the empirical literature on the effects of FDI in Chapter 7 of this volume. He concludes that FDI on the whole has positive economic effects in host countries.

References

Agrawal, Pradeep, Subir Gokarn, Veena Mishra, Kirit S. Parikh, and Kunal Sen. 2000. *Policy Regimes and Industrial Competitiveness: A Comparative Study of East Asia and India*. London: Macmillan.

Balasubramanyam, V. N., M. Salisu, and D. Sapsford. 1996. "Foreign Direct Investment and Growth in EP and IS Countries." *Economic Journal* 106: 92–105.

Blejer, Mario I., and M. Khan. 1984. "Government Policy and Private Investment in Developing Countries." *IMF Staff Papers* 31: 379–403.

Blinder, Alan S., and J. E. Stiglitz. 1983. "Money, Credit Constraints and Economic Activity." *American Economic Review* 73: 297–302.

Brecher, Richard A., and C. F. Diaz-Alejandro. 1977. "Tariffs, Foreign Capital and Immiserizing Growth." *Journal of International Economics* 7: 317–22.

Cardoso, Eliana. 1993. "Private Investment in Latin America." *Economic Development and Cultural Change* 41: 833–48.

Edwards, Sebastian. 1996. "Why Are Latin America's Saving Rates So Low? An International Comparative Analysis." *Journal of Development Economics* 51: 5–44.

Fry, Maxwell J. 1993. "Foreign Direct Investment in Southeast Asia: Differential Impacts." ISEAS Current Economic Affairs Series. Singapore: Institute of Southeast Asian Studies, ASEAN Economic Research Unit.

———. 1995. *Money Interest and Banking in Economic Development*, 2nd ed. Baltimore: Johns Hopkins University Press.

———. 1998. "Saving, Investment, Growth and Financial Distortions in Pacific Asia and Other Developing Areas." *International Economic Journal* 12: 1–25.

Gopinath, T. 1997. "Foreign Investment in India: Policy Issues, Trends and Prospects." *Reserve Bank of India Occasional Papers* 18(2 and 3; special issue): 453–70.

Granger, C. W. J. 1969. "Investigating Causal Relations by Econometric Models and Cross-Spectral Methods." *Econometrica* 55: 251–76.

Greenaway, David, and D. Sapsford. 1994. "What Does Liberalisation Do for Exports and Growth?" *Weltwirtschaftliches Archiv* 130: 152–73.

Kumar, Nagesh. 1994. *Multinational Enterprises and Industrial Organisations—The Case of India.* New Delhi: Sage Publications.

Ram, Rati. 1985. "Exports and Economic Growth. Some Additional Evidence" *Economic Development and Cultural Change* 33: 415–25.

Salvatore, Dominick, and T. Hatcher. 1991. "Inward Oriented and Outward Oriented Trade Strategies." *Journal of Development Studies* 27: 7–25.

Servén, Luis, and Andres Solimano. 1992. "Private Investment and Macroeconomic Adjustment: A Survey." *World Bank Research Observer* 7: 95–114.

Van Wijnbergen, Sveder. 1982. "Stagflationary Effect of Monetary Stabilization Policies: A Quantitative Analysis of South Korea." *Journal of Development Economics* 37: 133–69.

World Bank. 1998. *World Development Indicators.* Washington, D.C.

AN INDIAN PERSPECTIVE ON WTO RULES ON FOREIGN DIRECT INVESTMENT

Satya P. Das

The World Trade Organization (WTO) is a living and growing organism. It was born with at least 16 "wings" (agreements) at various stages of completeness. The functioning of the WTO affects the economic life of all countries around the globe. It is not concerned only with international trade—meaning exports and imports of goods and services in the traditional sense—but with "international business" in general, and that includes foreign direct investment (FDI). Indeed, in recent decades FDI in the global economy has grown much faster than has trade in goods. Between 1973 and 1995, the annual outflow of funds as FDI has grown more than 12-fold compared with a 9-fold increase in the value of merchandise exports (Drabek 1998).[1]

The provisions on FDI in the WTO framework are contained in two agreements: the General Agreement on Trade in Services (GATS) and the Agreement on Trade-Related Investment Measures (TRIMs) in relation to trade in goods. Undoubtedly at some time in the future these are going to be integrated and, more important, they will evolve into simply investment measures (IMs). In other words, the FDI wing of the WTO is likely to spread over time. Whether some form of FDI is trade related would be an irrelevant issue. All forms of FDI would come under the jurisdiction of the WTO.

In that context, the objective of this chapter is to assess the gains to India from existing and potentially new WTO rules on FDI. I hope it will provide some basis for articulating negotiating objectives and strategies from the Indian perspective and, to some extent, from the perspective of developing countries.

The next section of the chapter offers a review of different policies that parent and host countries have adopted over time, the existing WTO provisions on FDI, and a summary of the official views of different countries, including India, on TRIMs and FDI in general. Because a truly forward-looking strategy should take into account the dynamics of FDI in India as well as the history of India's FDI policy, the second section of this chapter presents a facts-and-figures review of the dynamics and history. The third section discusses the potential benefits and costs of FDI. Findings from various empirical studies are presented in the fourth section. Of particular interest will be those findings pertaining to India. All of these materials are background for the main query—what should be the optimal strategy for India? The fifth section presents a view that the arguments against freer FDI and against multilateral rules on such investment are weak. The final section proposes that, contrary to the current policy stand, India should support a regime with more multilateral rules.

FDI Policies, and the WTO on FDI Thus Far

Over time FDI has been subject to various types of policies by both host and parent countries—from extremely negative policies like nationalization or appropriation to positive incentives like tax holidays. Some of these policies are summarized in table 7.1. Nationalization is a rare occurrence, but the threat of it has real effects (Eaton and Gersovitz 1984). Relatively common negative incentives include restrictions on foreign equity share, domestic content requirements, production or export requirements, restrictions on remittances of profits, and so forth.

As one would expect, there are more restrictions on FDI in developing countries than in industrial countries. Member countries in the Association of Southeast Asian Nations (ASEAN) in which FDI has played a major role in growth use a screening, negative list (sectors into which FDI is not permitted or permitted only with substantial restrictions); foreign equity caps; and land-ownership limitations. India uses these restrictions plus balancing requirements (details are given below). Most of the restrictions on FDI by less developed host countries stem from their perception that multinational firms, the principal conduits of FDI activity, engage in restrictive and predatory business practices, whereas the countries do not have the institutional setup to enforce competition policies effectively. Industrial countries use screening and the negative list much less commonly than do developing countries. In some Organisation for Economic Co-operation and Development (OECD) countries these have been practically abolished.

TABLE 7.1 FDI Policies over Time

Positive Incentives	Negative Incentives
• Guarantee against nationalization • Tax holidays • Tax treaties to avoid double taxation • Exemptions on import duties on capital goods and intermediate goods • Other exemptions or relaxation of rules in priority sectors • Subsidized loans, reduced rent for land use, accelerated depreciation • Special promotion of exports, for example, through export processing zones	• Nationalization or appropriation • Double taxation • Domestic content requirement in terms of intermediates • Domestic employment restrictions • Export requirements and foreign currency earning targets • Screening • General foreign equity limits • Sectoral foreign equity limits • Land ownership restrictions • Division of management within a joint venture • Restrictions on remittance of profits • Transfer of shares • Restrictions on liquidation of the company

Source: Author's compilation from various sources.

Against this background, among the four categories of agreements reached under the GATT (which evolved into the WTO)—that is, agreements on goods, services, intellectual property rights, and dispute settlement—by the end of 1994 two categories contained some disciplines on FDI: the agreements on goods and on services. In the goods category, the agreement on FDI, called TRIMs, seeks to abolish FDI policies that supposedly hamper trade. There is, however, a lack of consensus on the definition of TRIMs. At least eight types of TRIMs can be classified:

1. Local content requirements
2. Trade balancing requirements
3. Foreign exchange restrictions
4. Export performance requirements
5. Local production requirements
6. Production mandates
7. Mandatory technology transfers
8. Limits on foreign equity and remittances.

Of these, the TRIMs agreement specifically mentions the first, the second, and a part of the third entry (Yu and Chao 1998).

The TRIMs agreement set up a committee to monitor the implementation of commitments. Industrial countries had two years (until the end of 1996) to eliminate these restrictions. Developing countries had five years (until the end of 1999) and the least developed countries had seven (until the end of 2001). It is important to note that the incidence of TRIMs is believed to be high in India, as well as in Brazil and Indonesia. It is interesting also that under the dispute settlement scheme of the WTO, there is an instance of TRIMs violation: namely, the European Union (EU), Japan, and the United States against Indonesia on its National Car Program initiated in 1996. Under this program, the Indonesian firms or firms located outside Indonesia but owned by Indonesian nationals obtained exemption from the luxury tax on cars and from some import duties as long as they met local content requirements. The WTO passed judgment in favor of the plaintiff countries.[2]

The GATS defines four modes of international services transactions:

1. Cross-border supply (e.g., provision of a technical report faxed by a foreign national)
2. Commercial presence (e.g., foreign banks operating in a host country)
3. Movement of business persons (e.g., computer software engineers moving to another country temporarily to complete a project)
4. Consumption abroad (e.g., tourism).

Among these modes, commercial presence involves FDI naturally. Unlike the broad range of sectors negotiated with respect to trade in goods, however, under GATS each country negotiated a list of GATS-exempted sectors. In principal in these sectors, FDI can be subject to substantial restrictions. In others, there is a de facto commitment (rule) on FDI policy. This contrasts with TRIMs in that in the goods sector there is no direct commitment on FDI policy. Local content, trade balancing, and so forth can violate WTO norms only insofar as they adversely affect trade in goods.[3] Hence there are inconsistencies between FDI policies embodied in the two agreements. In any event, this was the state of FDI liberalization under WTO at its inception in 1995.

The next set of policy initiatives with respect to FDI came during the second WTO Ministerial Meeting held in Singapore in 1996. It was decided to establish three working groups mandated to undertake "educative work" in three areas, one of which is the relationship between trade and investment.[4] The report of the working group was submitted in December 1998; it recommended further studies on several aspects of FDI.

Discussions about multilateral rules on FDI were scheduled for the WTO Ministerial Meeting in Seattle in 1999, and more than 150 documents by various countries were submitted in preparation. The following is a brief summary of various viewpoints expressed there:

- It was generally agreed that FDI is a major means of enhancing global production and efficiency. Countries other than Brazil, Colombia, and India stated that transparency and fairness are critical in attempting to encourage FDI, and that those can be achieved by formulating rules.
- At the same time, the countries held that the growth and development of developing countries should be a major consideration in formulating disciplines on FDI. The EU even proposed that some characteristics of the development process itself should be built into the WTO framework.[5]
- No country document was specific about where the line between international rules and individual national goals may be drawn or, in other words, how comprehensive the rules ought to be.
- Also, they were silent on the time frame. Should FDI be included in the fast-track agenda? Or should it be allowed to take a building-block approach?
- India was among the minority in opposing *any* kind of multilateral rules. It wanted TRIMs to be permitted insofar as they could be justified from the viewpoint of growth and development. Its document stated that "domestic content is an extremely useful and necessary tool from the point of view of developing countries." Similar views were expressed by Brazil and Colombia.

As is well known, the Seattle Ministerial Meeting remained inconclusive for various reasons. The next ministerial meeting was held in Doha in 2001. Before that, in May 2001, member countries met to discuss how the FDI issue should be taken up during the Doha gathering. Members such as Chile, Costa Rica, the EU, Japan, and the Republic of Korea supported a multilateral investment agreement. It is interesting that the United States heard out the arguments and counterarguments and remained passive. The Arab Republic of Egypt, India, and Malaysia (constituting what has been termed the "Like-Minded Group"), on the other hand, were opposed to it, citing loss of sovereignty and lack of flexibility that would be associated with a rules-based regime. A quid pro quo middle ground was advanced by Argentina, Australia, and Brazil: negotiations on FDI rules would be conditional on concessions to be granted to concerned countries in agriculture and on commitments made in the area of market access to industrial countries.

Not much progress was made in the Doha Meeting but countries agreed that negotiations will take place after the Mexico Ministerial Meeting in September 2003. WTO will cooperate with other organizations, such as the United Nations

Conference on Trade and Development (UNCTAD), to provide technical assistance and capacity building to developing and least developed countries in evaluating their objectives and development policies. The organization has also called for further study of the various ramifications of FDI rules, including dispute settlement.

India remains opposed to further liberalization of FDI and to any set of multilateral rules at the WTO level. The question is whether this policy stance is the right one for the country's self-interest. To answer that question it is necessary to review (a) India's policy toward FDI and the status of FDI flows into India, (b) the various sources of benefits and costs associated with FDI, and (c) the empirical findings that bear on these benefits and costs.

FDI and FDI Policies in India: Facts

There are many published studies on the history of Indian FDI policy from the time of independence until the beginning of (or a couple of years into) the liberalization era (1991–94), for example, Athreye and Kapur (1999b), Bhattacharya and Palaha (1996), and Kumar (1994). Thus our review of this period will be short. More emphasis will be placed on postliberalization years.

The Years 1947 to 1991

As Kidron (1965) has put it, in the initial period after independence, between 1947 and 1957, an uneasy triangle prevailed among individual businesses, industry associations, and the government. To assess technology, industrialists preferred foreign collaboration. The actions of industrial associations were colored, however, by the proclaimed virtues of the Swadeshi (Nationalist) Revolution. The official position of the government was a relatively open-door policy toward FDI, but in intent it was nationalist. Ambivalence toward foreign capital prevailed very starkly at the industry and government levels. This was understandable in view of the memory of the East India Company's rule evolving into the British Empire and on the heels of independence from the empire.

The following decade, from 1957 to 1967, can be termed (following Kumar 1994) an era of gradual liberalization.[6] An ambitious program of industrialization was envisaged in the Second Five-Year Plan. It required massive doses of investment, much beyond what domestic sources could garner. And it was recognized that, unlike domestic projects, investment from foreign sources would not "use up" much foreign exchange. Consistent with the objective of the Second Five-Year Plan and the concept of planning itself, the government followed a policy of selectivity in terms of sectors. Manufacturing received most of the foreign capital.

The situation changed drastically by the late 1960s. The foreign exchange shortage became acute. The rupee was devalued, but the balance-of-payments deficit continued. (This was similar to the experience of many other countries in the Bretton Woods system.) Economic thinking turned to a more socialistic philosophy. Major banks were nationalized. There was a wholesale policy shift toward exchange rate management and FDI. The (in-)famous Foreign Exchange Regulation Act (FERA) came into existence in 1973.[7] Foreign equity was restricted to 40 percent, in the sense that:

(a) If the joint venture was to be treated without discrimination vis-à-vis domestic firms, the foreign equity share must not exceed this limit.
(b) The conditions under which the foreign equity share could exceed 40 percent were quite stringent and the decision as to whether such a venture would be allowed (even if it met all conditions) was left to the discretion of the government.

Different sectors were identified in which foreign collaboration was deemed unnecessary, where only technological collaboration was considered desirable and FDI was permissible. The period from 1967 to 1980 may therefore be called an era of severe (draconian!) restriction.

Policies were eased in the 1980s. In the wake of the oil price shocks it was probably realized that the country needed to increase its exports considerably and, for various reasons, domestic firms alone would not be up to the task. FERA restrictions were relaxed for 100 percent export-oriented units. Four export processing zones were set up. In 1984 and 1985 many capital goods were moved to the Open General License (OGL) list. In 1986, the tax rate on royalty payments was brought down from 40 percent to 30 percent. FDI regulations continued to fall at a gradual rate throughout the 1980s.

1991 Onward: The Liberalization Era

A structural break from the past policy regime came in 1991. As with other aspects of India's economic policy, 1991 and onward can be called the postliberalization era or simply the liberalization era. Similar to other major policy shifts in the past, the change was initiated partly because of outside shocks. The Gulf war in 1991 led to a massive exodus of Indians working in the region and it severely curtailed the flow of foreign exchange to India. In the international loan market, India's credit rating plummeted. There was an exodus of nearly US$1 billion dollars from nonresident Indian (NRI) deposits. For the first time the country faced a serious prospect of defaulting on foreign loans. Assistance from the International Monetary Fund and the World Bank was sought and those institutions insisted on reforms.

In 1991 the rupee was devalued by 20 percent. Import liberalization took place over a large spectrum of goods. For example, automatic clearance of capital goods up to 25 percent of total value of plant and equipment or Rs. 2 crores—whichever is less—was granted. Foreign equity proposals would no longer have to be tied up with a technology agreement. A Foreign Investment Promotion Board (FIPB) was set up to consider large investment proposals. It could also negotiate and would give single-window clearance.

The Monopolies and Restrictive Trade Practices Act requirement that expansion of foreign ventures needed prior approval was lifted. Foreign brand names could be used by domestic industry having connections with foreign firms. Over time, the size of the negative list of exports and imports shrank. Previously there was a dividend-balancing requirement for foreign ventures, which meant that dividend payments to a foreign party over the first seven years from the date of commercial production had to be balanced by export earnings. That requirement was lifted except for 24 consumer goods industries. Many restrictions on acquisition of immovable property were removed.

In January 1994 India became a full-fledged member of the Multilateral Investment Guarantee Agency (MIGA). As a result, all investments approved by the government are insured by MIGA against expropriation or nationalization.

A minerals policy was introduced in 1993. The minerals sector was no longer restricted to the public sector; private domestic firms or firms with foreign equity not exceeding 50 percent could participate. Many "core" or priority sectors have been defined in which FDI is "encouraged." As of the end of the financial year 1999–2000, there is automatic approval of up to 100 percent of equity in three special categories of industries—power, transport, and totally export-oriented units—unless the magnitude of foreign equity exceeds Rs. 1,500 crores. (The maximum allowable limit is 100 percent whether or not FDI qualifies for automatic approval.) In mining, there can be 100 percent foreign equity, but automatic approval is given in case of 50 to 74 percent of equity, depending on particular subsectors. In core industries, automatic approval is given as long as the foreign equity share does not exceed 51 percent. In the petroleum sector, the maximum foreign equity allowed is 100 percent but a license is required; there is no automatic approval. Even in small-scale industries, FDI is allowed (subject to licensing) with foreign equity not exceeding 24 percent. There are a few sectors in which FDI is not permitted: arms and ammunitions; railways; atomic energy; coal and lignite; and mining of chrome, copper, diamond, gold, gypsum, iron, manganese, sulphur, and zinc.

India's FDI Approval System

An FDI proposal requires approval. There are two approval bodies: the Reserve Bank of India (RBI) and the SIA/FIPB (Secretariat for Industrial Assistance and FIPB for Foreign Investment Promotion Board). The RBI gives automatic approval to proposals in high-priority sectors where foreign equity does not exceed 51 percent and in the mining sector as long as it does not exceed 50 percent. Automatic approval is given in two weeks. This is subject to the following conditions, however:

- Capital goods and machinery imported from abroad have to be new, not secondhand.
- The (import) cost of such goods must be borne from foreign equity.
- Fees and royalties need to conform to some norms.

SIA/FIPB deals with other proposals, such as where foreign equity exceeds 51 percent the industry is not on the list of high-priority sectors, or foreign equity does not cover the import of capital goods. Proposals are cleared in four to six weeks. Unlike the RBI, SIA/FIPB can initiate and carry on detailed negotiations with foreign firms. The secretary of the Department of Industry is the chairman.

FDI Flows into India

We now present data on FDI flows into India. Table 7.2 shows total FDI flows from 1997 to 2001 into various countries. As we see, the United States is the largest importer and exporter of foreign capital, followed by the United Kingdom and China. It is interesting that Japan and Korea have received almost equal amounts of foreign capital. India lags behind not only Japan and Korea but also

**TABLE 7.2   Total FDI in Selected Countries, 1997–2001
(in Millions of US$)**

Country	Investment Amount
United States	986,555
United Kingdom	365,877
China	215,925
Brazil	131,663
Mexico	77,948
Japan	33,628
Korea, Rep. of	30,040
Thailand	18,902
Malaysia	17,275
India	14,142
Israel	13,713

Source: UNCTAD 2002.

TABLE 7.3   Flow of FDI into India and Other Countries, 1997–2001 (in Millions of US$)

Country	1997	1998	1999	2000	2001
Brazil	18,993	28,856	28,578	32,779	22,457
China	44,237	43,751	40,319	40,772	46,846
India	3,619	2,633	2,168	2,319	3,403
Israel	1,628	1,760	2,889	4,392	3,044
Japan	3,224	3,193	1,2741	8,322	6,202
Korea, Rep. of	2,814	5,412	9,333	9,283	3,198
Malaysia	6,324	2,714	3,895	3,788	554
Mexico	14,044	11,933	12,534	14,706	24,731
Thailand	3,626	5,143	3,561	2,813	3,759
United Kingdom	33,229	74,324	87,973	116,552	53,799
United States	103,398	174,434	283,376	300,912	124,435

Source: UNCTAD 2002.

behind Thailand and Malaysia. It has attracted only a little more than 6 percent of the total foreign direct investment that China has received.

The amounts of investment capital that flowed into India and a group of other countries from 1997 through 2001 are presented in table 7.3. Notice that the FDI generally has grown over time (except from the year 2000 to 2001). It is understandable that Malaysia and Thailand saw a declining trend from 1998 to 2000, given the financial crisis they went through, and despite the worldwide recession since 2000 FDI inflow to Thailand increased from the year 2000 to 2001. Even though India was insulated from that crisis, it is noteworthy and a bit disturbing that FDI inflow to India declined from 1997 to 1999, although it has since trended upward again.

Although the emphasis in this chapter is on the *in*flow of foreign capital, multilateral FDI policy from any single country's perspective would affect *out*flow of capital as well. Table 7.4 presents both inward and outward flows as a percentage of gross capital formation. For industrial countries, FDI is pretty much a two-way flow. For India, FDI outflow is only a trickle, but it has an increasing trend. Among the developing countries, Malaysia's outward orientation is the largest.

We now concentrate on India only. The time series from 1970 to 1998 (except for the year 1990) is given in table 7.5. We see that in the 1970s there was a fluctuating and very modest growth pattern of FDI—thanks to FERA. More consistent growth has occurred since 1980 in response to the gradual liberalization of policies. Approval data are available since 1991 only.[8] It is striking that the actual-to-approved ratio is very poor except in 1991.

TABLE 7.4   Inward and Outward FDI Flows as a Percentage of Gross Fixed Capital Formation, 1997–2000

Country		1997	1998	1999	2000
Brazil	In	11.8	18.6	28.2	28.4
	Out	0.7	1.8	1.7	2.0
China	In	14.6	12.9	11.3	10.5
	Out	0.8	0.8	0.5	0.2
India	In	4	2.9	2.2	2.3
	Out	0.1	0.1	0.1	0.3
Korea, Rep. of	In	1.7	5.7	8.3	7.1
	Out	2.7	5.0	3.7	3.8
Malaysia	In	14.7	14.0	22.2	16.5
	Out	6.2	4.4	8.1	8.8
Mexico	In	18.0	13.6	12.3	12.2
	Out	1.4	1.5	1.4	0.8
Thailand	In	7.1	20.5	13.9	10.4
	Out	0.9	0.5	1.3	0.2
United Kingdom	In	15.1	30.2	34.9	46.4
	Out	28.0	49.9	80.0	101.0
United States	In	7.8	11.9	18.0	17.5
	Out	7.2	8.9	11.1	9.6

Source: UNCTAD 2002.

The sectorwise breakdown is given in table 7.6. FDI is most concentrated in the infrastructure sector, which is consistent with the government's policy of giving this sector the highest priority. The actual-to-approved ratio, however, is the lowest in this sector (as is also true of the chemicals sector)—only 13 percent. The ratio is highest in drugs and pharmaceuticals—92 percent. Econometric analysis taking into account industry-specific characteristics and policies is needed to explain such wide variation.[9]

It seems useful at this point to recap what has been covered so far in this chapter. Suggestions by various countries, including India, concerning what investment rules should be permitted in the WTO have been summarized. India's FDI policy over time since independence has been reviewed, and various facts and figures on FDI in India have been presented. The next step is to evaluate India's policies—and, more important, to determine what future policies may be warranted. But before we get to that stage we need to have an understanding of the benefits and costs, in terms of welfare, of FDI in general and of multilateral rules, and of what has been found empirically. We begin with theory.

TABLE 7.5   Inflow of FDI into India

Year	Actual Inflow		Approved Inflow		Ratio of Actual to Approved Amounts
	In Crores of Rs.	In Millions of US$	In Crores of Rs.	In Millions of US$	
1970			2.45		
1971			5.84		
1972			6.22		
1973			2.81	3.85	
1974			6.71	9.19	
1975			3.20	4.38	
1976			7.27	9.96	
1977			4.00	5.48	
1978			9.41	12.89	
1979			5.69	7.79	
1980			8.92	12.22	
1981			10.87	14.89	
1982			62.81	86.04	
1983			61.87	84.75	
1984			113.00	154.90	
1985		173.00	126.00		
1986		147.00	107.00		
1987		148.00	108.00		
1988		327.00	239.00		
1989		433.00	316.00		
1990					
1991	350	166.00	534.00		0.66
1992	680	237.00	3,887.00		0.17
1993	1,787	550.00	8,859.00		0.20
1994	2,970	973.00	14,187.00		0.23
1995	6,370	2,144.00	32,071.00		0.21
1996	8,440	2,426.00	36,147.00		0.23
1997	12,040	3,351.00	54,891.00		0.22
1998	9,210	2,258.00	30,813.00		0.30

Sources: Confederation of Engineering Industries 1992; author's compilation of data available from SIA.

FDI in Theory

The theoretical literature on the welfare effects of FDI is vast. This, however, is not the occasion to present a review of this rich literature. Only a brief summary is presented below at the risk of not assigning due acknowledgment to many scholars.

TABLE 7.6   Sectorwise Breakdown of FDI in India, 1991–98 (in Crores of Rupees)

Sector	Actual Investment	Approved Investment	Ratio of Actual to Approved Amounts
Infrastructure	10,898	86,341	0.13
Services	4,475	17,964	0.25
Drugs and pharmaceuticals	735	801	0.92
Chemicals, not including fertilizers	3,473	27,418	0.13
Food and food processing, including sugar	2,105	10,549	0.20
Electrical equipment	3,931	9,427	0.42
Other	8,893	28,573	0.31
Total	34,510	181,073	0.19

Note: These figures do not take into account NRI investment because the sectoral allocations of such investment are not available. Here, infrastructure includes fuel, telecommunications, transport, and cement; services includes consultancy, service (financial, banking, nonfinancial, hospitals and diagnostics, and others), hotel and tourism, and trading; food and food processing includes sugar, fermentation industries, food processing industries, and vegetable oil and vanaspati. Other industries are defined as single entries in the SIA publications.

Source: Author's compilation of data available from SIA.

Benefits from Freer FDI

In the absence of *any* kind of distortions, the basic gains from FDI arise from its expansionary effect on a country's production possibility frontier (PPF) because more capital as a primary factor of production is now available. As a consequence, starting from a situation with a relatively restrictive regime of FDI, an increase in FDI, given diminishing returns to capital, leaves more output *net* of repatriation. The decrease in the return to capital with foreign capital at work can be seen as a terms-of-trade gain as the country is importing capital.

The PPF can also shift out as FDI in capital and infrastructure goods as well as services increases the aggregate supply/endowment of these inputs for production. The preceding refers to sources of expansion of the PPF through market channels. Probably a still greater benefit from FDI for a developing country stems from PPF expansion by the technology-spillover effects associated with FDI. It works via demonstration effects, labor turnover, and learning of superior technical and managerial skills, for which arm's-length trading is costly. It is also believed that FDI from industrial countries brings in more environment-friendly technology and hence would improve the environment in capital-importing developing countries.

Benefits from Multilateral Rules

The present international order of FDI activity is not prohibitively restrictive or nearly so. However, at issue is whether we want more multilateral disciplines that are binding across the board. There are at least four general benefits that may accrue from multilateral rules. First, rules themselves imply FDI liberalization or reforms by breaking any political inertia of discretion or "rent-keeping" inertia of inaction. Second, rules provide further and "third-party" insurance to foreign investors via implicit commitment, policy credibility, and reputation for liberal, nondiscriminatory policy—in that incidence of deviation from commitments can be challenged on a neutral ground like the WTO rather than in the courts of host countries. Third, at present there are about 1,600-plus bilateral investment treaties in the world economy. Multilateral rules under the WTO would substantially reduce the transaction costs of abiding by multiple bilateral treaties and hence would ensure greater efficiency. Fourth, rules can also be devised so as to deter wasteful and costly competition in terms of providing subsidies by potential host countries in attracting FDI.

Costs of Freer FDI

There is an extensive discussion in the "pure" theory of international trade and investment on how, in the presence of distortions, foreign capital inflow may lower welfare. For example, Brecher and Diaz-Alejandro (1977) argued that in a tariff-distorted, small Heckscher-Ohlin economy, capital inflow would lower welfare if the import-competing sector were capital intensive. As the economy is small in world trade, the product-price ratio and hence the factor prices are unchanged in such an economy. Thus an inflow of capital affects welfare only through changes in tariff revenues. If the import-competing sector were capital intensive, capital inflow would increase the output of this sector (by the Rybczinski theorem) and hence tend to reduce the volume imported. This would reduce tariff revenues (at any given level of positive tariff) and consequently aggregate welfare. In a small, open economy with unemployment (a result of distortion in the labor market), Batra (1986) has shown that the entry of multinational firms in capital-intensive industries would reduce the economywide demand for labor and thereby exacerbate the problem of unemployment and lower total welfare. Similarly in the absence of effective competition policy, FDI channeled through major multinational companies may lead to a greater exercise of market power and hence result in loss of welfare in terms of consumer surplus as well as domestic profits. Such arguments belong to the generic theory of second best, which suggests that as long as there are some given distortions in an economy, attempts to minimize other distortions (i.e., encourage FDI) can adversely affect welfare.

In light of the theory of second best, the possible positive effects of TRIMs on welfare can be seen as a cost of freer FDI. Consider, for example, the export performance requirement in a tariff-ridden small economy (see Rodrik 1987). Given that this requirement is binding, it induces more production in the exportable sector and less in the importable sector—hence more imports and more tariff revenues. This is a source of welfare gain as in Brecher and Diaz-Alejandro (1977).

Probably the biggest concern about more FDI that is felt by less developed countries involves market power. Most FDI is channeled through multinational corporations (MNCs) that are powerful in the global market. The fear is that when they get a foothold in a market they will wield considerable market power. Furthermore, by driving out domestic firms through predatory practices, they can even exert absolute monopoly power in the future.

FDI adversely affects domestic entrepreneurship and particularly infant industries. It can do so in two ways: directly through more competition and indirectly by increasing the cost of scarce resources, for example, a domestic source of raw material and finance. It is argued that FDI in cultural industries (such as music, or rice for Japan, for that matter) may "pollute" a country's unique culture.

MNCs have a global perspective in mind and care about their growth in the global market. Hence they may use a particular host country just as a production or distribution location. The growth of such a host nation may not be significantly affected by the presence of FDI through MNCs.

There may be informational problems as well. Free entry to foreign markets would help MNCs recycle their outdated technologies to uninformed and unsuspecting host countries. In other words, there may be *technology dumping*. On the other side, because of their lack of information MNCs also may make wrong, inefficient locational choices.

Inefficient competition in attracting FDI among potential host countries may emerge, forcing host countries to offer tax holidays and thereby worsening the budgetary position of developing countries.

International trade and FDI may be substitutes for each other. By inducing international prices to converge, free international trade in goods would narrow the differences in factor rewards (through product and factor-market linkages) and would reduce the incentive for capital to move across countries. The reverse argument also holds.

There is also the *pollution haven hypothesis*. FDI would encourage firms from industrial countries to move their outdated, polluting plants to the "South." This would worsen the environment in the South as well as the global environment.

FDI into skill-intensive sectors in the developing countries would increase the relative demand for skilled workers and thereby raise the skilled–unskilled wage gap. Thus the income distribution in these countries, presumably more unequal than in industrial countries, would be further "worsened."

Costs of Multilateral Rules

The cost of rules in policymaking generally lies in the lack of flexibility in the face of new information. While a country is following some sort of prioritization, given some information set, unanticipated changes may occur that require corrective FDI policy in the short run for welfare improvement, but in the presence of rules such corrections cannot be executed unilaterally and in time.

Furthermore, developing countries have offered particular reasons from their perspectives as to why multilateral rules on FDI are not a good idea now. One argument is that there are not many studies on the measurement of welfare gains from FDI to the recipient countries. Another argument is that although there may be potential gains from FDI, in a bargaining framework, further global liberalization of such investment should be opposed until labor mobility (movement of natural persons) is brought to the negotiation table as a quid pro quo.

Empirical Evidence about FDI

So much exists in theory. What does empirical evidence suggest? I have organized various findings in two subsections. The first relates to FDI and growth in cross-sectional studies and the second relates to empirical studies on FDI in India. Our review, again, will be very brief but we will be more formal in terms of assigning results to respective studies.

Empirical Studies on FDI and Growth and FDI and Knowledge Spillover in Cross-Sectional Studies

Casual empiricism suggests that the FDI–growth link is not well established. Korea and Taiwan, China, have done well without much emphasis on FDI. China and Thailand have experienced high growth by resorting to high levels of FDI. Sub-Saharan Africa has witnessed low FDI and low growth. Latin American countries have also experienced relatively open FDI policy but with modest growth. In technical terms the evidence on causality from FDI to growth in cross-section studies is rather weak. Blomstrom, Lipsey, and Zejan (1994) found that it runs more from growth to FDI than vice versa. De Mello (1997) has suggested that perhaps causality should be studied in the context of country-specific effects.

On the other hand, Borenszstein, de Gregorio, and Lee (1995) found that FDI has a positive effect on domestic capital formation: a dollar increase in FDI results in more than one dollar increase in total investment. It is interesting that the effect of FDI on growth works through other variables. For example, the impact of the education variable becomes greater in the presence of FDI. Hence, except for causality tests, the general implication is that FDI contributes positively to economic growth.

Eaton and Kortum (1995) found positive spillovers from foreign sources on the economic growth of host countries. Positive spillover effects from the operation of multinational firms in the host countries are apparent in Blomstrom, Kokko, and Zejan (1994), Blomstrom and Persson (1983), and Schive (1990).[10]

With regard to the environment, the evidence on the pollution haven hypothesis has been negligible or even negative. Mani and Wheeler (1997) found that, over the period 1960–1995, pollution shifting from industrial to developing countries has "not been a major phenomenon." The study by OECD (1997) found that the total investment flow into less developed countries in pollution-intensive sectors was less in 1992 than in 1972.

Studies on India

Studies on India are limited in number. They can be divided into three categories: those estimating the extent of foreign control in production, those concerned with the effects of technology transfer in terms of purchase and spillover, and those investigating the link of FDI to growth.

Foreign Control in Production   This was studied by Kumar (1994) and later by Athreye and Kapur (1999a). Foreign control is defined in terms of voting shares owned by foreigners in a company. In Kumar (1994), a firm is considered to be foreign controlled if 25 percent of its shares are held abroad. A somewhat different definition is used by the RBI; there is foreign control if 25 percent of equity is held by a single foreign investor or 40 percent of shares is held by a single foreign country. Using this definition over the sample period 1970 to 1990 Athreye and Kapur (1999a) found that foreign control in the manufacturing sector rose from 1970 to 1976 and then fell gradually until 1990.

Technology Transfer   For selected industries during the 1960s Deolalikar and Evenson (1989) found that the flow of foreign technology had a positive effect on inventive activity (in terms of the number of Indian patents) in India. Basant and Fikkert (1996) found that there is a high rate of return to Indian firms from technology purchased from outside. Research and development activity in India, although quite small compared with industrial countries, is complementary to technology purchase, and there are positive international spillover effects on the productivity of Indian firms. Their sample period covers the early 1980s. Product quality estimates of different firms in the Indian computer industry in the 1980s and 1990s were examined by Das (1998), who found that foreign firms generally offer better quality computers in the market.

The Linkage of FDI and Growth Aggregate growth effects of FDI—in terms of causality tests—in the postliberalization era have been studied by Dua and Rashid (1998). Using monthly data on actual FDI inflow and approvals, they discovered no causality links between actual FDI and the growth rate of industrial production (as a proxy for real gross domestic product [GDP]). But FDI approvals Granger-cause industrial production. This is explained in terms of the possible positive expectations that approvals may generate for business in general. The lack of significant effect of the actual FDI flow, however, could result because the FDI coming to the country in any particular month would affect the output only after several months. In other words, with month as the unit of time, the standard lags taken in the causality test ($t-1$, $t-2$, $t-3$, and so forth) may not capture any effect at all.

Keeping that in mind, I have done a simple regression analysis to find lagged effects of (actual) FDI on industrial production. Taking available data from March 1999 backward until December 1994, I found a significant relationship when FDI with a lag of five months is included; lags up to four months contribute very little. The index of industrial production was first deseasonalized and then first-differenced in logs (because the unit root hypothesis could not be rejected). The data on FDI (measured in millions of U.S. dollars), however, were stationary and subject to seasonal correction only. (The results differed very little between seasonalized and deseasonalized FDI data.) Hence the growth rate of industrial production (IP) was regressed on FDI. The results are reported in table 7.7 with the constant term, IP growth rate, at one-month lag and FDI at five-month lag as the explanatory variables. This is, however, a very preliminary exercise. Other macro effects of FDI need to be investigated in order to judge how robust the lagged effects of FDI are.

On balance, then, if one were to make an overall judgment on the nature of empirical conclusions with regard to the effects of FDI, it is positive.[11] We now argue that in principle the rationales behind FDI-restricting policies are rather weak.

TABLE 7.7   FDI and the Growth Rate of Industrial Production in India from December 1994 to March 1999: Regression Results

	Coefficient	Standard error	t-Statistic	Probability
Constant	−0.011328	0.008780	−1.290158	0.2037
Industrial production (−1)	−0.335726	0.136054	−2.467587	0.0176
Foreign direct investment (−5)	8.12E−05	3.94E−05	2.061175	0.0452
R^2	0.199617	Mean dependent variable		0.004213
Adjusted R^2	0.163236	Standard deviation dependent variable		0.020904
Standard error of regression	0.019122	Akaike information criterion		−5.014273
Sum of squared residual	0.016088	Schwarz criterion		−4.896178
Log likelihood	120.8354	Durbin-Watson		1.895988

Limitations of Arguments against FDI

To be sure, no country, including India, is against FDI per se. It is a question of whether to be more or less open to FDI, compared with the present system. Those who support multilateral rules are championing the cause of even freer FDI. Those who are not (e.g., India) support the status quo or even wish for a rollback (TRIMs indefinitely). Hence "against FDI" must be interpreted as against freer and more uniform and transparent policy intervention toward FDI than exists currently.

We begin by noting that there is in principle a fundamental similarity between the case for freer trade in goods and freer FDI. The central proposition of the theory of international trade is that in a frictionless, distortion-free, global-market economy, free trade is the best policy. But no economy in the world is free from these problems. How is it then that the industrial and the developing countries alike tend to support free trade in goods and services? Implicitly it amounts to accepting two (sensible) principles of policy practice (PPPs):

1. Following the important works by Bhagwati, Ramaswami, and Srinivasan (1969) and Bhagwati (1971), distortions should be handled by appropriate policy instruments that *most directly* deal with the respective distortion. There is thus no need to unnecessarily burden trade policy with "other" objectives.

For example, tariffs cannot be justified on the grounds that they raise revenues for the government. If revenues are scarce they should be mobilized more efficiently through direct taxes than through trade taxes.

2. If there is no forceful theoretical support for welfare-enhancing effects of a policy intervention, the benefit of the doubt belongs to the market, not to policy activism. That is, no intervention is the preferred choice.

The same PPPs should apply to FDI policy as well. Consider, for example, the pollution haven hypothesis. Apart from the lack of empirical evidence, pollution can be regulated more directly and effectively by setting appropriate pollution standards. Restricting FDI to check pollution is clearly inefficient. In this light it follows that the arguments against the free flow of FDI are rather weak.

Perhaps the single most important reason for the resistance toward a more open FDI policy is the presumed market-power effect of MNCs. However, a more open and transparent FDI policy would not invite just one MNC but many and thereby would foster competition not only between domestic and foreign firms but among MNCs themselves. Hence the scope to exercise market power will be self-constraining. The Indian auto market is a highly visible example of this. If there is evidence of predation, let this be handled by competition or antitrust policy. Lack of an effective institutional framework of competition policy should not be taken as a refuge for imposing restrictions on FDI. A more open FDI policy itself may indeed act as a catalyst toward the development of these institutions. In any event the first PPP applies.

Crowding out or scaling down of domestic entrepreneurship is another concern. Although such effects are true, it is equally true that downsizing of *inefficient* domestic firms improves rather than worsens welfare because, on one hand, there would be rationalization and, on the other, consumers would have a spectrum of qualities among which to choose. Those domestic firms unable to undertake technological innovation would be relegated to serve the lower end of the market, whereas those who are willing and able to do so would serve, along with the foreign firms, the high end of the market. The Indian auto market is again a good example here. Moreover, through mergers and acquisitions and by infusing new technology FDI can prevent some domestic industries from being wiped out. Some recent research (Markusen and Venables 1999) also suggests that FDI actually may encourage domestic entrepreneurship through favorable linkage effects.

Similarly, apart from FDI encouraging domestic investment (as is seen empirically in some cases), a partial crowding out of domestic investment should not be a concern. What should matter for welfare is the total volume of investment. Furthermore, there is little rationale for rationing FDI because it may substitute for trade. In theory, perfect substitutability between trade in goods and factors is based on the premises of factor-price equalization. Otherwise the differences in factor prices tend to narrow as a result of free trade in goods, but they do not vanish. What remains generally true is that free trade in commodities reduces—*not eliminates*—the incentive to engage in FDI. If so, this would make FDI a self-limiting activity, endogenously determined by market forces. There is no valid reason to restrict FDI just because it may restrict trade.

Consider technology dumping. It is a more probable occurrence in case of a pure technology transfer than in the case of FDI because FDI, unlike a simple technology transfer, involves more risk sharing by the technology-providing foreign firm, and so it is in the interest of MNCs to provide good technology. The moral hazard problem in providing technology and intangible assets is solved more efficiently with FDI than without. Put differently, FDI acts as insurance against such dumping.

Foreign equity restrictions on joint ventures with an aim toward protecting national interest or somehow containing market power seem misplaced, too. Recent research has illustrated that the concept of joint venturing arises as a response to moral hazard problems—in the provisions of inputs for which arm's-length transactions are very costly. Equity distribution is an efficiency parameter, *not a distributive one*, so restricting foreign equity share (or for that matter domestic equity share) reduces the joint economic surplus and lowers the welfare of the foreign country and the host country (as shown in Das and Katayama 2002).

Multiple bidding for FDI by host countries through offers of tax breaks, tax holidays, and other incentives is clearly inefficient. There is, however, some rationale for tax holidays in a world of asymmetric information about the "fundamentals" of a potential host country (Bond and Samuelson 1986), but in this age of the information technology revolution, such informational problems are likely to mitigate quickly over time. Hence competitive tax-advantage offers are dispensable. An FDI rules–based system would help eliminate these inefficiencies.

It is true that, compared with those on FDI, there are many more studies on welfare gains from free trade in commodities. But most of them relate to industrial countries. There are relatively few such studies on developing countries. Thus when free trade in goods is acceptable in the absence of sufficient empirical estimates, lack of adequate empirical studies on gains from FDI does not seem to be a valid argument.

The argument for bunching FDI liberalization with labor mobility does not seem to have much bite either as long as the industrial economies possess technological superiority and developing countries *need* foreign investment and technology to sustain a high-growth path. Given that nearly two-thirds of all world trade is concentrated among industrial countries and huge volumes of foreign investment flow among them, the "threat point" of no capital and no labor mobility is much worse for the developing countries than for the industrial ones.

Turning to the environment, it is quite possible that FDI would increase pollution (apart from the fact that studies to date show no such effects). But this has to be weighed against the economic benefits from FDI. Recent research by Das and Mehra (1999) showed that the benefits of FDI are likely to more than offset the costs in terms of environmental deterioration and thus higher global welfare results from FDI moving from North to South countries. The environment is a legitimate concern, of course, but using FDI restrictions to check pollution is inefficient.

With particular regard to TRIMs, both PPPs apply. If there is market imperfection in the form of market power, an effective competition policy is a more efficient instrument to use than TRIMs. Second, the transitional period for retention of tariff and nontariff barriers to trade would be over soon for many developing countries, including India. Hence the scope of welfare-enhancing effects of TRIMs is likely to be minimal at best.[12]

So far I have reviewed the possible negative efficiency effects of FDI. In regard to distribution, recent research (Das 2002) has indicated that in the long run FDI in skilled, labor-intensive sectors may not lead to more unequal distribution of wages in a developing country. Assuming that, in addition to foreign firms, domestic skilled workers (not unskilled workers) are potential entrepreneurs, an increase in FDI activity would lead to a partial crowding out of domestic entrepreneurs, thereby increasing the total pool of skilled workers for production and lowering the relative wage. The not-so-obvious point is that such an effect is likely to outweigh the initial positive impact on wage inequality.

Policy Recommendations for India

It is obvious that an inward-looking, domestic market–oriented growth strategy has not been and would not be successful. An export-oriented, global-market strategy with proper harnessing of modern technology is the ideal path to follow for any country, including India, that aspires to be an economic force in the world. There is already a realization of the benefit of that approach and a realization that FDI is an important component of India's overall growth strategy. All of this is fine. But the problem lies in the unwillingness and resistance to embrace further FDI reform and multilateral rules—especially the latter.

It is true that, unlike trade in goods and services, FDI is correctly viewed by both industrial and developing countries as a more direct instrument of development and growth. (Whether or how it is related to international trade is a subsidiary issue.) And growth strategy should vary from country to country, depending on factor endowments, technology and so forth. Hence FDI policy ought to be country specific to some extent.

The key broad question here is, What kind of outward development strategy is best suited for India? Is there a country that should serve as its role model? Policymakers and economists associated directly with policymaking in India generally are quick to pinpoint differences between India and any other proposed model economy, but they offer no clear alternative strategy.[13] I believe that in terms of its basic characteristics the Chinese economy is most similar to the characteristics of India. Because the Chinese real growth rate has averaged better than that of India and FDI has played a very prominent role in the recent Chinese fast-track development experience, I recommend that India adopt a very proactive, liberal approach to FDI.

The next question then concerns at which sectors FDI should be targeted. It is evident that infrastructural problems continue to be India's biggest bottleneck, and this is where FDI is most wanting. On the occasion of a World Bank–sponsored conference on India in Paris in 1998, Yashwant Sinha, then India's finance minister, observed that India needed US$25 billion per year for investment in its infrastructure sector.[14] The sectoral breakdown of GDP shows that 5 percent to 6 percent of India's GDP goes toward investment in this sector. For the year 1999–2000 this translates into $21 billion (at $1 = Rs. 45). Hence there is a shortfall of $4 billion in investment capital per year. Given the fiscal deficit and the relative inefficiency of public sector investments, the shortfall has to be financed by private investment. Because of the nature of technology, the scale of operation, and the risk involved, however, it is unrealistic to expect domestic sources to fill the gap. Thus FDI remains the only viable option for a rapid growth of this key sector in India.

The next and almost equally important target area should be India's export sector. In a world of free trade India must not merely specialize in the primary sector in which it has had comparative advantage traditionally. The aim should be to develop a new base of comparative advantage—a niche—in the manufacturing and services sector (including software). This is where the crucial role of FDI enters. Rather than attempting to build a diversified, efficient, growing, and sustained export-market base from scratch, it would be wise to encourage multinational corporations, which have established global networks, to enter and build India's export base in the manufacturing and high-tech sectors. Again this is similar to the Chinese model.[15]

It is important to note that prioritization has been the hallmark of Indian planning. But during the "planning era," it meant having a complex and heterogeneous system of regulations. Breaking away from this legacy has been rather slow. The current FDI policy is no doubt much more liberal in many aspects than that of the past, but it still entails a long and varying list of positive and negative regulations— what can or cannot be done—across different sectors. Those regulations still smack of complexity and heavy-handed discretion. There remains a lack of adequate understanding that international investors weigh their *current* rate of return from investment opportunities in competing host countries—historical progression matters little in that calculation. Reform should aim for simplicity, for example, removing many arbitrarily set caps on foreign equity in different sectors so as to make the rate of return for international investors more attractive than their other options.

Danger still persists with regard to any valid argument for prioritization insofar as it allows costly discretion to last long. A long-term timetable must be set and preparations made for removing prioritization schemes. This is where the virtues of multilateral rules come in. All four merits of multilateral rules discussed in the third section above apply to India. There are examples already in India of circumstances in which liberalization has been introduced or quickened precisely because of WTO obligations, for example, the amendment of the Patent Act of 1970. The same would be true for FDI reforms. Furthermore—and quite important—as we have seen, there is a yawning gap between FDI approvals and actual inflow in India. Since liberalization in 1991, the ratio of actual FDI to FDI approvals is no more than 25 percent! It should be kept in mind that there was an *absolute decline* in FDI into India from 1998 to 2000, despite the facts that India was largely immune from the "Asian crisis" and that FDI into a crisis-stricken country like Thailand increased during that period. It is heartening that FDI into India picked up in 2001. But the variability probably indicates the uncertainty in the minds of international investors about the returns to their investments in India. Further assurance and security to foreign investors are needed and can be obtained from WTO rules. Moreover, multilateral rules limiting subsidies would help India attract FDI without having to offer a tax holiday, as is currently being offered in the power sector or in 100 percent export units, for example.

Between 1995 and 2001, India concluded bilateral investment treaties (BITs) with 41 countries.[16] A set of multilateral rules will simplify and streamline the numerous procedures and provisions and therefore should reduce the transaction costs for India in dealing with international investors and for international investors in their dealing with India.

More concretely, India should support a design of conduct codes on the MFN principle, aiming at gradual, time-bound removal of restrictions on FDI—whether or not these are in the form of TRIMs—with the proviso that any alleged deviation from its commitments may be contestable in the dispute-settlement process. India also should stipulate strictly defined prioritization deadlines for different developing countries. A safeguard provision must be included, but only as a well-defined temporary deviation from free foreign entry and only on grounds of industry-specific ills, not macro problems.[17]

Overall, in my view, there is a strong case for simplicity, commitment, and reputation building, all of which are possible only through the adoption of international rules. It is high time to shed the notion that the drive for comprehensive liberalization has to wait until industrial countries do it first, or until some specified number of years have elapsed.

In closing, I must draw attention to the point that these recommendations are based on the two PPPs outlined earlier. For example, they presume the strengthening of antitrust legislation and enforcement. Lack of such institutional arrangements has been offered as an excuse for too long in justifying discretionary, distortionary, and essentially arbitrary interventions in different spheres of economic activity. In turn, such interventions have formed the basis for the lack of collective effort to build procompetitive, effective institutions. This is a kind of "prisoner's dilemma"—in a somewhat different sense than usual—that has led to an equilibrium in which institutional failures and distortionary interventions prevail in a developing country like India. Multilateral rules on FDI are a potent instrument to break this dilemma.[18]

Endnotes

1. Since 2000 the world volume of FDI (both inflow and outflow) has declined, as the global economy has been in recession.

2. Indonesia was targeted because its policy came into existence after the TRIMs agreement was reached.

3. This point was clarified for me by Aaditya Mattoo.

4. The other two are trade and competition policy and trade and government procurement.

5. During the Seattle meetings, however, the EU seemed to tone down its demand for a comprehensive multilateral rules system.

6. Kumar (1994) actually took the whole period from independence to 1967 as this era.

7. It is interesting that India went to a highly regulated, fixed exchange-rate system when the global economy abandoned the Bretton Woods fixed-exchange rate system in 1973.

8. For early years until the 1980s there is probably a minor difference between the approval amount and the actual inflow.

9. Note that the overall ratio of 19 percent is not entirely consistent with table 7.5. This is probably because the sectoral breakdown of investments by nonresident Indians is not available and hence not included in table 7.6.

10. Aitken, Hanson, and Harrison (1997) is an exception.

11. This conclusion is borne out also by Agrawal's econometric research in Chapter 6 of this volume.

12. From the perspective of MNCs that face these TRIMs, Hoekman and Saggi (1999) cited survey results showing that only 6 percent of foreign affiliates of U.S. firms felt constrained by TRIMs. Thus TRIMs are often not binding. If so, such redundancy should be eliminated.

13. This partly explains a lack of clear development strategy in India even now.

14. For details, see www.worldbank.org (countries and regions; India; news and events; and features).

15. There are two other priority areas that are already recognized by the government, namely, the general services sectors (e.g., financial and insurance industries) and the agricultural input sector (e.g., machinery, chemicals, and fertilizers for agriculture).

16. The source is the UNCTAD BIT/DTT database.

17. India's dispute with the United States on the length of the transition period to keep quantity restrictions on grounds of external-payments difficulties and the WTO ruling in favor of the United States suggest that such a provision may be ineffective anyway.

18. Agrawal offers somewhat more guarded recommendations for India's investment policies in Chapter 6 of this volume.

References

The word "processed" describes informally produced works that may not be available commonly through libraries.

Aitken, Brian, Gordon H. Hanson, and Ann E. Harrison. 1997. "Spillovers, Foreign Investment, and Export Behavior." *Journal of International Economics* 43: 103–32.

Athreye, Suma S., and Sandeep Kapur. 1999a. "Foreign Controlled Firms in Indian Manufacturing: Long-Term Trends." Working Paper. Manchester School of Management and Birkbeck College, Manchester, U.K.

———. 1999b. "Private Foreign Investment in India: Pain or Panacea?" Working Paper. Manchester School of Management and Birkbeck College, Manchester, U.K.

Basant, Rakesh, and Brian Fikkert. 1996. "The Effects of R&D, Foreign Technology Purchase, and Domestic and International Spillovers on Productivity in Indian Firms." *Review of Economics and Statistics* 78: 187–99.

Batra, Ravi N. 1986. "A General Equilibrium Model of Multinational Corporations in Developing Economies." *Oxford Economic Papers* 38: 342–53.

Bhagwati, Jagdish. 1971. "The Generalized Theory of Distortions and Welfare." In Jagdish Bhagwati, Ronald W. Jones, Robert A. Mundell, and Jaraslov Vanek, eds., *Trade, Balance of Payments, and Growth: Papers in International Economics in Honor of Charles P. Kindleberger*. Cambridge, Mass.: MIT Press.

Bhagwati, Jagdish, V. K. Ramaswami, and T. N. Srinivasan. 1969. "Domestic Distortions, Tariffs, and the Theory of Optimum Subsidy: Some Further Results." *Journal of Political Economy* 77: 1005–13.

Bhattacharya, B., and S. Palaha. 1996. *Policy Impediments to Trade and FDI in India*. New Delhi: Wheeler Publishing for Indian Institute of Foreign Trade.

Blomstrom, Magnus, Ari Kokko, and Mario Zejan. 1994. "Host Country Competition and Technology Transfer by Multinationals." *Weltwirtschaftliches Archiv* 130: 521–33.

Blomstrom, Magnus, Robert Lipsey, and Mario Zejan. 1994. "What Explains Developing Country Growth?" Working Paper W-4132. National Bureau of Economic Research, Cambridge, Mass.

Blomstrom, Magnus, and Hakan Persson. 1983. "Foreign Investment and Spillover Efficiency in an Underdeveloped Economy: Evidence from the Mexican Manufacturing Industry." *World Development* 11: 493–501.

Bond, Eric, and Larry Samuelson. 1986. "Tax Holidays as Signals." *American Economic Review* 76: 820–26.

Borenszstein, Eduardo, Jose de Gregorio, and Jong-Wha Lee. 1995. "How Does Foreign Investment Affect Economic Growth?" Working Paper 5057. National Bureau of Economic Research, Cambridge, Mass.

Brecher, Richard A., and C. F. Diaz-Alejandro. 1977. "Tariffs, Foreign Capital and Immiserizing Growth." *Journal of International Economics* 7: 317–22.

Confederation of Engineering Industries. 1992. "The Role of Foreign Direct Investment in Economic Development: Comparison of Selected Asian Countries." In *Foreign Direct Investment and Technology Transfer in India*. Washington, D.C.: United Nations.

Das, Sanghamitra. 1998. "Foreign Versus Domestic Technology, Private Versus Public Ownership and Product Quality." *Journal of Quantitative Economics* 14: 97–121.

Das, Satya P. 2002. "Foreign Direct Investment and Relative Wage in a Developing Economy." *Journal of Development Economics* 67: 55–77.

Das, Satya P., and Seichi Katayama. 2002. "International Joint Venture and Host Country Policies." *Japanese Economic Review.*

Das, Satya P. and Meeta Mehra. 1999. "North-South Capital Movement and Global Environment." Indian Statistical Institute, New Delhi. Processed.

De Mello, Jr., Luiz R. 1997. "Foreign Direct Investment in Developing Countries and Growth: A Selective Survey." *Journal of Development Studies* 34: 1–34.

Deolalikar, Anil, and Robert E. Evenson. 1989. "Technology Production and Technology Purchase in Indian Industry: An Econometric Analysis." *Review of Economics and Statistics* 71: 689–92.

Drabek, Zdenek. 1998. "A Multilateral Agreement on Investment: Convincing the Skeptics." Working Paper ERAD-98-05. Economic Research and Analysis Division, World Trade Organization, June.

Dua, Pami, and Aneesa I. Rashid. 1998. "Foreign Direct Investment and Economic Activity in India." *Indian Economic Review* 33: 153–68.

Eaton, Jonathan, and Mark Gersovitz. 1984. "A Theory of Expropriation and Deviation from Perfect Capital Mobility." *Economic Journal* 94: 16–40.

Eaton, Jonathan, and S. Kortum. 1995. "Engines of Growth: Domestic and Foreign Sources of Innovation." Working Paper 5207. National Bureau of Economic Research, Cambridge, Mass.

Hoekman, Bernard, and Kamal Saggi. 1999. "Multilateral Disciplines for Investment-Related Policies?" Paper presented at the Conference on Global Regionalism, February, Rome.

Kidron, Michael. 1965. *Foreign Investment in India.* Oxford: Oxford University Press.

Kumar, Nagesh. 1994. *Multinational Enterprises and Industrial Organization: The Case of India,* 2d ed. New Delhi: Saga Publications.

Mani, Muthukumara, and David Wheeler. 1999. "In Search of Pollution Havens? Dirty Industry in the World Economy, 1960–1995." Policy Research Working Paper. World Bank, Policy Research Department, Washington, D.C.

Markusen, James R., and Anthony Venables. 1999. "Foreign Direct Investment as a Catalyst for Industrial Development." *European Economic Review* 43: 335–56.

OECD (Organisation for Economic Co-operation and Development). 1997. "Foreign Investment and the Environment: An Overview of the Literature." Report of the Negotiating Group on the Multilateral Agreement on Investment. December.

Rodrik, Dani. 1987. "The Economics of Export-Performance Requirements." *Quarterly Journal of Economics* 102: 633–50.

UNCTAD (United Nations Conference on Trade and Development). 2002. *World Investment Report* 2002. Division on Investment, Technology and Enterprise Development.

Yu, Eden S. H., and C-C. Chao. 1998. "On Investment Measures and Trade." *The World Economy* 21: 549–61.

8

INDIA AS USER
AND CREATOR OF
INTELLECTUAL PROPERTY:
THE CHALLENGES
POST-DOHA

Arvind Subramanian

For India, no aspect of the Uruguay Round has engendered as much concern, acrimonious debate, and vitriol as TRIPS (trade-related intellectual property rights). With some exaggeration, it came to symbolize all that was wrong with the World Trade Organization (WTO), as well as multilateral engagement, greedy multinationals, and even globalization as a whole. As with most impassioned rhetoric, although there was some misunderstanding and misrepresentation, an essential kernel of truth underlay the rhetoric. On balance, the TRIPS agreement on its own will impose welfare costs on India, at least in the key pharmaceuticals sector.[1]

Today, of course, the mood on intellectual property (IP) is vastly different. At Seattle the presence of the IP lobby was token and concerned more with preventing serious backsliding on TRIPS than with advancing a new IP agenda. So the good news about TRIPS for India is that in the near future, external pressure on IP issues is going to be minimal. This is so for four reasons.

First, there is the strong influence of civil society groups within industrial countries championing causes that can be argued to be at odds with IP protection. For example, the sanctity of human and animal life is perceived to be at variance with efforts to patent biotechnological inventions, and technologies such as the terminator gene are felt to run counter to environmental protection and the preservation of biodiversity.

Second, there is the inevitable intellectual/ideological backlash to the headlong embrace of free markets associated with the last 10–15 years. As the pendulum swings back, there is a greater focus now on the *abuse* of IP protection and a corresponding emphasis on competition and contestability. The recent IP-related cases in the United States involving the prosecution of Microsoft, Intel, and the class action suit against Monsanto exemplify this new climate.

Third, private sector pressure in IP-related industries has diminished in the last few years, reflecting the success of the Uruguay Round. Many of the key commercial issues, at least the big-ticket items such as pharmaceuticals and chemicals, were resolved in TRIPS to the broad satisfaction of IP-related companies. Although issues and concerns remain, they are not of the same order of magnitude as those that existed prior to the Uruguay Round.

Finally, developing countries have successfully conveyed the sense that the Uruguay Round was imbalanced in its outcome, with TRIPS contributing critically to that imbalance. It would simply be too difficult now to force developing countries to swallow more of the TRIPS pill.

On the other hand, the more sobering news is that many challenges on intellectual property lie ahead for India and they will need to be addressed, even without the external pressure. The Doha declaration can be read as a clear signal that any pressure for increasing levels of IP protection around the world is unlikely in the foreseeable future. And in the case of pharmaceuticals, the declaration arguably can be seen as a political reaffirmation that TRIPS can be used flexibly by developing countries to mitigate the impact of IP protection without eliciting pressure—bilateral or through the WTO dispute settlement process—from industrial-country trading partners.

The next phase of issues is going to differ from the previous one in one key respect. In the past, India's main task in IP was defensive: to resist external pressure. Although obviously difficult, given the magnitude of the pressure, it was easy to know what had to be done. Now, however, India has "to do" rather than "not do," which entails its own set of challenges. These challenges affect India in each of its locations on the knowledge-creation spectrum: as net user, potential net creator, and net creator. This chapter argues that the challenges are fivefold:

1. To use TRIPS as a mechanism for enforcing India's market access rights in the WTO
2. To develop policies and mechanisms that serve to mitigate the most egregious effects of the TRIPS agreement
3. To seek changes in the TRIPS agreement that allow India to contribute constructively and significantly to public health crises in developing countries, such as the AIDS crisis in Africa

4. To identify where India's interests lie in relation to the new technologies (plants, biotechnology) and appropriately adapt intellectual property rights (IPR) legislation as well as complementary institutions that would allow the benefits of those technologies to be harnessed while minimizing attendant risks

5. To create workable institutions domestically that protect intellectual property and resources created in India and would serve as a basis for seeking their replication internationally.

With a few exceptions, those challenges will be domestic and will need to be met constructively. In this chapter, suggestions are offered on how this might be accomplished in some areas, but in other areas more questions are raised than are answered.

The chapter is organized as follows. The next section elaborates a proposal on the use of TRIPS obligations as an enforcement mechanism. The third section offers suggestions on how domestic policies need to be adapted to cope with the TRIPS agreement. The fourth section describes how TRIPS rules must be changed so that Indian companies can provide affordable drugs to countries that experience public health crises such as the AIDS epidemic afflicting Africa. The fifth section poses some questions that need to be answered before arriving at policy positions in relation to the new technologies and it draws attention to the regulatory challenges. Issues related to IP created in India are discussed next. The seventh section addresses certain issues that have elicited strong positions in India, but that should be spared time and effort because they are not of any real significance for India. Section eight presents some data on patenting activity by developing countries that shed light on India's prospects for increasing inventive activity.

TRIPS as an Enforcement Device[2]

There are widespread fears that the quantitative restrictions imposed on textiles and clothing products by industrial countries will not be eliminated by 2005, as required by the Uruguay Round Agreement on Textiles and Clothing (ATC). The stakes are high for India. Given the right domestic policy environment, India stands to gain from the elimination of the quotas or to lose if there is backtracking by trading partners. Does India have the means to ensure compliance with commitments or must the country resign itself to ineffectiveness, believing outcomes are beyond its power to influence?

I believe that India does have the means to ensure compliance, but the country must change its draft-patent legislation to allow for retaliation in TRIPS for noncompliance by partner countries in areas affecting India's exporting interests. As I demonstrate below, if designed with care such retaliation can be feasible, effective, and legal. It is noteworthy that recently Ecuador has requested and been granted authorization by the WTO to retaliate against the European Union (EU) in the area of services and IP in the controversial bananas dispute.

Why TRIPS Is a Good Retaliatory Weapon

An effective retaliatory action must possess two features: it must inflict loss or pain swiftly on the party being retaliated against, and to be credible it must be beneficial to the country taking the action. Does retaliation through TRIPS satisfy those two conditions?

Effectiveness   India has undertaken serious commitments on TRIPS from which large, multinational corporations based in industrial countries stand to benefit enormously. For example, the requirement to grant patent protection for pharmaceutical products will begin to reap profits for large, European and U.S. research-based companies in the early years of the new millennium as the first protected products come onto the market. Axiomatically, withdrawing TRIPS benefits would be costly and painful for them. Calculations by Subramanian (1995) and Watal (1998) have shown that the benefits of TRIPS commitments to large pharmaceutical producers alone could be in the millions of dollars. The first condition of retaliation is therefore satisfied.

Credibility   So too is the second condition, namely, that retaliation will actually make the retaliating country better off in welfare terms. Support for this proposition comes from the many analyses showing that, under most circumstances, higher IP protection accorded by India makes it worse off.[3] Conversely, withdrawing TRIPS commitments, or reducing the strength of IP protection, must make India better off.[4] This lends credibility to the threat of retaliation. It must be noted, however, that for this proposition to hold, the withdrawal of TRIPS benefits must be accompanied by measures to ensure alternative sources of supply to the market—supply that had hitherto been precluded by the IP protection (see below).

Targeting, Proportionality, and Pointedness   In relation to the first condition of inflicting pain, TRIPS also possesses other desirable properties. First, the retaliatory action can target the noncompliant partner country. If, for instance, the European Union fails to eliminate a textile quota affecting India, the Indian authorities can target IP rights granted to EU nationals as the objects of retaliatory action. Second, the principle of proportionality—that the retaliatory action should be commensurate with the offending action—can be respected. The variables for achieving proportionality would be how many IP rights owners to affect and for how long. The third really compelling advantage of such retaliatory action is its ability to create pressure on noncomplying constituents to revert to compliance with WTO obligations. A typical process of political economy following the threat of retaliatory action would be as follows. Say India threatens nonacceptance of the patent applications of Pfizer and others in retaliation against U.S. textile quotas not being removed as scheduled; Pfizer and others would then have a very strong incentive to lobby the politicians supporting the textile industry and force remedial action. The more pointed the retaliatory action, the greater the incentive for the affected party to take remedial action—and that renders TRIPS an effective retaliatory instrument.

Difficulties with TRIPS as a Retaliatory Weapon

Four difficulties present themselves: the private nature of rights, the exclusivity of the rights conferred, the possible constraints imposed by WTO dispute settlement rules, and the possible deterrence of foreign direct investment (FDI).

The Private Nature of Rights   Although it is possible to retaliate by abrogation of IP rights, the tactic has problems because there are crucial differences between conventional retaliation in goods and retaliation in intellectual property. Intellectual property rights are private rights justiciable domestically in the country granting them. Once the rights have been conferred through domestic legislation and pursuant to an act of parliament, their withdrawal can be challenged as illegal or unconstitutional by the affected parties in the domestic courts. On the other hand, when tariffs are raised in retaliation, the affected foreign supplier has no direct right that he can challenge in the retaliating country's courts. Raising a tariff in most countries can be done through an act of the executive. Private IP rights granted through legislation cannot so easily be withdrawn by the executive.

Exclusivity of Rights   A practical complication arises when retaliating in TRIPS: benefits will accrue to the retaliating country only if alternative sources of supply quickly substitute for the product whose patent right has been withdrawn. Thus, the retaliation must be such as to ensure quick alternative supplies to the market that will dilute or eliminate the legal monopoly granted. Another complication is that the retaliatory action must not create uncertainty for the alternative suppliers. For example, if the retaliatory action has to be reversed because partner countries come back into compliance, then WTO rules would require the restoration of IP rights. This would mean that alternative suppliers would have to cease production, and that may cause such uncertainty that alternative suppliers would not enter the market in the first place.

WTO Rules on Cross-Retaliation Do WTO rules allow cross-retaliation (for example, TRIPS for textiles)?[5] The WTO Dispute Settlement Understanding (DSU) deals with compensation and the suspension of concessions in Article 22. It lays down a sequential procedure for cross-retaliation, which can only be resorted to if within-sector retaliation is not feasible or practicable.

The issue is whether such procedures could unduly circumscribe the use of TRIPS as retaliation when partner-country infringements are in goods. This depends very much on the interpretation of what is deemed "effective" and "practicable." On both criteria, especially the second, complainants in developing countries can reasonably argue that retaliating in the same sector—say, other goods for a textiles-related dispute—is ineffective because of the size of the market; moreover, such action would amount to inflicting economic harm on themselves. Hence, easy recourse to welfare-improving retaliation as in TRIPS should be allowed. The outcome of the arbitration requested by the EU against the authorization granted by the Dispute Settlement Body (DSB) to Ecuador allowing retaliation under the General Agreement on Trade in Services (GATS) and TRIPS in the bananas dispute would be interesting to set the tone for the future use of such cross-retaliation. If the arbitration comes out against Ecuador on this issue, India should seriously consider options for renegotiating the DSU in this regard.[6]

Deterring Foreign Direct Investment The concern exists that the possibility of retaliation will deter FDI. However, as long as the legislation is carefully drafted to spell out the exact circumstances for retaliation and its withdrawal and is consistent with international rules, FDI need not be affected. The legislation and its judicious implementation can reassure investors that India is not intent on expropriating foreign property, but is merely seeking to enforce its rights in a manner that is internationally sanctioned.[7]

Design of Retaliation

The difficulties described above are not insuperable. India's draft-patent legislation can be carefully designed to ensure that the difficulties are addressed or overcome.

The Private Nature of Rights The fact that IP rights are private rights conferred under domestic law requires that their revocation—partial or complete (discussed below)—must also be built into the law, particularly in countries where international law is not self-executing. India's domestic legislation implementing the TRIPS agreement must clearly specify that the country's executive reserves the right to revoke or dilute these rights in the event that partner countries are found to be noncompliant with commitments that affect India's interests. The retaliation provisions should not engender the perception of India as a renegade state, acting outside the pale of reason. Rather, they should be broadly consistent with international trading rules, which will ensure their good standing in the international arena and confer legitimacy on the retaliatory actions if they ever are used.

Exclusivity of Rights   What form should retaliatory action take, considering the problems arising from the exclusive nature of rights that are conferred? It is important to note that retaliation merely by delaying the grant of the patent will not satisfy the first principle of retaliation—inflicting harm on the affected party. In the case of pharmaceuticals, for example, delaying a patent grant may not reduce the effective economic life of the patent because regulatory approval is typically obtained long after the patent is granted. Several feasible options present themselves.

First, retaliatory action can include the suspension of acceptance of patent or design applications from the targeted country for the time of noncompliance. However, nonacceptance of applications must not result in loss of priority rights because the punitive measure would result in a loss of IP rights over the entire duration of the right, and that action may not be proportional to the nullification and impairment for which compensation is sought.

Second, retaliatory action could take the form of awarding compulsory licenses. The legislation could clearly specify that they will be granted in cases where foreign countries do not comply with WTO obligations affecting India. In granting such licenses, the conditions that would normally be applied to them, specified in Article 31 of TRIPS, need not be respected. Clearly, if such compulsory licenses were granted in pharmaceuticals or chemicals, marketing approval for these products would also need to be granted expeditiously.

Another possibility is for the government to choose products that are reaching the end of their patent life and to shorten or terminate their protection so that competitors can quickly enter the market. In these cases, the problem of reversal of the retaliatory action would not arise because the patent may expire by the time the dispute is settled. Yet another possibility is to target copyrights and trademarks where copying is swift and easy.

WTO Consistency   The language on retaliation in domestic legislation should be carefully drafted to ensure that the discretion to use or authorize retaliation is typically exercised only after the multilateral dispute-settlement process has worked its way through the dispute and has decided in favor of the developing country. If it is further specified that this discretion can only be exercised after explicit authorization is granted by the DSB, retaliation would be strictly WTO consistent.

Of course, domestic legislation need not preclude entirely the possibility of retaliatory action where partner countries are so egregiously in violation of their commitments that retaliatory action would be warranted even in the absence of explicit authorization by the WTO DSB. The kind of situation envisaged here resembles that of the EU in the banana dispute. Noncompliance has been so protracted and the balance of legitimacy so overwhelmingly against the EU that it is hard to imagine retaliatory action being seriously questioned in the WTO.

If the arguments made about the effectiveness of such retaliatory action are right, its threat—its very presence in domestic legislation—could lead to improved compliance by industrial countries that would typically be the targets of such action. The threat may seldom have to be converted into a reality.

One obstacle to effective implementation of such retaliation could be the hurdles implicit in the procedures on cross-retaliation specified in WTO dispute-settlement rules. It may be necessary to clarify the rules to ensure that easy access to cross-retaliation is permitted. Of course I would strenuously insist that such clarification is unnecessary because the rules, particularly the "practicable" and "effective" conditions, would permit a case to be made in favor of easy recourse to retaliation in TRIPS.[8]

Developing Domestic Policy Instruments and Institutions

One of the key challenges of TRIPS will be to develop domestic policies and institutions so that the benefits from IP protection can be maximized and the potential costs minimized. The policies and institutions relate to a number of areas.

Coping with TRIPS: Compulsory Licensing and Competition Policy

As mentioned above, TRIPS will impose costs, at least in the pharmaceutical sector. Sometime around 2005, when the first patented products come onto the market, prices of patented drugs will be higher than they otherwise would have been by margins that are uncertain but nevertheless positive. How should India cope?

The two most important policy instruments available to developing countries to mitigate some of the effects of the high levels of patent protection are compulsory licensing and competition policies. In principle, the flexibility associated with compulsory licensing can be exploited to dilute some of the effects of patent protection. This flexibility comes in two forms. First, countries are virtually unrestricted in the circumstances under which they can grant compulsory licenses.[9] Second, while a number of conditions need to be fulfilled when these licenses are granted, there is sufficient discretion available to national authorities to meet these conditions while diluting the monopolistic impact of the proprietary protection granted in the first place (Watal 1998).

From a TRIPS perspective, the advantages of deploying competition policy are twofold. First, there is a wide degree of latitude in determining the optimal degree of protection that balances the need to foster innovation while ensuring technological diffusion. And it is understood, even in industrial countries, that this balance—often blurred and always shifting—is determined by the joint action of IP rights and competition policies. Put crudely, the standards set for anticompetitive practices can dilute the effects of IP rights protection without running foul of the minimum standards laid out in the TRIPS agreement. For example, what constitutes abusive pricing is a question with a wide variety of answers. India can exploit this latitude through enactment of competition policies and the mechanisms to implement them.[10]

The second advantage of using competition policies follows from the language of the TRIPS agreement. In two key respects that could be usefully harnessed by developing countries, there is even greater flexibility in the use of compulsory licenses when they are granted to remedy anticompetitive practices. When compulsory licenses are used to remedy anticompetitive practices, the TRIPS agreement provides that (a) no case must be made that the patentee was unwilling to license the patent on reasonable commercial terms as a precondition for granting the compulsory license, and (b) the principle that remuneration for the compulsory license should be "adequate" need not be respected.

In the light of the above information, two key tasks face India. First, the country needs to strengthen the patent law and implementation apparatus so that India is able to use compulsory licensing effectively.[11] A number of specific questions must be answered in creating an effective system of compulsory licensing. What guidelines need to be provided so that the minimum procedures that TRIPS requires—making efforts to obtain a voluntary license—are met? Is it enough if the potential compulsory licensee writes a letter to the patent holder seeking a voluntary license or must a minimum period of delay be allowed for a response? How long should such a period be? TRIPS allows enough discretion for India to write these guidelines in a way that can make the process efficient, but these guidelines must be elaborated and enacted expeditiously.

Another important question relates to the number of compulsory licenses that are awarded. There should be a presumption in favor of having more than one compulsory licensee to ensure a more competitive market outcome. How will the licensees be chosen and by whom? What expertise and market information will the granting authority need to have before making decisions on compulsory licenses? How will the royalty payment be determined? Article 31 (h) of TRIPS makes clear that royalty rates should be conditioned by the value of the compulsory license rather than the value of the patent. This would allow royalty to be related to the final price charged by the licensee. The larger the number of compulsory licenses, the lower will be final prices, thus yielding lower royalty payments.

Effectiveness of compulsory licensing will require minimizing legal uncertainty for the licensee. If, for example, appeals against the grant of compulsory licenses become routine and litigation protracted, the compulsory licensees will not be able to start production, which will thwart the objective of diluting monopoly protection. India should consider creating a special administrative tribunal to hear appeals related to compulsory licenses and dispose of them expeditiously. In fact, a general presumption should be created that production under compulsory licenses can take place even if an appeal is pending before the relevant administrative authority. Safeguards to protect the interests of the compulsory licensees, provided for under Article 31 (g) of TRIPS, need to be built into the guidelines that would create an economic climate relatively free of uncertainty and thereby make production under compulsory licensing an attractive proposition.

Finally, India will need to address the question of how to design regulatory approval procedures in the event that compulsory licenses are generously awarded so as to facilitate the easy marketing of drugs produced under such licenses.

The second task is to expeditiously implement a strengthened competition policy and institutions so that adequate experience is gained by the time competition laws have to be used to offset the impact of the TRIPS agreement.

Changing TRIPS Rules to Address Public Health Crises in Developing Countries[12]

Under the TRIPS agreement developing countries could invoke the public health/interest exception in the TRIPS agreement to grant compulsory licenses for the domestic production of relevant drugs, as indeed South Africa has provided for in its law. (The law is currently challenged in South Africa's courts as being too permissive and hence inconsistent with the TRIPS agreement.) Although this is a feasible option for large, technologically advanced developing countries (such as India) that can easily produce the patented drug, it may be less feasible for the smaller African countries that would have to *import* the drugs. Therefore, African countries will have to issue a compulsory license for importing the drug. But where could they find these drugs at reasonable prices (that is, at lower than monopoly prices) if the rest of the world is TRIPS compliant? There are two possibilities:

1. From those countries that are outside the TRIPS agreement
2. From those WTO countries in which a similar compulsory licensing exception has been invoked.

Because the membership of the WTO is becoming comprehensive (even China has joined the WTO), the first possibility is increasingly ruled out.

The key point here is that African countries cannot import from other WTO countries unless the latter also have invoked a similar compulsory licensing exception. In other words, a country such as India cannot issue compulsory licenses to its firms just to export AIDS drugs to African countries. Article 31 (f) of the TRIPS agreement rules out this possibility because it requires compulsory licensing to serve "predominantly" the local market (that is, in the country where the license is issued). Because IP laws are territorial, the right to import does not become a right to export unless laws in the country where production for export takes place authorize such production.

The consequences of this restriction are not theoretical. Take the recent case of the Indian company, CIPLA, that offered to sell AIDS drugs to Kenya at $650 per dose. This offer was legal in India because the drugs in question were not covered by the TRIPS agreement. They were inventions made prior to 1994, the cutoff date for protection around the world. But in a year or two, when new AIDS drugs are covered by the TRIPS agreement, the Indian company will not be able to make such an offer. To do so they will have to obtain a compulsory license to serve the Indian market; when such a license is obtained they can then export to Africa some of their total production (much less than 50 percent, given Article 31 (f) of the TRIPS agreement).[13]

If providing affordable access to Africa is indeed a serious imperative, even this possibility that is left open under the TRIPS agreement is a very slim one. For example, a country like Zimbabwe can obtain drugs under competitive conditions only if *other* countries have successfully cleared the following hurdles for compulsory licensing:

- Potential compulsory licensees must have attempted to obtain a voluntary license from the patentee on reasonable commercial terms and have been refused within a reasonable period of time
- The patentee should be paid reasonable compensation for the compulsory license
- Decisions by a government to grant compulsory licenses must be subject to judicial review.

Even if those hurdles could be cleared, the delays involved could be enormous and militate against swift responses to what is a serious crisis. What is needed is a legal situation that clearly allows and legitimizes third-country governments (that is, other than governments of importing countries) to grant compulsory licenses for export so that firms such as CIPLA in India can sell AIDS drugs to African countries in crisis. This would require a change in TRIPS rules.

It is important to note that a needed change in the legal situation still may not be sufficient if extralegal pressures are exerted to prevent realizing the outcomes at which the legal changes aim. For example, if an Indian company is willing to sell AIDS drugs to African countries at close to marginal costs, it is easy to imagine that both the company and the Indian government would come under pressure of an implicit or explicit threat from the United States not to grant compulsory licenses for export. If India or the Indian pharmaceutical company succumbs (as happened recently to CIPLA when it offered to sell drugs to Ghana), the losers will be the AIDS victims in Africa.[14]

The need for legal clarity cannot be overemphasized as recent experience indicates. South Africa's parallel import regime came under severe pressure from the United States and its pharmaceutical companies despite the fact that parallel imports were so clearly permitted by WTO rules. In the end, of course, the United States relented but only after substantial countervailing pressure was exerted by nongovernmental organizations. Of course the WTO rule helped but it was not enough in itself to stave off pressure.

Some have argued that the TRIPS agreement requires no changes because it allows countries to grant broad, sweeping exceptions to IP laws in the event of an emergency, as indeed the AIDS crisis could be argued to be. But for the reasons spelled out above, such an exception will not help African countries because even if they suspended their IP laws, they would still have to obtain the AIDS drugs from partner countries. Those partner countries cannot invoke similar emergency exceptions unless the emergency is a domestic one; that is, India cannot suspend its IP laws because of an AIDS crisis in Africa.

To be sure, any change in IP rules should not become or be seen as a license for widespread infringement of patent rights. Appropriate safeguards can be designed to prevent that. First, third-country production of drugs under compulsory licenses for export can be restricted both to countries in real need and to multilaterally certified (by the World Health Organization [WHO]) instances of public health problems. Second, patent holders should be provided reasonable compensation for third-party use of the patent, which could be specified in advance to avoid legal uncertainty. And finally, countries should be assigned responsibility to prevent drugs produced under compulsory licenses from leaking into other markets and undermining legitimate patent protection.[15]

Thus the proposal to change TRIPS rules would run along the following lines. In the event of a WHO-certified public health crisis in a developing country, governments in other countries should be free to grant compulsory licenses to their pharmaceutical companies to export the necessary drugs to the country in crisis. Compliance with the normal procedures for granting such licenses specified in Article 31 of the TRIPS agreement, particularly paragraph (f), should not be necessary;

however, patentees affected by the compulsory license should be provided a nominal remuneration of 2 to 4 percent. The country or countries granting the compulsory license should cooperate with trading partners to ensure that drugs produced under such licenses do not find their way into markets other than those affected by the crisis. The international community, under the aegis of the WHO, should make concerted and expeditious efforts to ensure that drugs produced under such licenses satisfy the regulatory criteria for marketing approval.

IP and Regulatory Policies for the New Technologies

India's draft legislation provides plant variety protection similar to that foreseen under UPOV (the International Union for the Protection of New Varieties of Plants) 1978. In the patent legislation there is an exclusion for "plants and animals and essentially biological processes for the production of plants and animals other than microbiological processes." Although this exemption for biotechnology is up for review under TRIPS, it does not seem likely that India will be under external pressure to close this exemption because of the unsettled nature of the debate in Europe in particular.[16] Nevertheless, regardless of these external influences, India will need to assess the costs and benefits of higher IP protection in these areas.

There may be reasons to believe that the economics of IP protection in relation to these new technologies may be different from that in the case of pharmaceuticals. In pharmaceuticals, the negative welfare impact arises from the likelihood that no real dynamic benefits will accrue to India to offset the static costs of a more monopolistic market structure resulting from higher IP protection. In principle there could be three dynamic benefits, which can be called the *knowwho, knowwhat,* and *knowwhere* benefits. Higher IP protection accorded *by* India could lead to increased research *by* Indian nationals (*knowwho*), *on* technologies or products of interest to India (*knowwhat*), or *in* India (*knowwhere*). Each of those variables creates benefits in terms of the higher profits accruing to India, the cheaper or increased variety of products, or the increased transfer of technology.

In pharmaceuticals there was reason to believe that the scope for inducing these benefits was small. By contrast, in agriculture there is greater scope for some if not all of these benefits to be realized. Pray and Ramaswami (2001) showed that sizable benefits result from private research in inputs, in the form of increased yields of maize, sorghum, and millet. Farmers received more than 80 percent of the benefits of increased yields. Much of this private research takes place in India, and although multinationals carry out most of the research, there is scope for indigenous involvement in this research capability. Thus, the dynamic benefits can be substantial. For sure, enhancing research in agriculture will require a multipronged approach, including greater public support and involvement (see Pray and Basant 2001), but the need for adequate proprietary protection should be considered more seriously.

On biotechnology, three points can be made, two relating to the IP aspect—namely, what level of IP protection should be accorded—which is distinct from that relating to the commercial *use* of products that have benefited from this technology. For India, biotechnology probably resembles pharmaceuticals more than agriculture in terms of the *knowwho* and *knowwhere* benefits. For the foreseeable future, serious research is likely to be undertaken by large foreign companies located outside India. The scope for the *knowwhat* benefits may be greater than in the case of pharmaceuticals because it is possible that protection by India could provide the incentives for greater research on genetically modified crops suited to Indian agroclimatic conditions. If such research is induced, the potential gains could be enormous. It could be the case that genetically modified technologies hold enormous promise for Indian agriculture and for alleviating rural poverty.[17] China and Argentina, and to a lesser extent Brazil, have become major users of these technologies. More work is therefore needed to ascertain the relevance of these dynamic benefits to India and hence to underpin policy positions relating to IP protection.

The second point relates to the consequences of firms being able to create technological protection as an alternative to legal protection.[18] (The terminator gene and the greater research in hybrids where second-generation seeds are genetically weak are examples of endogenously chosen technological protection.) The implication is that ultimately countries may not be able to influence the final market structure in cases involving such technologies. If legal protection is denied, firms may be able to secure it through technological means. Either way, creators of these technologies will have strong market power. In such a situation, countries may need to reevaluate their approach to IP protection. Legal IP protection could be moot or it could be merely the lesser of two or more evils if its absence leads to extra effort and cost in creating technological protection that will eventually be passed on to consumers and users of such technologies. Again, more research is necessary to understand the consequences of technological protection as an alternative to legal protection.

The third point refers to the commercial use of biotechnology. Concerns have been expressed in India as in the developed countries about the ethical, environmental, and safety risks associated with the new technologies. These concerns are very real and need to be addressed. Public policy choices will have to be made based on complex tradeoffs between economic benefits and noneconomic risks, where the benefits and risks may be subject to deep uncertainty and arouse strong emotions. For these choices to be made and command the public's trust and confidence, there must be strong and transparent domestic institutions that ensure that these technologies and the products derived from them are appropriately regulated and the risks minimized. Institutions must provide for public processes that promote reasoned debate and allow competing claims to be heard and assessed. Creating these institutions or strengthening existing ones will be a major challenge ahead.

There also may be an international challenge to the use of new technologies. Civil-society groups in industrial countries have mounted a serious and often successful campaign against the development of some new technologies. They have also managed to portray their causes as universally supported. It is possible that India assesses the tradeoff between economic benefit and noneconomic risk differently from the industrial countries so that India's interests may well lie in encouraging—subject to appropriate regulatory safeguards—rather than freezing these technologies. If that is the case, India and Indian civil society will have to engage in this debate internationally to ensure that their interests are adequately represented. Failure to do so may well lead to civil-society "imperialism" with costly consequences.

Harnessing India's Intellectual Property

Leading up to the December 1999 WTO Ministerial Meeting in Seattle, India made proposals in the WTO seeking international protection for two types of IP created in India: indigenous/traditional knowledge and genetic resources and geographical indications such as Darjeeling, Basmati, and so forth. These are very sensible and long overdue proposals, but a note of caution may be in order here. Although seeking protection of genetic resources and traditional knowledge is important, it is not clear at this stage how valuable in economic terms such protection will turn out to be, even if it can be feasibly implemented. This uncertainty should condition how much India is willing to give up in any future international negotiation to attain its goals in this area.

Genetic Resources and Indigenous Knowledge

India has advanced the notion of farmers' rights and their right to remuneration for the use of endoplasm, seeds, and other genetic material used by foreign companies in the pharmaceutical and biotechnology sectors (see Shiva 1993). In an ironic reversal of the rhetoric of the 1980s when developing countries were accused of piracy, it is now the industrial countries that stand accused of "biopiracy."

The Convention on Biological Diversity (CBD) makes a useful start in requiring registration systems that would identify and document the sources of genetic material and indigenous knowledge. This could provide the basis for the sharing of benefits from the use of such material and knowledge. The requirement in the CBD that those who use such material should obtain the prior informed consent of the country of origin of the material is also a useful step. One way of reconciling the TRIPS agreement and the CBD is for TRIPS to incorporate this obligation of prior informed consent as a condition for obtaining a patent that uses genetic resources.[19]

These, however, are just starting points. The goal in this area must be to devise a system of internationally recognized proprietary rights for genetic resources and indigenous knowledge. Such a system could represent a market-based response for international cooperation. Its logic would be to address a potential market failure in relation to the maintenance and creation of genetic resources and indigenous knowledge (see Cottier 1998, Sedjo 1992, and Subramanian 1992). To be sure, there are several unresolved issues relating to the feasible implementation of this idea and that is where India should devote greater time, energy, and research effort.

As a starting point, India and other developing countries must attempt to create *domestic* systems for the protection of traditional knowledge, including farmers' rights. India's efforts at pioneering legislation entailing registration of traditional knowledge and the establishment of a National Community Gene Fund are significant developments, although it is disappointing that the notion of farmers' rights (as opposed to farmers' privilege) does not feature prominently in the draft plant-variety law. If such systems can be shown to work domestically, that will strengthen India's case for seeking to replicate internationally. It is insufficient now to complain against biopiracy without simultaneously offering concrete suggestions for preventing it.

Implementing such a scheme will run into opposition from industrial countries. First, it will be argued that property rights cannot be accorded to things found in nature—this principle underpins patent systems all over the world. But the riposte must be that this legal principle does not always accord with the economic rationale for proprietary protection, which is to reward any effort whose fruits are ex post appropriable and hence subject to market failure. And the case for proprietary protection for traditional knowledge and genetic resources can be shown to be a response to this type of market failure. Second, there will be advocacy of the voluntary cooperation route, letting pharmaceutical companies enter into contracts with countries and communities that possess such resources, as in the case of Merck and Costa Rica. But voluntary cooperation, though welcome, cannot be guaranteed in all instances; moreover, the terms of such cooperation will necessarily be influenced by whether there are prior rights to such resources. If these rights are internationally recognized and infringements credibly punishable, the reward for maintaining the resources will be higher than it otherwise would be.

Geographical Indications

The EU is seeking extra protection for geographical indications originating in its territories, such as those relating to wines and spirits. India, as mentioned, has sought similar protection for names such as Basmati and Darjeeling. Here, too, the principle embraced by India is appropriate. The problem will be to demonstrate how such names, which have been in the public domain for years, can be restored to proprietary protection. The case of the patenting of Texmati in the United States also served to demonstrate how inadequately prepared India is and how weak its own case was in preventing the appropriation of Indian intellectual property. For example, because of divergence of interests domestically, India was unable to establish that Basmati was a valid geographical indication domestically. India needs to ensure that all potentially valuable geographical indications are registered and protected domestically, which could then serve as the basis for seeking higher protection for Indian indications along the lines foreseen in Article 23 of TRIPS.

Second-Order Issues

A number of other issues have generated a lot of controversy in India. In this section I will explain why they may be relatively unimportant and will suggest that scarce resources be more effectively deployed elsewhere.

Extension of the "Nonviolation" Exemption

Under TRIPS, IP matters can be subject to "nonviolation" complaints as of the year 2000. To understand what this means it is useful to recall that WTO dispute-settlement rules provide two avenues or bases for challenging partner-country actions (or claiming that there has been "nullification and impairment of benefits"). The first basis for a challenge is the partner country's breaching the rules of the WTO (the "violation" route). The second basis is a partner country's taking action that may lead to nullification and impairment even though a rule may not have been explicitly breached. Although somewhat arcane as a legal concept, the essential point to note is that the hurdles for successfully mounting nonviolation complaints are many and nearly insurmountable.[20]

Developing country fears on this issue stem from the perceived vulnerability of price controls and other drugs-related policies, which, although not in overt contravention of TRIPS rules, could be challenged for impairing the benefits under the agreement. A successful nonviolation complaint may be particularly difficult in TRIPS because IP rights are negative rights; that is, they are rights that allow action against infringement by third parties. IP rights themselves do not confer positive rights, such as the right to produce or market a product. To be sure, a price control dilutes the value of the monopoly but legally IP rights do not guarantee a monopoly. Hence, a price control, as long as it is implemented in a manner that ensures that other producers do not infringe the patent, cannot be seen as nullifying and impairing benefits. Of course, disallowing the nonviolation avenue as a source of complaints would provide a cast-iron guarantee for developing countries to preserve such domestic policy options as price controls. But if the reasoning described above is correct, the chances are not high that nonviolation complaints would ever seriously threaten important domestic policies. Hence, although it would be useful to foreclose this option, the value of such foreclosure may not be too great.

Transfer of Technology

India has expended a lot of effort over decades seeking international mechanisms for the transfer of technology. This is a laudable objective. But the experience of the last 20 years in international forums suggests that there has been some lack of clarity on how this is to be concretely achieved. For a long time, developing countries such as India were persuaded that the vehicle for attaining this objective was multilateral action on restrictive business practices and transfer-of-technology provisions. But it was always clear that those actions could in any case be taken by India domestically through its own competition laws. Specific answers to the following questions need to be provided before a cogent position on what we should seek internationally can be formulated: (1) what can international action do that India cannot do on its own to ensure the transfer of technology? and (2) what concrete actions of industrial-country governments that do not involve coercion of their private sector corporations or that are otherwise unrealistic will help achieve transfer of technology? It is possible that international cooperation can help in securing improved transfer of technology by addressing negative spillovers from industrial to developing country markets. Instances of such spillovers and the appropriate remedial action need to be clearly identified by India and placed on the negotiating agenda.[21]

Parallel Imports

The TRIPS agreement allows countries to choose whether to allow or disallow parallel imports (that is, imports that are put on the market in another country with the consent of the patent holder). At stake here is whether rights holders can prevent parallel imports and sustain price discrimination across markets or be forced into a uniform monopoly. India holds a very strong position on this issue, in favor of preserving the right to allow parallel imports. At first blush, that position appears to be paradoxical. First, theory would suggest that for a small market with a higher elasticity of demand, prices would be higher under a uniform monopoly than under a discriminating monopoly. India should therefore argue against parallel imports. Second, theory also suggests that it is the regime in the larger (industrial-country) market that determines whether price equalization or discrimination will prevail. Developing countries' regimes appear to be irrelevant in determining the final price outcome. Thus developing countries should not be arguing for *their* right to allow parallel imports but, paradoxically, should be arguing against the right of industrial countries to allow parallel imports. In this instance, notwithstanding their best efforts, the wishes of developing countries seem to have been granted (at least in the patent area) because of the workings of political economy in which industrial-country producer interests (against parallel imports in their market) have prevailed.

Standing against these theoretical arguments there seems to be the empirical perception that developing countries can find lower-cost sources of parallel imports (South Africa is a recent example). Given these contrasting considerations, it is difficult to have a strong view in either direction. On balance, therefore, India should probably not expend too much effort attempting to change or even resist pressures to change the status quo.

Compulsory Licensing for Nonworking

Recently, developing countries have been attempting to resurrect the right to grant compulsory licenses if patent owners do not "work" the patent (that is, produce the patented product) locally. India should resist raising this Lazarus from the dead for three reasons. First, from a systemic perspective it would not be an efficient allocative principle if all countries required that production be located in their jurisdiction: comparative advantage could not be reasonably exploited.

Second, in the area of pharmaceuticals where compulsory licenses are most frequently employed, a nonworking provision is either misguided or probably a noncredible threat. It is misguided because it assumes that a domestic monopoly is significantly better than an import monopoly. As an example let us say that in response to the threat of compulsory licensing for nonworking, a pharmaceutical company decides to locate in India to "work" the patent. The provision would have achieved its objective of securing working but without addressing the underlying problem of monopolization. Working is therefore not the objective to aim for, and especially not in the case of pharmaceuticals because technology transfer can be effected through imitation rather than requiring local production. On the other hand, where technologies cannot be easily imitated the threat of compulsory licensing is not credible: even if the patent owner refuses to comply with the provision, alternative sources of production may not be easy to find.

Finally, TRIPS disallows compulsory licensing on grounds of nonworking, and seeking to reverse this for little obvious gain could again represent an inefficient use of negotiating coinage.

Caveat to External Pressures

Although external pressures on India in the field of IP are going to be minimal, there is one caveat to this general presumption. This caveat relates to developments in WTO dispute settlement on IP. Ambiguity permeates the TRIPS agreement. It is up to the dispute-settlement process either to resolve this ambiguity or to entrust the task to the political (negotiating) process. There is increasing concern that the dispute-settlement process in the WTO may be tending toward judicial activism that may have ramifications for TRIPS and developing countries. India will therefore need to keep a watchful eye on how TRIPS provisions are interpreted. A few cases currently going through the dispute-settlement process will be particularly important to monitor. They relate to the ability of countries to facilitate quick entry of generics upon patent expiration (Canada versus EU) and to the protection that needs to be accorded to test data (Argentina versus the United States). If TRIPS rules are consistently interpreted to favor high IP protection, some offsetting political initiative may have to be mounted by India.

Domestic Inventive Activity: Whither India?

What scope is there for India to become a creator of knowledge and IP, and can IP protection help? These are very difficult questions to answer because they have multiple aspects relating not just to IP protection, but more importantly to science and technology policy, public sector involvement in research, education, climate for investment, openness, and so forth.

Figure 8.1 and table 8.1 shed some light on where India stands relative to other developing countries in terms of inventive activity and the evolution in such activity across time. The data capture patenting activity in the United States by selected developing countries, which should be a broadly appropriate gauge of underlying research and development activity. The three parts of table 8.1 clearly highlight the technological gap between industrial and developing countries, which is especially pronounced for the United States and Japan.

FIGURE 8.1 Data on Patenting in the United States for Selected Developing Countries, 1985–98

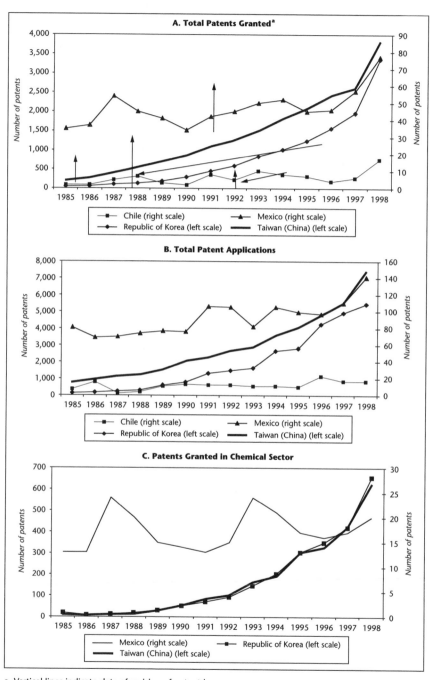

a. Vertical lines indicate date of revision of patent law.

Source: U.S. Patent and Trademark Office.

TABLE 8.1 Data on Patenting in the United States by Selected Countries, 1985–98

Economy	1985	1986	1987	1988	1989	1990	1991	1992	1993	1994	1995	1996	1997	1998
A. Total Patents Granted														
Brazil	30	27	35	37	39	45	66	43	59	61	70	69	67	88
Chile	2	2	5	7	3	2	8	5	10	8	7	4	6	17
China	1	11	23	48	52	48	52	41	53	48	63	48	66	89
Hong Kong (China)	66	111	91	104	134	151	209	159	182	220	248	247	261	372
India	11	18	12	14	15	23	24	24	30	28	38	37	48	94
Japan	13,351	13,864	17,294	16,989	21,106	20,743	22,402	23,164	23,411	23,517	22,871	24,059	24,191	32,119
Korea, Rep. of	50	55	105	126	183	290	449	586	830	1,008	1,240	1,567	1,965	3,362
Mexico	35	37	54	45	41	34	42	45	50	52	45	46	57	77
Taiwan (China)	199	269	411	536	688	861	1,096	1,253	1,510	1,814	2,087	2,419	2,597	3,805
United States	43,394	42,177	47,916	44,728	54,760	52,976	57,789	58,791	61,221	64,345	64,510	69,419	69,922	90,699
Total	77,273	77,041	89,598	84,439	102,690	99,219	106,842	107,511	109,890	113,704	113,955	121,806	124,146	163,206
B. Total Patent Applications														
Brazil	78	68	62	71	111	88	124	112	105	156	115	145	134	165
Chile	7	16	2	4	11	13	12	12	11	11	10	23	17	17
China	24	112	83	122	112	111	126	129	135	100	144	142	117	181
Hong Kong (China)	56	66	82	86	108	86	132	150	155	219	163	222	207	274
India	25	36	26	41	50	58	51	64	54	70	91	115	137	180
Japan	21,431	22,895	24,516	28,357	31,791	34,113	36,846	38,663	34,816	37,768	39,872	39,510	41,767	45,260
Korea, Rep. of	129	162	235	295	607	775	1,321	1,471	1,624	2,654	2,820	4,248	4,920	5,452
Mexico	81	69	70	74	77	76	106	105	82	105	99	97	110	141
Taiwan (China)	760	959	1,182	1,246	1,507	2,035	2,252	2,667	2,874	3,560	4,054	4,766	5,492	7,412
United States	63,874	65,487	68,315	75,192	70,380	73,915	76,351	80,650	74,788	82,624	88,419	88,295	94,812	107,579
Total	117,006	122,433	127,917	139,825	152,750	164,558	164,306	173,075	174,743	189,857	212,377	195,817	215,257	243,062

TABLE 8.1 *(Continued)*

Economy	1985	1986	1987	1988	1989	1990	1991	1992	1993	1994	1995	1996	1997	1998
C. Total Patents Granted in Chemical Sector														
Brazil	10	3	7	5	8	9	11	9	11	14	21	12	13	19
Chile	n.a.	n.a.	n.a.	n.a.	n.a.	n.a.	n.a.	n.a.	n.a.	n.a.	n.a.	n.a.	n.a.	n.a.
China	1	1	8	10	20	14	16	19	24	19	22	22	36	41
Hong Kong (China)	n.a.	n.a.	n.a.	n.a.	n.a.	n.a.	n.a.	n.a.	n.a.	n.a.	n.a.	n.a.	n.a.	n.a.
India	7	13	11	11	10	18	15	16	25	17	26	22	35	67
Japan	3,730	3,637	4,113	4,274	5,437	5,467	5,810	6,242	6,793	6,419	6,115	5,940	6,130	7,392
Korea, Rep. of	9	7	11	13	29	52	83	102	164	189	302	328	424	624
Mexico	13	13	24	20	15	14	13	15	24	21	17	16	17	20
Taiwan (China)	19	9	13	19	31	51	71	93	146	202	304	349	420	656
United States	11,520	10,496	11,374	11,204	13,782	13,075	14,107	15,424	16,048	15,401	15,185	16,446	18,338	21,537
Total	21,192	19,624	21,640	21,740	26,943	25,954	27,586	29,361	30,629	29,181	29,311	30,605	33,736	40,445

n.a. Not available.

Source: United States Patent and Trademark Office.

In comparison with other developing countries, India does not fare too badly. In 1998 it ranked fourth among all developing countries in terms of the number of patents obtained, behind the Republic of Korea, Taiwan (China), and Hong Kong (China)—the three leading nations—but ahead of Brazil, China, and Mexico. It is interesting that in the chemical sector—which accounts for the bulk of all patents—and in biotechnology—one of the cutting-edge sectors—India ranks fourth among developing countries. Moreover, in biotechnology, the gap between India and countries ahead of it is not large.

Perhaps, a more interesting issue from India's perspective is the experience of other developing countries that have strengthened their IP protection over the last decade. Figure 8.1 depicts the patenting activity of four developing countries— Chile, Korea, Mexico, and Taiwan—that undertook revisions to their patent legislation over the last 10 to 15 years. Panels A and B refer, respectively, to patent grants and applications, and Panel C depicts patents granted in the chemical sector.[22] The panels illustrate that, although Korea and Taiwan, China, witnessed a surge in patenting after their IP regimes had been strengthened (registering 20-fold and 30-fold increases since the mid-1980s), no such effect was discernible in Mexico or Chile, which continue to be characterized by a very low level of inventive activity.

Clearly, therefore, strengthening IP protection does not appear to be a sufficient condition for increased inventive activity. But is India more likely to fall into the pattern set by Korea and Taiwan, China, or that set by Mexico and Chile? Like the former group India has a diversified industrial and technological base, a well-educated and highly skilled workforce (at least in selected sectors), and some core-research capability. Looking ahead, it is possible that the strengthening of India's patent laws will lead to developments that resemble more closely those of Korea and Taiwan, China, than those of Mexico and Chile.[23] Realizing this objective will require a more concerted policy effort that goes beyond IP protection, but with the right set of policies there may be grounds for guarded optimism.

Conclusion

Although external pressure to change intellectual property regimes has abated, India faces other challenges—as a net user, potential net creator, and net creator of knowledge and intellectual property. The challenges are unique in each area. As a net user, an important challenge is to mitigate the most egregious impacts of the TRIPS agreement, particularly in the case of pharmaceuticals. Compulsory licensing and competition policy offer the most promising avenues for meeting the challenge, and India needs to implement them expeditiously and render them effective in the near future. As a net user India can use its TRIPS obligations to enforce its market-access rights in the WTO. Accordingly, consideration should be given to revising the draft IP legislation to allow for retaliation in TRIPS for failure by trading partners to adhere to their market-access commitments affecting India.

On the new technologies, particularly in agriculture, India must identify its location on the technology spectrum. There is some evidence that it could be a potential net creator of IP. Based on such an assessment, IP rights legislation should be designed appropriately. At the same time, strengthening complementary regulatory institutions would allow the benefits of new technologies to be harnessed while minimizing attendant risks.

As a net creator of technology (in the area of genetic resources, traditional knowledge, and geographical indications), the challenge is to establish workable domestic systems for protecting such technology. Those systems could then serve as the basis for seeking their protection internationally.

Finally, the recent experience of developing countries that share India's knowledge-generation characteristics suggests that India should not be overly pessimistic about its potential to move up the knowledge spectrum even in areas, such as pharmaceuticals and chemicals, where it is currently a net user of intellectual property.

Endnotes

1. See Subramanian (1994, 1995) and Watal (1998) for illustrative estimates of the magnitude of these welfare costs.

2. This section draws heavily on Subramanian and Watal (2000).

3. A lucid theoretical demonstration of this proposition is presented in Deardorff (1992). Watal (2000b) placed maximum annual welfare losses in India from pharmaceutical patents alone at around US$140 million. See also Subramanian (1995).

4. It should be noted that in the context of retaliation, which will be isolated instances of, rather than systematic, dilution of IP protection, the question of the dynamic effects—of innovation and R&D generation—will not arise. Reducing IP protection will therefore confer the static benefits without leading to any dynamic efficiency losses.

5. I am grateful to Aaditya Mattoo for alerting me to this potential problem.

6. Paradoxically, in the Uruguay Round it was India that was in the forefront arguing against cross-retaliation as a "safeguard," fearing that it would be used to enforce obligations on TRIPS and GATS. These "safeguards" are, of course, counterproductive to their interests. India was unable to see a key characteristic of an asymmetric system: that compliance by the weak cannot be avoided, with or without retaliation, but that rules and effective retaliation may be necessary to ensure compliance by the strong. It was therefore not recognized that (1) industrial countries would not need to go as far as cross-retaliation in goods for securing compliance by developing countries in TRIPS, and (2) developing countries had potential power through cross-retaliation in the very TRIPS obligations that many of these countries perceived to be burdensome.

7. Most bilateral investment treaties require that intangible assets, such as IP, be protected in accordance with national law. As long as national law also specifies clearly the circumstances under

which IP protection can be modified, these treaties would not be affected by the proposal on retaliation.

8. TRIPS as retaliation offers one tantalizing possibility. Although India should use retaliation in a manner that is strictly compatible with WTO rules, India could also choose to emulate the infamous "Section 301" of the U.S. trade law and enlarge the scope of such retaliation to cover other situations of potential detriment to it. Just as Section 301 prior to the Uruguay Round was wielded to cover IP rights that were then beyond the scope of world trading rules, India could provide for retaliation if partner countries sought to impose excessive labor or environmental standards that are currently outside WTO rules. A difficult question is whether it is in India's or the system's interest to counter vigilantism with its own image.

9. The only basis on which compulsory licenses cannot be granted is nonworking of the patent locally, as discussed above.

10. Of course, competition policies should be motivated by the wider concern of making markets competitive.

11. Although India's patent laws have provided for compulsory licensing, no serious need to use it ever arose because of the level of IP protection.

12. This section draws heavily on Subramanian (2001).

13. As long as the number of AIDS sufferers in Africa exceeds those in the countries that could be sources of supply for cheap drugs, Article 31 (f) of TRIPS will be restrictive.

14. The cooperation of the international community in facilitating supply by the Indian company may need to go even further. For example, drugs manufactured in third countries will need to obtain regulatory approval either in the country of production (under compulsory license) or by other countries or the WHO.

15. In discussions of differential pricing, legitimate concerns are expressed by the pharmaceutical companies about the leakage of "parallel goods" into rich-country markets, undermining patent protection there. However, it should be noted that this threat existed in a more serious form in a pre-TRIPS world and was dealt with rather successfully. As long as rich-country markets have good enforcement capability the leakage problem need not be serious. The arrival of the Internet and the attendant increase in Internet-based sales, of course, make national enforcement more difficult, underlining the need for greater cooperation among countries.

16. Although Europe has formally closed this exemption, the situation has become muddied because of the decision of the Netherlands, which voted against the European Directive, to challenge the directive in the European Court of Justice (see Watal 2000a).

17. It was recently announced that genetically modified rice could help reduce iron-deficiency anemia or vitamin A deficiency.

18. Although MONSANTO has recently announced a policy that the terminator technology would not be further developed, this issue of technological protection is not likely to disappear.

19. Alternatively, as proposed by Watal (2000), the obligation of prior informed consent can be imposed before commercialization of the patent.

20. In the entire history of the General Agreement on Tariffs and Trade/WTO, there have been only 8 nonviolation complaints (out of a total of more than 300 complaints) and none has been successful. The recent U.S. complaint against Japan's domestic distribution system was dismissed by a WTO panel.

21. For example, abuses of IP rights in foreign markets (through patent pooling or acquisition of other rights) can inflict welfare losses on developing countries. These abuses could be more effectively addressed at their source than at their destination, requiring the cooperation of the large countries. This cooperation can then be embodied in multilateral rules.

22. It is interesting to look at the chemical sector because IP protection has been shown to have a more significant impact on research and development activity in this sector than in others.

23. Lanjouw (1997) cites cases of increased research and development activity in the Indian pharmaceutical and chemical sectors.

References

Cottier, Thomas. 1998. "The Protection of Genetic Resources and Traditional Knowledge: Toward More Specific Rights and Obligations in World Trade Law." *Journal of International Economic Law* 1:555–84.

Deardorff, Alan. 1992. "Welfare Effects of Global Patent Protection." *Economica* 59:35–51.

Lanjouw, Jean. 1997. "The Introduction of Pharmaceutical Product Patents In India: Heartless Exploitation of the Poor and Suffering?" Working Paper 6366. National Bureau of Economic Research, Cambridge, Mass.

Pray, C. E., and R. Basant. 2001. "Agricultural Research and Technology Transfer by the Private Sector in India." In Carl E. Pray and Keith O. Fuglie, *Private Investments in Agricultural Research and International Technology Transfer in Asia.* ERS Agricultural Economics Report 805 (November).

Pray, C. E., and B. Ramaswami. 2001. "Technology, IPRs, and Reform Options: Case Study of the Seed Industry with Implications for Other Input Industries." *International Food and Agricultural Marketing Review* 2(Special Issue):407–20.

Shiva, Vardana. 1993. "Farmers' Rights, Biodiversity, and International Treaties." *Economic and Political Weekly* (April 3).

Subramanian, Arvind. 1992. "Genetic Resources, Biodiversity, and Environmental Protection: An Analysis and Proposals towards a Solution." *Journal of World Trade* 26:105–09.

———. 1994. "Putting Some Numbers on the TRIPS Pharmaceutical Debate." *International Journal of Technology Management* 2:252–68.

———. 1995. "Trade-Related Intellectual Property Rights and Asian Developing Countries: An Analytical View." In A. Panagariya, M. G. Quibria, and N. Rao, eds., *The Global Trading System and Developing Asia.* Cambridge, U.K.: Cambridge University Press.

———. 2001. "The AIDS Crisis, Differential Pricing of Drugs, and the TRIPS Agreement: Two Proposals." *Journal of World Intellectual Property* 4:323–36.

Subramanian, Arvind, and Jayashree Watal. 2000. "TRIPS as an Enforcement Device for Developing Countries in the WTO." *Journal of International Economic Law* 3:403–16.

Watal, Jayashree. 1998. "The TRIPS Agreement and Developing Countries—Strong, Weak or Balanced Protection." *Journal of World Intellectual Property* 1:281–307.

———. 2000a. *Intellectual Property Rights in the World Trade Organization: The Way Forward for Developing Countries.* Oxford, U.K.: Oxford University Press.

———. 2000b. "Pharmaceutical Patents, Prices and Welfare Losses: A Simulation Study of Policy Options for India under the WTO TRIPS Agreement." *The World Economy* 23:733–52.

9

TRADE, INVESTMENT, AND COMPETITION POLICY: AN INDIAN PERSPECTIVE

Aditya Bhattacharjea

Although the relationship between international trade and competition policy has been discussed in India for several years, two developments recently have given it a new focus: the passage of a new competition law and the likelihood of negotiations to bring aspects of competition policy into the World Trade Organization (WTO) framework after the Fifth Ministerial Conference (Cancun) in late 2003, despite India's strenuous opposition to such negotiations. A brief recapitulation of how these developments came about is necessary to provide the background to this chapter.

The issue of trade, investment, and competition policy first came into prominence in 1996 when the WTO Ministerial Conference (Singapore) resolved to set up two working groups—one "to examine the relationship between trade and investment" and the other "to study issues raised by members relating to the interaction between trade and competition policy, including anticompetitive practices" (WTO 1996, para. 20).[1] Expert groups on these subjects were set up by the Government of India shortly thereafter, followed by the establishment of another high-powered committee to suggest changes in Indian competition law and policy in light of the changed environment consequent to India's economic reforms and the WTO regime. A new competition bill, designed to replace the Monopolies and Restrictive Trade Practices (MRTP) Act of 1969, was tabled in the Indian parliament in August 2001, studied by a parliamentary standing committee for a year, and finally passed with several amendments in December 2002. At the time this chapter was last revised (March 2003), however, the government had not yet issued the official notification that would bring the new Competition Act into force.

Government statements indicate that for the first year of its life, the new Competition Commission (which is still to be appointed) will undertake purely educational activities and the various sections of the Competition Act will be brought into effect thereafter in phases.

With many other developing countries at the Doha Ministerial Conference in 2001, India insisted that the "Singapore issues" still required further study and could not be taken up for negotiation until developing countries' concerns about the implementation of existing agreements were addressed (WTO 2001). Ultimately a compromise was worked out: negotiations on both investment and competition will take place only after the Fifth Ministerial Conference in 2003, with modalities to be decided by explicit consensus. In almost identical paragraphs on the two issues, the Doha declaration recognized the needs of developing countries for enhanced support for technical assistance and capacity building, and set out separate agendas for continuing study by the working groups.

The Working Group on Competition Policy, which is my main concern, has so far submitted six annual reports. Following the unusual wording of its mandate, however, it has confined itself to reporting the very different opinions of member countries on various issues, with many of the same conflicting arguments being repeated from one report to the next. India and many other developing countries have emphasized the need to respect their diversity in terms of stages of development, socioeconomic circumstances, legal frameworks, and cultural norms. They have drawn attention to the dangers of transplanting a system that has evolved over many years in industrial countries into economies lacking in experience, expertise, and institutional memory. Virtually every specific proposal has met with opposition at the working group, including a proposal to extend the fundamental WTO principle of nondiscrimination to competition policy. Consensus seems to be emerging only with respect to the need to control international cartels, to enhance voluntary cooperation among national authorities, and to provide technical assistance for developing countries. There is considerable disagreement, however, on whether even such limited measures should be under the aegis of the WTO.[2]

Irreconcilable differences have emerged more recently on the interpretation of the decision at Doha. The European Union (EU), which has been the major proponent of the Singapore issues, claims that the Doha declaration commits all members to negotiations, with consensus required only on "modalities"; India maintains that negotiations cannot proceed without such a consensus, which it is not prepared to join. As of early 2003, the state of play at the WTO suggests that any agreement will be limited to enshrining only a few key principles in the national competition laws of members, with provisions for special and differential treatment for developing countries, and possibly a framework for voluntary international cooperation in investigations.

Both the precise shape of India's new competition regime and the fate of competition policy negotiations at the WTO are thus undecided at the time of writing. Even if no WTO agreement finally emerges, however, competition policy in India must now operate in an economy that is far more open to international trade and investment than it was in 1969 when the MRTP Act was passed. To contribute to this ongoing discussion, this chapter draws on the lessons of India's trade and industrial reforms, particularly its less-than-satisfactory experience with competition policy, together with insights from the theoretical literature on trade and industrial policies under imperfect competition. I will be concerned here mainly with trade and competition policy and only tangentially with trade and investment in the course of discussing mergers and entry policy. I do not intend to go into competition policy issues arising from the agreements on government procurement and trade-related aspects of intellectual property rights (TRIPS), which have been ably dealt with by Srivastava and Subramanian in this volume. After a review of certain background issues in the next section of this chapter, the third section reviews the important changes in India's trade, investment, and competition policies, with particular emphasis on the country's experience with the MRTP Act. The fourth section then undertakes a compressed survey of the relevant theoretical literature and uses it to evaluate the Indian economic reforms. The fifth section examines the road ahead. This involves an assessment of the new Competition Act, followed by suggestions for what our priorities should be in preparation for the next ministerial conference and in any negotiations thereafter. The final section concludes the discussion.

Background

In this section I review in an extremely compressed manner the existing international agreements on competition policy, the recent literature on trade and competition, and Indian official positions on the subject.

International Agreements on Competition Policy

At present no multilateral agreement exists. A "Set of Multilaterally Agreed Equitable Principles and Rules for the Control of Restrictive Business Practices" was agreed at the United Nations Conference on Trade and Development (UNCTAD) in 1980 and is reviewed periodically, but it remains nonbinding and unenforceable. International cooperation in competition policy takes the form of bilateral, regional, or sectoral arrangements. The EU and the United States have adopted a policy of "positive comity" in investigating each other's complaints of anticompetitive conduct by firms in their jurisdiction against the interests of parties in the other jurisdiction. Competition policy clauses, which require various degrees of consultation, coordination, and harmonization, figure in several regional agreements, notably the North American Free Trade Agreement, the Andean Common Market, and one between Australia and New Zealand. The process has gone furthest in the EU, which now also requires countries in Central and Eastern Europe to conform entirely to its competition principles as one of the preconditions for accession. Less rigid templates for a wider multilateral agreement involving developing countries could include the 1998 Panama communiqué signed by the United States, Canada, and nine developing countries in the Western Hemisphere, affirming their intention to cooperate in dealing with cartels; or Article IX of the General Agreement on Trade in Services (GATS), which deals with restrictive business practices but requires only "full and sympathetic consideration" of requests by other members for consultations, and with supply of "publicly available non-confidential information."

A Review of the International Literature

Turning to the recent literature on the relationship between trade and competition policies, three main themes stand out.[3] The first theme is the complementarity or substitutability between trade liberalization and competition policy. Trade restrictions facilitate anticompetitive conduct by providing a focal point or "facilitating practice" for collusive behavior between foreign and domestic firms in the home market. Supposedly they also enable domestic firms to engage in predatory pricing by selling exports at less than cost, cross-subsidized by profits earned in protected home markets. Anticompetitive practices can in turn limit the benefits of trade liberalization. For example, export cartels, which are exempted by the competition law of most countries, can adversely affect importing countries, whereas import cartels and exclusionary vertical arrangements in distribution can be used to deny market access to foreign suppliers, even after trade barriers are dismantled.

These arguments suggest that trade liberalization and competition policy are complementary, but they may also be substitutes in some respects. Exposure to import competition has long been seen as a means of imposing "market discipline" on domestic producers of tradable products, forcing them to price competitively even if domestic competition policy is absent or ineffective. Conversely, competition policy may be a superior substitute for trade policy in the specific case of antidumping measures, which have been used increasingly in place of other protectionist policies that were outlawed or sharply circumscribed after the Uruguay Round. Several scholars have suggested that rules against predatory pricing could be less susceptible to misuse, although, as I show below, that has not been the case in India.

The second theme that figures in the literature relates to changes in the structure and conduct of international business. Foreign monopolization, concentration, and collusion are matters of growing concern because of stronger patent protection under the TRIPS agreement, a wave of mega-mergers with cross-border spillovers on competition, and a trend toward pooling and cross-licensing of patents, with many technology licensing agreements featuring restrictions on licensing, pricing, or exporting to third-country markets. Competition policy authorities in the EU and the United States also have uncovered evidence of price-fixing and international market sharing by large firms, notably in recent cases involving vitamins and steel tubes.

Third, various arguments have been made in favor of international action on competition policy. National authorities would have very different assessments of international cartels or of the balance of positive and negative effects of a merger, depending on how producers and consumers are distributed across countries. The actions of foreign firms are difficult to regulate through the extraterritorial application of national competition laws, especially in developing countries where such laws and their domestic enforcement are weak or nonexistent. Even if national laws are applicable, international cooperation is required for carrying out investigations in foreign countries. It is also argued that competitive relaxation of competition policy by different countries in order to attract foreign investment might encourage a "race to the bottom," as allegedly can happen in the case of environmental policies. All these reasons make a case for international action, ranging from consultation, technical assistance, sharing of confidential information, and coordinated investigations by national authorities at one extreme, through harmonization of national competition laws, to an international agreement on what are sometimes referred to as TRAMs (trade-related antitrust measures), to establishment of a supranational authority to enforce such measures at the other extreme. An international competition policy is seen to benefit developing countries, especially in curbing antidumping actions against their exports and (more speculatively) in restraining collusive behavior by foreign suppliers.

Official Indian Perspectives

Official Indian documents on trade and competition policy articulate several contradictory positions, which have little to do with the issues discussed above. The stand of the two Indian committees on the subject was that more vigorous competition is always a goal worth pursuing. The first committee (Government of India, 1999; hereafter referred to as the Chakravarthy committee) boldly declared that *"COMPETITION SHOULD INFORM ALL TRADE AND MARKET POLICIES"* (para. 2.7.5, double emphasis in the original). However, it also argued for competition policy to "inhere a development dimension," which it does not define. It further calls for competition policy to safeguard the "public interest," which it defines as follows:

> Consumer interest and public interest *are not necessarily mutually exclusive social goals.* While public interest will take into account *efficiency facets* like cost minimisation, profit maximisation, optimal use of resources, etc., consumer interest will emphasise equity facets like free competition in the market, but these are not necessarily antithetical. [para. 1.4.12; emphasis in the original]

Insofar as any meaning can be discerned in that statement, it seems to see the public interest being served by bringing about the conditions under which the First Theorem of Welfare Economics holds (although it mixes up the theorem's assumptions and conclusions), without any regard to second-best issues, not to mention well-known alternative perspectives that see a tradeoff between market power and economies of scale or dynamic benefits from innovation. Its conflation of consumer interests with equity and "free competition" is equally incomprehensible.

The second committee (Government of India, 2000) followed a similar course in seeking to establish conditions for free entry everywhere, extending its mandate to recommend abolition of import restrictions and product reservations for small-scale industries and the public sector. It presents a mixed bag, with some paragraphs betraying the same Olympian emphasis on balancing "public interest" against "consumer interest," and others that are much more incisive and show considerable awareness of both recent economic theory and regulatory practice in other countries. It is no more helpful than the Chakravarthy committee, however, in defining the public interest as "something in which society as a whole has some interest, not fully captured by a competitive market. It is an externality" (para. 3.2.0).

An Indian submission to the WTO Working Group on Competition Policy in 2001, like the Chakravarthy committee a year earlier, seemed to visualize the goal of competition policy as bringing about conditions for the first-best welfare optimum, but questions this objective on the grounds that these gains from allocative efficiency are once-and-for-all in nature. Developing countries instead seek dynamic gains from total factor productivity growth. The gains from international trade, although potentially beneficial, had been cornered by those countries that used "beggar thy neighbor" industrial policies unrestrained by competition policy—notably Japan. The submission also expresses skepticism about developing countries' ability to make use of positive comity or even information-sharing arrangements, given their lack of experience with competition policy (WTO 2000). In a subsequent submission to the working group, India has asserted the need to take action against mergers and cartels involving foreign firms, while supporting an East Asian–style industrial policy of promoting "national champions" to take on multinationals, and permitting mergers and rationalization cartels that would allow orderly restructuring in the face of trade liberalization. This action would violate the core WTO principle of national treatment, against which the Indian submission argues strongly in the context of competition policy (WTO 2002a). On the other hand, the Competition Act that was passed just a few months later made cartels a violation per se, and contained no provisions for discrimination between domestic and foreign firms.

Yet another perspective is that of the official competition agency under the MRTP Act, the Monopolies and Restrictive Trade Practices Commission, which in a number of recent judgments identified the "public interest" as protecting the interest of workers and investors in Indian firms threatened by foreign competition, and stated that this "public interest" should prevail over consumer interests.[4]

In all these conflicting descriptions of the "public interest," there seems to be no recognition that there is a standard measurement of social welfare in economics—that is, the sum of consumer surplus and producer surplus—which is widely used to reconcile conflicting interests, especially in analyses of trade and competition policy. Because this is blind to distributional issues, many critics of reform dismiss it, although I will show in the next section that applying this criterion to competition policy actually calls into question the way in which reforms have been going. I state my position on national treatment in the fifth section of the chapter, and return to distributional considerations and the public interest at the very end.

Indian Experience

I now turn to a discussion of India's experience with investment and competition policy.

Foreign and Domestic Entry

Doing away with restrictions on entry has arguably been the oldest and most far-reaching aspect of India's economic reforms. Years before privatization, financial sector liberalization, or a more accommodating policy toward foreign investment became even a remote possibility, reform of entry restrictions began in the mid-1980s with gradual relaxation of the extensive and dysfunctional system of investment licensing that had been in force since the 1950s. This system required government approval for establishing a new unit, expanding an existing unit, diversifying into new products, and relocating a plant. Controlling the concentration of economic power (in the form of interconnected firms under the common control of a business group) and abuse of market dominance were among the system's ostensible objectives. But in practice the licensing system clearly served as a barrier to new entrants and reinforced the very industrial concentration it was supposed to inhibit, because large business groups engaged in preemptive acquisition of licenses as an entry-deterring strategy. To oblige different business groups and regional politicians, licensed capacity was fragmented and distributed in noneconomical sizes.[5] The 1969 MRTP Act reinforced this by requiring an additional layer of investment approvals for firms that were either "large" (in the sense of belonging to a group whose assets exceeded a certain threshold), or "dominant" (in the sense of commanding a market share in excess of one-fourth). With expansion of their individual firms thwarted by the licensing regime, the groups often engaged in conglomerate overdiversification, or set up nominally independent rival firms in the same industry. We will see that this has a bearing on recent merger trends.

Early reform measures in the 1980s included automatic endorsement of capacity installed in excess of the licensed amount; delicensing of 25 industries; and "broadbanding," or allowing flexibility of product mix within a capacity limit, for other industries. The threshold defining "large" undertakings under the 1969 MRTP Act was quintupled in 1984, which removed a large number of firms from the further investment approvals required by the act. In 1991 this liberalization of entry restrictions accelerated dramatically in several ways. First, all but 18 industries were removed from the purview of capacity licensing (this list was further reduced in stages, to 6 at present). Second, the additional approvals required of large or dominant firms under the MRTP Act were abolished altogether. Third, the number of areas reserved for the public sector was sharply reduced (from 18 to 8 in 1991 and to 3 now). Fourth, controls on issues of equity capital were considerably relaxed.

Restrictions on foreign direct investment (FDI) were also reduced substantially. Under the Foreign Exchange Regulation Act (FERA) of 1973, foreign firms had been restricted to an equity stake no greater than 40 percent, except in technology-intensive or export-oriented activities. The 1991 reforms allowed for automatic approval of proposals involving up to 51 percent foreign equity in 48 industries, and provided lists of designated priority industries in which up to 74 percent or 100 percent foreign equity would be granted automatic approval. These industry lists have been expanded progressively so that only agriculture, mining, petroleum refining, and a few service sectors are now subject to equity caps. Even FDI proposals involving higher foreign shareholding can be approved on a case-by-case basis by the interministerial Foreign Investment Promotion Board.

Major obstacles to private investment remain in the reservation of almost 800 items for a conservatively defined "small-scale" sector.[6] Entry is also hampered at the level of state (provincial) authorities who must be approached for water and power connections, land acquisition, and environmental clearance. FDI is still restricted in sectors under industrial licensing and in sectors where the foreign party already has a joint venture. There is no doubt, however, that policy-created barriers to entry have been lowered significantly.

Trade liberalization, also relevant to the competitive environment, has proceeded more slowly. Because Chapter 2 of this volume provides a detailed summary, I will be brief here. Import licensing for intermediate and capital goods was gradually dismantled during the 1980s, but sharp increases in tariffs in the late 1980s and a substantial real depreciation of the rupee between 1985 and 1993 blunted import competition. Tariff reductions were phased in gradually, with Indian tariff levels even now remaining higher than in most developing countries. In the late 1990s special additional duties and a surcharge resulted in a slight reversal of the downward trend in average tariffs (although the surcharge was revoked in 2001). Furthermore, as Chadha and coauthors noted in Chapter 2, the persisting high tariff and nontariff barriers on imports of consumer goods actually raised the effective protection of their domestic market as tariffs on inputs were brought down. Stringent quantitative restrictions on the import of almost all consumer goods were selectively relaxed only in recent years, and abolished in 2001, after India lost its case for retaining quantitative restrictions on balance-of-payments grounds. Most manufactured consumer goods imports remain subjected to a tariff rate of 25 percent. Much higher rates are applied in highly oligopolistic sectors such as wines and spirits (166 percent) and automobiles (61 percent for new cars; 105 percent for second-hand vehicles; and 26 percent for completely knocked down kits—giving very high effective protection to assembly operations). This poses competition policy issues that do not seem to be getting recognized, and to which I return below.

Competition Policy

In this section I will examine the working of the MRTP Act, and in the following section the provisions of the new Competition Act. This two-pronged approach is necessary because the chapter is being revised on the cusp of the old and new regimes and because the new Competition Commission will probably inherit the investigative staff and possibly some of the members of the present MRTP Commission, and therefore many of its perspectives. In any case the new act provides that competition cases initiated under the MRTP Act will continue to be adjudicated under its provisions by the new commission, and in appeals to the Indian Supreme Court.

The MRTP Act covered a wide range of anticompetitive practices and provided for fines for violation of its provisions, and criminal penalties for noncompliance with Commission orders. It armed the designated agency—the Director-General of Investigation and Registration—with extensive investigative powers and provided for a statutory MRTP Commission to decide cases. Of particular significance to the interface with international trade, Section 14 of the Act provided for orders against "any party to such practice [who] does not carry on business in India...with respect to that part of the practice which is carried on in India." This provision is similar to the "effects" doctrine followed in Europe and the United States, whereby foreign firms can be prosecuted for violations of competition law that have adverse effects in the domestic jurisdiction. However, as I show below, a recent judgment of the Indian Supreme Court has severely qualified this power, holding that the MRTP Act has no extraterritorial application. Section 15 prevented the commission from passing orders with respect to monopolistic or restrictive trade practices that restrict "the right of any person to export goods from India, to the extent to which the...practice relates exclusively to...such export"; this too is similar to exceptions made in other countries. I take up three policy issues for detailed discussion, with special attention to their international dimension: mergers (which were dealt with in Chapter III of the MRTP Act, under the rubric of "Concentration of Economic Power"), cartels, and predatory pricing (both of which figured among the "restrictive trade practices" of Chapter V.A of the act).[7]

Concentration of Economic Power   Several sections of Chapter III were deleted when the act was amended at the outset of the reforms in 1991 to remove the additional investment approval required of "large" and/or "dominant" firms. Among these was Section 23, which required government approval of mergers, amalgamations, and takeovers involving such firms. The Securities and Exchange Board of India also regulates "substantial acquisition of shares and takeovers," but again mergers are explicitly excluded as are substantial acquisitions approved by a majority of the shareholders of the target firm. These provisions regulate the market for corporate control, but not through the prism of market power.

In 1994 the Indian Supreme Court put its imprimatur on the situation resulting from the 1991 amendment. A merger of the multinational firm Hindustan Lever Ltd. (HLL) with the Indian firm TOMCO, both significant players in the market for soaps and detergents, was challenged on various grounds by the HLL employees' union. The issue that concerns us here is that the provisions of the MRTP Act had not been adhered to, and the commission had erred in refusing to grant an interim injunction against the merger. The Supreme Court ruled that after the 1991 amendment deleted the relevant section of the Act, no government approval was required because no other provision of the act could be construed to require such approval. The merger could be questioned only if it was not carried out in accordance with the provisions of the Companies Act, or involved fraud or illegality. Beyond the provisions of the MRTP Act, the plaintiffs also argued that the merger would result in a large share of the market being controlled by a multinational company, and that consumer interests might be adversely affected. On these grounds they sought to invoke the "public interest," which in recent years the Court had used to provide an expansive interpretation of fundamental rights in areas such as environmental law. In the present case, however, the Court held that the merger could not be stopped on the grounds that it violated public interest or public policy. The majority judgment held that the MRTP and FERA amendments were specifically intended to allow foreign firms to do business in India more easily, and "what has been expressly authorised by the statute cannot be struck down as being against the public policy." Consumer interests could be taken into consideration only after the fact: "As a result of the amalgamation, if it is found that the working of the Company is being conducted in such a way which brings it within the mischief of the MRTP Act, it would be open to the authority under the MRTP Act to go into it and decide the controversy as it thinks fit."[8] The problem with this legally unexceptionable position is that the residual Section 27 (which survived the 1991 amendment of the act's Chapter III on concentration of economic power and allowed the government to order division of an undertaking or severance of interconnections between undertakings) had never been used.[9] And as will be noted below, important sections dealing with the abuse of dominance were limited in their effectiveness.

After the 1991 amendment and 1994 judgment, merger control—a subject of both lively debate and serious enforcement in industrial countries—presented an egregious gap in Indian competition law and economic analysis, even as the reality changed dramatically. By far the most comprehensive database on mergers in India has been compiled by Agarwal (2002). Figure 9.1 identifies three phases based on the annual intensity of merger activity, such that the highest number of mergers in a year in one phase is lower than the lowest number in the immediately succeeding phase. A high level of merger activity has continued in 2001 and 2002 ("The ET-CMIE M&As Survey" 2003).

Recent research on this subject can be summarized as follows. Figure 9.1 suggests that the legislative changes (both delicensing and MRTP amendments) of 1984/85 and 1991 reviewed above had a distinct impact on the frequency of mergers, with a lag that can be attributed to the time required for negotiating the merger and getting through the legal process. Using both industry and firm-level data, Agarwal (2002) found econometrically that capacity utilization was significantly positively related to merger activity, which indicated that mergers were undertaken for expansionary motives. Almost all investigators found that most mergers have been horizontal. In the initial years after the 1991 amendment,

FIGURE 9.1 Distribution of Merger Activity, 1973–74 to 2000–01

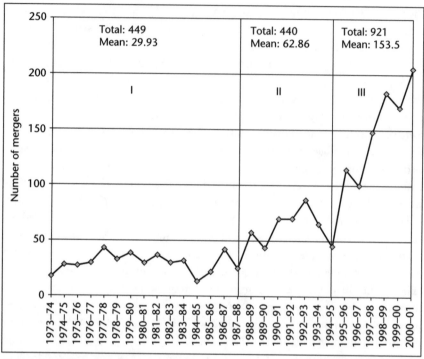

Source: Agarwal 2002.

mergers usually involved consolidation of companies by Indian business groups striving to undo the fragmentation of the licensing era. Foreign firms have been especially active since 1996, although more through acquisitions (not included in figure 9.1) than through outright mergers (Basant 2000; Beena 2003). Their participation is especially marked in branded consumer goods (most of which were on the negative list for imports until 2001), in services (notably financial, advertising, and travel), and in pharmaceuticals. This is often a consequence of the merger of their parent firms, or (as documented in the UNCTAD's 1997 *World Investment Report*) as part of a new trend in developing countries whereby multinational corporations (MNCs) prefer entry through merger rather than "greenfield" investment in new capacity. A parallel trend, especially in automobiles and household appliances, has involved MNCs entering into joint ventures with established Indian business groups and then buying out the domestic groups' stake when they are unable to come up with the financial resources for expansion plans. Both strategies give an MNC rapid access to complementary country-specific assets that it lacks, especially market knowledge, distribution networks, and contacts in government.

MNC acquisitions often have involved financially weak or loss-making Indian firms, or the spin-off of firms from an overdiversified Indian business group. Khanna (1999) attributed the vulnerability of Indian companies and partners to the mismanaged financial sector reforms in the early years of liberalization, which resulted in both banks and individual investors burning their fingers and a subsequent drying up of both debt and equity markets. Poor macroeconomic management and the consequently higher cost of capital also were significant (Basant and Morris 2000). Kumar (2000) argued persuasively that such mergers have adverse consequences for capital formation, the balance of payments, technology transfer, and competition.

On this last issue, market share data compiled from company annual reports by the Centre for Monitoring Indian Economy (CMIE 1999) showed that HLL's market share in soaps rose from 19.7 percent in 1992/93 (the year before the merger with TOMCO) to 26 percent in 1997/98; in synthetic detergents and scouring agents it rose from 33.1 percent to 46.7 percent, although CMIE (2001) indicated that it has dipped in recent years. Market research data (Naidu 2000) put its share of toilet soaps and shampoos at over 60 percent and detergent bars at 45 percent. Other mergers and acquisitions have given HLL market shares of 60 percent in talcum powder, 70 percent in color cosmetics, 75 percent in jams, more than 40 percent in ketchups, and 45 percent in packaged tea. Other important mergers involving foreign firms have been in carbonated drinks (effectively a Coke–Pepsi duopoly, with a few minor players), storage batteries (where the Herfindahl index of concentration has risen from 0.268 in 1994/95 to 0.483 in 1999/2000), shaving products (0.04 to 0.33 in the same period), and cement (where significant merger activity began only in 1999 and data are not yet available).[10]

All of these amalgamations have involved market shares of a magnitude that would attract the attention of competition authorities in most industrial countries, but in India all this merger and acquisition activity was beyond challenge.[11] And these are not products for which economies of scale or technological progress would justify greater concentration; indeed HLL outsources production of many of these items to several independent firms and markets them under its brand names. Note that almost all of these industries involve consumer goods, for which effective protection has if anything increased (see Chapter 2). I should also acknowledge, however, that apart from cases like those mentioned above, the industrywise Herfindahl indexes calculated by Basant and Morris (2000) for 1992–98 and those reported for more recent years (presented in CMIE 2002) indicate that there has been no widespread increase in industrial concentration; in fact, concentration seems to have declined in many sectors, although to levels that are still high by international standards. On the other hand, Beena (2003) found for a much smaller sample that the Herfindahl index did increase in most product lines in which mergers occurred. It is difficult to say anything definite on this subject because the data source used by all such studies covers only firms listed on the Mumbai stock exchange. Concentration indexes based on these data would therefore underestimate concentration because they exclude fully state-owned and fully foreign-owned firms and joint ventures (which would be much larger than the average for the industry), and overestimate it because they leave out unincorporated enterprises and private limited companies (which would be relatively small) and imports.

Restrictive Trade Practices   Restrictive trade practices (RTPs) were defined in broad terms in one section of the act, with an illustrative list of agreements that must be registered and deemed to be prejudicial to the public interest given in another section, and a list of "gateways" or permissible defenses in yet another section. The impugned agreements covered a range of horizontal and vertical restraints, as well as price discrimination and predatory pricing. Unlike the cases of concentration of economic power in which the MRTP Commission could only review mergers referred to it by the government and recommend action, in the case of RTPs it could initiate inquiries and pass its own orders. Those orders could either require the violator to "cease and desist" from the practice or modify the practice suitably. Sandesara (1994) and Singh (1999) documented the track record of uneven enforcement. Because fines for noncompliance were modest and jail terms never awarded the orders were often ignored. Most investigations have pertained to vertical restrictions, especially tying and resale price maintenance, and instances of individual consumer dissatisfaction. Practices such as price fixing and predation that have a bearing on the focus of this chapter were involved in only a small minority of cases, with "inquiry closed" being the reported result more often than not.

The cases tabulated by Sandesara and by Singh cover the period from the inception of the MRTP Act until 1991 and were compiled from the annual reports that the commission is statutorily required to submit to parliament. It is not possible to say much about the post-reform period because reports after 1993 do not provide the necessary information about the distribution of cases by type of RTP. However, a few quick points can be made. First, the number of inquiries initiated each year declined in the 1990s, and a perusal of the published judgments of cases decided (a small fraction of those initiated) shows that vertical restrictions continued to predominate between 1991 and 1998 (Basant and Morris 2000). Second, with discussions at the WTO now focusing on international cartels, it is revealing that my scrutiny of cases decided and reported between 1998 and 2002 shows that only three involved allegations of price fixing. In none of them could the charge be sustained, even though the alleged participants were domestic companies against which evidence should have been easier to obtain. The law's inability to deter even hard-core cartels was highlighted recently by a price fixing arrangement made by several leading cement manufacturers in 2000/01 that persisted despite the commission's notice of inquiry. The names of the participants and details of their decisions were reported in the press, but no effective action has been taken.

Third, other government policies actually encourage price fixing. In such highly oligopolistic sectors as fertilizers, petroleum products, and many pharmaceuticals, the government itself fixes prices. And a basic tenet of anticartel policy is undermined in India by other legislation that forces producers of packaged goods to label them with the maximum retail price. This is obviously a measure to protect consumers from being overcharged, and under the resale price maintenance clause of the act, the commission frequently has cited firms that prevent their distributors from charging lower prices. However, publicly declared prices are well known to facilitate oligopolistic collusion by reducing the threat of secret discounts and price wars. This labeling requirement has acquired a trade dimension because after abolishing the remaining quantitative restrictions on imports in 2001, the government extended the requirement to imported goods to ensure a level playing field for Indian producers. This well-intended move will certainly facilitate collusion.

Fourth, regarding vertical restrictions, RTPs by Indian firms do not appear to create a "Japan problem" by inhibiting market access to foreign suppliers. According to the United States Trade Representative's (USTR's) Report on Foreign Trade Barriers for 2000 (pp. 166–67):

> Both state-owned and private Indian firms engage in most types of anticompetitive practices with little or no fear of reaction from government overseers or action from a clogged court system. India suffers from a slow bureaucracy and regulatory bodies that reportedly apply monopoly and fair trade regulations selectively. These practices are not viewed as major hindrances to the sale of U.S. products and services at this time.

The USTR's complaint is thus directed against the MRTP mechanism rather than the practices it is supposed to regulate. The USTR's 2001 report reproduces the same paragraph and then adds the following: "…although U.S. industry (e.g., soda ash) has been denied access to the Indian market as a result of an adverse ruling by the government of India's monopolistic and restrictive trade practices commission" (p. 187). An examination of this particular dispute is instructive. The following discussion summarizes and updates the more detailed treatment in Bhattacharjea (2000), which provides extensive citations from the MRTP Commission orders and press reports.

Predatory Pricing   In September 1996 the MRTP Commission imposed an interim injunction order on the American Natural Soda Ash Corporation (ANSAC), restraining it from cartelized exports to India, on a plea by the Alkali Manufacturers Association of India (AMAI), alleging infringement of several sections of the MRTP Act, including cartelization, predatory pricing, and exclusion from the American association.[12] In 1997 the commission rejected ANSAC's review petition. It held that ANSAC was prima facie (at first view) a cartel and asserted that Section 14 of the MRTP Act gave the commission jurisdiction "with respect to that part of the practice which is carried on in India," even though the cartel itself was formed outside India. It confirmed its earlier injunction, and at the same time allowed the individual American firms to export to India (which ANSAC rules did not permit) but not as a cartel. The commission indicated that a letter from an executive of ANSAC setting lower prices for exports to India than to other countries gave rise to a possible inference of predatory pricing, but it made no final determination on the issue. Nor did it rule on the question of public interest and gateways, but it suggested that the possible closure of Indian producers and the unemployment of their workers would be considered relevant to the public interest.

In February 2000, with the final verdict still out and the injunction in force, the case became a live international political issue. In a joint letter, the USTR and U.S. secretary of commerce asked the Indian minister for commerce and industry to address the obstacles to market access that ANSAC was confronting, including high tariffs and the "de facto embargo" created by the injunction. They linked the satisfactory resolution of the problem with renewal of benefits for Indian exports under the Generalized System of Preferences. In March 2000 the commission again upheld the maintainability of the proceedings. It dismissed ANSAC's fresh contention that the case involved dumping rather than predatory pricing and as such did not come under the MRTP Act. It held that the allegations of cartelization and predatory pricing, as well as the public interest dimension of the case, brought it under the act. It reiterated that ANSAC was prima facie a cartel, and that the impugned practice had an effect in India. Conflicting evidence on predatory pricing submitted by the parties was found to be inconclusive, but the commission again recorded a possible inference in support of the allegations.

With American soda ash thus effectively shut out of the Indian market in 1996, other suppliers entered the picture. In 1997/98, 60 percent of soda ash imports came from China. And in April 1998 the commission passed orders on another petition by the AMAI—this time against a Chinese firm, restraining it from exporting at a price below "fair market value." A year later the AMAI asked the commission to fix the fair market value, and in its order of May 13, 1999, finding from the material placed before it that the Chinese firm's selling price in its domestic market was US$132 per metric ton, the commission did so in the following terms:

> The export price would certainly be slightly higher keeping in mind the margin of profit and other factors. It would therefore be quite proper to consider the fair and normal price of Chinese Soda Ash to be imported into India at US$150 per Metric Tonne... It is hereby clarified that the respondents shall not be permitted to export into India any Chinese Soda Ash below the fair and normal value of US$150 per Metric Tonne [*Alkali Manufacturers' Association of India* 1999, paras. 10 and 13].

In a third case, involving imports of float glass from Indonesia, the commission again restrained imports at predatory prices, this time accepting the Indian industry's data on foreign costs because the respondents did not appear before the commission to dispute them. The two-member majority also expressed considerable concern about the loss of jobs and investors' funds in the Indian float glass industry, which they held to be against the public interest. The chairman of the commission felt that even though the imports in question supplied less than 2 percent of the Indian market, "in the long run this trickle will be transformed into a flood" (*All India Float Glass Manufacturers' Association* 2000, para. 21) if unchecked, and that Indian consumers could very well afford to pay more for domestically produced float glass, which was about 12 percent more expensive than the Indonesian product. The concurring member opined that there was no reason to expect that Indonesia possessed comparative advantage in the production of float glass. A dissenting member found no evidence of pricing below costs or of intent to eliminate competition, and held that injury to the domestic industry, even if it could be proved, was relevant for claiming an antidumping remedy rather than one under the MRTP Act.

As I have argued at greater length in Bhattacharjea (2000), these rulings were inconsistent with earlier practice and with much of the economic analysis that suggests that predatory pricing laws require a higher standard and are hence less vulnerable to the kind of protectionist capture that has been witnessed in antidumping cases. I return to this in the next section. In a far-reaching verdict delivered in July 2002, however, the Indian Supreme Court overturned the MRTP orders in the ANSAC and float glass cases. It did not go into the allegations of cartelization or predatory pricing, but instead held that the wording of the MRTP Act did not give it any extraterritorial jurisdiction. The commission could therefore not take action against foreign cartels or the pricing of exports to India, nor could it restrict imports. Action could be taken only if an anticompetitive agreement involving an Indian party could be proved, and that only after the goods had been imported into India. Contrary to the commission's alignment of the public interest with that of the domestic industry, the Court declared that Indian industry needed to gear up to face the challenge of foreign competition.[13] I discuss this judgment in greater detail in Bhattacharjea (forthcoming). The most immediate effect of the decision has been a government-sponsored amendment of the new competition bill that explicitly arms the proposed Competition Commission with the power to restrict imports. This is discussed in greater detail below.

Some Insights from Theory

This section complements the descriptive material in the one that preceded it, retaining its emphasis on competition policy as applied to international trade and investment in the specific areas of entry, mergers, and predatory pricing. Social welfare and efficiency, as usually defined, will be the criteria for judging outcomes. The analytical framework to be employed is thus firmly within the mainstream paradigm used to analyze both trade liberalization and competition policy, although in this case it delivers results that are at variance with current fashions. Central to this discussion will be an important feature of developing countries: the small size of domestic markets relative to the costs of setting up production and marketing facilities.

Entry

An extensive body of theoretical literature from the 1980s has established what is sometimes known as the "excess entry theorem" in the presence of oligopoly and economies of scale. Using the standard measure of social welfare, entry has a positive effect on consumer surplus (through lower prices and greater variety), but that effect can be outweighed by a negative effect on producer surplus as each entrant "steals business" from existing producers and forces them to operate on a smaller scale. Although this possibility was demonstrated in special cases by several authors, it was shown to be quite robust by Mankiw and Whinston (1986). There is an even older literature that assesses this problem in an open economy, which should be at the heart of the current debate on competition policy. An early paper by Eastman and Stykolt (1960) and an empirical investigation by Cox and Harris (1984) attributed inefficient excess entry to high levels of protection, and argued that trade liberalization would bring additional gains from trade by eliminating monopoly distortions and encouraging exit and "rationalization" of such industries, with the surviving firms able to produce on a larger scale. Although their articles were based on Canadian experience, they conform to the perceived reality of most developing countries as far as competitively supplied imports are concerned. In this "small open economy" setting, free trade is the standard prescription, and excess entry could therefore be blamed on wrong-headed protectionist policies.

Exposure to import competition imposes "market discipline" on imperfectly competitive domestic firms, forcing them to act as price-takers with respect to the world price. Entry then displaces only imports or yields additional exports with no theft of business from incumbent domestic firms.

If the number of foreign firms is limited, however, so that prices are greater than domestic marginal costs, the business-stealing effect reappears. The first author to recognize excess entry in an international oligopoly setting was Dixit (1984), who showed that there could be a case for some reduction in the number of home firms via mergers even under free trade if the share of imports was small. The larger profits earned by a more concentrated domestic industry at the expense of foreign firms (and foreign consumers, if some output is exported)[14] could outweigh the loss to domestic consumers over some range.

As Dixit himself showed, however, free trade is not optimal under international oligopoly. The literature on "strategic trade policy" that also emerged during the 1980s demonstrated that tariff protection could be used to shift profits from oligopolistic foreign exporters to domestic firms and governments. Such optimal tariffs are typically decreasing in the number of domestic firms, and should therefore dampen the tendency to excess entry. However, in Bhattacharjea (1995) I showed that even domestic entry conditioned on a rationally anticipated, time-consistent tariff appropriate to the post-entry market structure can result in excessive (welfare-decreasing) entry. Indeed, with Cournot competition, although the first domestic entrant into a market served by a foreign monopolist always improves welfare, free domestic entry in this setting is socially excessive if it results in any market structure more competitive than duopoly.

Nor is excess entry easily reversed by trade liberalization. If entry costs are sunk (nonrecoverable), then the damage cannot be undone, and exposing the industry to import competition may not get rid of the unwanted firms because the level of profit that triggers exit is less than that which encouraged entry.[15] The superfluous entrants may then remain in the industry, with that part of their fixed costs that is not sunk remaining a recurring social burden. Even if exit does occur, there is no guarantee that the survivors will produce on a larger scale. As Head and Ries (1999) have shown, with imperfect competition both the theoretical predictions and empirical evidence on the impact of trade liberalization on firm scale are ambiguous.

The mirror image of excess domestic entry is limited foreign entry in the form of imports from or direct investment by oligopolistic foreign firms. A number of authors recently have shown that the advent of the first few foreign firms in competition with a domestic oligopoly *decreases* welfare below the autarky level. Here the business-stealing effect dominates the procompetitive effect. I provided a detailed survey of this literature and a unifying theoretical framework in Bhattacharjea

(2002), which also showed that the welfare decline is steeper if foreign firms have lower costs, if the domestic industry is highly concentrated, or if the private costs of domestic production exceed social opportunity costs, all of which are likely to occur in developing countries.[16] Welfare begins to rise again only after a certain crucial amount of foreign entry, giving a J-shaped relationship between welfare and the number of foreign firms. With Cournot competition, linear demand, and constant costs, I showed that welfare eventually regains the autarky level only when foreign firms capture at least 80 percent of the home market.[17] I also showed that an optimal tariff conditioned on the market structure prevents the initial welfare decline in the case of import penetration, although for various reasons stated there this cannot be used as a practical guide to policy, and is in any case unavailable if foreign entry takes the form of FDI. In fact, protection can encourage "tariff-jumping" FDI, which, as Levy and Nolan (1992) and Bhattacharjea (2002) have shown, is more likely to be welfare reducing, even if it brings in better technology and greater product variety.

All of the models reviewed above treat FDI and exports simply as alternative means of entering the domestic market, differing only in the possibility of border taxes on imports. But critics might object that if the foreign firms are part of a multinational corporation, this framework is not adequate. An established tradition in the economic analysis of MNCs recognizes that firms invest abroad to exploit intangible assets that inherently give them market power. UNCTAD (1997) provided an even-handed review of the issues that arise out of this for developing countries. It can be argued that it is precisely these proprietary assets of MNCs that make their advent desirable for developing countries because such assets are costly to develop and often take the form of firm-specific tacit knowledge that cannot be unbundled and acquired through transfer at arm's length. Proponents of FDI argue that spillovers of such know-how benefit domestic firms.

Evidence on spillovers is mixed, however, and suggests that if there is limited domestic competition, or if domestic firms lack the ability to imitate, foreign presence can lead to negative spillovers on domestic productivity by forcing them to contract (see Blomstrom and Kokko 1998; and Aitken and Harrison 1999). MNCs also have financial "deep pockets" and the resources to engage in modes of non-price competition and restrictive business practices that may be new to the host country, making for foreign entry leading to greater concentration (UNCTAD 1997). However, the preceding analysis shows that the effects of foreign entry are ambiguous even if FDI leads to a *reduction* of concentration by increasing the total number of firms, and the foreign firms behave no differently from their domestic counterparts. This insight needs to be set off against the undeniable benefits of FDI. The finding that limited foreign entry is unambiguously bad for domestic welfare, especially if foreign firms have a cost advantage, only reinforces the argument by UNCTAD (1997) that developing countries should be cautious about giving "market power inducements" in the form of exclusive production or marketing rights to attract FDI. This is especially important in infrastructure activities like power and telecommunications, where import competition is absent and firms may deny access to their distribution networks (where natural monopoly conditions prevail) and thereby block the entry of rivals at the potentially more competitive generation/switching stages.

This analysis puts a question mark over the Indian government's policy of case-by-case clearance of FDI proposals involving more than 51 percent foreign equity, without any apparent concern that foreign firms should provide competition for each other—obviously in price and quality, not in advertising wars such as those between Coke and Pepsi. This policy was especially misguided in infrastructure, where import discipline is absent, and in consumer goods, where imports were restricted until recently and remain subject to high tariffs. Clearly the guaranteed price *and* off-take promised to foreign firms for some of the early post-reform power projects on the basis of negotiations rather than competitive bidding look especially bad in this framework. These early mistakes are being rectified now.

Empirical application of the kind of models surveyed above usually takes the form of calibrated partial equilibrium models, where "outside" estimates of costs and demand are combined with data on market structure to reproduce observed price and output behavior, with the implied conjectural variation parameter being obtained endogenously. Even practitioners are unhappy with this procedure, and because it is designed to estimate equilibrium relationships, it is probably not suitable for an economy in transition. I offer indirect evidence of excess entry instead. A number of sophisticated econometric studies recently have shown that rates of total factor productivity growth (TFPG) in Indian industry have been lower and even negative in the post-reform period (see Balakrishnan and Pushpangadan 1998; Balakrishnan, Pushpangadan, and Kumar 2000; Srivastava 2001; Das 2001; and Unni, Lalitha, and Rani 2001). TFPG measures the increase in output minus the increase of a weighted sum of inputs. Although there could be various explanations for this deterioration of performance, it is consistent with excess capacity creation, as the first and last of the articles actually have suggested. This is because the new entrants reduce the output of existing firms without proportionately reducing their fixed stocks of labor and capital.[18]

Recent research by Banga (2003) shows that in the second half of the 1990s TFPG was higher in industries without FDI than in those with FDI. Her econometric analysis with various control variables and foreign presence disaggregated by source shows that TFPG was negatively related to U.S. equity participation in an industry, whereas Japanese presence had a positive effect. Firm-level analysis showed that higher Japanese equity participation was associated with higher TFPG in the firms in which it was present and with positive productivity spillovers to Indian firms in the same industries. U.S. presence had neither effect. On the basis of other evidence she compiled, Banga attributes these results to the American firms' relatively larger size, to technology gaps vis-à-vis domestic firms, and to their concentration in highly oligopolistic industries with more significant economies of scale. These factors would make their output-displacement effect stronger and the technology spillover effects weaker than those of Japanese FDI.[19]

As to more informal sources, reports in the business press have blamed on excessive entry the recessionary conditions prevailing in industries like steel, cement, soda ash, and automobiles. Industry observers believe that comprehensive restructuring through exit and merger is inevitable in the near future, but with official help these industries are resisting the inevitable. Commercial imports of cars, which were released from quantitative restrictions in 2001, have been subject to high rates of import duty so that the industrial structure will remain fragmented and continue to operate at suboptimal scales of production. The cement industry began consolidation through mergers in 1999, but has more recently organized a successful cartel. The soda-ash industry succeeded in obtaining MRTP injunctions (and, more recently, antidumping duties) to protect itself from imports. Steel similarly has been protected by antidumping duties and successive bailouts by public sector financial institutions.

Mergers

A growing body of theoretical literature uses the number of home and foreign firms in an international oligopoly model as policy parameters representing the strength of merger policy. Despite tractable results being obtained only with Cournot models with constant costs (and usually linear demand), no robust conclusion has emerged. Depending on the relative numbers of home and foreign firms; on whether the firms compete in the domestic market, the foreign market, or both; on the countries' trade policies; and on the importance of economies of scale, a country may want to increase or decrease the number of home firms, given the number of foreign firms (or vice versa), and to change the number of home firms in the same or opposite direction as that of its trading partners (see Dixit 1984; the articles summarized in Lloyd 1998; and Horn and Levinsohn 2001).

A problem with these approaches is that they deal only with small changes in the number of firms, although it is well known that a horizontal merger among Cournot competitors with constant costs is unprofitable for the firms themselves because of the free-riding and expansion of output by "outsider" firms, unless it brings about a cost reduction or unless a substantial proportion of the firms in an industry internalize the externality by merging. The latter action adversely affects consumers but benefits firms, including the outsiders, whereas cost savings can result in welfare gains, despite their adversely affecting rival firms. When firms and consumers are distributed across countries, national competition authorities may see different tradeoffs between the benign and malign effects of a merger. A model by Head and Ries (1997) showed that mergers may be approved because they increase welfare in their home jurisdictions even though they reduce world welfare. This is more likely when the cost savings, home consumption, and post-merger number of firms are small.

Bhattacharjea (2002) showed in the linear/Cournot framework that if domestic oligopolists do not export—which is a more accurate description of developing countries—then foreign mergers can actually reduce home welfare below the autarky level. I further showed that imposing an optimal tariff can mitigate the consequences of foreign mergers, but the optimal tariff rate is typically inversely related to the number of foreign firms and to their costs. Thus foreign mergers that result in cost reductions (the sort that are profitable for the merging firms and that foreign competition authorities are likely to approve) will entail higher optimal tariffs and thereby put pressure on tariff bindings. As I indicated earlier, tariffs also can induce inefficient tariff-jumping FDI, which not only leads to a loss of tariff revenue but also forces the foreign firm(s) to relocate production to a higher cost environment. In the case of mergers between foreign-owned subsidiaries operating in the host country, the tariff remedy is unavailable and the original conclusion applies: having too few foreign firms can be worse than having none. With regard to the home government's optimal response in the number of domestic firms to change in the same or opposite direction to changes in the number of foreign firms, I show that there is more likely to be international discordance in merger policy when home firms do not export, compared with the reciprocal oligopoly result presented in Horn and Levinsohn (2001).

This analysis can be integrated with the earlier one on foreign entry as follows. Whereas limited foreign entry involves descending the left branch of the J-shaped curve relating welfare to the number of foreign firms, mergers between foreign firms involve descending the right branch. If fixed costs relative to market size limit the number of firms, a country that turns a blind eye to entry and foreign mergers might end up wallowing in the trough of the J, worse off than under autarky.

Predatory Pricing

Here I will not review the large body of theory that exists (see Ordover [1998], Tharakan [2000], and Bhattacharjea [2000] for surveys). Much of it shows that, contrary to the early skepticism of the Chicago School, "rational predation" is a distinct possibility. But it also reveals that the commonly used Areeda-Turner test (which involves checking to see whether the price is below the alleged predator's average variable costs) is neither necessary nor sufficient to establish predation. Although there is no consensus about what other standard to apply, it is argued that the commonly used criteria for a finding of predatory pricing do set a stricter standard than do existing antidumping procedures. For one thing, the criteria usually require evidence of predatory intent and market power on the part of the alleged predator, whereas no such evidence is required in antidumping actions. Second, the Areeda-Turner test is more exacting than the test required in dumping cases, which can be satisfied by evidence of either international price discrimination (a legitimate business practice that can even be beneficial to consumers in low-income countries), or of pricing below a constructed value that typically includes overheads (which is again normal in periods of depressed demand). Finally, predatory pricing requires demonstration of injury to competition, rather than to competitors as is required in antidumping suits.[20]

Authorities in the United Kingdom routinely investigate the market structure of the industry concerned because forcing the exit of a rival firm is fruitless if the victim or other firms can easily (re-)enter the market. An even stricter standard is used in the United States. Possibly influenced by game-theoretic analyses advanced by expert witnesses in the *Matsushita* (1986) and *Brooke Group* (1993) cases, the U.S. Supreme Court examined the alleged predators' prospects for recouping losses sustained during the predatory campaign. These insights from theory were explicitly rejected by the European Court of Justice, however, which held in a significant decision that a "price set below average variable cost must always be considered abusive.... Predatory pricing may be penalised whenever there is risk that competitors will otherwise be eliminated without requiring additional proof that the undertaking in question has a realistic chance of recouping its losses."[21]

Even if we ignore the recoupment rule, it is clear that the Indian cases reviewed above yielded outcomes that were considerably more favorable to the Indian firms than what they could have obtained through antidumping suits.[22] In looking at evidence of price discrimination rather than pricing below costs and intent to eliminate competition, and expressing concern at injury to the Indian industries, the MRTP Commission applied a dumping standard rather than one on predatory pricing. Evidence of severe financial injury, or even the possible closure of the target firm(s), is not sufficient to establish predation, and concern for the interests of workers and investors in the endangered industries ignores those of the downstream industries that use their products. Furthermore, even if the Indian firms had shut down, the alleged predators would not have acquired dominant positions.

As I have argued in Bhattacharjea (2000), the soda-ash imports that were interdicted represented less than 2 percent of Indian consumption, and in the relevant years, nonnegligible quantities were supplied to India by several countries other than the United States and China—whose exports were targeted by AMAI. The same was true of float glass imports from Indonesia. Nor are these products for which brand loyalties or switching costs may lock in a dominant position acquired by successful predation. The soda-ash cases were more in the nature of dumping, for which WTO-compatible remedies exist.

The relief granted in *ANSAC* effectively shut out soda-ash imports from the United States. In the case against the Chinese industry it took the form of a minimum import price set above the exporter's domestic market price, whereas antidumping duties would at most have offset the dumping margin, allowed consumers to benefit from further reductions in the foreign price, and brought revenue to the government. I certainly am not arguing that predatory pricing never occurs. The standard "long purse" story based on unequal financial resources may well describe the situation in recent years, when increased competitive pressures and crippled financial markets made Indian firms vulnerable to merger bids by multinational corporations in industries with significant barriers to domestic and foreign entry. It is ironic that whereas the soda-ash imports were restrained although they were unlikely to have been predatory, the possibility of predation for merger in other industries was never examined.

The Road Ahead

With WTO negotiations on competition policy on the horizon, the institutional backdrop in India has been transformed by the December 2002 passage of the Competition Act. The act is a distinct improvement on the MRTP Act in many ways. It covers with a much more modern approach the usual three areas of anticompetitive agreements, abuses of a dominant position, and mergers, and wisely avoids such areas as monopolistic pricing, control of firm size, and "unfair trade practices." Most anticompetitive practices are now clearly defined. Predatory pricing is now under the section dealing with the abuse of a dominant position, and is explicitly defined as "the sale of goods or provision of services at a price which is below costs, as may be determined by regulations, of production...with a view to reduce competition or eliminate the competitors." Several criteria are listed for judging whether an agreement is anticompetitive, a market position is dominant, or a merger will have an adverse effect on competition. Criteria for determining the relevant geographical or product market are listed. The act provides for several regional benches of the Competition Commission, as well as specialized merger benches. It also provides for professionals to serve on the commission and in the director general's office, and for hearing expert testimony. The fines are substantial: 10 percent of turnover or three times the profits from cartelization.

On the international front, the act provides for cooperation between the Competition Commission and foreign agencies. Section 3(5), like Section 15 of the MRTP Act, exempts agreements exclusively relating to exports. Section 32 restates the "effects" doctrine that was embedded in Section 14 of the MRTP Act, establishing jurisdiction over foreign anticompetitive practices that have an effect on the relevant market in India. In response to the Supreme Court judgment in *Haridas Exports*, this has now been reinforced by an amendment inserting subsection 33(2), explicitly giving the commission the power to restrain imports. In reinstating the merger review powers that were deleted from the MRTP Act, the new act defines "combinations" that are subject to challenge on the basis of alternative thresholds for domestic and international assets or turnover. Although it boldly asserts that "no person or enterprise shall enter into a combination which causes or is likely to cause an appreciable adverse effect on competition within the relevant market in India and such a combination shall be void," it is unlikely that the Competition Commission will be able to challenge offshore mergers. At best it can challenge the merger of their local subsidiaries, and India can free ride on U.S. and EU authorities blocking or modifying mergers in their own and each other's jurisdictions.

Although the act is a distinct improvement over its predecessor, I share the reservations of several commentators concerning the actual implementation of its provisions. The multifarious criteria (13 each for determining dominance and the anticompetitiveness of mergers!) will be of little help to a body that lacks institutional memory or theoretical understanding of their significance. Fortunately, the Competition Act does not have the MRTP Act's provisions on unfair trade practices (see note 7), and transfers pending cases involving such practices to the consumer courts to be dealt with under the Consumer Protection Act. But with its energies devoted to those issues, which are not part of competition law as it is normally understood, the investigative, prosecutorial, and adjudicatory wings of the commission were unable to develop an understanding of the important economic arguments required for the enforcement of a modern competition law. The judgments I have studied show a lack of appreciation of basic distinctions, such as those between marginal costs and average total costs, comparative and absolute advantage, predatory and discriminatory pricing, producer interests and the "public interest," and the partial and general equilibrium consequences of import competition for employment. Firms were subjected to inquiries for engaging in normal business practices, such as underutilization of capacity or raising prices disproportionately to costs.

One may legitimately ask, then, where is the expertise required to implement the new law in all its complexity? The revival of merger review powers in particular has come about as an unsatisfactory compromise. The initial proposal for mandatory review of proposed mergers over a certain asset or turnover threshold faced tremendous criticism from business lobbies, and was diluted by making premerger notification voluntary, with a proviso that approval would be deemed to have been granted if no decision is reached in 90 days. But the act empowers the commission to look into a merger up to a year after it is completed and to undo or modify it if it sees fit to do so. The unscrambling of firms' assets is likely to be a hugely costly operation for which there is no official expertise, thanks to the nonenforcement of Section 27 of the MRTP Act. Expertise is lacking even with regard to ex ante evaluation. For more than a decade there has been no merger regulation in India, and prior to that regulation focused more on preventing the concentration of industrial ownership than on market power.

These problems are likely to be compounded by several amendments that were introduced by the government when the bill was being passed in December 2002. I have discussed these at length in Bhattacharjea (forthcoming), but some need to be mentioned here. One amendment allows an efficiency defense for joint ventures, introducing yet another criterion that will be difficult to operationalize. Another amendment allows a "meeting the competition" defense for price discrimination, without comprehending that this can serve as both an entry-deterring strategy and a facilitating practice for collusion, and inexplicably extends this defense to predatory pricing.

Another amendment, which is obviously a direct response to the Supreme Court judgment overturning the MRTP injunctions on imports, inserts a new subsection 33(2) that allows the commission to issue temporary injunctions to restrain any party from importing goods, if the import is likely to contravene the act's sections on anticompetitive agreements, abuse of dominance, or combinations. Such injunctions can be given without hearing the other party. This amendment will be a boon for domestic producers hankering for the good old days of import control when they could shut out import competition altogether, thanks to the requirement that a prospective importer produce a certificate to prove that the product was not available in India. A similar power—on different grounds and only with respect to imports from particular sources—will now be vested in the Competition Commission, which does not have to hear the importer at all. The MRTP Act at least provided gateways for the defense of RTPs. Sections 3 and 4 of the Competition Act, in contrast, make certain types of collusive agreements and abuse of dominance illegal per se, subject only to the dubious defenses mentioned above, but even they cannot be effectively considered at the injunction stage if the opposing party is not given a hearing. And as illustrated by the two cases that were finally decided by the Supreme Court, the injunction can remain in force for several years during the regular hearing, the review hearing, and the appeal to the Supreme Court.

There is no way the exporter, the importer, and the ultimate consumers can be compensated for the losses they have suffered in the intervening period.

Even if collusion or abuse of dominance can be proved, an import prohibition is surely the wrong remedy. Imports might be targeted for being priced too high (as by a foreign merger or cartel) or too low (as by a dominant foreign firm engaged in predatory pricing). If the prices are too high, then further restricting competition by shutting out imports amounts to cutting off one's nose to spite one's face (although the *threat* of an import restriction could be helpful to compel foreign defendants to cooperate with the investigation and comply with the ultimate verdict). If the prices are too low, an import restriction likely will be held to be inconsistent with Article VI of the General Agreement on Tariffs and Trade and the Uruguay Round Antidumping Agreement, which established a procedure for dealing with low-valued imports and which require that domestic laws be brought into conformity with that procedure. In 2000 the WTO Dispute Settlement Body held that the U.S. 1916 Antidumping Act was inconsistent with these requirements and could not be exempted on the grounds that it was a national competition law. Ironically, India included itself as a third party in that case, on the side of the complainants, the EU and Japan. The saving grace is that by introducing explicit cost and dominance criteria for predatory pricing, the Competition Act will make it more difficult to obtain the kind of injunctions against imports that were obtained in the MRTP regime. But with both the EU and the United States implacably opposed to replacing antidumping rules with competition principles of this kind (see note 20), the literature on this point reviewed in the preceding sections is now moot as far as a multilateral agreement is concerned.

Where does that leave us? With a competition act that contains problematic provisions, a lack of expertise to interpret them, inordinate delays in delivering judgments, and the very different understanding of competition matters displayed by the MRTP Commission in the predatory pricing cases, it is hardly likely that India will succeed in obtaining the benefits of reciprocal positive comity with advanced countries. Many of the anticompetitive practices dealt with in the debates on trade and competition policy appear to be insignificant in India—for example, export and import cartels and exclusionary vertical arrangements that restrict market access to imports. This again means that we have little to offer in terms of positive comity, little even to put on the table in multilateral negotiations. Moreover, by making hard-core cartels intrinsically illegal, and by not allowing differential treatment of domestic and foreign firms (thus providing de jure national treatment, despite India's arguments against it at the WTO Working Group), the Competition Act has already satisfied the requirements of the EU, which has been spearheading the move for a competition agreement at the WTO (WTO 2002c). Perhaps for this reason, the EU trade commissioner recently declared that India's competition regime was already "WTO-plus-plus," and that the country's opposition to negotiations was purely tactical ("FDI behind India's Stance: Lamy" 2003, p. 2). India thus seems to be going to the 2003 Fifth WTO Ministerial Conference with an intransigent position on competition, without much to bargain with except perhaps an offer to bind the provisions already enshrined in the Competition Act in exchange for other concessions.

I believe that a more proactive approach is required. One idea is to bring into force various sections of the act at staggered intervals, as provided for in the act itself. A good place to begin would be the section on cartels, on which there is considerable international consensus. In fact it is the only specific anticompetitive practice mandated by the Doha declaration for study by the working group. Doing so would help to draw on the promised technical assistance from foreign agencies and expose Indian investigators to international practices. Provided that agricultural marketing boards and associations of small exporters can be exempted, India could easily subscribe to an international agreement rescinding the exemptions regarding export cartels in national competition laws, because India is more likely a victim than a promoter of such cartels.

Merger review for domestic firms should be kept in abeyance for the time being. Apart from the commission's lack of expertise to evaluate mergers, Indian industry needs to restructure after a decade of excess entry. A certain amount of consolidation is also required to overcome the legacy of the earlier control regime, which fragmented capacities among firms and regions and forced business groups into excessive conglomerate diversification by checking their expansion in any one line. A permissive approach to mergers may be required as a concomitant to further trade liberalization, particularly because closures seem politically out of the question and the existing policy toward what are called "sick industries" simply keeps resources unemployed throughout extremely protracted winding-up proceedings. On the other hand, in expanding sectors like consumer nondurables, where neither scale economies nor technological change is significant enough to justify greater concentration, concentration probably has gone too far already, as the market share data cited earlier show. Advertising, brand loyalties, and extensive distribution networks will make the incumbents difficult to challenge.

The preceding analysis suggests, however, that both entry and mergers involving *foreign* firms will continue to require greater scrutiny. In particular, India must resist an investment agreement that would entail pre-establishment national treatment (NT) for FDI. If the market will remain oligopolistic, the theoretical insights of the preceding section show that there is a case for denying entry to foreign firms that will compete with Indian firms in the home market, unless there is clear evidence of technological spillovers. This prohibition should be applied at the sectoral level rather than to individual firms, not only because firm-by-firm review will invite inefficiency and corruption but also because it will reinforce the problem of limited foreign entry that represents the worst of all possible worlds. Theory also suggests that mergers of foreign subsidiaries should be subjected to a stricter standard because the terms of the tradeoff between higher profits and reduced consumer surplus become more adverse with some of the profit going abroad. Therefore, post-entry NT should be resisted as well, at least with regard to merger policy. As a beginning, to reconcile this with the hands-off approach recommended for domestic mergers, the relevant sections of the act can be implemented, but only mergers involving local subsidiaries of foreign firms should be investigated, thereby economizing on the commission's limited resources. (If such discriminatory treatment is not possible because of de jure NT, the balance effectively could be tilted by reducing the thresholds for international assets while raising those for domestic assets.) Exposure to the kind of evidence brought by foreign firms in their defense will itself be valuable for the commission and for Indian firms. Remedies to safeguard competition, such as divestiture of brands, plants, and shareholdings, or licensing of patents, should be applied before rather than after the merger.

The sooner we start, the better. Having the new law in force, with some experience and expertise in its implementation, will strengthen our bargaining position when negotiations begin, even if some of the more assertive postures have to be surrendered in the give-and-take process. It is important, however, that the government's power to exempt sectors (as provided for in Section 54 of the Competition Act) be stoutly defended in negotiations, by pointing out that such exemptions are widely used in developed countries[23] and if necessary insisting on "special and differential treatment" as in other WTO agreements. It goes without saying that this power should be used judiciously, with the exemptions being reviewed periodically.

These domestic exemptions could be combined with a GATS-type positive list approach in a multilateral agreement, which would limit commitments to particular sectors. Exempting NT for some of them (as in GATS), or keeping NT out of a competition agreement altogether, would also allow India to rethink the principle it has conceded in the Competition Act. Both the EU and the United States have double standards on nondiscrimination in competition policy: they oppose most-favored-nation status for cooperation in investigations, and they violate NT in defending the exemption of their export cartels. As the Indian government's submission to the working group itself points out, the arguments that make NT a vital component of a trade agreement cannot be carried over to competition policy because not all competition policy issues are trade distorting. Keeping NT out would allow developing countries to join the emerging consensus against international cartels while permitting domestic cartels to rationalize production and enable orderly downsizing in the face of greater import competition. If anything, the level playing field supposedly afforded by nondiscriminatory treatment of domestic and foreign firms is actually tilted in the latter's favor. Because competition authorities in developing countries will find it difficult to prosecute firms based abroad, domestic firms might bear the brunt of enforcement activities while foreign firms get away with similar infractions. Also, even if the rules are nondiscriminatory, the costs of compliance will be higher for firms that are unfamiliar with them, thereby putting firms in developing countries at a competitive disadvantage.[24]

Summary, Conclusion, and a Caveat

Following the introductory material, the second section of this chapter traced the parallel developments on the subject of trade and competition policy at the WTO, in bilateral and regional agreements, in the international academic literature, and in Indian official circles. The third section recounted the major economic reforms that have occurred in India in the areas of investment and trade policy, and then undertook a detailed analysis of the working of the MRTP Act, especially with regard to mergers and restrictive trade practices. That discussion showed that merger and acquisition activity increased substantially, with a growing proportion of foreign participants, after the relevant sections of the act were dropped and restrictions on FDI were relaxed in 1991. As we saw, the MRTP Commission's regulation of cartels and predatory pricing left much to be desired. The review of the theoretical literature in the fourth section showed that more competition is not always better in an oligopolistic setting, and thus liberalizing both foreign and domestic entry can reduce welfare. It also cited recent empirical evidence on industrial productivity growth that indirectly supports the contention that liberalization has led to excess entry. The theoretical literature on mergers suggested that amalgamations of foreign-owned firms could be harmful, while the literature on predatory pricing only reinforced the skepticism of the preceding section. The fifth section appraised the new Competition Act, welcoming its positive features, but warning against the lack of expertise to implement its numerous technical provisions, and expressing concern over the amendment reinstating the commission's ability to restrict imports. I then set out an agenda for improving India's bargaining position on competition policy at the WTO, involving careful scrutiny of cartels, entry, and mergers involving foreign firms, a more relaxed attitude to domestic mergers, and consequently a case for resisting the NT clause in possible agreements on investment or competition.

If there is a common strand running through this chapter, it is a case for greater economic input to the formulation and enforcement of competition policy.

At a minimum, given the limited expertise that is available, economic analysis can suggest screening devices based on empirically verifiable aspects of market and product characteristics that will help to narrow the list of cases for investigation and prosecution. At the subsequent stage, given that antitrust enforcement worldwide has moved away from holding certain practices illegal per se, economics can provide one kind of reasoning to support "rule of reason" judgments. Ex post, economic (and even statistical) analysis of judgments can help highlight systemic failures. Analyses of this kind show that competition policy enforcement in industrial countries is not always consistent, based on economic logic, or immune to politics. It is not as though Indian practice has been especially inept on these counts. Economic inputs should lead to the formulation of amendments to the competition law and guidelines for its enforcement, operationalizing the multiple criteria in the new act. These guidelines should be widely publicized and replace subjective case-by-case interpretations of an undefined "public interest" in arriving at verdicts. This would reduce uncertainty, delays, and legal costs.

Theorists argue that quantifiable "bright line" criteria to identify anticompetitive practices, such as the Hirschman-Herfindahl concentration index for merger review or the Areeda-Turner test for predatory pricing, are unsatisfactory. However, a more general criterion emerges from the analysis of the apparently very different issues of entry, mergers, and predation in this chapter. Barriers to entry create preconditions that are conducive to "inefficient" foreign entry, sustainable horizontal mergers and cartels, and rational predation. This suggests, as a rough first approximation, that infrastructure and branded consumer goods (which are likely to benefit from high effective protection for the foreseeable future) should be high on the watch list for the competition authority. I have also suggested a quantifiable criterion for entry barriers in Bhattacharjea (2000).

At the same time I would not completely blinker legal (and ultimately political) judgments with economic theory, for there are many policy objectives that are outside the ambit of the theoretical framework employed here, which privileges "efficiency" (in the form of maximization of a particular metric of social welfare) above all else. This has not been decisive even in industrial countries. Section 84 of the UK Fair Trading Act of 1973, for example, recognized balanced distribution of industry and employment as a legitimate criterion in assessing abuse of a monopolistic position and in reviewing mergers, and section 10 of its RTP Act (copied with minor changes as Section 38 of the Indian MRTP Act) allowed the prevention of reductions in employment or exports to be pleaded as gateway defenses of RTPs. In Europe and Japan "crisis cartels" were permitted until fairly recently to protect declining industries, and mergers were encouraged to create "national champions." Even in the United States, merger policy until the 1970s, as well as laws to control price discrimination (such as the Robinson-Patman Act and state laws on fair trading), were designed to protect small businesses, regardless of efficiency. And vigorous prosecution of price discrimination in the EU has more to do with the political objective of enforcing a single market than with efficiency.

It is ironic that although the EU is leading the charge to have hard-core cartels made illegal, during Europe's 19th-century industrialization cartels were actually promoted by the state in Germany and restrictive agreements were upheld by the courts in Britain and France. Active prosecution began in these countries only in the last 50 years (Chang 2002). The essays in Evenett, Lehmann, and Steil (2000) expose the wide divergences on competition policy that even now remain between the United States and the EU, and the continuing European ambivalence about promoting "efficiency," despite considerable convergence in the past decade.

As Scherer (1994) clearly documented, the practice of competition policy in advanced countries often has been inconsistent within and between countries and over time, and frequently ignorant of simple economic logic. It is unlikely that whatever common principles they agree on at their current levels of economic and institutional development will be in the interests of countries at much lower levels. In India, which lacks even rudimentary unemployment insurance, protection of employment will remain a live political issue, manifested in the various pro-producer interpretations of the "public interest" that were cited above, and in the government's continuing inability to reduce tariff barriers further or to introduce labor market flexibility by amending the laws that make retrenchments and closures so difficult.

This chapter has used the most narrow "efficiency" definition of social welfare, only because it is the one that informs most theoretical approaches to the issue of competition and market-friendly reforms. Although I take distributional goals more seriously than most writers on this topic, I share their reservations about using competition policy for meeting those goals. Not because I believe that market outcomes are benign or that I believe in the mythical lump-sum taxes and transfers that economists use to dodge the issue, but because it is difficult to redress the inequities of the market with a law intended to promote competition. Active prosecution of the exclusionary practices of large firms could help, as could carefully monitored rationalization cartels, but these actions require high levels of commitment and expertise, which have been lacking in India's policy toward declining industries.

My more pressing concern is that requiring recourse to an expensive judicial process, which allows for only "win-lose" outcomes, inevitably tilts competition policy against people who are less well-off. Why should only those who can resort to this process be protected from the rigors of liberalization, transferring the burden to others? In particular, injunctive relief in the form of an import prohibition, as I argued above, is a remedy that worsens the disease. It tackles a private anticompetitive practice by a further judicially directed restriction of competition, in a manner that is more protectionist than an antidumping duty, and possibly violates WTO antidumping rules. By the same token, it inflicts costs on ultimate consumers, on firms that use the product as an input, or on exporters in totally unrelated sectors who might have to suffer the retaliation of other WTO members. Many of these potential losers are likely to be less well-off than the large business houses who can move the competition mechanism.

Furthermore, an unfamiliar and complex legal regime disproportionately burdens small firms with the costs of compliance, placing them at a competitive disadvantage relative to larger domestic and foreign rivals in a manner that has nothing to do with "efficiency." One way out would be to limit enforcement to large firms. This is already mandated by the thresholds for merger review, and is implicit in the criteria defining dominant positions. But it could be further strengthened by granting blanket exemptions to sectors with predominantly small producers, or establishing a de minimis rule for participants in anticompetitive agreements, thereby enabling the Competition Commission to concentrate on the larger players. A more positive route would be to follow the South African Competition Act in incorporating provisions that promote businesses owned by historically disadvantaged people.[25] Even if there is a tradeoff between efficiency and equity, there is no particular justification for insisting on a corner solution.

Endnotes

1. All numbered WTO documents cited in this chapter are available at the WTO Web site, www.wto.org.

2. The reports of the working group are available as WTO documents WT/WGTCP/1-6.

3. In what follows I have drawn on Scherer (1994), Utton (1995), Levinsohn (1996), Perroni and Whalley (1996), Lee (1998), and Lloyd (1998), as well as UNCTAD (1997), WTO (1998-2001), OECD (1998, 2000), and Government of India (1999). Several popular publications of the Consumer Unity and Trust Society have been very informative as well.

4. See Bhattacharjea (2000) for more excerpts from the committee reports and the MRTP Commission's judgments, which show that there are many contradictory interpretations of what constitutes the "public interest" in competition policy.

5. See Bhagwati and Desai (1970) for a thorough early critique of the licensing system.

6. A 1998 relaxation of this measure allowed larger firms to produce these items, provided they exported at least half their output; in 2000 the textile sector, which was vital for exports, was removed from the list.

7. I will not go into the so-called monopolistic trade practices in Chapter IV of the act, which were defined as any practice that "unreasonably" increases prices, costs, or profits, or "unreasonably" prevents or lessens competition. That chapter has fallen into disuse in recent years (see Singh 2000). Nor do I intend to go into the "unfair trade practices" that were unwisely inserted as Chapter V.B by the 1984 amendment. That insertion led to the MRTP Commission's limited resources being substantially diverted to dealing with cases of individual consumer dissatisfaction relating to deficiency in service (often nondelivery of apartments or cars booked with dealers) or to adjudicating allegations of false advertising or misleading prize schemes. Consumers found the MRTP route far more effective than

resorting to the Consumer Protection Act, and most of the cases now pending before the commission fall into categories that should not have been part of a competition law in the first place.

8. *Hindustan Lever Employees' Union v. Hindustan Lever and Others*, 1995 SCC 499. Quotations are from paragraphs 73 and 71 of the majority judgment. The majority judgment also invoked an argument similar to the "failing firm defense" provided for in the United States. TOMCO was ailing and would probably have closed down had it not merged into the stronger firm. The public interest was identified with that of its shareholders and employees. Another judge gave a separate but concurring judgment, acknowledging that when a merger involved a foreign company, there could be broader public interest issues involved, but that judge found no grounds for interfering in the merger under consideration. See Singh (2000) for a slightly different interpretation of this judgment.

9. Only two cases had been referred to the commission. One was a blatantly political move to muzzle a newspaper that was critical of the authoritarian 1975–77 state of emergency; the reference was retracted by the successor government. The other case was struck down by the courts.

10. The Herfindahl index, as reported in CMIE (2001), is the sum of firms' squared market shares, which are taken as shares of the aggregate domestic sales of the industry. (Imports of all the consumer goods mentioned in this paragraph were negligible in the 1990s.) The index ranges from zero for an industry with many producers to one in the case of monopoly.

11. The conference that led to this volume had a South Asian focus, so it might be appropriate to point out that although the merger of Lipton and Brooke Bond into HLL's parent Unilever passed unchallenged in India, the Pakistan competition authority succeeded in getting Unilever "to withdraw one of its brands and reduce its shareholding in Brook Bond Pakistan to 40 per cent" (UNCTAD 1997, p. 199).

12. Promoted as an export joint venture by six producers, ANSAC was recognized by the U.S. government under the Webb-Pomerene Act's exemption from American antitrust laws, whereas three of the leading members of AMAI were under investigation for cartelization by the MRTPC.

13. *Haridas Exports v. All India Float Glass Manufacturers' Association*, 2002 6 SCC 600.

14. This reasoning also provides a theoretical justification for the exemptions from competition laws that most industrial countries grant to their firms with regard to export sales, as long as the anticompetitive conduct does not adversely affect the home market. Because firms in developing countries seldom have monopoly power in their export markets, this is not particularly relevant here, although as importers, developing countries may be legitimately concerned about anticompetitive conduct by their foreign suppliers.

15. This situation is quite apart from political economy problems involving the forced exit of unwanted firms and their workers; in fact, extremely cumbersome procedures relating to bankruptcy and transactions in land in India effectively make expenditures on several other assets sunk costs.

16. In industries that have been protected for a long time, equipment is likely to be obsolete and organized labor succeeds in getting wages higher than those prevailing in the unorganized sector. Indian industry also has been subjected to a high interest rate regime. The private costs of labor and capital are therefore higher than the opportunity costs of these resources to society.

17. Most of the results discussed in this paragraph are derived in a homogeneous-product framework. Although one would expect product differentiation to moderate the business-stealing effect of foreign entry, as well as to provide an additional source of welfare gains in the form of greater variety, the problem does not go away. Several authors cited in Bhattacharjea (2002) have recently shown that limited foreign entry can reduce welfare in various differentiated product models as well.

18. In the context of organized manufacturing in India, a substantial proportion of labor input must be considered a fixed factor because of legal restrictions on retrenchment.

19. Banga also showed that the picture is reversed for export performance: U.S. presence had positive direct and indirect effects, whereas Japanese presence had no significant effect.

20. See especially Scherer (1994), Utton (1995), and Tharakan (2000). Some members of the WTO Working Group also expressed similar opinions, although it is significant that both the EU and the United States argued against replacing antidumping with competition policy standards on the grounds that antidumping was primarily a response not to exporting firms' behavior but to government policies,

such as import restrictions and weak competition policy enforcement that enabled exporters to charge higher prices in their home countries (WTO 1998, paras. 39, 48, and 49; discussions recorded in the 1999 report went over much the same ground).

21. *Tetra Pak SA v. EC Commission*, 1997 CMLR 662. It should also be noted that even *Matsushita* was decided by a narrow majority (five to four), with the minority rejecting the recoupment standard.

22. AMAI later succeeded in getting antidumping duties imposed as well.

23. See Khemani (2002) for a useful compilation, with economic arguments in favor of such exemptions.

24. These arguments are advanced in the Indian communication (WTO 2002a).

25. This proviso would also exonerate the anticompetitive practices of large firms, provided they had this desirable effect (WTO 2002b).

References

The word "processed" describes informally produced works that may not be available commonly through libraries.

Agarwal, M. 2002. "Analyses of Mergers in India." M.Phil. dissertation, University of Delhi.

Aitken, B. J., and A. E. Harrison. 1999. "Do Domestic Firms Benefit from Direct Foreign Investment? Evidence from Venezuela." American Economic Review 89: 605–18.

Alkali Manufacturers' Association of India v. Sinochem International Chemical Company and Nahar Industrial Enterprise. 1999. Comp LJ 326.

All India Float Glass Manufacturers' Association v. P.T. Mulia Industries and Others. 2000. CTJ 252.

Balakrishnan, P., and K. Pushpangadan. 1998. "What Do We Know about Productivity Growth in Indian Industry?" *Economic and Political Weekly* 33: 2241–46.

Balakrishnan, P., K. Pushpangadan, and M. S. Kumar. 2000. "Trade Liberalisation and Productivity Growth: Evidence from Firm-level Panel Data." *Economic and Political Weekly* 35: 3679–82.

Banga, R. 2003. "The Nature, Pattern and Impact of Japanese and U.S. Foreign Direct Investments in Indian Manufacturing." Ph.D. dissertation, University of Delhi.

Basant, R. 2000. "Corporate Response to Economic Reforms." *Economic and Political Weekly* 35: 813–22.

Basant, R., and S. Morris. 2000. "Competition Policy in India: Issues for a Globalising Economy." Indian Institute of Management, Ahmedabad. Processed. Executive summary published in *Economic and Political Weekly* 35: 2735–47.

Beena, P. L. 2003. "Understanding the Latest Phase of the Merger Wave in India: A Comparative Perspective." Paper presented at the Conference on Globalisation in India, sponsored by the School of Management of the Indian Institute of Technology, January, Bombay.

Bhagwati, J. N., and P. Desai. 1970. *India: Planning for Industrialisation*. Delhi: Oxford University Press.

Bhattacharjea, A. 1995. "Strategic Tariffs and Endogenous Market Structures: Trade and Industrial Policies under Imperfect Competition." *Journal of Development Economics* 47: 287–312.

———. 2000. "Predation, Protection and the 'Public Interest.'" *Economic and Political Weekly* 49: 4327–36.

———. 2002. "Foreign Entry and Domestic Welfare: Lessons for Developing Countries." *Journal of International Trade and Economic Development* 11: 143–62.

———. Forthcoming. "India's Competition Policy." *Economic and Political Weekly*.

Blomstrom, M., and A. Kokko. 1998. "Multinational Corporations and Spillovers." *Journal of Economic Surveys* 12: 247–77.

Chang, H.-J. 2002. *Kicking Away the Ladder: Development Strategy in Historical Perspective*. London: Anthem Press.

CMIE (Centre for Monitoring Indian Economy). Various years. *Industry: Market Size and Shares*. New Delhi.

Cox, D., and R. Harris. 1984. "Trade Liberalization and Industrial Organization: Some Estimates for Canada." *Journal of Political Economy* 93: 115–45.

Das, D. K. 2001. "Some Aspects of Productivity Growth and Trade in Indian Industry: Exploring the Trade Liberalization–Productivity Link." Ph.D. dissertation, University of Delhi.

Dixit, A. 1984. "Trade Policy for Oligopolistic Industries." *Economic Journal* 94: 1–15.

Eastman, H., and S. Stykolt. 1960. "A Model for the Study of Protected Oligopolies." *Economic Journal* 70: 336–47.

"The ET-CMIE M&As Survey." 2003. *Economic Times* March 7: 13.

Evenett, S. J., A. Lehmann, and B. Steil, eds. 2000. *Antitrust Goes Global: What Future for Transatlantic Cooperation?* Washington, D.C.: Brookings Institute/Royal Institute of International Affairs.

"FDI behind India's Stance: Lamy." 2003. *Business Standard*, March 15–16, p. 2.

Government of India. 1999. *Report of the Expert Group on Interaction Between Trade and Competition Policy.* Ministry of Commerce.

———. 2000. *Report of the High Level Committee on Competition Policy and Law.* Ministry of Law, Justice and Company Affairs.

Head, K., and J. Ries. 1997. "International Mergers and Welfare under Decentralized Competition Policy." *Canadian Journal of Economics* 30: 1104–23.

———. 1999. "Rationalization Effect of Tariff Reductions." *Journal of International Economics* 47: 295–320.

Horn, H., and J. Levinsohn. 2001. "Merger Policies and Trade Liberalisation." *Economic Journal* 111: 244–76.

Khanna, S. 1999. "Financial Reforms and Industrial Sector in India." *Economic and Political Weekly* 34: 3231–41.

Khemani, R. S. 2002. "Application of Competition Law: Exemptions and Exceptions." United Nations document UNCTAD/DITC/CLP/Misc25.

Kumar, N. 2000. "Mergers and Acquisitions by MNEs: Patterns and Implications." *Economic and Political Weekly* 35: 2851–58.

Lee, K. U. 1998. *Competition Policy, Deregulation and Economic Development.* Seoul: Korea Institute for Industrial Economics and Trade.

Levinsohn, J. 1996. "Competition Policy and International Trade." In J. Bhagwati and R. Hudec, eds., *Fair Trade and Harmonization: Prerequisites for Free Trade.* Cambridge, Mass.: MIT Press.

Levy, S., and S. Nolan. 1992. "Trade and Foreign Investment Policies under Imperfect Competition: Lessons for Developing Countries." *Journal of Development Economics* 37: 31–62.

Lloyd, P. J. 1998. "Globalisation and Competition Policies." *Weltwirtschaftliches Archiv* 134: 161–85.

Mankiw, N. G. and M. Whinston. 1986. "Free Entry and Social Inefficiency." *Rand Journal of Economics* 27: 48–58.

Naidu, R. 2000. "Where Size Matters." *Business Standard Smart Investor* April 17: 6–7.

OECD (Organisation for Economic Co-operation and Development). 1998. *Complementarities between Trade and Competition Policies.* Joint Group on Trade and Competition. Paris.

———. 2000. *Hard Core Cartels.* Paris.

Ordover, J. A. 1998. "Predatory Pricing." In P. Newman, ed., *The New Palgrave Dictionary of Economics and the Law.* London: Macmillan Reference.

Perroni, C., and J. Whalley. 1996. "Possible Developing Country Impacts from a Competition Policy Negotiation." In V. N. Balasubramanyam and D. Greenaway, eds., *Trade and Development: Essays in Honour of Jagdish Bhagwati.* Basingstoke, U.K.: Macmillan.

Sandesara, J. C. 1994. "Restrictive Trade Practices in India, 1961–91: Experience of Control and Agenda for Further Work." *Economic and Political Weekly* 29: 2081–94.

Scherer, F. M. 1994. *Competition Policies for an Integrated World Economy.* Washington, D.C.: Brookings Institute.

Singh, J. 1999. "Some Aspects of Industrial and Labour Markets in India: Perspectives from Law and Economics." Ph.D. dissertation, University of Delhi.

————. 2000. "Monopolistic Trade Practices and Concentration of Economic Power: Some Conceptual Problems in MRTP Act." *Economic and Political Weekly* 35: 4437–44.

Srivastava, V. 2001. *The Impact of Economic Reforms on Industrial Productivity, Efficiency and Competitiveness: A Panel Study of Indian Companies.* New Delhi: Industrial Development Bank of India. Processed.

Tharakan, P. K. M. 2000. "Predatory Pricing and Anti-dumping." In G. Norman and J.-F. Thisse, eds., *Market Structure and Competition Policy: Game Theoretic Approaches.* Cambridge, U.K.: Cambridge University Press.

UNCTAD (United Nations Conference on Trade and Development). 1997. *World Investment Report: Transnational Corporations, Market Structure and Competition Policy.* New York.

Unni, J., N. Lalitha, and U. Rani. 2001. "Economic Reforms and Productivity Trends in Indian Manufacturing." *Economic and Political Weekly* 36: 3914–22.

USTR (United States Trade Representative). 2000. *National Trade Estimate Report on Foreign Trade Barriers.* Washington, D.C.

————. 2001. *National Trade Estimate Report on Foreign Trade Barriers.* Washington, D.C.

Utton, M. A. 1995. *Market Dominance and Antitrust Policy.* Cheltenham, U.K.: Edward Elgar.

WTO (World Trade Organization). Various years. *Reports of the Working Group on the Interaction between Trade and Competition Policy to the General Council.* WT/WGTCP/1-6. Geneva.

————. 1996. "Singapore Ministerial Declaration." WT/MIN(96)/DEC. Geneva.

————. 1998. "Report on the Meeting of 27–28 July 1998." WT/WGTCP/M/5. Geneva.

————. 2000. "Communication from India." WT/WGTCP/W/149. Geneva.

————. 2001. "Communication from India." WT/GC/W/459. Geneva.

————. 2002a. "Communication from India." WT/WGTCP/W/216. Geneva.

————. 2002b. "Communication from South Africa." WT/WGTCP/W/220. Geneva.

————. 2002c. "Communication from the European Community and Its Member States." WT/WGTCP/W/222. Geneva.

10

INDIA'S ACCESSION TO THE GOVERNMENT PROCUREMENT AGREEMENT: IDENTIFYING COSTS AND BENEFITS

Vivek Srivastava

The Government Procurement Agreement (GPA)[1] is currently a plurilateral agreement with 27 signatories. Although virtually no developing country, including India, is a signatory to the present agreement, even industrial countries, such as Australia and New Zealand and some Organisation for Economic Co-operation and Development (OECD) countries, remain outside its purview. This raises two important questions. First, what are the considerations for a developing country (such as India) in considering becoming party to this agreement? Second—and this question is largely connected with the first—what needs to be done to multilateralize the agreement? This chapter will focus on the first question because a better appreciation of the issues is important for answering the second question.

There are two potential sources of benefit for signatories to the GPA. First, as a result of the transparency requirements and competition resulting from the agreement, the tax-paying public could get better value for money spent on government purchases. The second benefit is an increase in export markets as a result of

I am grateful to Aaditya Mattoo, A. N. Varma, J. L. Bajaj, Sunil Chaturvedi, Deepak Sanan, Ajay Mahal, and Agneshwar Sen for their material help and encouragement during the writing of this chapter. Suchita Mehta and Rukma Biswas provided the research assistance for the original version. Prasun Bhattacharjee provided excellent support in updating the chapter.

purchases by governments of other member countries. The general perception is that the second source of gain is likely to be small for developing countries, so it is important to estimate the potential gains from achieving transparency in procurement procedures and from nondiscrimination in the purchase of goods and services. It is unfortunate that economic theory does not provide clear answers. There are cases in which discrimination can be shown to be welfare enhancing. In addition, the benefits of conforming to the discipline of the GPA may be outweighed by the costs.

The apparent position of the Indian government is that although it is willing to negotiate an agreement on transparency in government procurement, it is opposed to extending this to a market-access agreement. Even with respect to this limited agenda, a major problem is the inclusion of state governments and public sector undertakings within the scope of the agreement. Although these costs have not been explicitly documented (most likely not calculated), implicit in this decision is the assumption that the costs of entering into an agreement like the existing GPA and of including state governments and public enterprises in a transparency agreement outweigh the possible benefits. There is a clear need for some concrete information if the issue of India's membership in the GPA or in a transparency agreement is to be discussed in a meaningful way. There is a gap in the literature with respect to these issues and virtually none of the relevant information is readily available for India. This chapter takes a first step toward filling this gap.

The rest of this chapter is organized as follows. The next section provides background by briefly outlining some of the theoretical considerations involved in an assessment of costs and benefits. The third section summarizes the salient features of the existing GPA. The fourth section describes the procedures for government procurement in India and the extent to which these procedures diverge from the requirements of the GPA. The fifth section discusses the Indian government's position on the GPA. The sixth section offers estimates of purchases by the government sector in India and, based on this, the seventh section summarizes the estimated costs and benefits. The last section concludes the chapter with a summary and the implications of the main findings and then a brief discussion of clarifications of and changes in India's position since this chapter was first prepared.

Theoretical Background for Assessing Costs and Benefits

There are three potential sources of gain from market access and transparency. It is a well-known theorem in the classical theory of international trade that any restriction on free trade reduces welfare. Thus any form of preferential treatment of domestic firms is likely to be welfare reducing. Second, nondiscrimination should increase competition and minimize procurement costs. Third, lack of transparency in procurement could lead to corruption and rent seeking. The last two possible gains supplement the traditional "gains from trade" argument.

What are the possible costs? First, there are the costs of switching over from the existing procurement regime. These costs depend on the divergence of the existing procurement policies from those required by the GPA and the number of entities involved. For India the costs could be high because of its federal structure, the number of subcentral entities, and the large number of central and state public sector enterprises. Debroy and Pursell (1997) have stated that although there would be no problem for India to have joined the Tokyo Round GPA, this is not true for the current GPA because of its extension to subcentral and other public entities and to the purchase of services. Attempts must be made to estimate the changes involved and to examine what exclusions, if any, might be justified on these grounds.

Second, there are some theoretically justifiable arguments for preferential treatment. The so-called New Trade Theory developed during the 1980s showed that, in the presence of imperfect competition and increasing returns to scale, interventions in trade could be used to shift profits to domestic firms or to generate positive externalities (see Krugman 1988, Helpman and Krugman 1986). Some of these arguments can be extended to the case of government procurement (for example, see Branco [1994]). In addition, there are some other possible justifications for preferential government procurement. These include the possibilities of increasing competition through price preferences (McAfee and McMillan 1989), reducing price-cost margins by expanding domestic output (Chen 1995), avoiding problems of contract enforcement (Laffont and Tirole 1991), and realizing economies in the presence of asymmetric information.[2] Although such "strategic" interventions are difficult to target accurately and their potential benefits are likely to be small, they are popular with governments and the business community (see Krugman [1987] for a discussion). For this reason it is important to identify the potential gains from such discriminatory policies.[3]

The third argument against the GPA suggests that discrimination does not significantly restrict trade and consequently the gains from nondiscrimination are small. Baldwin (1970, 1984) and Baldwin and Richardson (1972) argued that if domestic and foreign goods are perfect substitutes, in the presence of perfect competition, preferential treatment for domestic industry will not have an effect on the level of imports, domestic prices, output, or employment. Mattoo (1996) has pointed out, however, that the benefits may be significant if government demand exceeds domestic supply, if domestic and foreign goods and services are not perfect substitutes, and if there is imperfect competition. Evidence suggests that, in a wide variety of cases, discriminatory procurement does have an adverse effect on trade.

Fourth, as markets become more competitive and trade becomes freer, it would become easier to conform to the discipline of the GPA. But, at the same time, the need for the GPA would become less pressing. With the public sector being subject to harder budget constraints, procurement by these entities is likely to become more efficient. On the other hand, with trade restricted through tariffs and non-tariff barriers, the GPA may not achieve much. Thus, there is the issue of whether the GPA is relevant in such a situation. Debroy and Pursell (1997) noted that the procurement policy regime in India has been reformed considerably since 1991.

Important Features of the GPA

The Agreement on Government Procurement—originally negotiated during the Tokyo Round—was renegotiated during the Uruguay Round. The revised GPA, signed in Marrakesh on April 15, 1994, entered into force on January 1, 1996. It is one of the World Trade Organization's (WTO) Annex IV or Plurilateral Agreements. Participation is restricted to WTO members, and it applies only to WTO members that have signed it.

Objective, Scope, and Structure

The objective of the new GPA is to contribute to the "liberalization and expansion of world trade" by eliminating discrimination against and between foreign products, services, and suppliers; by enhancing the transparency of laws and practices; and by ensuring fair, prompt, and effective enforcement of international provisions on government procurement.

Its scope is wider than that of the Tokyo Round agreement. It covers procurement of goods, services (including construction services), and lease, rental, and hiring arrangements. It has been extended to purchases by subcentral government entities as well as other government entities and to such enterprises as public utilities.[4]

One of its central features is that, in government purchases covered by the agreement, signatories must give *most-favored-nation (MFN) treatment (nondiscrimination)* and *national treatment* to products and services of the other signatories. It specifies the need to comply with detailed procedures to ensure that potential foreign suppliers are given a real chance to compete for government contracts.

Transparency and Tendering Procedures

Transparency is a key element of the agreement, and the requirements are listed in a comprehensive set of rules that form the bulk of the agreement. These requirements include rules regarding technical specifications, tendering procedures, qualification of suppliers, invitation to tender, selection procedures, time limits, documentation requirements, procedures for award and negotiation, limited tendering, transparency, and publication of awards and of reasons why tenders have failed.

Three methods of tendering—open, selective, and limited—are permitted, with open and selective tendering being the preferred methods. All three may be complemented by competitive negotiation. Under open tendering, any interested supplier may submit a bid in response to a call for tenders. Selective tendering involves preselected potential suppliers and usually is intended to speed up the tendering process. Under limited tendering procedures, the buyer contacts specific suppliers individually. This is only permitted under special circumstances and may not be used as a means of reducing competition, discriminating among suppliers, or providing protection to domestic producers or suppliers.

Special Treatment of Developing Countries

Article V of the agreement provides for special consideration to be given to developing countries. The provisions of this article recognize the needs of developing countries to safeguard their balance of payments, promote the development of domestic industry in rural and backward areas, foster the development of other sectors, support industrial units dependent on government procurement, and encourage economic development through regional or global arrangements. In this context, developing countries can negotiate exclusions from national treatment. Industrial countries are expected to provide technical assistance, on request, to developing countries.

Challenge Procedure

A unique feature of the agreement is the challenge procedure that is independent of the WTO's dispute-settlement mechanism. This procedure allows firms to protest during as well as after completion of the decisionmaking process. Each member country is required to set up a reviewing procedure using a court or some independent review authority. Suppliers who feel that a purchasing entity has not lived up to the rules can pursue a complaint with that entity. Procedures must allow rapid interim measures to be taken, including suspension of the procurement process if necessary. The signatories must provide for correction of a breach of the agreement or compensation for loss or damages suffered. Multilateral monitoring and the threat of the WTO dispute-settlement procedures put pressure on purchasing entities to abide by the disciplines of the agreement.

Procedures and Practices in India

In principle, the government procurement system is set up to ensure the purchase of good-quality products in the most economic and efficient manner. The stated procurement policy is expected to allow the maximum level of competition among bidders and to make the processes of bidding and decisionmaking transparent. In spite of this policy, government purchases often are the subject of controversy and are a potential source of corruption (Debroy and Pursell 1997). As Hoekman (1998) has pointed out, it is difficult to estimate the extent to which the actual practice diverges from the formal rules and procedures.

The central government, the state governments, and the three tiers of local government—village, intermediate, and district—make up the various levels of government in India. In addition to these strata, there are the centrally and state-owned enterprises. There is no single uniform law governing procurement by all of these government entities. In this section I will discuss briefly some of the features of the procurement system that are relevant to this chapter.[5]

Although there is no legal definition of government procurement, as exist for most other activities of government, there are fairly detailed sets of procedures and rules governing procurement and procurement by government entities. The general principles governing procurement by the central government are laid down in the General Financial Rules (GFRs) of the Ministry of Finance. The purchase procedures followed by various government departments have evolved in line with these general principles. The Directorate General of Supplies and Disposal (DGS&D) under the aegis of the Department of Supply is the central purchasing organization of the Government of India. As a result of decentralization in the 1970s, the role of the DGS&D is restricted to finalizing rate contracts for "common use" items. The role of the DGS&D has been declining gradually and, even in nominal terms, purchases by the directorate have fallen from Rs. 24.0 billion in 1995/96 to Rs. 16.6 billion in 1998/99. Other ministries and departments and departmental undertakings have been delegated powers enabling them to make their own purchases. Similarly, the procedures followed by state governments are based on the states' financial rules and a number of states have the equivalent of a central-stores purchasing organization.[6]

Procurement Methods

The rules provide for purchases based on advertisements (open tender), direct invitation to a limited number of firms (limited tender), invitation to one firm only (single tender), and negotiation with one or more firms.[7] Tender notices are generally publicized through the *Indian Trade Journal*, a monthly bulletin issued by the DGS&D, and are now available on the NIC-NET of the National Informatics Centre (NIC). For global tenders, notices are also published or disseminated through Indian embassies. In the case of the railways, all tenders above a value of Rs. 0.3 million are invited by open advertisements in the national newspapers.

The specifications for procurement normally are quite comprehensive and generally are drafted on the basis of national or international standard specifications.[8] There is a well-defined registration procedure to establish "reliable and regular sources" of supply for government purchases. The DGS&D registers firms interested in government purchases as approved contractors for supply of stores of various descriptions. Similarly, the National Small Industries Corporation registers such firms in the small-scale sector, and Indian Railways also has an analogous registration procedure.

Preferential Treatment

According to the purchase policy, all the suppliers—whether domestic or international—are to be treated at par and no preference is given to domestic suppliers.[9] According to the Indian government, "domestic bidders are treated on par with foreign bidders and the ultimate price available to the user department is the determining criterion."[10] However, with a view to encouraging the small-scale sector, village industries, certain kinds of women's organizations, and public enterprises, some preferential treatment is allowed. Generally such preferential treatment discriminates against domestic as well as foreign firms not belonging to these categories and, in this sense, foreign firms get "national treatment." Debroy and Pursell (1997) provided a comprehensive review of the policy and an analysis of its impact. I will discuss here the main features of this policy and some recent changes.

Preference for the Public Sector

As is well known, a large public sector developed in India as a result of the policies initiated in 1956.[11] Prior to the reforms initiated in 1991, public sector enterprises (PSEs) were not only protected from competition through reservation, but there were also policies that mandated that both central government departments and public sector enterprises apply price and purchase preference in favor of the public sector. The preference for the public sector also applied to construction and service enterprises and was extended to state-level PSEs.

Since that time some significant changes have occurred. The list of industries reserved for the public sector has now been reduced significantly. The system of price preferences has been discontinued, although the practice of using private sector bids to allow public sector units to submit a fresh bid continues. This system of "purchase preference" has been extended, with some modifications, to orders placed until March 31, 2000. Under this provision a government enterprise whose bid is within 10 percent of that of a large private unit is allowed to revise its price downward and is eligible for a parallel-rate contract. Given the emphasis on privatization and reform of the public sector, such purchase preferences are now an anachronism.

Preference for the Small-scale Sector

Policies aimed at protecting and promoting artisans and small-scale firms have constituted an important element of India's traditional economic policies. These include reserving a large number of products for production by small-scale firms. The small-scale sector also is protected through compulsory purchase and price preferences on procurement imposed on central government ministries, departments, and PSEs. The purchase-preference system requires that specified products be procured exclusively from small-scale firms. In addition, a system of price preference exists: if the price offered by the small-scale unit is not more than 15 percent above the price offered by a large unit, the product has to be purchased from the small-scale sector. This condition applies not only to central ministries and departments, but also to central public undertakings. If the competition is with the duty-inclusive price of imports, the implied preferential margin is higher with respect to the duty-free price of imports. As in the case of the public sector, the small-scale sector is exempted from the payment of earnest money and tender fees. So far, the protection of artisans and small-scale firms, and the subsidies and preferences directed to them, have not been touched by the reforms. Between 1994/95 and 1998/99, purchases by DGS&D from the small-scale sector were about 8–10 percent of the directorate's total purchases.[12]

Preferences for Indigenous Production

Before 1991 foreign firms' direct investment in India was discouraged. The maximum foreign equity permitted in joint ventures was 40 percent. There were complicated clearance procedures and controls over the terms of technical agreements between local and foreign firms. Government procurement was used directly to favor indigenous production over imports. Both a price and purchase preference in favor of domestic production used to exist. The system of price preference was abolished in 1992. Purchase preference was also scrapped. In some cases, however, the preference for Indian providers of services, if not of goods, continues to apply.

Redress of Grievances and Settlement of Dispute

According to the government, regular interaction is maintained with the suppliers as well as tenderers so as to have necessary feedback and also to remove the grievances of the suppliers. The primary objective is to provide "guidelines and counseling" in all procedural and contractual matters pertaining to DGS&D procurement. The grievances relating to delays in action concerning purchases and inspection are resolved. There is also a Standing Review Committee functioning under the DGS&D. Unresolved issues pertaining to contracts are settled through arbitration, which is part of the general conditions of the contract.

India's Procurement Policy and the GPA: Areas of Divergence

The major differences are with respect to the national treatment, transparency, and challenge and review provisions of the GPA. With a number of price and purchase preferences still in place, India's policies are at odds with the requirements of Article III. Although Article V provides some flexibility to developing countries, and exclusions are possible, the long-term objective of the GPA is do away with any kind of preferential treatment in purchases. To promote greater transparency in transactions, Article XVIII requires that information on winning contracts be made public. It also makes it mandatory for each entity, on request, to provide pertinent information concerning the reasons for rejection and the characteristics and relative advantages of the selected tender. This could be a major problem area because the procurement policies in place in India do not have any such provision. In general India has the reputation of being one of the most opaque countries in which to do business. As noted in the previous section, the GPA lays down a detailed challenge procedure (Article XX), which has no parallel in the existing rules and procedures in India insofar as there is no independent adjudicating authority, and the concerned department generally deals with disputes. An aggrieved party obviously always has access to a regular court of law.

India's Position[13]

Like most other developing countries, India did not sign the Tokyo Round GPA and is not a signatory to the current GPA. India, however, has dropped its opposition to a multilateral agreement on transparency in government procurement, a long-standing demand of various multilateral agencies as well as some of its trading partners ("Not Good Enough" 1999). This is one of the new issues that has arisen from the initiatives of the Singapore Ministerial Conference of December 1996 and is likely to be part of the Millennium Round negotiations. The Working

Group on Transparency in Government Procurement had been set up by the Singapore Ministerial Conference to study the existing practices and develop elements for inclusion in a suitable agreement.

India's biggest problem with any government procurement agreement is with the "national treatment" requirement. As noted above, the procurement policies of the government give preference to various categories of companies based on size and location. Such practices are based on the view that government procurement is an important instrument for directing investment to "desirable" sectors, less privileged social groups, and underdeveloped regions of the country. In view of these concerns, the Indian government is only willing to go along with a suitable transparency agreement that steers clear of market-access issues.

Two other important areas of concern for India are the definition and scope of government procurement and the issue of procurement methods. With regard to the former, it is felt that a broad definition that includes government entities at the subcentral level and other public entities would be difficult for a quasi-federal state like India with multiple levels of government and with a large number of public sector enterprises. Any agreement should be restricted to the central government. It is also held that the service sector and lease arrangements should be beyond the purview of the agreement. Further, it is believed that the methods of procurement have no bearing on transparency, and that there should be no restriction on the choice of procurement method other than those placed by domestic legislation. In addition, it is felt that existing domestic review and appeal procedures are available and should not be a part of any transparency agreement. Last, India maintains that the proposed transparency agreement should recognize the special needs of developing countries and should incorporate a special clause in this regard.[14]

India clearly is not ready to negotiate any agreement that goes beyond transparency. In fact, it is feared that the transparency agreement might be the forerunner for an agreement involving "national treatment." As noted above, the position is that this would deprive the government of an important instrument of development policy. Although the existing plurilateral GPA provides for exemptions from national treatment for certain categories of industries, these exemptions have to be negotiated with the other members. Finally, the government feels applying the WTO dispute-settlement mechanism to any transparency arrangement is unwarranted, and that effective domestic review procedures should suffice in any such agreement.

Participants at the Doha (Fourth) Ministerial Conference in November 2001 agreed that negotiation on the GPA will take place after the Fifth Session of the Ministerial Conference and will build on progress made in the Working Group on Transparency in Government Procurement. *It has been agreed that negotiations will be limited to transparency aspects and will not restrict the scope for countries to give preference to domestic supplies and suppliers.*

Estimating the Value of Government Purchases

In this section I present estimates of the total value of government procurement in India, with separate estimates for the central government, state governments,[15] and public sector undertakings (PSUs). No estimates of the value of government purchases are available for India. The estimates presented here are largely based on publicly available data and should only be treated as being broadly indicative of the scale of government purchases. Although there is scope for improving these estimates, beyond a point the increase in accuracy is not likely to be commensurate with the effort involved in achieving it.

Central Government Purchases

Estimates of purchases by central government ministries and departments are provided in table 10.1. In view of the large scale of their purchases, and the fact that purchases of goods and services (primarily construction contracts) account for a larger share of their expenditures, estimates for the ministries of railways and telecommunications are presented separately.[16] Defense purchases are also excluded because these are exempt from the provisions of the GPA.

It is reasonably straightforward to arrive at the estimate of central government expenditure with some government procurement component (row 14 of table 10.1).[17] Based on this, the expenditure on purchase of goods and services is estimated to be Rs. 128.21 billion (US$2.9 billion) in 1999/00 and Rs. 186.37 billion ($4.0 billion) in 2000/01.[18] Without additional data at the ministry/department level it is not possible to estimate exactly what proportion of spending will be above the GPA thresholds. However, expenditures on individual items are likely to be small in the case of "office expenses," "motor vehicles," "clothing and tentage," and "minor works." If these items are excluded, the remaining items account for about 80 percent of total purchases. Two sets of estimates, provided in the last two rows of table 10.1, are based on the assumptions that about 40 percent ("Subject to GPA–1") and 60 percent ("Subject to GPA–2") of these purchases would be above the GPA thresholds.[19]

Railways and Telecommunications

The estimates for purchases by railways and the telecommunication departments are presented in tables 10.2 and 10.3.

TABLE 10.1   Central Government Expenditures, Excluding Railways and Telecommunications (in billions of rupees)

	1998/99 (RE)	1999/00 (RE)	2000/01 (BE)
GDP at current prices	17,626.00	19,504.51	21,809.86
Nonplan expenditure	2,135.42	2,243.43	2,503.87
Share of GDP (percent)	12.0	12.0	11.0
Plan outlay (including IEBR)	884.80	963.09	1173.34
Share of GDP (percent)	5.0	5.0	5.0
Total expenditure by government departments and ministries	3,020.22	3,206.52	3,677.21
Share of GDP (percent)	17.0	16.0	17.0
Total expenditure on railways and telecommunications	209.40	228.50	294.04
Total expenditure by government departments and ministries (excluding railways and telecommunications)	2,810.82	2,978.02	3,383.17
Nonplan expenditure with no central government procurement component	1,888.38	1977.96	2232.41
Plan expenditure with no central government procurement component	301.08	357.35	368.25
Total expenditure with no central government procurement component	2,189.46	2,335.31	2,600.66
Pay and allowances (including travel) of central ministries (excluding railways and telecommunications)	151.89	215.34	161.29
Central government expenditure with some government procurement component	469.47	427.37	621.22
Share of GDP (percent)	3.0	2.0	3.0
Expenditure on purchases of goods and services	140.84	128.21	186.37
Purchases subject to GPA–1 (at 30%)	42.25	38.46	55.91
Purchases subject to GPA–2 (at 50%)	70.42	64.11	93.19

BE budget estimates; GDP gross domestic product; GPA Government Procurement Agreement; IEBR internal and extrabudgetary resources; RE revised estimates.

Source: Ministry of Finance 1998, 1999, 2000.

Railways   The railway budget provides data on items that involve purchase of goods and services. The expenditure on items 2, 3, 4, and 5 (table 10.2) adds up to about Rs. 113.74 billion for 1999/00 (US$2.6 billion),[20]—about 37 percent of the total expenditure of Rs. 309 billion ($7.1 billion)—and Rs. 133.33 billion for

**TABLE 10.2   Estimates of Purchases by Railways
(in billions of rupees)**

	1998/99 (RE)	1999/00 (RE)	2000/01 (BE)
Total working expenses	284.00	309.09	355.52
Purchase of miscellaneous stores	5.23	5.06	6.35
Purchase of fuel	13.42	15.91	19.22
Purchase of stores for maintenance	—	39.08	41.77
Budget for new construction	—	59.65	73.32
Expenditure with government procurement component	—	113.74	133.33
Share of total expenditure (percent)	—	37.0	38.0
Subject to GPA–1	—	37.91	44.44
Subject to GPA–2	—	75.83	88.89

BE budget estimates; GPA Government Procurement Agreement; RE revised estimates.

—Not available.

Source: Ministry of Railways 1999a,b, 2000a,b.

2000/01 ($2.9 billion)—about 38 percent of the total expenditure of Rs. 355.52 ($7.6 billion). Based on the assumptions that one-third or two-thirds of the purchases will be above the GPA thresholds, I present two estimates for the value of purchases likely to be subject to the GPA (see table 10.2).

Telecommunications   To make the estimates for the department of telecommunications I have relied on information provided in the central government budget. The estimates presented in table 10.3 are based on the assumption that the expenditures on the capital account on items 1 to 6 have a purchase content of 75 percent, and that the revenue expenditure on "engineering" has a procurement content of 30 percent. Adjustments for thresholds are as in the case of the railways.

State Government Purchases

In the case of state governments, the share of expenditure on procurement in total expenditure is likely to be higher than for the central government because state governments spend less toward loans and grants to lower tiers of government. In view of this I have estimated the share of purchases in total expenditures at the rate of 5 percent to 6 percent.[21] The estimates for the consolidated expenditure of state governments on the purchase of goods and services are presented in table 10.4.[22] In view of the smaller scale of operations of individual state governments, and the

**TABLE 10.3   Estimates of Purchases by Department
of Telecommunications (in billions of rupees)**

	1998/99 (RE)	1999/00 (RE)	2000/01 (BE)
Capital expenses:			
Telegraph systems	0.15	0.19	0.17
Local telephone systems	77.85	94.59	121.80
Long-distance switching systems	1.60	1.60	1.73
Transmission systems	16.00	23.04	26.59
Ancillary systems	1.10	2.59	2.98
Land and building	2.30	2.30	3.40
Revenue expenses:			
Engineering	23.10	22.71	24.27
Total	**122.10**	**147.02**	**180.94**
Expenditure with government procurement component	81.18	100.04	124.78
Subject to GPA–1	**27.06**	**33.35**	**41.59**
Subject to GPA–2	**54.12**	**66.69**	**83.19**

BE budget estimates; GPA Government Procurement Agreement; RE revised estimates.

Note: It is assumed that 75 percent of capital expenses and 30 percent of the engineering expenses are for purchase of goods and services.

Source: Ministry of Finance 1999, 2000, vol 2.

higher threshold limits for subcentral entities provided in the GPA, I have estimated the value of purchases likely to be subject to the GPA to be between 20 percent and 40 percent of the total purchases.

Purchases by Public Sector Enterprises   There are about 240 central PSEs and more than 1,000 state-owned PSEs in India. Data regarding the purchases of PSEs have been obtained from the Prowess database of the Center for Monitoring Indian Economy. The Prowess database provides data on the purchase of domestically sourced and imported raw materials. It is also possible to obtain estimates of the purchase of capital stock by looking at the change in the gross fixed assets of a balanced sample of firms from one year to the next. Although the set of firms represented in the Prowess data is not exhaustive, the data on PSEs appear to be representative of the central PSEs. State PSEs are generally quite small and their purchases are not likely to be significant. The central PSEs in the oil, wholesale trade, and steel sectors account for the bulk of the sales and purchases of all PSEs and these are represented in the data. The aggregate purchase figures are presented in table 10.5.[23]

**TABLE 10.4   State Government Expenditures
(in billions of rupees)**

	1996/97	1997/98	1998/99	1999/00 (RE)	2000/01 (BE)
Development expenditure	1,320.08	1,452.68	1645.04	1983.22	2083.32
Nondevelopment expenditure	620.95	717.67	864.74	1101.37	1254.84
Other expenditure	86.66	111.00	153.83	171.75	169.51
Total expenditure	2,027.69	2,281.35	2,663.61	3,256.34	3,507.67
Estimated expenditure on purchase of goods and services:					
At 5% of total expenditure	101.38	114.07	133.18	162.82	175.38
At 6% of total expenditure	121.66	136.88	159.82	195.38	210.46
Subject to GPA–1	24.33	27.38	31.96	39.08	42.09
Subject to GPA–2	48.66	54.75	63.93	78.15	84.18

BE budget estimates; GPA Government Procurement Agreement; RE revised estimates.

Note: The "Subject to GPA" estimates are based on the assumptions that 20 percent (GPA–1) to 50 percent (GPA–2) of expenditures are likely to be above the GPA thresholds.

Source: Reserve Bank of India 1999, 2000.

**TABLE 10.5   Purchases by Public Sector Enterprises
(in billions of rupees)**

		1991/92	1997/98
Public sector	Total raw materials	669.00	1,400.04
	Imported raw materials	175.10	261.80
	Share of imports (percent)	26.0	19.0
	Change in fixed assets	—	346.20
	Imports of capital equipment	—	24.90
	Total procurement	—	1,746.60
	Subject to GPA–1	—	383.95
	Subject to GPA–2	—	593.23
Private sector	Total raw materials	506.95	1,453.20
	Imported raw materials	43.80	217.50
	Share of imports (percent)	9.0	15.0

—Not available.

Source: Center for Monitoring Indian Economy Prowess database.

According to the Public Enterprises Survey 1997/98, the purchase of finished goods, raw materials, and stores and spares by all central PSEs was Rs. 1,399 billion (US$33 billion) and capital accumulation was Rs. 325 billion ($7.7 billion) during that year (Department of Public Enterprises [1998], table 1.12 and statement 1A). These figures compare reasonably well with those obtained from the Prowess database. Table 10.5 also presents data on the imports of raw materials by PSEs and by comparable private sector enterprises.[24] Although the share of imported inputs for PSEs has come down and that for private enterprises has increased since 1992, the share of imported inputs used by the PSEs continues to be higher than that for the private enterprises.[25]

Without more information, it is difficult to estimate what proportion of these purchases would be above the thresholds laid down in the GPA. I present two sets of estimates in table 10.5. The first is based on the assumption that 20 percent of the value of raw materials used and 30 percent of capital formation would be subject to the GPA, and the second estimate assumes that 30 percent of the value of raw materials used and 50 percent of capital formation would be above GPA thresholds.

Potential Benefits and Costs

In this section I discuss the potential benefits and costs of being a signatory to the GPA and then present estimates of the benefits and costs.

As noted earlier, there are potentially two sources of benefit for signatories to the GPA. First, the tax-paying public could get better value for the money spent by the government on its purchases as a result of the transparency, competition, and discipline imposed by the GPA. Second, there are potential gains through access to larger export markets resulting from the purchases of other member governments. The pessimistic position on this is that gems and jewelry, textiles, yarn and fabrics, and ready-made garments and clothing make up 40 percent to 45 percent of India's current exports, and that these are unlikely candidates for government purchases. With respect to construction services, most Indian construction companies are unlikely to meet international qualification criteria. On the other hand, there is likely to be a large potential for the export of software services and possible gains from South-South trade. In the analysis that follows I do not attempt to estimate these gains. Rather, the estimated net gains depend on the total quantum of government purchases and on the assumptions regarding the social welfare function.

If all individuals (firms) have equal weights in the social welfare function, then the payment of higher prices for purchases made with public money, or the receipt/payment of bribes, does not have any effect on aggregate social welfare (unless foreigners gain), although there is an impact on distribution. There are, of course, other channels through which the prevalence of corruption can have an adverse impact on social welfare. To the extent that transparency in government procurement leads to a reduction in rent-seeking activities and lower levels of corruption, and to the extent that corruption lowers economic growth, impedes development, and undermines political legitimacy,[26] there are gains to be had on this account. Because malfeasance in the award of government contracts and purchases is only one of many sources of corruption, it is not possible to separate the impact of this source of corruption from the "public bad" generated by corruption in general. For this reason I focus here on the direct gains that could accrue exclusively as a result of the reduction in procurement costs that result from the disciplines imposed by the GPA. I do not attempt to estimate the gains from a possible reduction in rent-seeking activities. The concern with corruption in public procurement is largely a concern with issues of distribution rather than efficiency. I will assume that social welfare is lowered if public spending buys fewer (and/or poorer quality) goods and services than what is possible even though this may be matched by private gains for politicians, bureaucrats, producers, or other individuals. Any gains on account of reduction in rent-seeking activities are excluded and, to the extent these are positive, the estimated benefits will be higher. I also do not attempt to estimate possible gains from trade resulting from nonpreferential procurement. As noted earlier, this depends on the relative scale of government purchases. Attempting an estimate of this is beyond the scope of the present exercise and is left as a subject for future research.

The extent of the social loss therefore depends on the relative weights attached to the losers and the gainers, the total quantum of public funds misused, and the total saving that could be generated. If we ignore the externalities associated with corruption, the upper bound to this loss is provided by the total value of government purchases subject to the discipline of the GPA.

These benefits need to be compared with the costs associated with acceding to the GPA. There may be some administrative costs related to switching over to the new system and adhering to its procedural requirements. In addition, as noted earlier, there could be some costs associated with the removal of preferential treatment.

Estimated Benefits

Estimates of the total value of government expenditure above GPA thresholds are consolidated in table 10.6. The estimates for government, including the state governments, range from about 0.78 percent to 1.6 percent of gross domestic product (GDP). The estimates for public sector enterprises are considerably higher, ranging from about 3.5 percent to 5.9 percent of GDP.

TABLE 10.6 Consolidated Government Procurement Estimates (in billions of rupees)

	1997/98		1998/99		1999/00		2000/01	
	Minimum	Maximum	Minimum	Maximum	Minimum	Maximum	Minimum	Maximum
Central government	—	—	42.25	70.42	38.46	64.11	55.91	93.19
Railways	—	—	36.35	72.71	37.91	75.83	44.44	88.89
Telecommunications	—	—	27.06	54.12	33.35	66.69	41.59	83.19
Total central government	—	—	**105.66**	**197.25**	**109.72**	**206.63**	**141.94**	**265.27**
Share of GDP (percent)	—	—	*0.6*	*1.1*	*0.6*	*1.1*	*0.7*	*1.2*
State governments	—	—	31.96	63.93	39.08	78.15	42.09	84.18
Total government	—	—	**137.62**	**261.18**	**148.80**	**284.78**	**184.03**	**349.45**
10% of government expenditure	—	—	13.76	26.12	14.88	28.48	18.40	34.95
20% of government expenditure	—	—	27.52	52.24	29.76	56.96	36.81	69.89
Share of GDP (percent)	—	—	*0.8*	*1.5*	*0.8*	*1.5*	*0.8*	*1.6*
Public sector enterprises	384.9	593.2	431.09	664.38	482.82	744.11	545.25	828.77
Grand total	—	—	**609.99**	**1,003.92**	**676.26**	**1,114.33**	**784.49**	**1,283.06**
Share of GDP (percent)	—	—	*3.5*	*5.7*	*3.5*	*5.7*	*3.6*	*5.9*
GDP	—	—	17,626.00	17,626.00	19,504.51	19,504.51	21,809.86	21,809.86

—Not available.

Note: Figures in italics are estimated or extrapolated.

Source: Author's calculations.

TABLE 10.7 **Potential Gains, Central Government Only (in billions of rupees)**

Relative Weight of Gainers	Savings		
	50%	30%	20%
100%	132.64	79.58	53.05
75%	99.48	59.69	39.79
50%	66.32	39.79	26.53

According to the estimates in table 10.6, the maximum value for this is Rs 265.3 billion (US$5.7 billion) for the year 2000/01 if only the central government is subject to the GPA. The numbers are accordingly higher if state government and PSE purchases are included. The matrix in table 10.7 presents different estimates of the potential social gain based on different combinations of the assumptions regarding the extent of savings of public funds and the relative weight attached to gainers. The estimates range from Rs. 26.53 billion ($568 million) to Rs. 132.64 billion ($2.8 billion) or between 0.1 percent and 0.6 percent of GDP. Realistically, the savings is unlikely to be greater than 30 percent. Based on Domberger, Hall, and Lee (1995), Hoekman (1998) has stated that competitive tendering and outsourcing could produce savings of about 20 percent without compromising quality. Transparency International (1997) notes that noncompetitive procedures may increase costs by about 30 percent. According to a recent study reported by the World Bank (2000), about 51 percent of the respondents stated that for government contracts they paid bribes either "always," "usually," or "frequently." According to 54 percent of the respondents, the payments amounted to between 2 percent and 9 percent of the contract value.

To the extent that discrimination is welfare increasing, the savings will be lower. If the entire savings is treated as a social gain, this amounts to about 0.36 percent of GDP. (Similar calculations, including the spendings of state governments and PSEs, are presented in Appendix 4.) The estimates of social gain, assuming that accession to the GPA results in a 30 percent savings, are presented in table 10.8. To put some further perspective on these numbers, I have also expressed them as a percentage of the fiscal deficit. These calculations show that the social gain would be between 0.36 percent and 1.76 percent of GDP. If these could be translated into savings for the central government, its fiscal deficit could be reduced by about 7.15 percent to 34.60 percent, depending on what entities are included.

TABLE 10.8 Estimates of Social Gain

Entities	Rupees (in billions)	As a Percentage of GDP	As a Percentage of the Fiscal Deficit
Central government only	79.58	0.36	7.15
Including state governments	104.84	0.48	9.42
Including public sector enterprises	384.92	1.76	34.59

Notes: The fiscal deficit used for these calculations is the budgeted fiscal deficit of the central government for 2000/01. To the extent that the actual deficit is higher, the gains will be lower.

Source: Author's calculations.

Estimated Costs

These benefits need to be compared with the costs of signing the GPA. The financial costs of implementing the requirements of the GPA are likely to be low. Undoubtedly, there will be costs associated with the procedural requirements of the GPA. But these are unlikely to lead at the margin to any significant additional expenditure because government entities in India are already subject to complex rules and procedures. Thus, although there will be a one-time switchover cost, any net additional recurring cost is likely to be small. In view of this, implementation costs cannot be an important concern.

Although there is no direct cost involved in doing this, the transparency requirements of announcing winners and providing reasons for rejection are probably the most awkward from the point of view of the government. From its stated position on transparency, however, it follows that the government has no objection to these provisions. In my view, there are likely to be some costs of litigation and delay resulting from the challenge and dispute-settlement procedures of the GPA. The domestic review provision has the potential to be misused by Indian companies. Some deterrents should be built into this mechanism so that it is not misused.

The government is currently using preferential treatment in government purchases as a tool of industrial policy. In keeping with the spirit of reforms, there is no need to continue with the preferential treatment of PSEs. The matter of the small-scale sector is more complicated. At this stage discontinuing preferential treatment may not be feasible politically, but it may be worth estimating the actual extent of the indirect subsidy to the small-scale sector in this way. Currently, the share of DGS&D purchases from the small-scale sector is about 8 percent to

10 percent of the total purchases. Even if all of these purchases involve a price preference of 15 percent (which they do not), the total "subsidy" to the small-scale sector is only about 1.2 percent to 1.5 percent of the total expenditure. If considered necessary, this easily can be paid out as an explicit subsidy through a suitable mechanism. The other sectors receiving preferential treatment are very small and insignificant, and getting exclusions for them should not be difficult.

Conclusion

The major requirements of the GPA are nondiscrimination, competitive tendering, and transparency, together with a domestic review mechanism and the WTO dispute-settlement mechanism. The possible benefits from such an agreement are two-fold. One source of gain is through better market access and gains from trade and the second source is through the cost savings and quality gains likely to result from the disciplines imposed by the GPA. To the extent that corruption is reduced, there are gains that follow from the reduction in negative externalities that arise from corruption. On the other hand, there are some potential benefits from discrimination. As things stand, India, like many other developing countries, is not in favor of the multilateralization of the GPA but is now willing to negotiate a limited transparency agreement. In this chapter I have attempted to identify and quantify (where possible) the costs and benefits to India of acceding to such an agreement.

In view of the composition of India's current export basket, I have assumed that the only significant source of gain can be from the potential savings in government resources that result from the disciplines of the GPA. The gains from market access are likely to be negligible. According to my estimates the maximum savings that is possible for central government purchases is Rs. 79.58 billion (US\$1.7 billion). This figure would increase to Rs. 104.84 billion (\$2.2 billion) if state governments were included and to close to Rs. 385 billion (\$8.2 billion) if all public enterprises were included. In my view, the inclusion of the latter is not justified. PSEs should be treated as commercial entities, and government decisions should not be forced on them. As these entities are privatized or increasingly subject to hard budget constraints over time, efficiency will follow. Although India has a federal structure and state government purchases are not subject to central government decisions, it should be possible (albeit somewhat difficult) to ask state governments to conform to the disciplines of such an agreement. At the first stage, as in the case of the United States, all states need not be included. Thus the realistic upper bound figure is probably close to Rs. 105 billion (\$2.2 billion). These gains chiefly follow from the transparency and competition-promoting provisions of the GPA. The gains will be larger to the extent that there are some indirect benefits resulting from the reduction of corruption in general.

Of course, the constitutional (legal) implication of the central government making a commitment on behalf of state governments is important. The central government will probably need to enter into agreements with individual states. The inclusion of state governments can only be voluntary and will, if at all, have to be done in stages. Purchases by local governments are likely to be small. In view of this, it should be easy enough to negotiate their exclusion. Failing this, they can easily be excluded through the thresholds.

Obviously there will be some costs of putting in place the appropriate processes and procedures. At present, there are fairly complex procedural requirements for purchases by government entities, so even though there will be a one-time switchover cost, any net additional recurring costs are likely to be small. Therefore, implementation costs cannot be an important concern. One possible cost could result from the misuse (overuse) of the domestic review provision in India, where there is a high propensity to litigate and where unsuccessful domestic firms are likely to overuse it. Some deterrent should be built in to minimize that possibility.

I have noted that there may be efficiency costs associated with the ultimate removal of preferential treatment. Although any significant social loss is unlikely to result from this, there may be significant political costs because both the small-scale sector and the public sector are powerful constituencies.[27]

Although corruption is an internal issue and not a trade issue, adopting transparent procedures can send positive signals for foreign investors. For some of the reasons that I have noted, although India may not be ready for the GPA, there should be no problem in negotiating a transparency agreement. When doing this, it needs to be borne in mind that any transparency agreement is, most likely, a precursor to a market access agreement. It also must be noted that, in view of the relatively small scale of its purchases, India's bargaining position on its own is not likely to be very strong. Because these exclusions have to be negotiated "the scope to pursue such policies is therefore inherently limited by the relative negotiating power of the country seeking to apply them" (Hoekman 1998, pp. 252–53).

India's opposition to the multilateralization of the GPA suggests that there are some positive net costs perceived to be associated with it. But it is not clear whether the perceived costs have been weighed against the potential benefits. Even if government procurement is used as a means of promoting domestic industry, it is important to estimate what the costs of doing this are and whether cost savings from nondiscriminating and competitive purchasing could be used for directly subsidizing this. I hope that the very preliminary estimates presented in this chapter will provide a starting point for such analysis.

Since this chapter was written, the Indian position on the GPA has been articulated more clearly, and there have been some changes in the stand now taken by

India against what is reported in the chapter. My understanding of the Indian government's current position on these issues is summarized here.[28]

- **Definition of terms**—"Transparency" is interpreted as meaning the provision of complete information on the procurement system and should not involve any obligation to follow specified procurement methods and procedures. The "content" should be best left to that prescribed in the applicable national laws or the procedures of the procuring entities.
- **Scope and coverage**—India has a multitiered and decentralized system of government and each level has its own procurement procedures. This decentralization is efficient and, hence, encouraged. In view of this structure, universal coverage of all procuring entities is neither required nor feasible. Moreover, procurement at lower levels of government is likely to be of low value. In addition, public sector enterprises and services should be kept outside the purview of any future obligations on transparency.
- **Information on national laws and procurement opportunities**—The requirement to provide information as a transparency issue is not contested, but prescriptions as to "what information" and "where it is to be made available" are not justified. Although providing information on individual procurement opportunities should be transparent, the rules should not be prescriptive and will vary according to the capacity of the member country. In the spirit of decentralization, the DGS&D has now been abolished.
- **Procurement procedures**—It is the government's case that there is already transparency in procurement methods, time periods, tendering methods, qualification procedures, decisions on qualifications, decisions on contract awards, and so forth, and there is no need for any additional (prescriptive) conditions for these procedures. Although, in practice, details of winning bidders are widely publicized, debriefing unsuccessful bidders will be cumbersome and costly.
- **Dispute settlement mechanism**—Because only the issue of transparency is being considered by the working group there is no need to link this with the WTO's dispute-settlement mechanism or understanding. This is a transparency (not an access) issue so punitive action such as the settlement mechanism is not justified.
- **Other matters related to transparency**—The government believes that the principles on which domestic systems are designed incorporate most of the suggestions expressed by members of the working group. For example, the procuring agencies that have the wherewithal have established Web sites not only for providing information but also for accepting applications, complaints, and so forth. These sites improve efficiency and add value for users of a

particular system, including adding value in the form of controlling the extent of graft. However, these systems have to reflect the local conditions and cannot be subject to overriding and externally imposed conditions.

Appendix 1: Other Examples of Government Procurement Practices

In this appendix I provide examples of government procurement practices for the State Government of Himachal Pradesh and the National Thermal Power Corporation.[29]

State Government of Himachal Pradesh

Government purchases in Himachal Pradesh (HP) are governed by the "Procedures and Rules for the Purchase of Stores by all Departments and Offices of the Government of Himachal Pradesh," which are published as an appendix to the HP financial rules. The purchase of stores by all departments of the state of Himachal Pradesh is generally made through a central agency called the Himachal-Pradesh Stores Department. As in the case of the DGS&D, the Stores Department enters into rate contracts for articles of common use.

Preferential Treatment   According to these rules there is a preference for stores produced and manufactured wholly or partially in India in general and in HP particularly. Up to some predetermined limit, the rules favor products of cottage and small-scale industries in HP over manufactured goods of large-scale industries of equal standard, even if the price of the former is higher. Currently, a 15 percent price preference is given to products of cottage industries and small-scale industrial units located in the state, whereas the corresponding figure for medium- and large-scale industrial units in the state is 3 percent. Items manufactured by government enterprises can be purchased directly by the concerned departments, provided these are not manufactured by any cottage or small-scale industries within HP. In general, a preference is given to HP over other states and to articles of domestic origin over those of foreign origin. Articles manufactured abroad, with a preference to Commonwealth countries (!), are imported only when suitable Indian products are not available.

Tendering Procedures   The limited tender system is adopted only for meeting urgent requirements. The emergency must be established and certified by the procuring office. These tenders can be invited only for indents of less than Rs. 10,000 (approximately US$220), and they require submission of tenders by at least six suppliers. For indents greater than Rs. 10,000 in value, tenders are invited through advertisement. It is specified in the tender notice that the power is reserved to reject any or all of the tenders received without assignment of reason. A period of three weeks from the date of publication is assigned for the receipt of tenders, except in the case of urgent demands when the period may be reduced to two weeks. The single-tender system is used in the case of articles of proprietary nature that are available from only one source. When accepting tenders other than the lowest, approval from higher authorities has to be sought.

Dispute Settlement Mechanism   There is a provision for a tenderer to make an appeal against the award of a rate contract to the Secretary (Industry) or any other authority as notified by the government. After the contract has been awarded, all disputes arising with respect to the contract or the rights and liabilities of the parties involved can be referred for arbitration to an officer appointed by the Government of Himachal Pradesh. The decision of the arbitrator is final and binding on the parties.

National Thermal Power Corporation

The stated objective of the procurement system is to make available the required equipment, materials, works, and services of desired quality at the right time and to ensure fair competition to all prospective bidders. The procurement process of a power project at the National Thermal Power Corporation (NTPC)—a PSE—divides the entire work into smaller well-defined groupings of equipment and services called "contract packages." The packages are classified according to the services required from the contractor (supply, supply-and-supervision of erection, supply-and-erection, civil and structural works, or consultancy), the availability of external assistance (from the International Development Association [IDA] or other financing agencies like the Asian Development Bank or World Bank), the mode of tendering to be adopted (international competitive bidding and domestic competitive bidding), and the extent of engineering coordination and value of the package (corporate contract package or site package).

Bidding documents define the responsibilities and liabilities of the owner and the contractor, and they include unambiguous instructions to bidders, technical specifications, and data requirements and forms for the bid proposal. Qualifying requirements indicate specific details of a bidder's requisite experience in addition to general requirements regarding his or her capacities and capabilities. The date and time of completion of the work, as stipulated in the bidding document, are incorporated in the Letter of Award. To ensure that the owner does not suffer due to the unavailability of spares during the full life of the equipment, the contractor has to ensure the long-run availability of spares. If unable to do so, the owner can purchase spares at the risk and cost of the contractor. In evaluating a bid, bidding documents are taken as the base. The contract is awarded to the lowest evaluated, qualified, and technically and commercially responsive bidder.

From 1981/82 until 1998/99 most of the contracts awarded by the NTPC used domestic competitive bidding as the mode of tendering. Even with international competitive bidding procedures, however, more contracts have been awarded to Indian bidders than to foreign bidders. Thus, under GPA rules, Indian companies may not lose too many contracts. The NTPC follows a purchase and price preference policy in accordance with central government regulations.

Finally, disputes that may arise between the contractor and the owner during the execution of the work are referred to the engineer concerned. In case he or she does not give a written notice of decision within 30 days or if either party is dissatisfied with the decision given, the matter may be referred for arbitration. The decision of the majority of the arbitrators is final and binding on the parties.

Appendix 2: Estimating Central Government Purchases

The starting points for these estimates are the central government budget documents for 1999/00 and 2000/01. I have relied primarily on the information on the nonplan expenditure by "Broad Categories," the plan outlays by "Heads of Development," and the detailed "Demand for Grants" contained in the "Expenditure Budget" volumes of the budget documents. This information is supplemented with information on grant-wise and object-of-expenditure-wise data for the two years. The relevant figures and calculations are presented in table 10.A.1. In view

TABLE 10.A.1   Shares of Total Expenditure for Items Involving Government Purchases

Item	Share (percent)
Supplies and materials	6.7
Major works	3.0
Minor works	1.5
Office expenses	1.3
Machinery and equipment	1.1
Motor vehicles	0.2
Clothing and tentage	0.1
Total	14.0

Source: Author's calculations.

of the large scale of their purchases and the fact that purchases of goods and services (primarily construction contracts) account for a larger share of their expenditures, the ministries of railways and telecommunications are excluded from these calculations.[30] Estimates for those departmental undertakings are presented separately.

The sum of the plan and nonplan outlays, including the internal and extra-budgetary resources (IEBR), gives the total expenditure by the different ministries and departments of the central government. This is estimated to be over Rs. 3,000 billion (over US$71 billion[31]) for the three years for which the estimates are presented and, at current prices, it works out to 16 percent to 17 percent of GDP. From this I subtract that part of the government expenditure on railways and telecommunications that is reflected in the central government budget. I also subtract those components of the plan and nonplan expenditures that clearly have no element of government procurement. In the case of the former, this is restricted to the plan assistance provided by the central government to states and union territories. For the nonplan expenditures, this includes interest payments, expenditure on subsidies, writeoff of state government loans, welfare payments, payments to the International Monetary Fund, and grants and loans to state governments and union territories. All defense expenditures are excluded because related purchases are outside the purview of the GPA. From this I also subtract the expenditure on pay and allowances of central government ministries and departments (excluding the provision for railways and telecommunications).[32] This leaves a total of about Rs. 427 billion ($9.8 billion) for 1999/00 and Rs. 621 billion ($13.3 billion) for 2000/01, a share of approximately 2 percent to 3 percent of GDP. This composite expenditure is on items for which further disaggregation is not possible, based on the budget documents, and clearly involves expenditures on items other than purchases of goods and services. In an attempt to sharpen the estimates further, I have used data on object-wise expenditures by central departments and ministries for the year 1998/99. The various objects of expenditure are listed in table 10.A.2. The items "supplies and materials," "major works," "minor works," "office expenses," "machinery and equipment," "motor vehicles," and "clothing and tentage" involve government expenditure on the purchase of goods and services.[33] I use these data to estimate the shares of these items in the total expenditure. To make the figures comparable, I excluded demand numbers 29 (interest payments), 30 (transfer to state and union territory governments), and 32 (repayment of borrowings) because the first two have been accounted for in the calculations and the third is an accounting entry. Data for demand number 16, pertaining to the department of telecommunications, were also excluded. In addition, I excluded expenditures on salaries and wages, overtime allowances, pensions, travel, and

TABLE 10.A.2   Objects of Expenditure

Demand Number	Item	Demand Number	Item
1	Repayment of borrowings	24	Advertising and publicity
2	Interest	25	Rents, rates, and taxes
3	Loans and advances	26	Suspense
4	Grants-in-aid	27	Wages
5	Share of taxes and duties	28	**Motor vehicles**
6	Subsidies	29	Arms and ammunition
7	Investments	30	Overtime allowances
8	Salaries	31	Foreign travel expenses
9	**Supplies and materials**	32	Other capital expenditures
10	Exchange variations	33	Other administrative expenditures
11	Other charges		
12	Pension charges	34	**Clothing and tents**
13	**Major works**	35	Petroleum, oil, and lubricants
14	Contributions		
15	Writeoffs and losses	36	Publications
16	**Minor works**	37	Reserves
17	**Office expenses**	38	Scholarships and stipends
18	**Machinery and equipment**	39	Secret service expenditures
19	Professional services	40	Royalties
20	Other contractual services	41	Rewards
21	Interaccount transfers	42	Lump-sum provision
22	Domestic travel expenses	43	Depreciation
23	Cost of rations	44	Deduct recoveries

Notes: Items in bold involve government purchases. Items are listed in order of importance.

arms and ammunition. Of the remaining expenditure, the share of the items involving government purchases is about 14 percent (see table 10.A.1). This, however, is likely to be an underestimate because subsidies, grants, and loans and advances are included in the denominator in these calculations although in part they have been accounted for before arriving at the composite figure in table 10.A.1. If those three objects of expenditure are also excluded, the share of the seven items involving procurement works out to about 38 percent. This is clearly an overestimate and the true value lies somewhere between the two percentages. Assuming the share to be 30 percent,[34] the government expenditure on purchase of goods and services works out to Rs. 140.84 billion ($3.32 billion) for 1998/99, Rs.128.21 billion ($2.94 billion) for 1999/00, and Rs. 186.37 billion ($3.99 billion) for 2000/01.

Appendix 3: Threshold Levels

	Goods		Services, Except Construction		Construction Services	
	Maximum	Minimum	Maximum	Minimum	Maximum	Minimum
Annex 1						
SDRs	130,000	130,000	130,000	130,000	8,500,000	4,500,000
Rupees (in millions)	7.75	7.75	7.75	7.75	506.56	268.18
Annex 2						
SDRs	355,000.00	200,000.00	355,000.00	200,000.00	15,000,000.00	5,000,000.00
Rupees (in millions)	21.16	11.92	21.16	11.92	893.93	297.98
Annex 3						
SDRs	400,000	150,000	400,000	130,000	15,000,000	5,000,000
Rupees (in millions)	23.84	8.94	23.84	7.75	893.93	297.98

SDR Special drawing rights.

Note: Annex 1 covers central government entities; Annex 2 covers subcentral government entities; Annex 3 covers all other entities, such as public enterprises and authorities.

Source: Available at http://docsonline.wto.org/GEN_searchResult.asp?RN=0&searchtype=browse&q1=%28@meta_Symbol++LTüURüA-4üPLURIü2%29+%26+%28@meta_Types+Legal+text%29.

Appendix 4: Potential Gains

Potential Gains, Including State Governments (in billions of rupees)

Relative Weight of Gainers	Savings		
	50%	30%	20%
100%	174.73	104.84	69.89
75%	131.05	78.63	52.42
50%	87.37	52.42	34.95

Potential Gains, Including Public Sector Enterprises

Relative Weight of Gainers	Savings		
	50%	30%	20%
100%	641.53	384.92	256.61
75%	481.15	288.69	192.46
50%	320.77	192.46	128.31

Endnotes

1. Contained in Annex 4, Multilateral Trade Agreement, Agreement on Government Procurement, of the Marrakesh Agreement Establishing the World Trade Organization, completed at Marrakesh on April 15, 1994. The signatories include Canada, the European Community and its 15 member states, Hong Kong (China), Israel, Japan, the Republic of Korea, Liechtenstein, the Kingdom of the Netherlands with respect to Aruba, Norway, Singapore, Switzerland, and the United States. In addition, 18 member countries have observer status (Government Procurement Committee, 2000 Report, available at http://www.wto.org/english/tratop_e/gproc_e/rep_00_e.htm).

2. Miyagiwa (1991) provided another example. The literature is reviewed in detail in Mattoo (1996), Hoekman (1998), and Hoekman and Mavroidis (1997b).

3. A simulation exercise by Deltas and Evenett (1997) suggests that the gains from preferential treatment are small.

4. The list of covered entities is provided by each signatory in the annexes to Appendix 1 of the agreement. The agreement applies only to government procurement contracts of a value above a specified threshold level (see Appendix 3 of this volume).

5. The discussion is based largely on Department of Supply (1999, 2000) and Debroy and Pursell (1997).

6. The central features of the procurement policies of Himachal Pradesh and the National Thermal Power Corporation are described as examples in Appendix 1 of this book.

7. These general rules apply to all departments regarding stores required for use in "the public service." Special rules apply to Defense, Railways, Post and Telegraphs, Public Works, Central Purchase Organization (DGS&D and supply missions in New Delhi, London, and Washington, D.C.), Survey of

India, Stationery and Printing, and other departments responsible for large purchases (Debroy and Pursell 1997).

8. Indian standard specifications are formulated by the Bureau of Indian Standards.

9. This is not true of all state governments. See, for example, the description of the practices in the state of Himachal Pradesh (Appendix 1).

10. See the Government of India's response to question 9 of the WTO Questionnaire on Government Procurement Services (document S/WPGR/W/11/Add. 14, dated January 17, 1997).

11. In March 1998 there were 240 central PSEs (see Department of Public Enterprises 1998) and almost 1,000 state PSEs, including electricity boards.

12. The year 1997/98 with a 13.3 percent share is an exception.

13. When this chapter was originally written, no official document describing India's position was available. The discussion in this section was based on newspaper reports, unofficial documents, and conversations with people familiar with the subject. Now, following the Doha Ministerial Declaration, India's official position is more clear.

14. Similar to Article V of the current GPA.

15. Although there are three levels of local government below the state governments, I have not attempted any estimates for these because no data are available. The value of purchases by these local governments is likely to be small and their transactions (except, possibly, in rare cases) are unlikely to be of values larger than the threshold levels in the GPA.

16. In any case, the railways budget is presented and voted separately from the central government budget.

17. The procedure is described in some detail in Appendix 2 of this book.

18. Rupees (Rs.) refers to Indian rupees and conversion to U.S. dollars is based on exchange rates of US$1 = Rs. 42.4 for 1998/99, $1 = Rs. 43.6 for 1999/00, and $1 = Rs. 46.7 for 2000/01.

19. These work out to be 30 percent to 50 percent of the total.

20. For the last item—"new construction"—I have assumed that 10 percent of the expenditure is for control and supervision.

21. According to the estimates presented in table 10.1, the central government expenditure on purchase of goods and services was 4.7 percent of total expenditure in 1998/99, approximately 4 percent of total expenditure in 1999/00, and is expected to be 5.1 percent of total expenditure in 2000/01. Available evidence for Himachal Pradesh shows that the main items involving purchases during 1998/99 were machinery and equipment (Rs. 272 million), materials and supplies (Rs. 466 million), and major works (Rs. 366 million). The estimated procurement content of these purchases works out to a little more than 5 percent of the state's total expenditure of Rs. 4.1 billion during that year.

22. The estimate of "net purchase of commodities and services" by administrative departments of the state governments (Rs. 123.6 billion for 1996/97) presented in the National Accounts Statistics (see CSO 1998) is somewhat higher than my high estimate of Rs. 121.7 billion. This is also true for the estimate of central government expenditure on the same item, which is estimated to be Rs. 221.1 billion during 1996/97 or about 6.1 percent of total expenditure.

23. It was not possible to get consistent data beyond 1997/98. These figures have been extrapolated to get the estimates for later years presented in table 10.6.

24. The comparison is with private enterprises in the same sectors.

25. The bulk of the difference is accounted for by the imports of crude oil and petroleum products.

26. These issues are discussed in detail in Elliot (1997) and Jain (1998).

27. This is reflected in the fact that there has not been any significant privatization in spite of a number of government initiatives in this direction. Also, there has been no serious debate within government regarding continuation of the reservations for the small-scale sector, although there is enough evidence to suggest that such reservation may be costly.

28. In the absence of any formal documentation of the official position, this is based on newspaper reports and discussions with government officials familiar with the subject.

29. The section on National Thermal Power Corporation is based on Bajaj (1995).

30. In any case, the railway budget is presented and voted separately from the central government budget.

31. The conversion rates for Indian rupees to U.S. dollars used here are US$1 = Rs. 42.4 for 1998/99, $1 = Rs. 43.6 for 1999/00, and $1 = Rs. 46.7 for 2000/01.

32. These data are also available in the Expenditure Budget volume of the central government budget documents.

33. The entire expenditure on these items cannot be assumed to be on purchases and contracts because these may include some expenditure on control and supervision.

34. This is probably marginally higher than the actual share.

Bibliography and References

Bajaj, Harbans L. 1995. "Managing Contracts for Power Projects." Paper presented at the International Conference on Contract Management in the Construction Industry, New Delhi.

Baldwin, R. E. 1970. "Restrictions on Government Expenditure." In R. E. Baldwin, ed., *Nontariff Distortions of International Trade.* Washington D.C.: Brookings Institution Press.

———. 1984. "Trade Policies in Developed Countries." In R. W. Jones and P. B. Kenen, eds., *Handbook of International Economics,* Vol. 1. Amsterdam: North Holland.

Baldwin, R. E., and J. D. Richardson. 1972. "Government Purchasing Policies, Other NTBs, and the International Monetary Crisis." In H. English and K. Hay, eds., *Obstacles to Trade in the Pacific Area.* Ottawa: Carleton School of International Affairs.

Branco, F. 1994. "Favoring Domestic Firms in Procurement Contracts." *Journal of International Economics* 37: 65–80.

Chen, Xianquin. 1995. "Directing Government Procurement as an Incentive of Production." *Journal of Economic Integration* 10: 130–40.

CSO (Central Statistical Organization). 1998. *National Accounts Statistics 1998.* Department of Statistics, Ministry of Planning and Programme Implementation, Government of India. New Delhi.

Debroy, Bibek, and Gary Pursell. 1997. "Government Procurement Policies in India." In Bernard Hoekman and Petros Mavroidis, eds., *Law and Policy in Public Purchasing: The WTO Agreement on Government Procurement.* Ann Arbor: University of Michigan Press.

Deltas, George, and Simon Evenett. 1997. "Quantitative Estimates of the Effects of Preference Policies." In Bernard Hoekman and Petros Mavroidis, eds., *Law and Policy in Public Purchasing: The WTO Agreement on Government Procurement.* Ann Arbor: University of Michigan Press.

Department of Public Enterprises. 1998. *Public Enterprises Survey 1997–98,* Vol. 1. Ministry of Industry, Government of India, New Delhi.

Department of Supply. 1999. *Annual Report 1998–99.* Ministry of Commerce, Government of India, New Delhi.

Department of Supply. 2000. *Annual Report 1999–00.* Ministry of Commerce, Government of India, New Delhi.

Domberger, Simon, Christine Hall, and Eric Ah Lik Lee. 1995. "The Determinants of Price and Quality in Competitively Tendered Contracts." *Economic Journal* 105: 1454–70.

Elliot, Kimberly Ann, ed. 1997. *Corruption and the Global Economy.* Washington, D.C.: Institute for International Economics.

Ganesan, A. V. 1999. "Seattle Ministerial Conference of WTO: Agenda for India." Discussion Paper. Indian Council for Research on International Economic Relations, New Delhi, August.

Helpman, Elhanan, and Paul R. Krugman. 1986. *Market Structure and Foreign Trade.* Cambridge, Mass.: MIT Press.

Hoekman, Bernard. 1998. "Using International Institutions to Improve Public Procurement." *World Bank Research Observer* 13: 249–69.

Hoekman, Bernard, and Michel Kostecki. 1995. *The Political Economy of the World Trading System: From GATT to WTO.* Oxford, U.K.: Oxford University Press.

Hoekman, Bernard, and Petros Mavroidis, eds. 1997a. *Law and Policy in Public Purchasing: The WTO Agreement on Government Procurement.* Ann Arbor: University of Michigan Press.

————. 1997b. "Multilateralizing the Agreement on Government Procurement." In Bernard Hoekman and Petros Mavroidis, eds., *Law and Policy in Public Purchasing: The WTO Agreement on Government Procurement.* Ann Arbor: University of Michigan Press.

Jain, Arvind K., ed. 1998. *Economics of Corruption.* Boston: Kluwer Academic Publishers.

Krugman, Paul R. 1987. "Is Free Trade Passé?" *Journal of Economic Perspectives* 1: 131–44.

————. 1988. *Strategic Trade Policy and the New International Economics.* Cambridge, Mass.: MIT Press.

Laffont, J. J., and Jean Tirole. 1991. "Auction Design and Favouritism." *International Journal of Industrial Organization* 9: 9–42.

Mattoo, Aaditya. 1996. "The Government Procurement Agreement: Implications of Economic Theory." *World Economy* 19: 695–720.

McAfee, R. Preston, and John McMillan. 1989. "Government Procurement and International Trade." *Journal of International Economics* 26: 291–308.

Ministry of Finance. 1998. *Expenditure Budget,* Vols. 1 and 2. Ministry of Finance, Government of India, June.

————. 1999. *Expenditure Budget,* Vols. 1 and 2. Ministry of Finance, Government of India, New Delhi, February.

————. 2000. *Expenditure Budget,* Vols. 1 and 2. Ministry of Finance, Government of India, New Delhi, February.

Ministry of Railways (Railway Board). 1999a. *The Demand for Grants for Expenditure of the Central Government on Railways, 1999–2000, Part I.* Government of India, New Delhi.

————. 1999b. *Explanatory Memorandum on Railway Budget 1999–2000.* Government of India, New Delhi.

————. 2000a. *The Demand for Grants for Expenditure of the Central Government on Railways, Part I.* Government of India, New Delhi.

————. 2000b. *Explanatory Memorandum on Railway Budget.* Government of India, New Delhi.

Miyagiwa, K. 1991. "Oligopoly and Discriminatory Government Procurement Policy." *American Economic Review* 81: 291–308.

"Not Good Enough." 1999. *Economic Times,* August 4.

Reserve Bank of India. 1999. *Handbook of Statistics on Indian Economy.* Mumbai.

Reserve Bank of India. 2000. *Handbook of Statistics on Indian Economy.* Mumbai.

Transparency International. 1997. *The TI Source Book: Applying the Framework.* Berlin.

WTO (World Trade Organization) Secretariat. 1999. *Guide to the Uruguay Round Agreements.* The Hague, Netherlands: Kluwer Law International.

World Bank. 2000. *India: Policies to Reduce Poverty and Accelerate Sustainable Development.* Report 19471-IN. Washington, D.C.

11

TECHNICAL BARRIERS TO TRADE AND THE ROLE OF INDIAN STANDARD-SETTING INSTITUTIONS

Mohammed Saqib

During the rounds of multilateral trade negotiations promoted by the General Agreement on Tariffs and Trade (GATT), especially since the Kennedy Round in the 1960s, the world has witnessed a significant reduction in import tariffs. Lately there also has been a reduction in the unilateral application of quotas and other forms of nontariff barriers (NTBs). A considerable number of NTBs still exist, however, in the shape of technical regulations and standards. Technical regulations and standards (including sanitary and phytosanitary controls) are not in themselves trade barriers, but their use or adoption may create new obstacles to trade and provide protection to domestic producers.

The Agreement on Technical Barriers to Trade (TBT) and the Agreement on Sanitary and Phytosanitary Measures (SPS) define the international rights and obligations of member countries with respect to the development or application of standards-related measures that affect trade.[1] They are based on the principle that countries have a right to adopt and apply such measures as long as they do not restrict international trade more than is necessary or unavoidable. Although these agreements have established certain standards for their application, disagreements among countries about these measures often involve complex issues not specifically addressed by the text of the agreements.

The perceptions and the institutional capacities of developing countries are significantly different from those of industrial countries in implementation of the TBT and SPS agreements under the World Trade Organization (WTO).

269

Developing countries fear that technical barriers may become increasingly important in the future and thereby become significant barriers to trade. Among the difficulties in the technical aspects of trade identified by the developing countries are the high cost of adaptation, the irrelevance of foreign standards to local conditions, the lack of timely and adequate information and consequent transaction costs, the difficulties in understanding the requirements and in testing for and monitoring them, the perceived lack of scientific data for specific threshold or limiting values, and the uncertainty that arises from rapidly changing requirements in overseas market.

The major issue facing developing countries is implementation, which leads to the question of domestic capacity building. This chapter reviews the existing institutional or infrastructure framework created to comply with the TBT/SPS Agreements and the approach for addressing NTB measures. It also highlights the areas in which India should seek international technical and financial assistance to fully implement the TBT/SPS Agreements.

The chapter is based on a preliminary survey of exporters, government and nongovernment institutions, and various regulatory authorities and reports of the Indian Government.

The first section of the chapter provides a literature survey and identifies some of the products that have met NTBs in the international market. The second section reviews the status of the domestic institutional structure responsible for implementing the TBT and SPS Agreements. The third section deals with the international institutional framework. The final section provides conclusions and policy recommendations.

Literature Survey

In this section I present a brief literature survey concerning standards as well as a discussion of the SPS and TBT Agreements and NTBs raised by these agreements.

Standards perform a number of vital functions if used fairly. They facilitate market transactions, reduce the cost of uncertainty, increase the elasticity of substitution, promote economies of scale, provide guidelines or focal points around which enterprises can organize their production processes, and serve as benchmarks of technological capabilities and guarantees of compatibility with other components or with networks (Maskus and Wilson 2000).

Standards, however, can become barriers to trade when they vary among countries. The cost of complying with standards may be higher for foreign than for domestic firms, and that implicitly creates a trade barrier. Where regulatory authorities require product testing in the importing country to ensure compliance with that country's health or safety regulations, foreign suppliers will find themselves at a disadvantage if their products are subject to stricter tests or higher fees than those required for domestic products (ITC/CS 1999). This process is referred to as "conformity assessment" and some would argue that it presents the largest potential technical barrier to trade (Maskus and Wilson 2000). Conformity assessment is vulnerable to nontransparency, delays, arbitrary inspection, and redundant tests and is susceptible to being used as protection by domestic firms. The costs of uncertainty in complying with such procedures may well persuade foreign enterprises to withdraw from key markets.

Developing countries generally are less likely to have well-developed testing facilities for certification and accreditation. They will be unlikely to reach mutual recognition agreements with other countries, and they may find it difficult to reach the standards set especially by developed market economies. Trade between developing countries may also be constrained by both the inability to meet internationally agreed standards and the refusal to recognize the standards of other countries. The solution to this problem lies in harmonizing standards at the international level and in developing guidelines for determining conformity to standards (ITC/CS 1999). It can be argued that international harmonization is virtually impossible, but some form of coordination has the potential to expand market access for developing countries (Maskus and Wilson 2000).

The SPS Agreement

The SPS Agreement establishes international rules on how to apply sanitary and phytosanitary measures. It acknowledges a country's right to protect itself from risks to human, animal, and plant life and health, and it confirms the need to constrain countries from using such measures as excuses to create unnecessary barriers to trade. In short, the purpose of the agreement is to enable the legitimate protection of life and health while not giving rise to illegitimate protectionism. Protectionism in this regard is defined as trade barriers beyond what is required to meet a country's desired protection levels. The approach taken to address these two issues simultaneously is to require that SPS measures be based on sound science. In this way, only measures truly aimed at protecting life and health are allowed, and measures that are either not related to life and health issues at all or that are excessively strict are ruled out.

The two basic principles of the agreement are nondiscrimination and scientific justification. The principle of nondiscrimination is described in Article 2.3 of the agreement: It states that a measure shall not discriminate against or between trading partners more than necessary to reach the goal of sanitary and phytosanitary protection. This principle is equivalent to the GATT basic principle of most-favorednation privileges. The principle of scientific justification of SPS measures is spelled out in Article 2.2: Any SPS measure must be backed by scientific justification.

The special concerns of developing countries are addressed explicitly in the agreement in several regards. The general functioning of the agreement is the same for industrial and developing countries. The differences occur mainly in the implementation of the agreement and in the obligations to provide technical assistance to other members.

The regulation of SPS measures can be divided into four cases:

1. In areas where international standards already exist, the agreement encourages international harmonization based on international standards. It must be clear that this does not necessarily imply identical worldwide standards but rather standards that have some basic relationship to the same reference points.
2. In areas where no international standards exist, measures for individual member countries are permitted if they are based on a risk assessment and are nondiscriminatory.
3. If a country does not find that the protection level provided by an international standard is high enough, it may implement stricter measures. Again, this right is conditional on a formal risk assessment and the obligation that measures are to be nondiscriminatory.
4. Finally, when not enough scientific evidence enables a proper risk assessment, temporary measures are allowed. This right is also conditional. Temporary measures must be reviewed after a certain time and the implementing country must seek additional evidence.

Technical assistance for developing countries (Article 9 of the SPS Agreement) encourages members to provide technical assistance to developing countries. It refers to general technical assistance to help developing countries comply with SPS measures in their export markets. It addresses the situation that exists when developing countries have to undertake "substantial investments" to fulfill the requirements of an importing member country. In such a situation the importer is encouraged to provide the technical assistance that will enable the developing country to maintain and expand its market access. But it does not contain any commitments.

This lack of technical assistance and commitments has been criticized by developing countries who believe that the existing level of assistance falls short of the immense needs, and that the types of assistance are often inappropriate (Henson and Loader 2001). Several developing countries have called for a more organized approach to the provision of technical assistance related to SPS requirements. Furthermore, it is argued that providing such assistance should be bound to specific commitments by the industrial countries (WTO 1998a, b).

An example of a specific proposal to address these issues is a proposal by the countries of the Association of Southeast Asian Nations to create a trust fund within the WTO that would channel technical assistance to developing countries. The Fourth WTO Ministerial Conference, held in Doha in November 2001, also addressed the issue of technical assistance. But the discussions led only to a repeated call for financial and technical assistance, without offering specific commitments (WTO 2001). It should be noted that some of the problems that developing countries face regarding SPS measures are related directly to their overall level of economic development. According to Henson and Loader (2001, p. 98), examples include "...the efficacy of prevailing systems of SPS controls, development of scientific and technical expertise and access to modern testing methods." Such problems will be difficult to solve by technical assistance measures that are more appropriate for isolated problems within an overall sound standards infrastructure.

Another major problem with SPS measures as they apply to international trade is that they are different in different countries and are often complicated and are subject to frequent changes. Exporters therefore face great uncertainty about the state of SPS legislation in their export markets. In the agreement, member countries are obliged to establish notification points as well as inquiry points. This obligation is aimed at improving access to information both for foreign exporters who wish to access the national markets and for the country's own exporters in need of information about foreign markets. Whereas notification and inquiry points were created rapidly in industrial countries, the process has been slower in developing countries, with many least-developing countries especially still not having established such points (Brouder, Loader, and Henson 2000).

Moreover, the transparency provision in the SPS Agreement is the obligation that a member country implementing SPS measures that differ from international standards or in areas where no international standards exist must notify the new measure to other WTO member countries. Increased transparency has given rise to more intergovernmental discussion of SPS measures. An example of that is the discussion in the SPS Committee that followed the notification of a proposal by the European Union (EU) to introduce new limits on aflatoxin in foodstuffs (Otsuki, Wilson, and Sewadeh 2001).[2]

One can conclude that, in principle, the SPS Agreement should help developing countries maintain and expand their market access for food and agricultural products by preventing the implementation of SPS measures that cannot be justified scientifically and by improving transparency and encouraging harmonization. However, it was the industrial countries that negotiated the agreement. The developing countries signed on without active participation in the negotiation process and without any deep understanding of the contents and implications of the agreement. Developing countries have come to realize that it is difficult and sometimes impossible for many of them to make sure that the disciplines agreed on are practiced.

There are two fundamental problems with the implementation of the SPS Agreement. First, there is a wide gap between the financial, human, and technical resources of a very large number of developing countries and the resources demanded if participation in the agreement is to be effective. The implementation costs of the agreement may be considerable. The issue of those costs leads to the second fundamental problem of the agreement—the extent of harmonization of international standards that is desirable from the perspective of a developing country. In the agreement, standards that achieve a higher protection level than international standards will be considered, but standards that achieve a lower protection level will be ruled out. This is contrary to developing countries' interest because the food safety problems they experience differ radically from the ones addressed by international standards. This problem is a major source of high implementation costs. The issue can and should be taken care of either by generous financial and technical assistance or by drafting exceptions for a limited number of poor countries.

Nontariff Barriers   The SPS and TBT Agreements were added to the WTO so that, at whatever levels are deemed appropriate, no country would be prevented from taking measures necessary to ensure the quality of its imports; human, animal, and plant life and the health of the environment would be protected; and deceptive practices would be prevented. But these agreements are subject to the requirements that measures are not applied in a manner that constitutes arbitrary or unjustifiable discrimination between countries where the same conditions prevail or a disguised restriction on international trade, and that measures are otherwise in accordance with the provisions of the agreements. Experience, however, has been contrary to those requirements. Barriers in the name of technical regulations exist along the boundaries of trading nations.

SPS and TBT technical specifications have been a major source of NTBs and are likely to continue to be so in the future.[3] This fact is not difficult to infer because the SPS Agreement specifies that a country may introduce or maintain a higher level of SPS protection than that achieved by an international standard if there is scientific justification or when the country determines that a higher level of protection would be appropriate. In fact, the latter is often chosen to explain many overly stringent SPS measures in the EU and the United States.

The following are some examples of the measures perceived by Indian exporters to be NTBs disguised under (arguable) logic on various grounds such as quality, manufacturing process, certification, testing methods, and environmental protection. The following discussion is based on the field survey that I conducted via personal interviews using an unstructured questionnaire.

Product-related Nontariff Barriers: Peanut Exports   Peanut exporters believe that foreign governments put NTBs on their imports of agricultural products in order to sustain their domestic agriculture. Exporters also may have to make distress sales when buyers refuse shipments based on domestic import standards. Indian exporters therefore may have to depend on the domestic market or the South Asian Association for Regional Cooperation for business sustenance. Their foreign customers have informed them that new and stricter regulations will apply after December 31, 2000.

Some of the problems faced by exporters appear to be genuine. For example, they find that different testing procedures and conformity assessment standards are required in different markets. Each test costs Rs. 6,000. Nobody has told them of the justification for most of the tests. In fact, the EU tests exports from the Arab Republic of Egypt and India, but not exports from Argentina and the United States.

Another problem is that although there is no import duty on 50-kg bags, there is a duty on 5-kg bags. This discrepancy is because the foreign governments want to discourage retail consignments. Exporters also face problems regarding genetically modified peanuts. Although some years ago one foreign government encouraged the use of genetically modified organisms (GMOs), another now has asked for an assurance that the peanuts supplied do not contain GMOs.

A more detailed study was done by the Joint Expert Committee on Food Additives (JECFA 1997) on the issue of aflatoxin in peanuts because this appeared to be a major threat to peanut exports. The European Commission in Brussels has specified tolerance limits for aflatoxin contamination in peanuts and has established testing methods. The proposed levels are 10 parts per billion (ppb) (5 ppb of B1 [a kind of pathogen]) for raw material and 4 ppb (2 ppb of B1) for consumer-ready products. The new proposed sampling plan is similar to the Dutch Code, that is, the analysis is to be done based on a three-test Dutch Code methodology from a randomly drawn 30-kg sample. The new testing procedure, which is much more rigorous than is currently in force, requires that the lot be rejected if any of the three tests are found to exceed the limit.

This step procedure is unwarranted from a scientific standpoint, according to various agencies and governments. Laboratory tests on small animals such as rats that were given feed highly contaminated with B1 on a daily basis have found that aflatoxin can cause liver cancer, but there is no clear evidence to prove that aflatoxins are carcinogenic in humans. This fact should be viewed against the possibility that aflatoxin contamination of some peanuts in a shipment does not signal aflatoxin contamination of the entire shipment. Statistically one would expect to find one contaminated nut in a sample of, say, 5,000–10,000 uncontaminated nuts.

Experts have concluded that 75 percent of the lots rejected under the proposed procedure would be below the established tolerance, that is, 75 percent of the rejected lots would be uncontaminated material.

Furthermore, in many supplying countries where peanut consumption is very high (such as Argentina, China, India, South Africa, the United States, and Vietnam), there have been no findings that aflatoxin in peanuts led to increases in liver cancer.

According to a report by the Joint Expert Committee on Food Additives (JECFA 1997) of the World Health Organization (WHO) and the Food and Agriculture Organization of the United Nations (FAO), aflatoxin contamination of foodstuffs is very low among EU nations and only a few members of the population suffer from hepatitis B. Considering the estimated risk at 20 ppb, there will be 0.0041 cases of cancer per 100,000 population annually. Considering the risk at 10 ppb, there will be 0.0039 cases per 100,000 population annually. Those statistics show that the downward adjustment of the standard from 20 ppb to 10 ppb would reduce the estimated cancer risk only by approximately two cancer cases annually per 1 billion people. It seems improbable that there would be any measurable risk differential between the hypothetical standards (20 ppb and 10 ppb) in populations with a low incidence of hepatitis B, as in the EU countries. This low risk can be compared with the possibility that denying export markets to farmers in a developing country like India could result in starvation deaths in multiples of the estimated harm to life in Europe.

The JECFA previously recommended that maximum permissible aflatoxin levels be fixed as low as possible. Now, however, on the basis of further data, the committee has modified its recommendation to reducing the intake as far "as is reasonably possible." Furthermore, it should be noted that the JECFA's risk estimates are based on data that made no allowance for the substantial reduction in aflatoxin contamination achieved by mechanical removal of the nut skins and by the use of optical and electronic methods for sorting the nuts. The risk computations thus are based on aflatoxin levels that are no longer applicable. The new data should be taken into account when the future EU tolerance limits are specified. For example, the Codex Alimentarius Commission had proposed a maximum limit of 15 ppb.

The European Snack Association's Nut Working Group has already expressed concern about the testing program and analytical methodologies through the CIAA (the European Food and Beverage Association). The American Peanut Council has submitted documents showing significant increase in costs and rejections arising from the use of a multisample system. In the United Kingdom, where approximately 25 percent of the peanuts imported into Europe are consumed, the Ministry of Agriculture has stated that the proposals were more stringent than were required by current U.K. regulations and could result in unacceptable costs to both industry and enforcement, without any prospect of improved consumer safety. Despite these protests, the revised draft of the sampling plan still recommends a multiple sampling system. It is evident that such a change will have very serious implications for the peanut industry. It is also important to note that the EU proposal may contravene the GATT/WTO agreement by erecting artificial barriers and seriously discriminating against a number of producing countries, particularly developing countries such as India.

Barriers Related to Production and Process Methods

Mango Pulp   Many codes of regulation as well as European SPS measures link the quality of a product with its production processes.[4] In India, where most primary production takes place in unorganized, small-scale units, such primary-level quality assurance is difficult to attain. Thus the EU demand that each mango farmer keep records of the use of its mangoes in processing mango pulp is cumbersome. The EU justification for this measure is that the farmer whose mangoes were bad can be traced in case a consignment of mango pulp is found to be harmful. However, as long as a pulp processor observes strict quality checks at the point where mango pulps from various orchards enter the processing unit, records of farmers may not be necessary. In such a situation, a pulp processor and exporter can ensure strict compliance with quality norms at the factory's entry point.

Milk Products   The EU standard for milk and milk products requires that checks originate from the level of primary production, and it lays down the conditions of maintaining animals, types of feed to be given, and the monitoring of these regulations. Under Indian conditions, a dairy farm may have just one or two draught animals, and milk from a number of such holdings is commonly pooled before it is processed. It is impossible to monitor every animal. Therefore, the quality is determined at the processing unit's entry point and the milk is appropriately treated to ensure the destruction of any pathogens. The final product is thereby safe. It is necessary to stress the quality of the final product, which may be attained through a flexible systems approach. It is neither feasible nor desirable to standardize a specific systems approach.

Likewise, the EU has directed that raw milk must originate from cows or buffalos, which in the case of cows yields at least 2 liters of milk a day. In the Indian situation this is simply impractical. Similarly, the animal-health requirements stipulated by the EU are far in excess of the requirements of the International Animal Health Code of the International Office of Epizootics (IOE).[5] The International Animal Health Code does not include any conditions specifically related to milk and milk products for diseases like rinderpest, *pestedes petits ruminants*, bluetongue, sheep pox, and goat pox. But EU animal-health-attestation conditions specify that the animals must belong to holdings that were not under restrictions due to foot-and-mouth disease (FMD). Therefore, whereas IOE requirements for FMD are specific in nature, the EU directives are general and have included the conditions for livestock diseases like rinderpest.

In 1997 the EU circulated a directive stating that, when dry milk was exported, the package should clearly mention that buffalo milk was used and that, ideally, there should be an illustration of a buffalo on the package. This is likely to create a psychological barrier in the mind of a consumer who is used to drinking cow's milk, although in terms of health both cow and buffalo milk are perfect substitutes for making milk powder. On opposition from countries like India, the EU directive was withdrawn.

Barriers Related to Testing Procedures: Egg Products   The acceptance of a sanitary standard is based on the acceptance of certain test results. Some test results, however, can be disputed. For example, in 1997 Company O, a Bangalore-based egg products–exporting company, sent egg powder to Japan. Japan reported BHC (beta isomer) levels in the Indian product far in excess of permitted levels of 0.01 parts per million (ppm). To investigate this report composite samples were analyzed in laboratories in Bangalore and Belgium. Both analyses reported that the BHC level was below the detectable limit of 0.01 ppm. The inference to be drawn from this case is that if laboratory results can vary, then products that have been tested as fit for export in Indian laboratories can be declared unfit for acceptance at international borders. When both parties stick to their test results, how can credibility be brought about in laboratory tests?

Barriers Related to Certifications: Tires   Brazil requires that tires being exported to Brazil have "En-Metro" (EM) marking on them. EM is the national standard for tires in Brazil, rather like the "Agmark" for foods in India. For the Indian tire exporter, however, obtaining EM certification is expensive. To receive the EM certificate, an Indian exporter must defray the lodging and miscellaneous expenses of a Brazilian team of experts who travel to India and visit the prospective exporter's tire plant. The Automotive and Tyre Manufacturers Association of India quotes the sum total of these expenses at an average of US$20,000 ($1,100 of which is the direct cost for the certificate). Certification lasts only one year, so the exporter must invite and pay for the Brazilian team of experts every 12 months! Except for a few major Indian tire manufacturers (e.g., Apollo, JK, and Modi Rubber), many smaller potential tire exporters from India cannot export tires to Brazil because certification is prohibitively expensive.

Assuming that Brazilian tire manufacturers also must be certified, it is apparent that the cost they would incur would total little more than the $1,100 for the certificate itself. It is interesting to note that although the EM team has been traveling from Brazil to do inspections in India every year, formal EM certificates have not been issued at all for the last two years, and exports of Indian tires to Brazil have continued.

Mexico offers another example of a certification barrier. Imported tires there must carry "Norm" certification, which is awarded to each tire imported rather than to the tire company. To get this certificate, $40,000–$50,000 has to be paid to different certifying agencies of Mexico.

Environmental Barriers: Steel   Australia and New Zealand have imposed extremely stringent environmental laws and raised objections to the usage of wooden dunnage by an Indian steel company. As a consequence the company has used treated wood and wood substitutes, which are more expensive and in short supply. Furthermore, fumigation of containers is required, and the cost for that is $400 per container.

Packaging, Marking, and Language Barriers   Barriers related to packaging, marking, and language include printing of minimum import prices in countries like Brazil and Syria, and the requirement that texturized yarn be supplied in equal-length packages in some European markets. It also has been reported that Germany poses significant problems for Indian exporters of engineering products because German technical regulations are rarely made available in English. Indian exporters employ translators at their own expense, but the Germans argue that the translations do not accurately present the German specifications. Indian exporters, therefore, are always apprehensive of falling short of German norms. This apprehension obviously damages export potential.

Domestic Institutional Framework

The domestic institutional framework is the most important aspect of implementing the SPS and TBT Agreements. A weak institutional framework adds to the woes of exporters who are already facing NTBs from other countries. In India trade is regulated by a plethora of policy announcements and multiple regulatory authorities. This section of the chapter, which describes the significant domestic policies and institutions, is based on interviews and government reports.[6]

Export/Import Policy of India

The Export and Import Policy (EXIM Policy) of India is drawn up for a period of five years, with some changes being effected in an annual review in April and other changes taking place when necessary. The current EXIM Policy is applicable for the years 2003–2008. There is a negative list for exports and for imports comprising prohibited, restricted (licensed), and canalized items.[7] India's domestic environmental concerns (related to health and conservation) and multilaterally agreed environmental measures (e.g., CITES and Montreal Protocol) are implemented through these lists. There are many export-promotion measures built into the EXIM Policy, including the grant of special import licenses for firms having ISO certification. There is a separate chapter on quality, where ISO-compliant firms are rewarded and quality complaints are addressed.

Export promotion councils and certain (commodity) boards and (export development) authorities are given special status in the EXIM Policy. They grant membership to exporters so that some exporters become eligible to receive certain licenses and benefits, such as duty-free advance licenses for inputs for export production. Other relevant incentives include duty concession on import of capital goods used for export production, duty-free imports for 100 percent export-oriented units and units in export-processing zones, some fast-track mechanisms for import clearances, and additional benefits for export and trading houses showing export performance beyond a certain threshold.

Rules and Regulations on Product Standards

The Ministry of Food and Consumer Affairs is the main government agency dealing with product standards, although each ministry or department also has its own system of framing and publishing product standards. State governments also have systems for adopting standards, notably in the area of weights and measures. For the products under consideration in this chapter, the main rules and regulations are contained in the Prevention of Food Adulteration Act, the Export Inspection and Quality Control Act, and regulations for spice quality. A notable point in product standardization in India is that, although the enforcement agencies have means of enforcing these rules in domestic units, there is little possibility of enforcing them on imported goods. One reason for this could be that the Indian consumer market was comparatively closed until recently, and few imported goods entered. With the passage of time, it would be advisable for the concerned agencies to devise systems to enforce the rules on imported goods. Today the producers of imported goods seem to receive even better than national treatment because they are seldom subjected to the same enforcement procedures as are the domestic producers of similar goods. A review of the packaging rules has been initiated by the Ministry of Food and Consumer Affairs in 1999 order to apply the same rules to imported goods as are applied to domestic goods.

Export Promotion Institutions

The Indian government has been emphasizing export promotion since the late 1960s. One result of this emphasis has been the proliferation of export promotion councils and authorities. These agencies have been playing a dual role for product promotion—first as nodal agencies for disbursement of export subsidies (a function that has declined considerably since liberalization and the removal of subsidies like the cash compensatory scheme), and second as the nodal points for interaction between the industry and the government. Some of these agencies, notably, the Marine Product Export Development Authority and Agriculture Produce Export Development Authority, have been actively involved in implementing policies related to product standards.

Standard-setting Bodies

Indian goods have repeatedly faced restrictions on entry into foreign countries because of alleged noncompliance with certain standards, norms, or regulations established by the importing country. Apparently products made under Indian standards were not fit to be accepted abroad, so either Indian standards and hence the products made under them were not good enough, or the Indian standards were reasonable, but the product was being harassed at international borders on the pretext of unduly stringent foreign standards.

There are approximately 24 standard-setting bodies (SSBs) and a host of regulating agencies at the central government level as well as at state levels. Some of the most important domestic standard-setting and implementation authorities are the Bureau of Indian Standards (BIS); the Food and Agriculture Department (FAD); the National Accreditation Board for Testing and Calibration Laboratories (NABL); the Central Committee for Food Standards (CCFS); the Ministry of Food Processing Industry; the Standardization, Testing and Quality Certificate (STQC); and the National Quality Council (NQC).

In the following discussion I will identify the procedures of standard setting, their implementation, and problems that occur with them. I also will note the coordination among various standard-setting bodies and how well equipped these organizations are to meet the challenges posed by the WTO.

Bureau of Indian Standards Of some 24 standard-setting bodies in India, the Bureau of Indian Standards (BIS) is the premier organization. It sets voluntary standards, which may be made mandatory by government action. The bureau's organizational hierarchy is depicted in figure 11.1.

The procedure for setting up a standard in the BIS is the same as anywhere in the world. The request for a standard comes from a consumer or organization.

FIGURE 11.1   BIS Organizational Hierarchy

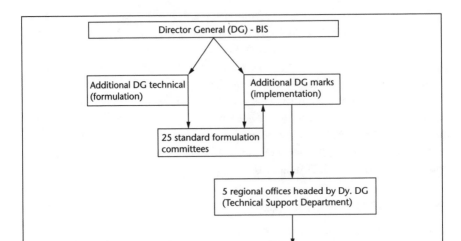

A divisional council of the BIS considers the request. The BIS then puts together a committee with a convenor and members from interested groups, and that committee drafts a standard. When approved, the standard is circulated for comments before its adoption. All BIS standards are voluntary unless they are adopted by the central government and made mandatory by the concerned ministry.

The BIS has been identified as the "enquiry point" for all TBT-related issues under Article 10.1 of the TBT Agreement, which states,

> Each member shall ensure that an enquiry point exists which is able to answer all reasonable enquiries from other members and interested parties in other member countries as well as to provide the relevant documents.

In the simplest terms, notification means that whenever an Indian SSB sets a technical regulation that differs from the existing international regulation on the same item, the rest of the world must be informed about it. This is helpful for any country wishing to export that item to India. Such notification informs the exporting country of the minimum technical requirements that it must meet specifically for the Indian market. Notification can be made to the WTO via the BIS or through the Ministry of Commerce, and it must be made in a format prescribed by the WTO and readily available from BIS or the WTO. According to Article 10.6 of the TBT Agreement,

FIGURE 11.2   BIS Notification Procedure

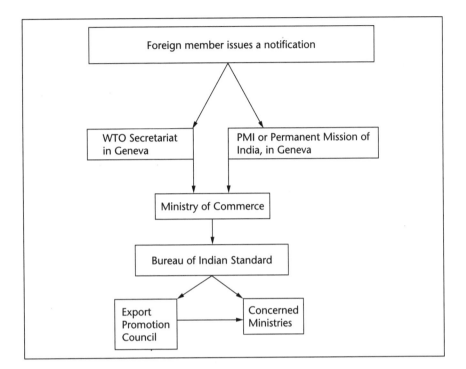

the WTO Secretariat will, when it receives notifications in accordance with provisions of this Agreement, circulate copies of the notifications to all members and interested international standardising and conformity assessment bodies.

The current route for such notification in India is depicted in figure 11.2.

Suggested alterations (deletions or additions) to the draft reach the concerned foreign member by the same route back. This is a tedious process so the BIS is trying to expedite the mechanism by enabling downloading of notifications directly from the Internet.

Only technical regulations (TRs) that are at slight or major variance with the prevalent international norm need to be notified.

Some basic infrastructure is needed for an organization entrusted with the responsible status of an inquiry point. Essentially, an inquiry point must be able to answer all questions regarding standards set within the country's national boundary. To the extent possible, SSBs should have a well-integrated information system to minimize the duplication of standards. Such a system also would prompt more harmonization of standards along the lines of international standards.

To this point, however, nothing much has been done about creating such an integrated process. The stark absence of a national notification system in India is noteworthy. The BIS reported an effort that it was making in conjunction with the Ministry of Commerce to create an awareness program for evolving a national notification system, but the response of other SSBs has been lukewarm.

Relative apathy has been observed toward Article 2.9.2 of the TBT Agreement. That article states the following:

> Whenever a relevant international standard does not exist or the technical content of the proposed technical regulation is not in accordance with the technical content of the relevant international standard, and if the technical regulation may have a significant effect on trade of other members, members shall notify other members through the WTO secretariat of the products to be covered by the proposed technical regulation, together with a brief indication of its objective and rationales. Such notification shall take place at an appropriate stage, when amendments can still be introduced and comments taken into account.

In India the body setting the new technical regulation can make such a notification either directly or through the BIS. On behalf of the WTO, the ISO/IEC (International Electrochemical Commission) produces weekly a roster of SSBs that have adopted a notification system.

All SSBs are obligated to adopt the Code of Good Practice (CGP) for preparing, adopting, and applying standards, as set out in Annex 3 of the TBT Agreement. Article C of Annex 3 states,

> Standardising bodies that have accepted or withdrawn this Code shall notify this fact to the ISO/IEC Information Centre in Geneva. The notification shall include the name and address of the body concerned and the scope of its current and expected standardization activities. The notification may be sent either directly to the ISO/IEC Information Centre, or through the national member body of ISO/IEC or preferably through the relevant national member or international affiliate of ISONET, as appropriate.

The CGP calls for transparency in preparing standards. To that purpose, Section J of Annex 3 states,

> At least once every six months, the standardising body shall publish a work programme containing its name and address, the standards it is currently preparing and the standards it has adopted in the preceding period. A standard is under preparation from the moment a decision is taken to develop a standard until that standard has been adopted. The titles of specific draft standards shall, upon request, be provided in English, French or Spanish. A notice of the existence of the Work Programme shall be published in a national or, as the case may be, regional publication of standardisation activities.

Apparently there is a twin obligation on the SSB. First it must notify the WTO that it has accepted the CGP, and then it must notify the WTO that it has prepared a work programme. According to Section J of Annex 3,

the work programme shall for each standard indicate, in accordance with any ISONET rules, the classification relevant to the subject matter, the stage attained in the standard's development, and the references of any international standards taken as a basis. No later than at the time of publication of its work programme, the standardising body shall notify the existence thereof to the ISO/IEC Information Centre in Geneva. The notification shall contain the name and address of the standardising body, the name and issue of the publication in which the work programme is published, the period to which the work programme applies, its price (if any), and how and where it can be obtained. The notification may be sent directly to the ISO/IEC Information Centre or preferably through the relevant national member or international affiliate of ISONET, as appropriate.

In India, only the BIS has duly accepted the Code of Good Practice and notified the WTO of that acceptance and of its work program. Surely it is not that the other SSBs have not notified the WTO because they maintain no record of standards they set. These SSBs must maintain an index, a catalogue, or some written documents to record their activities. Those records might not be called a work program, but their contents would contain more or less the requisites of the work program. So what has stopped them from giving notice? Apparently it is apathy and lack of consciousness about their responsibilities toward the WTO.

Whereas notification signifies disparity between a national and an international standard, equivalence between a national and an international standard is denoted by the term "harmonization." According to Article 2.4 of the TBT Agreement,

where technical regulations are required and relevant international standards exist or their completion is imminent, members shall use them or the relevant parts of them, as a basis for their technical regulations except when such international standards or relevant parts would be an ineffective or inappropriate means for the fulfilment of the legitimate objectives pursued, for instance because of fundamental climatic or geographical factors or fundamental technological problem.

Obviously such a clause has been added to bring down trade barriers regarding standards. Harmonized standards (technical regulations actually) enable all concerned trading partners to decipher the rules or technical regulations in the same way. Harmonization involves a careful analysis of the Indian standards vis-à-vis the international ones. Thereafter, the Indian standard is harmonized, to the extent feasible. Of course, not all items have international standards, and even when an international standard exists local conditions may propel the Indian SSB to set a national standard that differs from the international one. In such a case, however, the onus lies on the SSB to justify the difference. Hence, harmonization can be done only on limited standards. Thus far, the BIS has harmonized more than 4,000 standards, in accordance with EU/ISO norms, and harmonization for many other standards is under way there.

Food and Agriculture Department The Food and Agriculture Department (FAD) was established in 1956 in the BIS. The FAD deals with standardization in the field of food and agriculture, including processed food, agricultural inputs, agricultural machinery, and livestock husbandry.

There is a committee for each product group. The committee consists of 30–40 members or participants who represent industries, consumer groups, research groups, exporters, and government ministries. The BIS sends only one member per meeting to serve as the technical secretary. All of the representatives have some expertise on the subject under the purview of the committee. The FAD maintains a database of resourceful people who could be invited to be members of each committee. Each committee must meet once a year and with a six-month interval between meetings. At each meeting, matters may relate to review of an existing standard, finalization of a standard on which work began after discussions at the last meeting, or a new standard to be set up because no standard on the subject exists.

Any member of the committee may put forward a proposal to establish a standard for a particular good that has not been done before because no need had been perceived. Such cases are now becoming particularly significant because, post-WTO, SPS-related issues have grown in importance, and many countries have begun to use SPS measures not only to protect the health and sanitation levels of their domestic consumers but also to erect NTBs. Committee members have realized that much work needs to be done to limit possible contaminants in food. There are standards and regulations for some of these under the BIS and the Prevention of Food Adulteration Act (PFA), but even the existing standards have to be reviewed in light of newer and stricter specifications being issued for exports by Codex Alimentarius and the EU. The BIS has set approximately 17,000 standards so far, and the FAD has set 1,720 standards. The FAD also harmonizes standards with Codex or EN. It must be remembered that these standards are voluntary.

Many standards have not been harmonized because local Indian conditions for producing these commodities require that differences be accommodated. Quite often, industry representatives on technical committees are reluctant to change a standard because the revision would entail a change in production procedures or equipment and thereby increase production costs. Such attitudinal rigidity has been observed but to date it has posed no major problem.

The FAD is currently certifying for ISO 9000 and ISO 15000 (the former deals with general quality control and the latter is the standards terminology for

Hazard Analysis Critical Control Point [HACCP]). At present, eight companies have taken up HACCP certification from the FAD. These include Mother-Dairy and Pepsi Foods Ltd. (Another agency that issues HACCP certificates in India is SGS India Ltd.) Members of the FAD are called in for consultations with the health ministry when a new technical regulation on food products is to be designed.

National Accreditation Board for Testing   NABL is India's premier laboratory accreditation center.[8] It performs testing and calibration of laboratories. The testing is repetitive in nature, that is, the tests may be done again, either under a surveillance program or otherwise. NABL exists under and is funded by the Ministry of Science and Technology. Following a period of five years, however, NABL is supposed to begin garnering its own resources, chiefly through revenues generated in the form of charges from laboratories seeking accreditation. An accreditation certificate expires after three years.

NABL accredits laboratories, not products. It does not certify research and development laboratories because tests in those facilities are not repeatable. (Standards for products are certified by the BIS.) Accreditation is provided by a team of experts who are either on the permanent payroll of NABL or are hired for their expert consultancy.

The TBT and SPS Agreements encourage use of international standards where such standards exist instead of reliance on national standards that are specific to only one market. Customers increasingly are using international standards when specifying technical requirements.

The International Laboratory Accreditation Cooperation (ILAC), which is an informal international forum of laboratory accrediting bodies, has played a major role in establishing international standards for laboratory testing. In 1993 the ISO/IEC published *ISO/IEC Guide 5B*, developed by ILAC, as the standard system for the accreditation of testing, calibration, and measurement laboratories. To avoid expensive and unnecessary retesting of goods, ILAC promotes the concept of bilateral and multilateral recognition arrangements among laboratory accreditation bodies in various countries. Multilateral agreements are based on international peer evaluation by an international assessment team of accreditation experts in quality assurance and experts in different technical fields.

Thus NABL's current role in facilitating international trade is rather nonfunctional. What good is lab accreditation if all goods have to be tested at both places—at port of exit and at port of entry? NABL must get its accreditation system recognized by more countries so that Indian goods carrying test reports issued by NABL-accredited labs are accepted readily without additional tests in foreign countries. Such recognition would greatly reduce the interim time between shipping and final consumption of Indian goods, thereby reducing the chances of decay and increasing the credibility of the Indian goods.

Central Committee for Food Standards   The CCFS, set up at the federal level, has nine subcommittees dealing with different subjects, such as cereals, oils and fats, milk and milk products, and so forth. The subcommittees first generate data to support a new proposal or a revision to existing standards in cooperation with laboratories, industry, and consumers. Then the proposal is sent to the CCFS, which is chaired by the director general of health services and comprises five consumer members, two government experts, three representatives from industry, and representatives from all states, the BIS, and related ministries. If the new or revised standard is agreed on at the CCFS level, a notice period of 60–90 days is open for public reaction before the standard is notified. Standards generated by this committee are mandatory, unlike those of the BIS.

The issue of harmonization is of special concern to developing countries interested in expanding their export markets, and it was discussed at the June 1998 meeting of the WTO. The standards imposed by the Codex Alimentarius Commission are used as guidelines by Indian SSBs, but for various reasons, participants from industrial countries have largely dominated the Codex. The Indian voice is often drowned out by the majority, which comprises representatives from industrial countries. Consequently, many Codex standards are not relevant to or feasible for India. For example, because of the differing dietary habits of industrial countries, India has chosen to adopt Codex limits for fruits and vegetables, but only half of those limits for food grains.

Codex standards, however, are relevant for India's exports and noncompliance may create disputes, as the following examples suggest:

- In 1955 India strongly objected to the requirement of labeling milk and milk products with the picture of a buffalo. India questioned the justification of such a measure.
- Codex reduced the permissible level of sulphur dioxide in sugar from 70 ppb to 20 ppb. As the world's largest exporter of sugar, India took strong exception to this measure. A paper was presented that illustrated the technological infeasibility of this requirement and the fact that the original level posed no significant health hazards.
- Codex fixed the permissible level of aflatoxin in milk and milk products at 0.05 ppb. The Indian level is 30 ppb. The Codex limit is based on the assumption that monthly per capita consumption of these products is 1,500 gm, whereas a realistic assumption for India would be 300–400 gm. The European Community won this case.

In some cases Indian standards are more stringent than international ones. The relevant factors in this respect are nutritional status, dietary practices, and technological feasibility. For instance, India does not allow the use of artificial sweeteners in chocolates or the use of artificial colors and flavors in edible oils. The permissible limits are calculated on the basis of Acceptable Daily Intake (ADI) per kilogram of body weight. Technological constraints and dietary status are as significant as safety considerations in determining food standards.

As far as exports are concerned, the Export Inspection and Quality Control Act is applicable. Information about this is available from the Ministry of Commerce and the Export Inspection Council of India. It is important to note that the violation of international standards by an individual exporter also affects the reputation of the exporting country. Hence, organizations such as the Agricultural and Processed Food Products Export Development Authority (APEDA) provide subsidies and other assistance to Indian exporters to ensure that standards are met.

The Ministry of Health maintains four central food laboratories, one each at Calcutta, Ghaziabad, Mysore, and Pune. The former two are under the ministry's direct administrative control, and the latter two are supported through annual grants.

Ministry of Food Processing   The Ministry for Food Processing Industry provides norms, technical regulations, and standards for fruit and vegetable processing. It thus specifies the following:

- That machine and equipment parts that touch the food be made of stainless steel
- That water for washing and cleaning should be potable
- That running water should be available at all times
- That there should be in-house laboratories
- That qualified food technologists must assess the quality of the food.

Standards for processed edibles are specified by section A16 of the 1954 PFA Act. Most of those standards pertain to chemical contents, physical characteristics, contaminant levels, and additive levels in food so as to ensure safety of consumers' health.

The ministry has made no efforts so far to harmonize their standards or to get in touch with the BIS to create a national notification system.

Department of Electronics Standardization, Testing and Quality Certification
STQC is India's premier testing and calibration agency for electronic items. Its 22 laboratories situated all over India are duly certified by the NABL and are well

equipped for testing electronic items. It is noteworthy that STQC itself does not set any standards. Rather, when a party comes to the STQC to acquire a certificate, the STQC asks that party with what standard it would like to comply. When the party has expressed its desired standard, the STQC tests and certifies the product against that standard.

Within India consumers do not ask for very high quality in electronic products and they are usually quite uninformed about existing standards, so not many producers for the domestic market seek this agency's certification. Exporters are its chief clients because the STQC tests and certifies against International Electrotechnical Commission norms (IEC). The STQC is considered a competent authority and foreign parties duly accept its certification. Moreover, the STQC enters into two types of international contracts—international certification schemes and mutual recognition agreements—both of which demand reciprocity. Therefore, if the STQC agrees to accept the certification of an equivalent body in the exporting country, then STQC certification of India's electronic exports would be duly recognized in that country.

The STQC's role in standard formulation is on an ad hoc basis directly and on an ongoing basis indirectly. The normal procedure for setting an international standard takes about six years and for setting a national standard two to three years, so when a standard is required quickly, the STQC addresses the standard much faster. It consults the manufacturers, consumers, and other SSBs about the standard. For example, because no standard for color televisions existed in India, the STQC quickly produced one that was later adopted by the Department of Telecommunications and the BIS. Although it does not set standards, it helps to construct standards that are later to be adopted by the agency involved. Likewise for personal computers, the first standards in the country were set up by the STQC. Although created by the BIS, almost all standards for electronic items are actually decided by the STQC (whose members dominate the BIS electronic experts committee), because STQC has a memorandum of understanding with the BIS.

Prior to 1991, manufacturers in small-scale industries (SSI) dominated the BIS committees because, by government policy, these products were reserved for SSI. SSI diluted product quality because it was too costly a proposition for them to aspire to superior quality, so the national standard remained less than superior. Now, however, with increasing export awareness, the standards are being formed according to IEC norms.

Because standards are not set by the STQC, there is little it can do in the harmonization process. It does, however, reserve an opinion on the current harmonization status of standards and technical regulations in the field of electronics. According to the STQC, much harmonization cannot be done in India because of the lack of facilities for testing and certifying harmonized standards. In fact, the basic infrastructure in the country does not permit much to be done. For example, the EU levels allow for standards with respect to electricity fluctuations of ±10 percent, whereas fluctuations allowed by Indian standards are ±20 percent. Of course, international standards often are far more stringent than those allowable by any level. The EU and the United States have some standards that are quite stringent based on the IEC norms. India clearly does not have enough laboratories to certify these standards. Generally there is a feeling that U.S. standards are not always justifiable, and there is international pressure on the United States to amend its standards. Where feasible, the STQC is following the EU norms. Because the EU asks for marking of "Compliance with EU," the STQC provides such marking on the EU's behalf. Under the WTO, procedures for certification or calibration have to be submitted by the STQC to the BIS. The STQC admits, however, that it has done nothing so far in that direction.

National Quality Council   A national scheme for the formation of national quality councils was prepared in 1992 to serve the following chief purposes:

- To mobilize resources to ensure that goods and services are designed to match consumer needs, expectations, and desires in terms of their specifications, delivery, and competitive price, and that goods and services produced consistently conform to standards and are produced at the optimum cost at which the consumer will buy.
- To raise quality consciousness in the country, both in industry (manufacturing and service) and among consumers, by launching a nationwide quality campaign and establishing a national standards information inquiry service.
- To encourage third-party certification of goods and services and third-party certification of quality-management systems (ISO 9000 standards or equivalent) at the enterprise level, with a view to minimizing the need for multiple assessments by the consumers.
- To facilitate the upgrading of testing and calibration laboratories and encourage the development of a unified national laboratory accreditation system to ensure that the test reports become acceptable in the world market.
- To raise the level of training for personnel engaged in quality control activities, including assessors and trainers, and to encourage their third-party certification.
- To obtain mutual recognition with similar national schemes of India's major trading partners.
- To meet effectively the challenge of new and demanding European accreditation standards and legislation. Its most advantageous aspect would be the fact that all efforts would be made to bring about maximum possible national and international recognition of the scheme. This would greatly help in increasing the acceptance of Indian goods abroad.

The structure of the NQC has been established, but its effects have not yet started to percolate at levels where it is required. At this time, it is nonoperational.

International Institutional Framework

World Trade Organization

The General Agreement on Tariffs and Trade has been the beacon of the multilateral trading system since 1948. As a result of the Uruguay Round of multilateral trade negotiations, the World Trade Organization came into being on January 1, 1995, subsuming GATT under it. Article XX of the GATT allows member countries to deviate from their obligations under the agreement in the case of three types of trade measures, among other things. Those measures are ones necessary to protect human, animal, or plant life or health; ones relating to the conservation of exhaustible natural resources if such measures are made effective in conjunction with restrictions on domestic production or consumption; and ones necessary to secure compliance with laws or regulations not otherwise inconsistent with GATT rules. Such unilateral measures, however, have to pass a composite trade test. The trade test has three components: no arbitrary discrimination, no unjustifiable discrimination, and no disguised trade protection. It is often called the least-trade-restrictiveness test. Jurisprudence has shown that the second type of trade measure has become the most potent tool for making GATT-compliant unilateral trade measures pursuant to environmental objectives.

International Organization for Standardization   The ISO is the most important of the international standard-setting organizations. It is a world federation of 123 national standards bodies, an international nongovernmental organization with a majority of its members coming from the public sector. Its core business is the development, approval, and promulgation of consensus-based international standards. Unlike the WTO, however, majority voting is practiced in this organization.

The ISO develops standards through 200 technical committees split into about 650 subcommittees and 2,000 working groups. It also develops guides for standard setting. In preparing these guides, the ISO works with specific users of standards, including those in the private sector. All of its standards and guides are voluntary in nature but, given the organization's international credibility and wide acceptance, its standards have considerable trade effects. Those who can afford it apply for ISO certification. The certification is a costly process by Indian standards. It may take Rs.100,000–Rs. 500,000 to get certified, apart from the cost of maintaining the certificate. The ISO 9000 series is the general quality certification standard, but there also is an environmental management standard—the ISO 14000 series. India has about 5,000 ISO 9000 companies; some 100 companies have received ISO 14000 certification.

Codex Alimentarius Commission   The Codex Alimentarius Commission, a U.N. body, compiles agreed standards, guidelines, and other recommendations into the Codex Alimentarius, the Codex Food Code (CFC). The CFC tries to create harmonized standards. Prior to the SPS Agreement, the CFC could be adopted, applied, or ignored at the discretion of a government. Within the agreement, however, CFC has been adopted as the benchmark. Therefore, countries that do not impose standards higher than those of the CFC have the right to seek these standards for their imports. The Codex Alimentarius has incorporated Hazard Analysis Critical Control Point (HACCP) plans and principles as an integral part of the CFC. Volume V of the Food Code sets standards for a number of specific fish and fish products. Marine export was banned by the EU in 1997 and HAACP was adopted officially as the standard by government agencies for the first time in the marine sector.

Hazard Analysis Critical Control Point System   The Hazard Analysis Critical Control Point system is being used increasingly as a food safety system all over the industrial world. When properly applied, it is a set of preliminary steps and principles that yields a systematic method for identifying significant hazards and properly applying preventive measures so that food-borne hazards are prevented, eliminated, or reduced to an acceptable level. With emerging international and national agreement on HACCP principles, their application would create a commonality of understanding of the development, implementation, and maintenance of a food safety system. Having these commonly understood principles, many food processors require their suppliers to have an HACCP system for producing the ingredients that they supply. Application of the system offers widely understood principles for identifying significant risks and means of controlling them. Being able to identify the most likely sources of food-borne hazards by implementing effective, documented systems will enable the industry to focus more attention on those sources.

Conclusions and Recommendations

The study on which this chapter is based indicates that Indian exports face a number of NTBs in the forms of very high standards, testing procedures, environmental considerations, packaging requirements, and so on. It is also evident from the survey that these prohibitive standards lack sufficient scientific proof of a protective effect on the health and environment of the importing country. But the impact of these barriers on the value of trade for a broad range of Indian exportable commodities is potentially extensive, results in a variety of trade effects, and creates additional costs for Indian industry and government. Therefore, India is increasingly concerned that certain technical and sanitary/photosanitary measures may be inconsistent with WTO provisions and may unfairly impede the flow of trade.

It is also evident from my research that the Indian government is not well positioned to address these issues. Trade associations and key government officials have identified these barriers as an increasingly important issue in trade, but they have difficulty defining the nature and scope of the problem, partly because of the complex nature of the issue itself and partly for other reasons. For example, they lack complete information on the number of measures that affect India's exports, they are unsure how many measures that have been identified may be inconsistent with WTO provisions, and they do not have reliable estimates of the effects such measures have had on exports.

Many government, trade, regulatory, and research entities have some responsibility for addressing such measures, but there is no single entity directing and coordinating overall government efforts. Some entities' roles and responsibilities regarding these measures are not clearly defined, and these entities have had difficulty coordinating their activities. Government entities lack comprehensive data on which to address these measures and they do not know what progress has been made to address them.

No process has been developed to jointly evaluate measures and determine which ones the government should address, and in what order. When the government decides to challenge a measure, multiple entities with conflicting viewpoints have made it difficult to develop a unified approach and to decide which cases should be referred to the WTO for dispute resolution. Coordinated goals, objectives, and performance measurements related to government efforts do not yet exist.

One important recommendation for all of the standard-setting and implementation bodies is to create an exclusive set-up for documenting data on WTO compliance activities. These organizations have to be made aware of their responsibilities in the WTO and they must learn how they can play a more active part in setting standards at the international level.

My survey also revealed that the lack of coordination among standard-setting bodies leads to duplication in standards and confusion in implementation. What is needed is integration among standard-setting bodies, harmonization, and national notification of standards.

The Bureau of Indian Standards as a nodal agency for standards coordination and notification for the WTO is well aware of its obligations under the TBT and SPS Agreements. But the BIS, structured today with multiple responsibilities and lacking authority and coordination with other SSBs, may find it difficult to cope with increasing demands of the WTO. Therefore a separate body—something like a national quality council in collaboration with the BIS—should be established so that there is a body fully committed to standard-related matters in the WTO.

To upgrade quality in India, expertise is needed from countries that have tested quality measures on their farms, but inviting such expertise is a costly proposition. Therefore I recommend that the WTO/FAO promote and perhaps sponsor experts to assist developing countries improve their quality.

India is inadequately represented in international standard-setting meetings. Repeatedly it has been reported that most of the Codex standards are set even when there is very little participation by developing nations, including India. The Codex committees are dominated by members from industrial countries so the standards set by them are most often not viable for the developing countries. Standards set by Codex are made with the food and agricultural practices of the industrial economies in mind, but those practices are vastly different from the practices prevalent in developing economies. India must be better represented in standard-setting procedures.

As far as testing facilities are concerned, India's existing laboratories are poorly equipped with machines and skilled manpower, and that has led to the poor reputation of test results in international markets. Exporters therefore resort to multinational testing facilities, which are more expensive. Laboratory accreditation is voluntary and carries no accountability, so the number of inappropriately equipped and staffed laboratories has mushroomed, and many of the labs resort to issuing fake certificates. India, therefore, should invoke technical and financial assistance provisions in the WTO agreements to upgrade its testing facilities.

And most important of all, India must set her house in order as far as WTO commitments are concerned. The seriousness of the WTO commitments is still not recognized by various government and semi-government authorities responsible for implementing these commitments. The lack of coordination, communication, and interaction among government agencies is leading to delays and duplication of efforts, and that leads to suffering of businesses unable to exploit the benefits of globalization. The government agencies responsible for standard setting and implementation should realize that it is too late to ask, "Why?" and time to inquire "How?"

Endnotes

1. The TBT and SPS Agreements are described in more detail below.
2. The notification led to a wide range of responses from WTO delegations, including from some African and other developing countries. The EU subsequently decided to amend its proposed legislation, thereby meeting some but not all of the criticism that emerged. Developing countries have nevertheless brought forward complaints about the functioning of the transparency mechanism. They have complained that the notification procedure does not work properly. Although industrial

countries generally notify changes in legislation, they rarely take into account developing countries' comments and the desire of developing countries for a formal mechanism for dealing with comments.

3. Technical specifications can be divided into three types of standards relevant to primary and processed goods. *Packaging standards* regulate a broad range of container attributes, from dimensions to biodegradability of packaging material, to realize a wide range of regulatory goals. *Process standards* (sometimes referred to as production standards) dictate the means (inputs, production technology, or both) by which firms are to realize different regulatory targets. *Product standards* specify the ends (characteristics of a product related to its size, weight, or any number of other attributes). A product standard for imported tea, for example, might state that the product must be free of any trace of residue, a status that could be objectively verified by phytosanitary authorities in the importing country by means of tests on shipments at the border.

4. A process standard alternatively might stipulate, for example, that a product must be processed by a specific method. Economists usually argue that product standards are more efficient regulatory tools than are process standards because the former allow heterogeneous firms to choose the technology that minimizes the resource costs of achieving a specific regulatory target but the latter do not. It has also been pointed out in the context of food safety regulations, however, that process standards can sometimes be the optimal regulatory option. A Hazard Analysis Critical Control Point system, which includes flexible process standards designed to reduce microbial contamination in food, might be superior to specific product standards, given the expense of microbiological tests and the recurrent nature of the pathogen hazard. The costs of enforcement and the degree of administrative discretion in enforcement are also important considerations in any evaluation of the relative efficiency of process or product standards.

5. According to Article 2.1.1.20 of the International Animal Health Code of the OIE, for import of milk and milk products from the countries considered infected with foot-and-mouth disease (FMD) or rinderpest, the veterinary authorities of exporting countries are required to produce an international sanitary certificate attesting that the exported products originate from herds or flocks that were not subject to any restrictions resulting from FMD at the time of milk collection and that products have been processed to ensure the destruction of the FMD virus according to the procedures laid down in the article.

6. Because of space limitations, many details of India's standards policies and institutions are not included in what follows. Further details are available from the author on request.

7. Canalized items are those items that can be traded only by a government agency like the State Trading Corporation.

8. Laboratory accreditation is the formal recognition, authorization, and registration of a laboratory that has demonstrated its capability, competence, and credibility to carry out the tasks it is claiming to be able to do. The body granting the formal recognition records the accredited laboratory in a register, which is published periodically. The accredited laboratory is authorized to issue certificates, test reports, and reports of chemical analysis, which are recognized and accepted under the logo of the international laboratory accreditation body. Accreditation provides an independent third-party assessment of a laboratory's technical competence and consistency in the interpretation of international standards.

References and Bibliography

The word "processed" describes informally produced works that may not be available commonly through libraries.

Anderson, Kym, B. Hoekman, and A. Strutt. 1999. "Agriculture and the WTO: Next Steps." Washington, D.C.: World Bank. Processed. <www.worldbank.org/trade>

Bhagwati, Jagdish. 1997. "The Demands to Reduce Domestic Diversity among Trading Nations." In Jadish Bhagwati and Robert E. Hudec, eds., *Trade and Harmonization: Prerequisites for Free Trade?* Vol. 2. Cambridge, Mass.: MIT Press.

Bhattacharyya, B. 1999. Non-Tariff Measures on India's Exports: An Assessment. Occasional Paper 16. New Delhi: Indian Institute of Foreign Trade.

Bredhal, Maury E., and Kenneth W. Forsythe. 1989. "Harmonizing Phytosanitary and Sanitary Regulations." *World Economy* 12(2): 189–206.

Brouder, Anne-Marie, Rupert Loader, and Spencer Henson. 2000. "Constraints to Small-Scale Food Processing in Sub-Saharan Africa." Conference presentation, April 14–17, University of Manchester, U.K.

Caswell, Julie A., and N. H Hooker. 1996. "HACCP as an International Trade Standard." *American Journal of Agricultural Economics* 78(3): 775–79.

CDR (Centre for Development Research). 1999. Reviewing the SPS Agreement: A Developing Country Perspective. Working Paper 2.3. Copenhagen.

Das, Bhagirath Lal. 1998. *An Introduction to the WTO Agreement: Trade and Development Issues and the World Trade Organization.* London: Zed Books and Third World Network.

————. 1999. *The World Trade Organization: A Guide to the Framework for International Trade.* London: Zed Books and Third World Network.

Dawson, Richard J. 1999. "Impact of WTO on Codex Alimentarius and Its Implications for the South Asian Region." In Benoit Blarel, Garry Pursell, and Alberto Valdes, eds., *Implications of the Uruguay Round Agreement for South Asia: The Case of Agriculture.* Washington, D.C.: World Bank.

Deardorff, Alan V., and Stern, Robert M. 1998. *Measurement of Non-Tariff Barriers.* Ann Arbor: University of Michigan Press.

Desai, B. M., V. K. Gupta, and N. V. Namboodiri. 1991. *Food-Processing Industries: Development and Financial Performance.* New Delhi: Oxford and IBH Publishing.

FAO (Food and Agricultural Organization). 1998. *Possible Implications of Sanitary and Phytosanitary Measures for Exports of Oilseed-Based Products to the European Union.* Rome.

————. 1999. "The Importance of Food Quality and Safety for Developing Countries." Report to the Committee on World Food Security. 25th Session, Rome, May 31–June 3. <www.fao.org/docrep/meeting/x1845e.htm>

FICCI (Federation of Indian Chambers of Commerce and Industry). 2000. "Study on Comparative Trade Policy Analysis to Assess Barriers to Trade." New Delhi. Processed.

Giles, J. A. 1997. *Trade Opportunities in the International Processed Horticultural Markets.* Geneva: UNCTAD.

Government of India, Ministry of Commerce. 1999. "Non-Tariff Barriers (NTBs) Faced by India: Preliminary Report." Economic Division. New Delhi. Processed.

Gulati, Ashok. 1999. "From Market Access to Domestic Policy." *Economic Times,* November 3, p. 7.

Gupta, Deepak. 1999. "Codex Alimentarius Commission and SPS Agreement." Delhi: Ministry of Health Unpublished paper.

Henson, Spencer, and Rupert Loader. 1999. "Impact of Sanitary and Phytosanitary Standards on Developing Countries and the Role of the SPS Agreement." *Agribusiness* 15(3): 355–69.

————. 2001. Barriers to Agricultural Exports from Developing Countries: The Role of Sanitary and Phytosanitary Requirements. *World Development* 29(1): 85–102.

Hooker, Neal H., and Julie A. Caswell. 1999. "A Framework for Evaluating Nontariff Barriers to Trade Related to Sanitary and Phytosanitary Regulation." *Journal of Agricultural Economics* 50(1).

Indian Institute of Foreign Trade. 2000. "WTO Consistency of Trade Policy of Select Partner Countries of India." New Delhi.

ITC/CS (International Trade Center, UNCTAD/WTO, and Commonwealth Secretariat). 1999. *Business Guide to the World Trading System,* 2nd ed. Geneva and London.

JECFA (Joint FAO/WHO Expert Committee on Food Additives). 1997. Paper presented at the Forty-ninth Meeting, June 17–26, Rome.

Lall, Sanjay. 1999. "India's Manufactured Exports: Comparative Structure and Prospects." *World Development* 27(10): 1769–86.

Martin, Will, and L. Alan Winters. 1996. *The Uruguay Round and the Developing Countries.* Cambridge, U.K.: Cambridge University Press.

Maskus, Keith E., and J. S. Wilson. 2001. "A Review of Past Attempts and New Policy Context." In Keith E. Maskus and J. S. Wilson, eds., *Quantifying the Impact of Technical Barriers to Trade: Can It Be Done?* Ann Arbor: University of Michigan Press.

Maskus, Keith E., and J. S. Wilson. 2000. "Quantifying the Impact of Technical Barriers to Trade: A Review of Past Attempts and New Policy Context." Washington, D.C.: World Bank. Processed.

Maskus, Keith E., J. S. Wilson, and T. Otsuki. No date. "Quantifying the Import of Technical Barriers to Trade: A Frame Work for Analysis." Washington, D.C.: World Bank. Processed.

Mehta, Rajesh. 1999. *Tariff and Non-Tariff Barriers of Indian Economy: A Profile.* New Delhi: Research and Information System for the Non-Aligned and Other Developing Countries.

Mehta, Rajesh, and S. K. Mohanty. 1999. *WTO and Industrial Tariffs: An Empirical Analysis for India.* New Delhi: Research and Information System for the Non-Aligned and Other Developing Countries.

Michalopoulos, Constantine. 1998. "The Participation of the Developing Countries in the WTO." Policy Research Working Paper. World Bank, Washington, D.C.

Mukerji, Ananda. 2000. "Developing Countries and the WTO." *Journal of World Trade* 34(6): 33–74.

National Research Council. 1995. *Standards, Conformity Assessment and Trade.* Washington, D.C.

OECD (Organisation for Economic Co-Operation and Development). 1997. *Indicators of Tariff and Non-Tariff Trade Barriers.* Paris.

Otsuki, Tsunehiro, John S. Wilson, and Mirvat Sewadeh. 2000. "A Race to the Top? A Case Study of Food Safety Standards and African Exports." Policy Research Working Paper. World Bank, Washington, D.C.

Panagariya, Arvind. 1999. "The WTO Trade Policy Review of India, 1998." In J. N. Bhagwati, A. Panagarya, and T. N. Srinivasan, *Lectures on International Trade.* Cambridge, Mass.: MIT Press.

Pederson, Jorgen Dige. 2000. "Explaining Economic Liberalisation in India: State and Society Perspectives." *World Development* 28(2): 265–82.

Porter, Michael. 1990. *The Competitive Advantage of Nations.* London: Macmillan Press.

Research and Information System for the Non-Aligned and Other Developing Countries, and the Association of Indian Automobile Manufacturers. 1999. *The WTO Regime and Its Implications for the Indian Automobile Industry.* New Delhi.

RGICS (Rajiv Gandhi Institute for Contemporary Studies). No date. "Report on TBT and SPS." Report submitted to the Ministry of Commerce, Government of India. New Delhi. Processed.

Roberts, Donna. 1998. "Preliminary Assessment of the Effects of the WTO Agreement on Sanitary and Phytosanitary Trade Regulations." *Journal of International Economic Law* 1(3): 377–405.

Saqib, Mohammed. 2000. "Technical Barriers to Trade and Role of Indian Standard Institutions." Working Paper 19. Rajiv Gandhi Institute for Contemporary Studies, Delhi.

Singhal, Anirudh. 2000. "The Sanitary and Phytosanitary Measures Agreement." Working Paper 12. Rajiv Gandhi Institute for Contemporary Studies, Delhi.

Trebilcock, Michael J., and Robert Howse. 1999. *The Regulation of International Trade,* 2nd ed. London: Routledge.

UNCTAD (United Nations Conference on Trade and Development). 2000. *A Positive Agenda for Developing Countries: Issues for Future Trade Negotiations.* New York: United Nations.

Unnevehr, Laurian J., and H. H. Jenson. 1996. "HACCP as a Regulatory Innovation to Improve Food Safety in the Meat Industry." *American Journal of Agricultural Economics* 78(3): 764–69.

Wignarajah, Ganesh, and G. Ikiara. 1999. "Adjustment, Technological Capabilities and Enterprise Dynamics in Kenya." In Sanjay Lall, ed. *The Technological Response to Import Liberalisation in Sub-Saharan Africa.* London: Macmillan Press.

WTO (World Trade Organization). 1998a. *The SPS Agreement and Developing Countries.* Geneva.

———. 1998b. *Trade Policy Review: India, 1998.* Geneva.

———. 1999. *Review of the Operation and Implementation of the Agreement on Application of Sanitary and Phytosanitary Measures.* Geneva.

———. 2001. "Preparation for the Fourth Session of the Ministerial Conference: Draft Ministerial Declaration." Revision. October 27.

12

TRADE AND ENVIRONMENT: DOHA AND BEYOND

Veena Jha

Enhancing understanding and strengthening policy coordination in the area of trade, environment, and development are of key interest to India. Since the beginning of the 1990s this has become particularly relevant for several domestic and external reasons, including the economic liberalization policy that India has followed since 1991, the increasing importance of the environment in influencing market access and export competitiveness, and the inclusion of the environment on the international trade agenda of the World Trade Organization (WTO).

On the other hand, the changing character of the international debate on trade and environment can be traced to three distinct streams of influence. The first stream is related to the ongoing discussions in the WTO Committee on Trade and Environment (CTE) that are fairly well structured around distinct agenda items with a well-defined work program. In fact, this has constituted the cornerstone for most debates on trade and environment for a good part of the last decade. The special sessions of the CTE have also explored on a preliminary basis the different negotiating issues. These negotiating issues, outlined in paragraph 30 of the Doha Ministerial Declaration, however, mark a departure from the theoretical debates on trade and environment in the CTE. The second strand of the debate has originated from disputes related to trade and environment that have been taken up by the WTO. These panels and the related appellate bodies have subtly but surely changed interpretations of articles contained in the General Agreement on Tariffs and Trade (GATT).

The third stream of influence originates from the new mandate, largely championed by the European Union (EU), that appears to be emerging from the WTO process itself. According to this new mandate, which is closely related to the discussions on agriculture, trade, and environment, linkages appear to have an evolutionary character—that is, the exact nature of the linkage will evolve according to the character of the trade agreements that emerge from the negotiations. Environmental considerations have also featured in the discussions on multifunctionality that has emerged in the context of discussions on agricultural liberalization. For example, environmental considerations in a possible multilateral agreement on investment would be substantively different from the way that they have been addressed in the Agreement on Trade-Related Aspects of Intellectual Property Rights (TRIPS). Of course, the bargaining processes as well as the interest groups that will emerge from these future negotiations are also difficult to determine. What is clear is that India will have to develop expertise on the environmental aspects of several trade agreements and not simply remain confined to the agenda items of the CTE. This need for expertise reinforces India's need for an integrated approach to trade, investment, environment, technology, and other aspects of globalization.

Keeping such a framework in mind, this chapter proceeds as follows. The first section briefly outlines the negotiating history of trade and environment in the WTO, emphasizing the position of the major players in the current debate on trade and environment. The second section outlines how India's agenda on trade and environment has evolved in part as a response to the interests of industrial countries and in part because of the problems that industrial countries have experienced. Outlined are those issues on which India has developed a defensive agenda and those on which it has developed a proactive agenda. The section also links India's position to its experiences in the area of market access and environmentally sound technologies because these explain the position that India has taken at the WTO.

The third section discusses the developments that have taken place outside the framework of the CTE. These include the developments through dispute-settlement processes and through the buildup to the Doha Ministerial Meeting of the WTO. These developments are important and may change the complexion of the discussions on trade and environment. Their implications and India's need to respond to the dynamic nature of this interface are briefly outlined there.

The fourth section lays down the fundamentals of India's environmental policy that has been enunciated without a consideration of its trade interests. It is a comprehensive body of legislation adequate to protect India's environment, thus showing that India's capacity to implement environmental laws is in no way subverted by its trade interests or its WTO obligations.

The final section contains recommendations on those specific items regarding trade and the environment for which India may wish to suggest changes in trade rules, and those on which it may wish to safeguard the status quo. The chapter also will outline further policy-oriented research activities that may be needed to foster India's more informed participation in the Doha Development Agenda of negotiations on trade and environment.

Negotiating History of Trade and Environment in the WTO

The discussion begins with some background and then considers recent developments.

Background

Since 1995 the WTO has subsumed the role of the GATT, which was formed in 1948, as the cornerstone of an open international trading system and forum for multilateral negotiations. For many years, the multilateral trading system essentially dealt with the evolution of rules for traded products. Concepts of sustainable development and environmental protection in trade rules only came to be recognized in the Uruguay Round (1986–93). The GATT Group on Environmental Measures and International Trade (EMIT Group), though set up in 1971, remained largely inactive until 1991 when the tuna–dolphin case brought environmental issues to the fore. As a result, the environmental policies leading to trade effects were examined.

In the new WTO, the EMIT Group was replaced by the Committee on Trade and Environment, following the decision to do so reached in Marrakesh in April 1994. The CTE's role is to examine the relationship between trade measures and environmental measures in order to promote sustainable development and to recommend appropriate modifications of the provisions of the multilateral trading system, whenever required. In addition to the areas covered by the EMIT Group, the CTE encompasses such new areas as services and TRIPS.

Paragraph 31 of the Ministerial Declaration at Doha (WTO 2001) states that

With a view to enhancing the mutual supportiveness of trade and environment, we agree to negotiations, without prejudging their outcome, on:

(i) the relationship between existing WTO rules and specific trade obligations set out in multilateral environmental agreements (MEAs). The negotiations shall be limited in scope to the applicability of such existing WTO rules as among parties to the MEA in question. The negotiations shall not prejudice the WTO rights of any Member that is not a party to the MEA in question;

(ii) procedures for regular information exchange between MEA Secretariats and the relevant WTO committees, and the criteria for the granting of observer status;

(iii) the reduction or, as appropriate, elimination of tariff and non-tariff barriers to environmental goods and services.

Here is the essential point that requires clarification in this negotiating proposal at Doha: although there has been no consensus in the CTE to negotiate these issues, how will the Ministerial Declaration bring about results that are different from the CTE? Does this proposal appear to suggest that, although the CTE has failed to achieve a consensus, the issue can be negotiated in a negotiating committee? Moreover, the CTE spent a lot of time, without success, trying to reach consensus on what constitutes an MEA. Therefore it is not clear what would come of negotiations on issues that have not been agreed to in the CTE. Despite several meetings of the special session of the CTE, a clear agenda has not emerged. Recent statements by the EU appear to suggest that environment may only be of some optical value in its negotiating position (see WTO Committee on Trade and Environment 2003b).

Concerns of Industrial Countries Versus Those of Developing Countries

There are divergent environmental concerns in the Doha Development Agenda (see UNCTAD 1999). Industrial countries generally are keen to include environmental and sustainable development considerations on the agenda for the new negotiations for the following reasons:

- There are renewed concerns about the possible environmental effects of further trade liberalization, which call for greater integration of trade and environmental regimes.
- In a broad process of trade negotiations covering a wide range of issues trade-offs can be identified. Hence, including environment in several agreements will make it easier for industrial economies to make gains elsewhere, especially on issues such as agriculture for the Cairns group.
- Policymakers in industrial countries realize that any negotiating agenda that does not pay adequate attention to the environment will not generate political support.

Developing countries generally are reluctant to engage in a new round of trade negotiations for the following reasons (Khor 1999):

- They believe that the Uruguay Round failed to improve market access for developing countries.

- They are dissatisfied with the way the new WTO rules have dealt with important development-related areas, such as the protection of intellectual property rights, special and differential treatment, and other implementation-related issues.
- Because they have inadequate capacities, developing countries have been unable to use the WTO system to pursue their interests.

Developing countries generally are even more wary of entering negotiations on the environment for the following reasons (Shaheen 1999):

- Their perception is that entering negotiations will lead to increased protectionism and unilateral measures directed against them.
- The current trade and environment debate seems inclined toward accommodation of measures to restrict, rather than promote, trade. The agenda on environmental goods and services is unlikely to yield substantial trade benefits for them. On the other hand, they risk getting in non-product-related process and production methods (PPMs) through the back door (see WTO Committee on Trade and Environment 2003a).
- Not much progress has been made in implementing Agenda 21 from the Earth Summit in 1992 in terms of providing supportive measures to developing countries, such as finance, access to environmentally sound technologies (ESTs), and capacity building.

India, however, has a very different agenda on trade and environment. Although some of the reactions are purely defensive, India is also pursuing a proactive agenda as outlined in the next section.

Issues That Figure Prominently on India's Agenda

In this section I discuss several aspects of India's policies on trade and the environment, including its resistance to WTO rule changes, ecolabeling, mainstreaming the environment, and environmental reviews.[2]

Defensive Agenda

India appears resistant to changes in the WTO rules in a number of areas, as noted here. Some developed countries, in particular the EU, may continue to press for an adaptation of GATT Article XX to further accommodate the use of trade measures specifically mandated by MEAs, although recent decisions by the Appellate Body in the *Shrimp–Turtle* case may have reduced such pressure. In this context India has indicated that allowing unilateral trade measures based on non-product-related PPMs could result in imposing domestic environmental policies on trading partners.[3] India's view is that current WTO rules and practices are adequate to address any inconsistencies that might arise between trade measures used in MEAs and WTO rules. After all, there has never been a dispute between WTO rules and MEAs, and the conflict is therefore more hypothetical than real. Moreover, such actions may lead to the use of trade measures for protectionist purposes and for pressuring countries to join MEAs, which may not serve their economic interests.

India has put forward the view that an MEA can only be regarded as multilateral if (a) it has been negotiated under the United Nations; (b) there has been effective participation in the negotiations by countries belonging to different geographical regions and by countries at different stages of economic and social development; and (c) the Agreement should provide procedures for accession of countries that are not its original members on terms that are equitable in relation to the terms of its original participants. India's proposal also includes an indicative list of specific trade measures contained in some MEAs. Thus India has attempted to define the scope of the mandate of the Doha Declaration (see WTO 2003).

Whereas environmental standards can properly be set at the national level for effects that are confined to national boundaries, the same does not apply when the domain of the effect is international, or even global. In the case of such issues as greenhouse gases, ozone-depleting substances (ODS), or the conservation of threatened species, international agreements are essential. They mandate specific actions to address the environmental problems that arise, and they specify how the responsibility for the actions is to be divided among countries. Frequently, the required actions include some form of restriction on trade.

For example, under the Montreal Protocol India has to phase out its production and consumption of chlorofluorocarbons (CFCs) by 2006. Just prior to the signing of the Protocol, heavy investment was made in the CFC industry, and many manufacturing plants have yet to complete their payback periods. The choice of substitutes also was not clear as much will depend on the market for substitutes. Information about CFC-free technology as well as new investment in non-CFC technology was urgently required. According to Das (2000), the incremental costs for the phase-out of ODS in India have been estimated by the India Country Programme at US$1.964 billion for all sectors. However, only about $49 million worth of proposals had been approved for funding by July 1998. Few foreign companies have shown a desire to share their CFC-free technology.

Although the alternative ESTs and finance may not be forthcoming, the negative trade effects immediately come into play. The adjustment costs relating to technology, substitute raw materials, and retooling range from 30 percent to

35 percent with respect to refrigerators and 10 percent in the case of automobile air conditioners. Because those costs are not readily coverable from the Montreal Fund, India's reluctance to enter into MEAs that entail significant costs is understandable. This also explains India's stand on the use of trade measures for environmental purposes as the country does not want to be coerced with trade measures into joining agreements. Although global environmental problems have to be addressed cooperatively, there is an emphasis on common but differentiated responsibilities for these problems that may or may not entail the use of trade measures.

Paragraph 6 of the Ministerial Declaration (WTO 2001) states

> We are convinced that the aims of upholding and safeguarding an open and non-discriminatory multilateral trading system, and acting for the protection of the environment and the promotion of sustainable development can and must be mutually supportive. We take note of the efforts by Members to conduct national environmental assessments of trade policies on a voluntary basis. We recognize that under WTO rules no country should be prevented from taking measures for the protection of human, animal or plant life or health, or of the environment at the levels it considers appropriate, subject to the requirement that they are not applied in a manner which would constitute a means of arbitrary or unjustifiable discrimination between countries where the same conditions prevail, or a disguised restriction on international trade, and are otherwise in accordance with the provisions of the WTO Agreements.

In its official briefing to the press following the Doha Ministerial the EU concluded that paragraph 6 of the Doha Declaration provides adequate cover for invoking measures on the basis of the precautionary principle (WTO 2001).

Ecolabeling

Ecolabeling programs are a fact of the international marketplace. In view of the growing importance of such programs in commercial transactions between industrial and developing countries and the increasing use of comprehensive life-cycle criteria and indicators for these programs, the challenge is how to accommodate ecolabeling programs in the Technical Barriers to Trade (TBT) Agreement without compromising basic GATT rules. The situation is complicated by the lack of an agreed interpretation on whether private, voluntary ecolabeling schemes are within the scope of the GATT/TBT.

Discussions in the CTE have focused on multicriteria, ecolabeling schemes, especially those that are based on non-product-related PPMs. Although the effects of "type-1" ecolabeling on the marketplace and international trade,[4] particularly imports from developing countries, have been limited, the interest in ecolabeling in the context of international trade appears at least in part attributable to the fact that, from a conceptual and trade policy point of view, it involves many complex issues, such as PPMs, the definition of international standards, and equivalency. Little progress has been made thus far in dealing with the PPM issue in the context of ecolabeling. In particular, the debates in the WTO and the International Organization for Standardization (ISO)[5] have made very little progress in developing the concept of "equivalency."

There may be some advantages for India in clarifying the status of ecolabeling with respect to the TBT Agreement, but there may be some disadvantages, too. Clarifying the status of ecolabeling with respect to WTO rules may result in greater WTO discipline in certain sectors (forest products, textiles, cut flowers) where Indian export competitiveness may be adversely affected by such schemes. According to a study conducted in India by Bharucha (1997), small producers are most likely to be adversely affected by ecolabeling schemes. In some cases, certification costs alone would amount to 50 percent of total production costs. It may provide an opportunity to force greater WTO discipline for purely private programs and nongovernmental organization (NGO) campaigns again in areas where trade has been adversely affected. It may reduce pressure for unilateral measures by providing information as an alternative to an outright ban; that is, let the consumer decide.

There is an equal risk in establishing precedents, particularly if such precedents apply to labor and human rights issues. There is also a risk that clarifying the status of ecolabeling schemes versus WTO rules would encourage the wider use of ecolabeling in international trade and thereby often foster protectionist intent. It also may become more difficult to challenge an ecolabeling measure.

Very few, if any, examples can be found where type I ecolabels have allowed India to obtain price premiums, improved market shares, or environmental performance. Ecolabels may have potentially adverse or at best neutral trade effects on India. It is arguable that India may actually turn the system to its advantage by marketing "ecofriendly" products such as "green cotton" labels and the possible use of natural fibres such as jute in packaging. Because Indian exporters do not possess the capacity to obtain certification, however, the possible negative effects may outweigh the potential benefits of clarifying WTO rules with respect to ecolabeling. Opportunities provided by ecolabeling and consumer sensitivity in Organisation for Economic Co-operation and Development (OECD) markets would in any case accrue to India with or without the clarification of trade rules in this respect. The rules as they exist provide greater certainty in case such measures become barriers to trade.

An added complication introduced in the context of ecolabeling has been the precautionary principle. This principle is usually invoked to justify protective measures taken in the absence of full scientific certainty, such as the potential health hazards of a pesticide. This principle has generated a lot of controversy in a

North-North context as well as the North-South context. The reason is whereas the EU upholds the principle, the United States feels all measures should be based on sound science, and overdependence on the principle could undermine sound science (WTO 1999).

It is also ironic that ecolabeling, which was strongly championed by Canada and the United States, is now being questioned by those countries in the context of genetically modified organisms (GMOs). The countries disagree that labeling requirements for products containing GMOs would be needed. The United States in particular asserts that there is no need for such labeling because the products are safe and testing for traces of GMOs would be prohibitively expensive and complicated. It would require segregating GMO from non-GMO crops during cultivation, transport, and any consequent industrial production. This separation would entail unnecessary costs. The irony is that when countries of the South had raised similar questions regarding ecolabeling of textiles and footwear, their arguments were dismissed on the grounds that, if consumer preference so dictated, then such consumer preferences should be catered to. It is interesting that the issue of consumer preference has not been given much emphasis in discussions on GMOs (ICTSD 1998, p. 2).

This issue is further complicated in cases of conflictual science. The beef hormones case is a clear example of such a conflict. The EU's Scientific Committee on Veterinary Measures said that there was a "substantial body of recent scientific evidence that hormones exerted both tumour initiating and tumour producing effects." Although such risk was nonquantifiable, the fact that it existed should be enough to undertake trade-restrictive measures. The United States, on the other hand, quoted a joint panel of scientific experts from the World Health Organization and the Food and Agriculture Organization of the United Nations, which reconfirmed that residues of the hormones in question would not have a harmful effect if administered in accordance with good veterinary practices (ICTSD 1999a,b).

Mainstreaming Environment

Calls for mainstreaming environmental considerations in the WTO and the forthcoming negotiations seem to be inspired by two concerns. One is the perceived lack of progress achieved in the CTE. Proponents of mainstreaming argue that transferring specific issues to negotiating bodies may prompt quicker progress. They also argue that tradeoffs can be identified in a process of negotiations covering a wide range of issues. The other concern is ensuring that trade liberalization fully enhances its potential contribution to sustainable development.

With regard to the first concern, India has argued that the trade and environment agenda requires greater balance if progress is to be made. The country has strongly opposed transferring issues from the CTE to negotiating bodies, and has constantly reiterated that this goes beyond the Marrakesh mandate. India's concerns include the following:

- Certain mainstreaming proposals appear to focus on the accommodation of measures that tend to restrict trade on environmental grounds, rather than to promote trade.
- Mainstreaming may affect the balance of interests between industrial and developing countries that was established in the CTE work program.
- Certain proposals on mainstreaming may affect the consensus-based process.
- Mainstreaming would diffuse the WTO work on trade and environment and make it more difficult for developing country experts with environmental expertise to participate effectively (see Jha and Vossenaar 1999b).

With regard to the second concern, India attaches importance to promoting the integration of trade and environment in the pursuit of sustainable development, and reiterates the view that such integration should take place nationally rather than through the multilateral trading system.

In assessing the effects of changes in the terms under which trade is carried out, it is important to recognize that observed increased levels of pollution are not themselves evidence that the policy is undesirable. If the liberalization policy is successful, there will be an increase in economic activity, which may well result in some increase in environmental damage. The important policy point is to ensure that the cost of such damage is kept to a minimum for any given increase in economic activity.

Because of the inward-looking import substitution policies followed in the past, India's trade is currently a little less than 0.7 percent of the total world trade (Government of India 2002). In 1991, however, India embarked on a new strategy of economic growth through trade liberalization. Major exports are leather products, tea, dyestuffs, agriculture and marine products, and textiles. The volume of trade is too low to have an impact on the environment. Moreover, India has a comprehensive set of environmental policies that can mitigate any possible negative consequences of liberalized trade. Given that trade liberalization is not an important causative factor of environmental degradation in India and that other domestic factors are of paramount significance, it is not surprising that India has resisted any effort to mainstream environment into WTO agreements and sees little purpose in conducting environmental reviews of trade agreements.

The Doha Declaration according to the EU has mainstreamed environment by giving a special role to the WTO CTE—sustainable development and environmental concerns throughout the negotiations. This is reflected in paragraph 32 of the Ministerial Declaration (WTO 2001):

We instruct the Committee on Trade and Environment, in pursuing work on all items on its agenda within its current terms of reference, to give particular attention to:

(i) the effect of environmental measures on market access, especially in relation to developing countries, in particular the least-developed among them, and those situations in which the elimination or reduction of trade restrictions and distortions would benefit trade, the environment and development;

(ii) the relevant provisions of the Agreement on Trade-Related Aspects of Intellectual Property Rights; and

(iii) labeling requirements for environmental purposes.

Work on these issues should include the identification of any need to clarify relevant WTO rules. The Committee shall report to the Fifth Session of the Ministerial Conference, and make recommendations, where appropriate, with respect to future action, including the desirability of negotiations. The outcome of this work as well as the negotiations carried out under paragraph 31(i) and (ii) shall be compatible with the open and non-discriminatory nature of the multilateral trading system, shall not add to or diminish the rights and obligations of Members under existing WTO agreements, in particular the Agreement on the Application of Sanitary and Phytosanitary Measures, nor alter the balance of these rights and obligations, and will take into account the needs of developing and least-developed countries.

Environmental Reviews

So far environmental impact assessments (EIAs) have been used mainly in the evaluation of projects. There is little practical experience, particularly in India, with EIAs of trade policies. The challenges are to promote the integration of environment and economics and to anticipate potentially adverse scale effects of trade liberalization. However, there is a need to avoid undue pressures to carry out overly complicated EIAs that might further adversely affect trade liberalization and distract from emerging efforts in India to integrate environmental considerations into economic policymaking.

Some points need to be stressed. First, it is generally recognized that any assessment of environmental effects should be carried out under the responsibility of national governments. Second, EIAs are not only a tool for minimizing negative environmental effects; their principal objective is to focus on and to be used in promoting sustainable development. In a broad sense EIAs promote the integration of environment and economics. Third, EIAs should not narrowly focus on scale effects, but should also examine income and technology effects. It also may be necessary to examine "with" and "without" scenarios, that is, to examine the environmental effects of economic growth patterns that would evolve in the absence of the proposed trade agreement.

Given these considerations, India has generally opposed mandatory environmental review of trade agreements. The Doha Declaration has allowed for voluntary EIAs and for exchange of assessment information among members.

Proactive Agenda: Promote Changes in WTO Rules

The issues discussed in this section include the Agreement on Trade-Related Aspects of Intellectual Property Rights (TRIPS), market access, domestically prohibited goods, and the Doha Ministerial Meeting.

The Agreement on Trade-related Intellectual Property Rights

Developed countries have emphasized that TRIPS is meant to foster innovation. It has been noted, however, that in several cases there may be a tradeoff between the positive effects of intellectual property rights (IPRs) on the generation of environmentally sound technologies and the negative effects of IPRs on dissemination of technologies.[6] Through its review mechanisms the TRIPS agreement must find ways and means of balancing these two effects. It is important to bring to the discussion the empirical evidence gathered on the dissemination of ESTs in relation to the use of IPRs. Trademarks and trade secrets may also affect the dissemination of ESTs.

India is concerned that the agreement and more specifically its implementation do not necessarily promote the dissemination of ESTs or the protection of biodiversity. The system of IPRs should also find a way to recognize indigenous technologies, knowledge, and systems of species preservation because these may be of considerable value in protecting biodiversity.[7]

Ironically the system of IPRs may obstruct research and development. First, innovations in biotechnology for the agricultural sector have traditionally been dependent on land races.[8] Without granting adequate protection to land races, as Halle (1999) noted, TRIPS may erode the very germplasm that forms the basis of biotechnological innovations. Secondly, granting protection to plant varieties would imply that plant breeders and researchers would be forced to buy patented material at exorbitant prices if they are allowed access to it at all. This would discourage research, especially in a country like India where there is a cash constraint. It is also to be noted that most research on plant varieties in South Asian countries largely takes place in the public domain and is not subject to patents. This makes it widely accessible to a number of agriculturists, and changing this system may even endanger national objectives, such as food security. Third, granting broad-based protection to life forms instead of genes that produce those characteristics would block further research into effective ways of producing those characteristics. This may lead to a crisis in the patents system, elements of which can be seen already in countries such as the United States. It would have a particularly chilling effect on public research for which funding is in most cases difficult to obtain and to justify (for further discussion, see Runnalls and Cosbey [1996]). Similarly, in the manufacturing sector TRIPS may

- affect technology transfer by restricting the use of compulsory licensing mechanisms by the Indian government. The procedures at best are cumbersome.
- increase the price of goods and technologies as industries become increasingly concentrated.
- adversely affect innovation, especially in the area of ESTs.

In view of those considerations, the WTO may need to take account of the following factors in the review of TRIPS:

- Shorten the life term of some EST patents.
- Make the procedures for compulsory licensing of ESTs less cumbersome.
- Exclude life forms from patentability and ensure compatibility between the Bio-diversity Convention and TRIPS.
- Grant protection for traditional knowledge through systems other than patents.
- Extend protection under geographical indications to products other than wines and spirits.

Under the Montreal Protocol India's experience with the technological aspect of the transition away from ODS use and production demonstrates the case of an ODS-producing country where this industry is dominated by domestically owned firms that are emphatic about wishing to purchase the alternative technology without losing their majority equity holding to technology suppliers.[9]

Among the affected sectors, India's experience demonstrates two distinct trends:

1. A smooth transition in which the alternative technology exists and is easily accessible, commercially viable, and not covered by IPRs. For example, this applies to the foam sector where alternatives exist and to the insecticide spray–manufacturing subsector of the aerosol sector where alternatives are economically viable.
2. A negative experience and difficulties in effecting a phaseout in sectors where the technology or processes linked with it are under IPRs, with only a few technology owners, and in sectors where the alternative technology is not yet well

established or is disputed. In the metered-dose inhaler subsector of the aerosol sector and the fire protection systems sector, the transition process has been stymied because the technology is covered by IPRs. In the refrigeration and air-conditioning sectors, the technology options are not clear-cut.

Moreover, because the technology owners are a few multinationals, the bargaining power of Article 5 nations such as India has been limited in the process of purchasing the alternative technology.[10] Prices are exorbitant and negotiations with technology suppliers do not get very far because the only options offered to domestic producers are export curtailment of the alternative or the provision of majority equity to the technology supplier.

There is an additional problem associated with financial support in the context of technology switch: the domestic development of such technology is not funded unless the nation agrees not to demand finance for the transfer of technology in the pertinent sector at any stage. In the face of such a strong commitment, Indian firms have preferred to self-finance the development of the alternative technologies. This explains the strong position India has taken on TRIPS and on dissemination of ESTs (see Government of India 1996).

There has been some acceptance of this view in the Doha Declaration (WTO 2001). Paragraph 19 of the declaration states the following:

> We instruct the Council for TRIPS, in pursuing its work programme including under the review of Article 27.3(b), the review of the implementation of the TRIPS Agreement under Article 71.1 and the work foreseen pursuant to paragraph 12 of this Declaration, to examine, *inter alia*, the relationship between the TRIPS Agreement and the Convention on Biological Diversity, the protection of traditional knowledge and folklore, and other relevant new developments raised by Members pursuant to Article 71.1. In undertaking this work, the TRIPS Council shall be guided by the objectives and principles set out in Articles 7 and 8 of the TRIPS Agreement and shall take fully into account the development dimension.

Market Access

Safeguarding market access for products exported by developing countries has been discussed extensively at the WTO and remains an issue of key concern for India. India may be more vulnerable to environmental measures because of the composition of its exports and because small and medium enterprises, which account for a large share of exports, may find it difficult to meet environmental standards.

The erosion of preferential market access and other trade preferences that may be accentuated as the result of a new WTO round may have adverse effects on the exports of countries such as India and may reduce their ability to achieve sustainable development through trade. Much emphasis has been placed in this context on identifying "win-win" opportunities in trade and environment. "Win-win" situations arise when the removal or reduction of trade restrictions (e.g., high tariffs, tariff escalation, and remaining nonobstacles to trade) and distortions has the potential to yield both direct economic benefits for developing countries and positive environmental results (WTO Secretariat 1996). Much of the discussion so far has concentrated on removing trade distortions in such sectors as fisheries, agriculture, and energy. More research is needed to explore win-win scenarios, which would be of benefit to India in the area of textiles and similar goods, instead of restricting such discussions to agriculture and fisheries. _{Au: year?}

There have been instances of Indian exporters having to make changes in their production methods and in input uses to meet the environmental standards of OECD countries. Examples of this are the following (see Bharucha 1997):

- A ban on pentachlorophenol (PCP), a fungicide used by the leather industry, that was initiated by Germany, resulted in a short-term setback for the Indian leather industry's exports. The Indian leather industry had to go through dramatic alterations in its changeover to substitute chemicals, and these PCP substitutes are roughly 10 times costlier.
- India's export of tea has been affected by concerns from importing countries regarding the pesticide residue levels in Indian tea.
- In the early 1980s Indian shipments of marine products were detained on account of salmonella contamination. Production methods had to be changed quickly to meet importers' standards.

There have been obstacles in the packaging requirements of importing countries. For example, aluminum packages have been replaced by paper packages in the case of Indian tea. Although India generally has been able to adapt to the changing requirements of the importers, in most cases there have been cost increases on account of switching over to other inputs and delays in export orders. There may be a resulting loss of competitiveness and consequent reduction in market access.

A 1999 study conducted by the United Nations Conference on Trade and Development (UNCTAD) focused on process-based standards, such as hazard analysis at critical control points (HACCP).[11] It showed that several such standards may be totally inappropriate for India and may even have serious social consequences. Of the 400-odd shrimp firms in India, only 80 would be able to comply with the standards. Many of the others would simply become subcontractors to those firms that have been able to meet the standard. Moreover, in a country where potable drinking water is difficult to obtain, the requirement that floors and ceilings of facilities certified by HACCP be washed with potable water can be considered excessively wasteful (see Kaushik and Saqib 2000).

The increasing number and variety and the frequent changes in the regulations cause problems, especially for smaller producers trying to keep themselves informed. Also, producers find the regulations to be cumbersome and complex, and the costs of meeting them make their exports noncompetitive. They also sometimes have the effect of reducing the price of the products or reducing added value, and may either be unnecessary for meeting the environmental objective or inappropriate to the conditions of the exporting country.

The Doha Declaration has increased the cover provided to environmental measures as can be seen from paragraph 6 of the Declaration. Although the traditional safeguards have been inserted, they are unlikely to prove adequate should environment be used as a disguised form of protectionism.

Domestically Prohibited Goods

India is concerned about the health and environmental effects of imports in cases in which the domestic sale of such products has been prohibited or severely restricted in the exporting country. Indian importers need adequate information about the risk that such products could pose to public health and the environment. Apart from information problems, they may also lack the infrastructure (including testing facilities) and other capabilities to monitor and control imports of domestically prohibited goods. Industrial countries, on the other hand, argue that a number of multilateral agreements and instruments already address this issue. Although duplication is to be avoided, there is a need to examine whether existing instruments, such as the prior informed consent procedure, are sufficient from India's perspective to prevent environmental damage from such imports, particularly with regard to product coverage and procedures (WTO 1998).

Evidence collected by UNCTAD and other agencies appears to indicate that there is some empirical basis for the positions taken by India, and that they do not stem merely from political fears (see Jha and Hoffmann 2000). Moreover, as the next section will show, trade concerns have not led to a "regulatory chill" in the environment field. India continues to maintain a comprehensive body of environmental legislation.

Developments at the Doha Ministerial Meeting

At the November 2001 WTO Ministerial Meeting at Doha, there was a significant shift of attention to environment in the Ministerial Declaration. Looking at the fine print of the declaration, it appears that environment has been mainstreamed. Paragraph 6 of the Ministerial Declaration states that

> We recognize that under WTO rules no country should be prevented from taking measures for the protection of human, animal or plant life or health, or of the environment at the levels it considers appropriate, subject to the requirement that they are not applied in a manner which would constitute a means of arbitrary or unjustifiable discrimination between countries where the same conditions prevail, or a disguised restriction on international trade, and are otherwise in accordance with the provisions of the WTO Agreements.

According to the official briefing by the European Commission (WTO 2001), this language provides enough cover for formulating measures on the basis of the precautionary principle and for the labeling of environmentally friendly products. The United States views this as giving it enough cover for unilateral measures, whereas India views it as the tradeoff that they had to make for getting the EU to reduce their agricultural subsidies. It is also India's view that putting in WTO safeguards from the chapeau of Article XX gives them enough protection against measures that could be designed to protect trade.

Environmental Regulation in India

The overall framework of environmental legislation in India is set by the National Conservation Strategy and Policy Statement on Environment and Development issued by the Ministry of Environment and Forests (MOEF) in June 1992. The Indian constitution enjoins the "States to take measures to protect and improve the environment and to safeguard the forests and wildlife in the country." It also makes it a "fundamental duty of every citizen to protect and improve the natural environment including forests, lakes and rivers and wildlife, and to have ecological compassion for the living creatures."

Recognizing the severe problems related to the issue of air and water pollution, the Policy Statement for Abatement of Pollution, 1992, identifies the following steps to integrate environmental considerations into decisionmaking at all levels:

- prevent pollution at the source
- encourage, develop, and apply the best available and practicable technical solutions
- ensure that the polluter pays for the pollution and control arrangements
- focus on protection of heavily polluted areas and river stretches
- involve the public in decisionmaking.

To ensure that the projects are adequately monitored, the following requirements have been put in place:

- Investors are required to report every six months on the implementation of the environmental safeguards stipulated in the clearance by the MOEF.
- Field visits by the MOEF and its regional offices are required to collect samples and data on the environmental performance of the cleared projects.
- In cases of inadequate compliance, the issue is taken up with the concerned state governments and nodal ministries.

The division of powers between the central government and the state governments with respect to environmental legislation is not entirely clear. In general it appears that the central government is the legislating authority and the state governments are the implementing agencies. Specific differences are however discernible with respect to the different pollution control acts outlined below. And, in step with their political mandates, governments may provide more or less power to the state governments.

India's Environmental Legislation

Different forms of environmental legislation have existed for more than years and are listed in table 12.1. The first such law to be enacted was the Water (Prevention and Control of Pollution) Act of 1974, amended in 1988. This was followed by the Forest Conservation Act of 1980 and the Air (Prevention and Control of Pollution) Act of 1981, both amended in 1988; and the Environment (Protection) Act of 1986. These form the main body of environmental legislation in India.

The Environment (Protection) Act, 1986, is an umbrella law that seeks to close the loopholes in earlier legislation relating to the environment. Several sets of

TABLE 12.1   India's Environmental Legislation

Legislation	Year
Wildlife Protection Act	1972
Water (Prevention and Control of Pollution) Act	1974
Water (Prevention and Control of Pollution) Cess Act	1977
Forest Conservation Act	1980
Air (Prevention and Control of Pollution) Act	1981
The Environment (Protection) Act	1986
Hazardous Waste (Management and Handling) Rules	1989
The Public Liability Insurance Act	1991

rules relating to various aspects of the management of hazardous chemicals, wastes, microorganisms, and so forth have been notified under this act. The law gives the central government the power to set quality standards for air, water, and soil in specified areas and for specified purposes. The act covers the maximum allowable concentrations of various environmental pollutants as well as the procedures and safeguards for handling hazardous substances and related restrictions, the restrictions regarding the location of industry, and the procedures and safeguards for preventing industrial accidents that may cause environmental pollution. If a particular state so desires, however, it may set *more but not less stringent standards* with respect to a specified category of industries within its jurisdiction. Those industries that must obtain consent under the Water Act, the Air Act, or both, or that need authorization under the Hazardous Waste (Management and Handling) Rules of 1989 must submit an environmental audit report to the concerned state authority by September 30th of each year, according to the Environment Protection Act (see also Jha 1998).

In addition to legislation covering water, air, and the environment, the nonenvironmental Factories Act, amended in 1987, made it mandatory for hazardous manufacturing units to submit to the government a detailed disaster management plan and an assessment of the unit's possible environmental impact. The amendments to this act also made the top nonexecutive officers—such as the chairpersons of these companies—liable for prosecution in case of an accident. These amendments followed the Bhopal gas disaster, when the Indian Government was unable to sue the top executive of Union Carbide posted in India at the time.

Other relevant legislation includes the Public Liability Insurance Act of 1991, which is a further strengthening of the government's powers to legislate. This act imposes on the owner of a company that handles hazardous chemicals the liability to provide immediate relief in case of death or injury to any person or of damage to property resulting from an accident that occurs while handling any of the specified hazardous chemicals. To meet this liability, the owner has to take out an insurance policy of an amount equal to its "paid-up capital" or up to Rs. 500 million, whichever is less. The policy must be renewed every year. The owner also has to pay to the central government's environment relief fund (ERF) an amount equal to its annual premium. The liability of the insurer is limited to US$10 million to $15 million per accident, up to a maximum of $30 million a year or up to the tenure of the policy. Any claims in excess of this liability will be paid from the ERF. Payment under this act is only for immediate relief; owners must provide the final compensation, if any, arising from legal proceedings. This law also was passed following the Bhopal disaster and was meant to ensure that the suffering undergone by the victims would never be repeated.

Fiscal Incentives to Encourage Control and Prevention of Pollution

To encourage conservation, donations given by the corporate sector for conservation of nature and natural resources are exempt from income tax. A depreciation allowance of 30 percent is also permitted on devices and systems installed in industrial units to minimize pollution or conserve natural resources. To encourage plants to shift from congested urban areas, capital gains made in moving from urban to other areas are exempt from taxes if they are used for acquiring land and building production facilities in nonurban areas. Excise and custom-duty exemptions or reductions are given for the use of environmentally friendly raw materials.

This formidable body of law is also meant to ensure that industrial development, including export industries, does not sacrifice environmental interests; that industries are accountable to citizens; and that polluting industries are made to pay in accordance with the polluter-pays principle. Therefore, linking trade with the environment would not serve India's environmental interests as much as increasing the capacity to implement its formidable body of environmental legislation. The country's existing laws and its interest in protection of the citizenry and the environment explain India's reluctance to engage in discussions on changes in trade rules for environmental purposes. India, however, may be forced to rethink this linkage because trade and environment disputes may change the balance of rights and obligations at the WTO.

Evolutionary Developments in Trade and Environment Outside the CTE

Dispute settlement is a mechanism through which the carefully created balance of the CTE may be disturbed. Successive interpretations by panels and appellate bodies have expanded the scope of subparagraphs (b) and (g) in Article XX, where there is no consensus to do so through the CTE. It is important to examine the impact of this evolutionary interpretation of Article XX, subparagraphs (b) and (g), on the trade and environment debate. The precedent-setting value is immense. Other panels and appellate bodies may find it difficult to ignore these interpretations especially because of pressure groups that have developed around trade and environment. This section of the chapter investigates the evolutionary aspects of the *Shrimp–Turtle* panel and how proposals in the WTO Dispute Settlement Understanding (DSU) seek to rectify some of the imbalances created by the *Shrimp–Turtle* and *Asbestos* panels (WTO Appellate Body Report 1998).

In 1997 India, Malaysia, Pakistan, and Thailand requested the establishment of a WTO panel to consider U.S. trade restrictions on shrimp imports. Under the authority of the U.S. Endangered Species Act (ESA), the United States imposed embargoes on the import of shrimp from a number of its trading partners in order to protect the sea-turtle population. Under the ESA, access to U.S. shrimp markets is conditional on a certification that a country has adopted conservation policies that the United States considers to be comparable to its own in terms of regulatory programs and incidental taking. The United States unsuccessfully argued that this trade measure satisfied GATT Article XX(g).

The panel issued its final report to the parties on April 6, 1998. It rejected the U.S. argument on the basis of its interpretation of the chapeau to Article XX, and Article XX(g) was not considered in particular. The panel found that the U.S. measure constituted unjustifiable discrimination between countries where the same conditions prevail. The United States appealed the panel's interpretation of Article XX(g).

The appellate body delivered its report on October 12, 1998. It found fault with the panel's interpretation; considered Article XX(g); and decided that although the embargo served an environmental objective that is recognized as legitimate under the Article, the measure was applied in a manner that constituted arbitrary and unjustifiable discrimination between members of the WTO, contrary to the requirements of the chapeau of Article XX.

In the *Asbestos* case the appellate body stated, "In justifying a measure under Article XX(b) of the GATT 1994, a Member may also rely, in good faith, on scientific sources which, at that time, may represent a divergent, but qualified and respected, opinion. A Member is not obliged, in setting health policy, automatically to follow what, at a given time, may constitute a majority scientific opinion." Thus while allowing members freedom, this freedom is qualified. In the amicus brief submitted to the appellate body, the Foundation for International Law and Development and others have stated, "Science is not the sole arbiter of objective, non-discriminatory policymaking. The precautionary principle, which informs the interpretation of this and other aspects of the WTO Agreements, entitles regulators to act with precaution without having to meet a set threshold of scientific certainty" (see Foundation for International Law and Development 2001).

But the appellate body does not seem to have given explicit permission for applying the precautionary principle beyond the provisions of the Technical Barriers to Trade Agreement. It still places emphasis on science although the countries are not bound by majority opinion. On the other hand, however, applying the precautionary principle is not a matter of scientific evidence, majority or minority opinion, so it is difficult to come to definite conclusions about the application of the precautionary principle from this appellate decision. In this case the scientific evidence was against asbestos and asbestos-based products, and it was relatively easy to substantiate the claim with scientific evidence. But in other cases it may not be so easy (WTO Appellate Body Report 2001).

An interesting dilemma emerges with the appellate body decision. Although its decision appears to have broadened the scope of measures that clearly would be considered acceptable under GATT Article XX and it has opened the way for seeking inputs from NGOs and perhaps other lobbyists, the decision also has brought to the fore the numerous grounds under which such measures would be considered discriminatory. In fact, there may be a plethora of reasons by which trade measures for meeting nontrade objectives may be de facto "arbitrary and unjustifiably discriminatory." It is not the panel or appellate body decision that is of great concern, but rather the trend toward judicial activism that panels may inadvertently encourage. Whereas committees of the WTO may fail to achieve something for lack of consensus, panels and appellate bodies set aside the need for consensus.[12]

And, although the DSU makes clear that the dispute-settlement process cannot add to or subtract from the rights and obligations of the members under the WTO and its annexed agreements, by a gradual process of citing earlier rulings and adopting them as their own, panels and the appellate body may be spearheading a process of judicial activism that eventually will change the balance of rights and obligations. The solution lies in a review of the DSU process that may also consider giving guidelines on such issues to the Dispute Settlement Body.

Conclusions and Recommendations

Whereas trade and environment issues were confined to a well-defined and balanced agenda by the 1994 Marrakesh Agreement in the Uruguay Round, the 2001 WTO Doha Ministerial Declaration appears to have mainstreamed environment in the WTO agenda. Mainstreaming may require very different skills and capacities in India. To date, India has adequately addressed its interests by focusing specifically on a few issues, but the evolving nature of discussions would entail the development of special capacities, including research into the environmental aspects of practically all negotiations. Although the research initially might focus on such areas as agriculture, TRIPS, the Technical Barriers to Trade Agreement, subsidies, investment, and other issues that are likely to be negotiated in the new round.

What follows are eight recommendations for a capacity-building agenda in India.

1. There is a need to improve implementation of supportive measures under multilateral environmental agreements and to examine to what extent the multilateral trading system can help remove possible obstacles to better implementation. Such improvement would be particularly relevant for the transfer-of-technology provisions in the MEAs. Sharing experiences with countries at

similar stages of development may help in better implementing supportive measures. This could be done both at the CTE and in the working group on technology transfer created by the Doha Ministerial Declaration. Submissions by India in both the CTE and the working group have highlighted this need. Work carried out by UNCTAD has indicated a key need to share research results between developing countries at the stage of developing technologies. The India's Department of Science and Technology could provide vital input to this process.

2. There is a need to examine the consistency of TRIPS provisions and the Biodiversity Convention, especially in the areas of biological resources and traditional knowledge systems.[13] The Government of India has proposed that the country of germplasm origin be indicated in all patent applications for biotechnological innovations. It should also be indicated whether prior informed consent was obtained for the biological genetic resource or traditional knowledge so that mutual benefit-sharing arrangements can be made. Such documentation should be attached to the patent application. To this end the government has registered a database on traditional knowledge with the World Intellectual Property Organisation. But because such databases cannot be comprehensive, it is important to devise systems that could prevent misappropriation and generate benefits. The national Biodiversity Action Plan has begun the task of collecting and recording information and the biodiversity law provides for prior-informed-consent mechanisms. India will need to work with other like-minded countries to generate a framework for unique mechanisms for protecting traditional knowledge.

3. There is a need to strongly resist unilateral measures on the grounds that all unilateral measures that are extrajurisdictional and based on nonproduct-related process and production methods would fail the chapeau test of GATT Article XX. A comparative evaluation of WTO jurisprudence in this context would be useful. India's Ministry of Commerce has begun discussion groups on the evolution of WTO law in this field, but India needs to generate public awareness of these issues and to develop a media strategy.

4. Implementation of TRIPS Articles 67 and 66.2 on transfer of technologies to developing countries and to the least-developed countries is needed. Article 67 obliges industrial country members to provide, on request and on mutually agreed terms and conditions, technical and financial cooperation to developing countries. Article 66.2 obliges industrial country members to provide incentives to enterprises and institutions in their territories for the purpose of promoting and encouraging technology transfer to least-developed countries. As these are binding obligations and not best-endeavor clauses, developing countries should call for a review of the policies that industrial

countries have formulated to implement the two articles. It is also necessary to examine how the DSU would regard nonimplementation of these articles. The role of the working group on technology transfer in the WTO will be vital in this context.

5. A mechanism should be devised under the existing code of good practices for voluntary measures to avoid the use of trade-discriminatory measures based on PPM-related requirements. UNCTAD has proposed to set up a consultative mechanism between developing and industrial countries to promote analysis, debate, and consultations to address the following issues:

   • The key trends in environmental policies (sectors, measures).
   • The most important ongoing and planned general initiatives concerning environmental and health protection that may result in new standards and regulations with potential significant implications for developing countries. Which sectors and products may be affected? What response measures are available? What are the conditions and needs of developing countries? How could relevant information on certification, private sector standards and codes, buyers' requirements, and supply-chain management be collected and disseminated?

6. There is a need to build consensus on certain concepts to be considered in developing and implementing newly emerging environmental measures with trade effects, particularly for India. The role of sound science and the concept of risks that nonfulfillment may create also need to be examined in greater detail, particularly with a view to understanding the appropriate balance between trade distortions and environmental and health risks.

7. It may be necessary to examine whether differential treatment for small and medium-size enterprises (SMEs) is available within the existing framework of WTO rules, because a large proportion of India's exports comes from SMEs. Several organizations that provide support services to SMEs could be involved in this process. Industrial clusters that support SMEs need to improve awareness on these emerging standards.

8. A lesson drawn from the ecolabeling discussions is that that there may be a need to define "an international standard," and that a true international standard requires effective and representative participation of WTO member states at all levels of development. Similarly, there is a need to support the effective participation of India in international standard setting.[14] In this context, discussions in the Bureau of Indian Standards and the Ministry of Health have highlighted the need for changing India's role from a "standard taker to a standard setter." This would require investing in technologies, entering into mutual recognition agreements and, above all, creating a substantial research fund.

There are encouraging indications in two sectors—leather and tea—that India is emerging as a standard setter there.

Endnotes

1. This draws on Eglin (1995). Eglin is a former director, Trade and Environment Division, WTO Secretariat.

2. The discussion on issues in this section draws heavily on Jha and Vossenaar (1999a).

3. "Obviously this would be a recipe for protectionism and restriction of market access for developing countries' exports—with inevitable negative consequences for sustainable development." See Governments of the Dominican Republic, Egypt, Honduras, and Pakistan (1999). This statement was supported by India.

4. Type 1 ecolabeling refers to ecolabels awarded by a third party for products that meet preset environmental criteria, according to the terminology used by the ISO. See Zarrilli, Jha, and Vossenaar (1997).

5. In the ISO, progress has been made in developing guidelines on transparency, conformity assessment, and mutual recognition.

6. See the findings of the IPR commission established by the Department for International Development, Government of the United Kingdom, which furnished its report in 2002. Its Web site address is iprcommission@dfid.gov.uk.

7. In accordance with the TRIPS Agreement, to be patentable an invention must be new, must involve an inventive step, and must be capable of industrial application. TRIPS seems to contemplate only the Northern industrialization model of innovation. It fails to address the more informal, communal system of innovation through which farmers in the South produce, select, improve, and breed crop and livestock varieties. Thus, Southern germplasm achieves an inferior status to that of contemporary biotechnologists' varieties. The intellectual property of Southern farmers is apparently denied recognition and hence protection. See WWF (1999).

8. Land races refer to the genetic diversity of species that farmers rely on for improving the genetic stock of seeds.

9. For comprehensive coverage of India's experience in accessing ESTs under the Montreal Protocol, see Watal (2000).

10. Article 5 of the Montreal Protocol includes a list of countries that are eligible for receiving assistance from the Multilateral Fund.

11. Hazard Analysis at Critical Control Points (HACCP) with Respect to the Shrimp Sector under a 1999 project for strengthening capacities to promote trade and environment policy coordination, jointly pursued by the Government of India, UNCTAD, and the United Nations Development Programme, under project IND/97/955.

12. See Pakistan's proposal on the review of the DSU submitted to the General Council (WT/GC/W/62).

13. The international law of treaties uses various criteria to determine which treaty takes priority. Under the rule that *later treaties take priority over earlier treaties*, the TRIPS Agreement (which was agreed to at the end of the Uruguay Round in December 1993 and signed in April 1994) would take priority over the Convention on Biological Diversity (CBD) (which was agreed to in May 1992). However, under the rule that *more specific treaties take priority over general treaties*, because the CBD's language on IPRs in the context of transfer of technology for biodiversity objectives is more specific than that of the TRIPS Agreement, the CBD would take priority. It is also to be noted that Article 16.5 of the CBD states: "The contracting parties, recognizing that patents and other intellectual property rights may have an influence on the implementation of the convention, shall cooperate in this regard subject to national legislation and international law *in order to ensure that such rights are supportive of, and do not run counter to, its objectives*" [emphasis added].

14. For example, if reducing the standard of aflatoxins from 5 to 2 parts per billion increases the risk of cancer by 2 per billion people, such a standard is appropriate.

Bibliography and References

Bharucha, Vasantha. 1999. "The Impact of Environmental Standards and Regulations Set in Foreign Markets on India's Exports." In Veena Jha, Grant Hewison, and Maree Underhill, eds., *Trade Environment and Sustainable Development: A South Asian Perspective*. London: Macmillan.

Das, Shipra. 2000. "India: Effects of Trade and Positive Measures in the Montreal Protocol on Selected Indian Industries." In Veena Jha and Ulrich Hoffmann, eds., *Achieving Objectives of Multilateral Environmental Agreements: Lessons from Empirical Studies*. Geneva: UNCTAD.

Eglin, Richard. 1995. "World Trade and the Environment Volume II, House of Commons, Session 1995-96, Environment Committee." Fourth Report: Memorandum by the WTO (WTE 14) Trade and Environment Division. London.

Focus on the Global South. 2000. "Why Reform of the WTO Is the Wrong Agenda." Bangkok: University of Bangkok.

Foundation for International Law and Development. 2001. Amicus Brief Submitted to Appellate Body. London.

Government of India. 1996. "The Relationship of the TRIPS Agreement to the Development and Transfer of Environmentally-Sound Technologies and Products." Non-paper for the WTO Committee on Trade and Environment. June. Geneva.

———. 2002. *Economic Survey of India 2002*. Delhi.

Governments of Cameroon, Côte d'Ivoire, Nigeria, Sri Lanka, and Zaire. 1998. Technical Note on Domestically Prohibited Goods. MTN.GNG/W/18, November 17.

Governments of the Dominican Republic, Egypt, Honduras, and Pakistan. 1999. "Trade and Environment: A Developing Countries' Perspective." Statement presented at the High-Level Symposium on Trade and Environment, March 15–16, Geneva.

Halle, Mark. 1999. "IPRs and CBD." Paper presented at the Conference on International Trade and Environment. Supported by the SEMA Project, April 9–10, Hanoi.

"Hazard Analysis at Critical Control Points (HACCP) with Respect to the Shrimp Sector," under a Joint Government of India/UNCTAD/UNDP Project on "Strengthening Capacities to Promote Trade and Environment Policy Co-ordination." 1999. Export of fresh, frozen, and processed fish and fishery products (Quality Control, Inspection Council of India, New Delhi).

ICTSD (International Centre for Trade and Sustainable Development). 1998. *Bridges between Trade and Sustainable Development*, Vol. 2, September, Geneva, Switzerland.

———. 1999a. *Bridges between Trade and Sustainable Development*, Vol. 3, January-February.

———. 1999b. *Bridges between Trade and Sustainable Development*, Vol. 3, March.

Jha, Veena. 1998. "Investment: Liberalization and Environment—Conflicts and Compatibilities in the Case of India." Copenhagen: UNCTAD and Copenhagen Business School.

Jha, Veena, and Ulrich Hoffman, eds. 2000. *Achieving Objectives of Multilateral Environmental Agreements: Lessons from Empirical Studies*. Geneva: UNCTAD.

Jha, Veena, and Rene Vossenaar. 1999a. "Breaking the Deadlock: A Positive Agenda on Trade, Environment and Development" In Gary P. Sampson and W. Bradnee Chambers, eds., *Trade, Environment and the Millennium*. Tokyo: United Nations University.

———. 1999b. "Mainstreaming Environment in the WTO Agreement." Paper presented at an UNCTAD Seminar on Trade and Environment in the Philippines, November 8–11, Los Banos, Philippines.

Kaushik, Atul, and Mohammed Saqib. 2000. "Market Access Effects of Environmental Standards." Paper prepared for a joint Government of India/UNCTAD/UNDP Project on "Strengthening Capacities to Promote Trade and Environment Policy Co-ordination, under Project Number IND/97/955.

Khor, Martin. 1999. "Trade, Environment and Sustainable Development: A Developing Country View of the Issues Including in the WTO." Context paper presented to the WTO High-Level Symposium on Trade and Environment, March 15–16, Geneva.

Runnalls, David, and Aaron Cosbey. 1996. "The Sustainable Development Effects of WTO TRIPS Agreement: A Focus on Developing Countries." Paper presented at the Second Annual Sustainable

Development Conference, sponsored by the International Institute on Sustainable Development, August 4–10, Islamabad.

Shaheen, Magda. 1999. "Trade and Environment: How Real Is the Debate?" In Gary P. Sampson and W. Bradnee Chambers, eds., *Trade, Environment and the Millennium.* Tokyo: United Nations University.

UNCTAD (United Nations Conference on Trade and Development). 1999. "Seattle Ministerial Conference—Trade and Environment: Current Proposals and Their Possible Implications for Developing Countries." Geneva.

Watal, Jayshree. 2000. "Transfer of Technology Issues under the Montreal Protocol." In Veena Jha and Ulrich Hoffmann, eds., *Achieving Objectives of Multilateral Environmental Agreements.* Geneva: UNCTAD.

WTO (World Trade Organization). 1994. Communication from the Chairman, Decision on Trade and Environment. Special Distribution (UR-94-0085). MTN.TNC/W/141, March 29.

————. 1997. Note by Secretariat on Environmental Benefits of Removing Trade Restrictions and Distortions on Committee on Trade and Environment. WTO/CTE/W/67, November 7.

————. 1999. Submission by the United States to the High-Level Symposium on Trade and Environment, March 15–16, Geneva.

————. 2001. WTO Ministerial Doha: Assessment of Results for EU. Memo, WT/MIN(01)/DEC/W/1 November 14. < http://trade-info.cec.eu.int/europa/2001newround/p14.php>.

————. 2002a. Note by the Secretariat on the Environmental Effects of Services Trade Liberalization on Committee on Trade and Environment. WT/CTE/W/218, October 3.

————. 2002b. Synthesis Report Contributed by UNEP on Committee on Trade and Environment, Enhancing Synergies and Mutual Supportiveness of MEAs and the WTO. WT/CTE/W/213, June 12.

————. 2003. Submission by India under Paragraph 31(i) of the Doha Work Programme. TN/TE/W/23, February 20.

WTO Appellate Body Report. 1998. *United States—Import Prohibition of Certain Shrimp and Shrimp Products.* WT/DS58/AB/R. U.S.C.A. 1531-44, October 12.

————. 2001. *European Communities—Measures Affecting Asbestos and Asbestos-Containing Products.* WT/DS135/AB/R, April 5.

WTO Committee on Trade and Environment. 2003a. Report to the Fifth Session of the WTO Ministerial Conference, First Draft. JOB(03)/73, April 10.

————. 2003b. Special Session. TN/TE/S/3/REV.1, April 24.

WTO Secretariat. 1996. Singapore Ministerial Declaration. WT/CTE/1, November 12.

WWF (World Wildlife Fund). 1999. "The UN Biodiversity Convention and the WTO TRIPS Agreement." Discussion Paper. Gland, Switzerland.

Zarrilli, Simonetta, Veena Jha, and Rene Vossenaar, eds. 1997. *Ecolabeling and International Trade.* London: Macmillan.

13

INDIA AND THE MULTILATERAL TRADING SYSTEM POST-DOHA: DEFENSIVE OR PROACTIVE?

Aaditya Mattoo and Arvind Subramanian

One of the more commented upon facts about the Indian economy is its small and dwindling importance in world trade. At the time of independence, India accounted for more than 2 percent of world exports and imports, but by the early 1990s this share had declined to about half a percent (figure 13.1). A plausible case can be made that India's economic fortunes have been related to this de facto international disengagement that is attributable, at least in part, to India's inward-looking economic and trade policies. Protectionist polices, in turn, have shaped India's attitude to participation in the multilateral trading system, in both the old General Agreement on Tariffs and Trade (GATT) and its successor, the World Trade Organization (WTO). India's stance in the GATT/WTO has always tended to be defensive, seeking freedom to use restrictive policies—two prongs of the so-called special and differential treatment embraced by developing countries as a whole.[1] Since the early 1990s India has embarked on serious trade and economic reform, without, however, a corresponding change in the nature of its multilateral engagement. This chapter examines whether India should adopt a proactive role in the multilateral arena founded on its recent adoption of more open policies.

The authors would like to thank Carsten Fink, Francis Ng, Marcelo Olarreaga, Natalia Tamirisa, and especially Garry Pursell and Randeep Rathindran for their valuable input. Thanks are also due to Malina Savova for providing excellent research assistance. The views expressed in this chapter do not necessarily reflect those of the institutions with which the authors are associated. Errors and excesses remain our own.

FIGURE 13.1   India's Share in World Imports and Exports (Percentage)

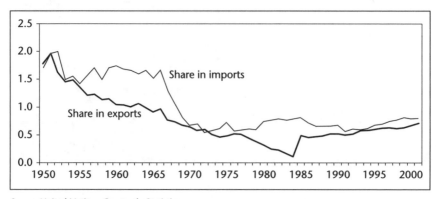

Source: United Nations Comtrade Statistics.

The launch of a new round of comprehensive multilateral trade negotiations in November 2001, two years after the debacle at Seattle, provides an opportunity for India to reassess its traditional strategy. India's position in the run-up to the launch was characteristically but perhaps not unjustifiably defensive. Among other things India sought to (a) keep out the new issues (competition, investment, and government procurement) altogether from the scope of future negotiations; (b) encourage progress in the implementation of Uruguay Round agreements, particularly accelerated liberalization of access in textiles and clothing; and (c) increase the flexibility afforded by the Trade-Related Aspects of Intellectual Property Rights (TRIPS) agreement in the use of compulsory licensing. India was not clearly associated with those voices pushing for greater and faster liberalization of global markets in goods and services. This chapter presents the case for a changed strategy.

In the following section we spell out the advantages to India of actively pursuing greater market openness in the current round of negotiations, while acknowledging the limits of such a strategy. The next section analyzes the issues that have emerged in some of the negotiating areas in the WTO. The third section offers concrete proposals that Indian negotiators might adopt in future discussions in the WTO.

Multilateral Engagement: Whether and How

A major challenge facing India is how to institute and sustain good economic policies. This challenge is a primarily domestic one. Good policy should be geared, first of all, to injecting competition in the domestic economy. In the area of goods, this will involve reducing trade barriers; in services, competition also requires eliminating barriers to entry. But good policy for both goods and services also includes judicious regulation, both to remedy market failures and to achieve social objectives efficiently.

It is clear that multilateral engagement cannot be an end in itself. Domestic policy priorities cannot be subordinated to the needs of such engagement nor must domestic reform be held entirely hostage to external bargaining imperatives. The important question is whether multilateral engagement can be harnessed to serve the ends of good domestic policies. Can it contribute meaningfully to overall policy reform, and if so how?

Multilateral engagement and the consequent international commitments undertaken by countries necessarily entail a loss in sovereignty—the freedom that countries possess to make unconstrained choices. Globalization is ultimately a process of erosion of sovereignty induced by conscious policy actions or forced by market and technological developments. But sovereignty is not an absolute, overwhelming consideration that should trump all others. It can be partially and strategically ceded to further domestic policy reform and to secure an open trading system, which India, as a large and growing trader, has some ability to shape. A number of factors argue in favor of a reassessment of India's approach to sovereignty and to the terms of its multilateral engagement.

Engagement as Facilitating Domestic Reform and Enhancing Access through Credible Bargaining

The GATT/WTO is a quintessentially mercantilist bargaining framework in which concessions to open each other's markets are exchanged between economies. These concessions are legally binding commitments not to make policies affecting market access more restrictive than a certain stated level. Thus a country may commit not to raise its tariffs on bananas above 20 percent or commit to allow at least five foreign banks to enter its market. It is important to recognize that actual conditions of access may be, and often are, more liberal than those that are legally bound—actual tariffs on bananas may be only 10 percent and more than five foreign banks may be allowed to enter. Traders and investors value both the actual liberalization of markets and the legal guarantee of access.

To see when multilateral engagement can both facilitate domestic reforms and make it possible to extract concessions from trading partners, it is useful to examine three situations.

If a country is wedded to self-sufficiency, as India and other developing countries were until recently, it cannot be a bargainer. If a country is not willing to open its markets, it does not have the most obvious means of inducing its trading partners to do so. Under so-called special and differential treatment, developing

countries sought—indeed, could only seek—limited preferential access as suppli-
cants because of their own unwillingness to liberalize, rather than genuine nonpreferential access as equal partners.[2]

Paradoxically a country credibly committed to reform and able to implement it
successfully cannot be a credible bargainer either. Partner countries can basically
free-ride on the internal commitment knowing that a refusal to engage in bargaining will not alter their market-access interests. The situation does not change
much if a reformer proceeds with liberalization unilaterally but refuses to bind the
openness under the WTO in the hope of extracting concessions because the value
to partner countries of a binding by a credible reformer such as Singapore or
Chile is small, given the low probability of policy reversal.

A third situation, and one that applies to India in the current context, arises in
relation to a willing reformer whose ability to implement reform is constrained by
domestic opposition. In this case, domestic reform could be facilitated if a government could demonstrate that domestic opening brought payoffs in terms of
increased access abroad. Those who gain from the increased access—whether
exporters of textiles, software, professional services, or other products—could
represent a countervailing voice to groups (import-competing industries) that are
resistant to reform. How effective such a strategy could be for Indian policymakers is unclear, but selling reform domestically should be that much easier if some
external payoffs can be demonstrated.

China's agreement with the United States on its accession to the WTO illustrates this political economy at work. In fact, in China's case the external payoff, at
least in the U.S. market, is really not in getting *increased* access but in securing
existing access because it already receives most-favored-nation (MFN) status in
the United States.[3] China considers that its task of domestic reform is easier to sell
and implement merely by pointing to the increased security of existing access.

Crucially, the need for improved foreign access to facilitate domestic reform
(by easing the domestic political constraints) makes a country a more credible
bargainer and enables it to extract more meaningful concessions from trading
partners.[4] Such a country can credibly say, "if I get less, I can deliver less domestic
liberalization" in a manner that neither an unwilling reformer nor a wholly credible reformer can say.

We would underscore here that the possibility of bargaining does not imply
that unilateral reform should be delayed or held back to secure market access benefits. Indeed, much of the reform is likely to be implemented unilaterally. However, this process can be facilitated by multilateral engagement, and, to that extent,
the latter becomes important to address.

The distinction made above between alternative situations is important
because there are some people who argue that India should focus on pushing

domestic reform without necessarily deepening its multilateral engagement. "Liberalize tariffs and investment unilaterally but don't necessarily bind them" is a typical line taken by such observers. To us, such a view is founded on a simplistic or overly sanguine view about the prerequisites for successful reform. It renounces the use of forces that could be harnessed to secure domestic reform. And it forsakes the possibility of credibly extracting concessions from trading partners.

Engagement as Commitment to Good Policies

Of course there is some value to multilateral engagement and ceding sovereignty even if concessions cannot be extracted from partners. Sovereignty or the freedom to choose could be the freedom to choose badly. Indian trade policymaking has been a sad testament to poor, unconstrained choices that might have benefited from being constrained. Such constraints foster good policies in two respects: by providing guarantees against reversal of current policies and by facilitating future reform.

Even if we ignore the dirigiste days of the 1960s and 1970s, there have been instances of policy reversal that might have benefited from some loss of sovereignty via a previous commitment to good policy. Despite undertaking commitments to bind tariffs in the Uruguay Round in 1994, India availed itself of large amounts of flexibility in the form of the wedge between the bound tariff and the actual tariff, particularly in agriculture. In 1996 and 1997, in the face of fiscal pressures, the government decided to raise tariffs and use up some of the water in the tariff. From the government's perspective, the decision to provide for a cushion or a maneuvering margin was vindicated by its subsequent actions. But from a welfare perspective, this freedom that the government had was counterproductive. Had the Uruguay Round bindings been really binding, they would have forced the government to choose a superior instrument—one that was neutral between imports and domestically produced goods—to meet its fiscal needs.[5]

One reason for the reluctance of the government to liberalize immediately is the perceived need to protect the incumbent domestic suppliers from immediate competition—either because of the infant-industry type of argument or to facilitate "orderly exit." And one reason for the failure of infant-industry policies in the past, and the innumerable examples of perpetual infancy, was the inability of the government to commit itself credibly to liberalize at some future date—either because it has a stake in the national firm's continued operation or because it is vulnerable to pressure from interest groups that benefit from protection. The WTO offers a valuable mechanism to overcome this difficulty. In the services negotiations, for instance, many governments precommitted to future liberalization, thus striking a balance between the reluctance to unleash competition immediately and the desire not to be held hostage in perpetuity to the weakness of domestic industry or to vested interests. But India failed to take advantage of this mechanism and committed only to review its policies in basic telecommunications at specified future dates.

Engagement as Enforcement of Rights

It is true that a rules-based system protects, albeit imperfectly, the weaker party in a situation of asymmetry. This is especially true when it comes to enforcement of rules that already have been established. Warts and all, the WTO dispute-settlement system has lived up to this requirement in offering recourse to developing countries to enforce their rights. Table 13.1 tabulates the complaints that have been publicized in the WTO. Developing countries account for about one-third of all the complaints and have been defendants in 40 percent of the complaints. Developing countries have won all the cases that they have brought against the industrial countries. India has successfully prosecuted each of three cases against industrial country partners. The fact that developing countries have been defendants in a lot of cases—even unsuccessful defendants—actually reaffirms the usefulness of the system as a safeguard, at least insofar as it reflects reduced extrasystemic pressure. Settling disputes within the system affords greater protection to the weaker party than does settling outside it.

TABLE 13.1   Summary Indicators of WTO Disputes, 1995–2001

	Defendant		
	Industrial Country	Developing Country	Total
All complaints			
Complainant:			
Industrial country	104	62	166
Developing country	37	39	76
Total	141	101	242
Completed panels			
Complainant:			
Industrial country	104	62	166
Developing country	37	39	76
Total	141	101	242

Note: Figures in parentheses indicate the number of cases in which complainants were successful.

Source: WTO (www.wto.org).

Although the experience of dispute settlement affords some comfort, it could be argued that, on the really big issues where real interests are at stake, there is still the possibility that developing countries will be ineffective at enforcing their rights. The banana and hormones disputes where compliance by larger trading partners has been delayed or absent warrant caution. More generally there is the perception that developing countries' ability to secure compliance by the larger traders is ultimately limited by the small size of developing country markets and by the consequential limited impact of any retaliatory actions.

This problem acquires fresh urgency in the current international trading context because of increasing fears that the quantitative restrictions imposed on textile products by industrial countries will not be eliminated by 2005, as required by the Uruguay Round textiles agreement. The stakes are high for India, which, given the right domestic policy environment, should stand to gain from the elimination of the quotas or to lose if there is backtracking by trading partners. Do developing countries such as India have the clout to ensure compliance with commitments or must they resign themselves to ineffectiveness, believing that outcomes are beyond their ability to influence? We argue below that India can wield an effective retaliatory weapon in the form of its TRIPS obligations and should seriously consider changing its intellectual property legislation to allow for this possibility.

Multilateral Engagement as a Bulwark against Regionalism

There are very few multilateral traders left in this world, and India has for the most part been one of those lone battlers.[6] Championing multilateralism is no longer a slogan because its erosion through regional agreements is having a serious if unrecognized effect on India's trade and could have similar consequences in the future. Over the last few years the trend toward regional integration has intensified, particularly with the United States seeking to negotiate such agreements with developing countries in Latin America, Asia, and Africa. We provide a particularly stark example below in relation to the North American Free Trade Agreement (NAFTA). Multilateral tariffs must come down if this policy-induced advantage is to be leveled, and India therefore has a strong interest in seeking to reduce tariffs on all industrial products including textiles and clothing.

A future area of concern for multilateral traders is the proliferation of mutual recognition agreements whereby countries choose to accept the standards of some but not all partner countries. These agreements are conceptually analogous to preferential trading arrangements with all the possible adverse impacts on those countries that are excluded from these agreements. Strengthening the provisions in goods and services on preferential trading arrangements is overdue.

Negotiating Pessimism

It is easy to be critical of the old obstructionist approach of developing countries that was founded on a belief in self-sufficiency and inward-looking policies. But a more complex question facing developing countries now is whether the liberal policies being pursued at home need to be multilateralized. Naysayers highlight the continuing asymmetry of bargaining power, which affects agenda setting and rule making, and they conclude a kind of negotiating pessimism. They accept that domestic liberalization could be used as negotiating coinage to obtain market access abroad. But they conclude that items of interest to India, such as improved market access for its services exports through movement of individuals as well as for textiles and clothing, will not be seriously addressed by trading partners. On the other hand, the agenda will be dominated by the interests of the economically powerful countries, ranging from TRIPS in the past, to labor and environmental standards, competition and investment policy, and government procurement in the future.

To some extent, this reluctance to engage more proactively is based on a certain justified diffidence to which the TRIPS experience has contributed. This fear, which can be dubbed the thin-end-of-the-wedge syndrome, attaches a certain cost to engagement and emanates from one particular view of the negotiating process. That is, when developing countries accede to the demand to *discuss* any of these issues there will be an irresistible tide that a country will not be able to control and that will inexorably lead to an outcome inimical to its interests. In such an environment, it is argued, it is simply not attractive to engage in bargaining.

With regard to negotiating pessimism, we would make several observations. First, India's negative approach to the introduction of new issues in the negotiating agenda needs to be reconsidered. It is essential to distinguish between issues in which the negotiating outcome will inevitably be inimical to India's interests and those in which even the worst-case scenario does not imply unfavorable consequences. It was right to resist insidious protectionism in the form of higher labor and environmental standards or rent transfer mechanisms such as the TRIPS agreement. But, as we argue below, it is difficult to justify the objection to the introduction of competition policy and disciplines on government procurement, unless we accept that complete national sovereignty is to be valued above improved policy at home and improved access to foreign markets.

Second, the prospects for significant gains in market access are not as bleak as they have been hitherto. Whereas the meeting in Seattle could have confirmed fears about negotiating pessimism, the launch of the Doha Round has lifted some of this pessimism. Labor standards have been successfully kept out of the negotiations. The declaration on environmental issues is, from the perspective of a developing country, fairly narrow. There is a commitment on the part of industrial countries to contemplate market opening in agriculture. Recently the United States proposed the complete elimination of tariffs on industrial products. There is a political reaffirmation that TRIPS should not impede access to essential medicines. Significantly, there is increasing recognition of the commonality of interests among industrial countries facing demographic challenges in the form of aging populations and rising dependency ratios, and developing countries in relation to the temporary movement of labor. And although a range of new issues—competition, investment, and government procurement—have been put on the negotiating agenda, we argue that these are not obviously issues that India should be defensive about. Of course there have been some disappointments—namely, the lack of commitment by industrial countries to consider or commit to faster and deeper liberalization in the textiles and clothing sectors. But, on balance, the Doha Ministerial Conference marks a notable change in the negotiating environment.

Negotiating pessimism is therefore an empirical proposition that needs to be tested seriously. India has never really done so because of its own unwillingness to make concessions and open its markets. And, internationally, India has aligned itself consistently with countries that have argued for closed rather than open policies. The way to test negotiating pessimism and even ameliorate it is for India to align itself with coalitions that form on a shared premise of liberal policies. Coalitions need not be fixed but could vary, depending on the issue. For example, India's natural allies should be the Cairns group in agriculture, Japan and Hong Kong (China) on antidumping, and the European Union (EU) on investment and competition policies.

Of course there is no guarantee of success in the short term. In the longer term, however, good arguments and proliberalization coalitions can be successful. Moreover, if India is identified as a strong and clear voice in favor of open competitive markets, its opposition to disguised protectionism in the form of inclusion of labor or environmental standards will be more credible. The opposition will be seen as founded on substance rather than ritual defensiveness. Under such circumstances India should now take advantage of the negotiations to try to secure the kind of outcomes outlined below on each of the issues based on a recognition of its interest in an open trading system.

Issues in Selected Sectors[7]

This section analyzes the issues that have emerged in some of the negotiating areas in the WTO.

FIGURE 13.2   Cross-Country Comparison of Average Tariff Rates

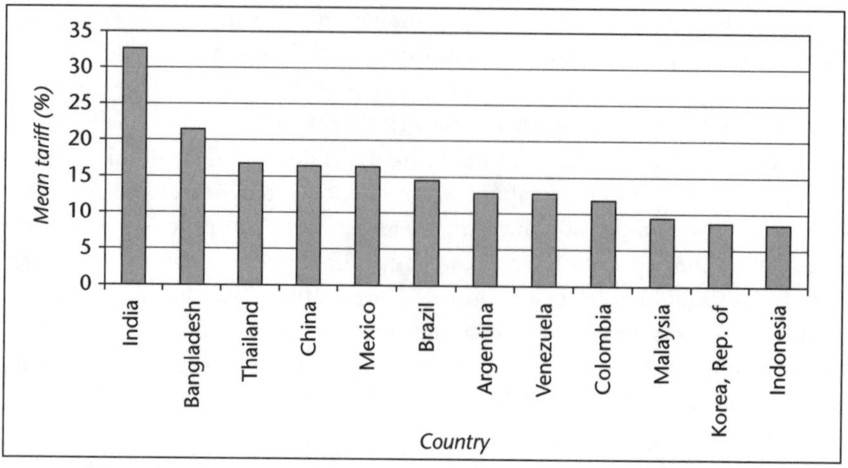

Note: Tariff data are for 2000, except for Malaysia (1997), India (1999), and the Republic of Korea (1999).

Source: World Development Indicators 2002.

Manufacturing

India has an unambiguous interest in actively seeking negotiations to bring down tariffs on industrial products.[8] The interest is fourfold. First, even following recent reform, India's tariffs today remain exceptionally high—among the highest in the world (figure 13.2).[9] Further liberalization is desirable but difficult for internal reasons, and this domestic situation could yield negotiating coinage in the Doha Round.

Second, even if the pace of further liberalization is divorced from external bargaining imperatives, India has a strong interest in reducing the level of tariffs that it bound in the Uruguay Round. The wedge between the applied and bound tariffs remains high and creates uncertainty and lack of predictabilty about trade policy (table 13.2). According to a 1999 survey, domestic investors appear not to have confidence in the stability of government policies (table 13.3). Bringing bound levels closer to current and future applied levels can engender confidence in the predictability of policies. For example, tariff policy increases—the special additional duty of 4 percentage points imposed in 1998/99[10] and the surcharge equivalent to 10 percent of the basic customs duty levied in 1999/00—illustrate the costs of not having tighter external discipline on trade policies. Had such discipline existed in the form of bindings that "bit," the government would have been

TABLE 13.2 Bound Tariff Rates and Effective Rates of Duty

	Effective Rate of Duty[a] 1993/94	Effective Rate of Duty[b] 1997/98	Effective Rate of Duty 2001/02	Bound Rate of Duty[c] by Year 2005
Average unweighted tariff (percent)				
Agriculture	43	26 (16)	33	94 (33)
Mining	70	25 (13)	22	36 (9)
Manufacturing	73	36 (10)	33	52 (41)
Whole economy	71	35 (15)	32	54 (42)
Average unweighted tariff by stage of processing (percent)				
Unprocessed	50	25 (16)	29	74 (40)
Semiprocessed	75	35 (9)	32	44 (23)
Processed	73	37 (17)	33	56 (51)

a. Following the reform package contained in the 1993/94 budget. The auxiliary duty was merged with the basic customs duty in the 1993/94 budget.

b. Effective MFN rate (i.e., actual rates applied where basic rates have been reduced by exempt rates). However, many exempt rates cannot be incorporated, such as where the exempt rate applies to only a part of the Harmonized Commodity Description and Coding System six-digit tariff line. The effective rate also excludes specific exemptions.

c. Included only items bound during the Uruguay Round. The bound rates do not include the commitments under the Information Technology Agreement.

Note: Standard deviation is provided in parentheses. Tariff averages consider only those tariff lines with ad valorem rates (year beginning April 1).

Sources: UNCTAD, World Bank, Government of India, and selected WTO Secretariat estimates.

forced to raise revenues through alternative, trade-neutral, and hence less costly measures.

Third, reductions in tariffs by partner countries will have important market-access effects for India. Further reductions, particularly in tariffs on textiles and clothing, are likely to improve India's terms of trade and to yield sizable welfare benefits. One particularly important aspect of these market access effects—and perhaps the most compelling reason for seeking cuts in tariffs in the textiles, clothing, and leather sectors—relates to *trade diversion*. In the current environment such reductions are necessary to arrest the trade diversion that MFN traders such as India have suffered as a result of regional agreements. We present one example—in relation to NAFTA in figure 13.3—that brings this impact home starkly. It is likely that there are similar effects in the EU market stemming from preferential arrangements between the EU on the one hand and Eastern European and Mediterranean countries on the other.

**TABLE 13.3   Predictability, Responses, and Availability
of Rules and Regulations**
(Percentage of respondent ratings under different categories)

	Strongly Agree	Agree	Slightly Agree	Slightly Disagree	Disagree	Strongly Disagree	Average Score 1999
Score	6	5	4	3	2	1	
Predictability of government rules and regulations	2	7	46	29	12	4	3.46
Predictability of policy changes in the annual central budget	2	3	45	33	9	8	3.32
Advance information to firms about the changes affecting them	0	18	11	35	25	11	3.00

Source: CII survey of 210 private sector firms (World Bank 2000).

Figure 13.3 shows the evolution in India's and Mexico's exports to the United States before and after NAFTA. Between 1994 and 2001, Mexico's manufacturing exports to the United States and Canada grew by about US$70 billion, whereas India registered an increase of US$5 billion. In clothing, where India is ensured a certain absolute quantitative outcome by virtue of the Multifibre Arrangement (MFA) quotas, India's share of total U.S. and Canadian imports declined after NAFTA: between 1994 and 2001, India's share declined by 0.5 percentage points, from 3.9 to 3.4 percent. Over the same period Mexico's share rose from 4.7 percent to 11.0 percent, an increase of more than 6.0 percentage points, translating into US$7 billion of *additional* exports. In the case of clothing, NAFTA opened up a preference margin for Mexico equal to the implicit tariff on India's export quotas. Even after the abolition of the MFA, when the implicit tariff comes down, the margin of preference will decline but will remain substantial—between 15 and 40 percent, depending on the product line. MFN tariffs must come down if this policy-induced advantage is to be leveled. India therefore has a strong interest in seeking to reduce tariffs on all industrial products, especially textiles and clothing.

Can these trade diversion costs be offset through alternative means (e.g., by disciplining the use of GATT Article XXIV? This is unlikely for two reasons: first, there already are too many large preferential traders who are likely to resist the

FIGURE 13.3   Exports of India and Mexico to the North American Market, 1990–2001

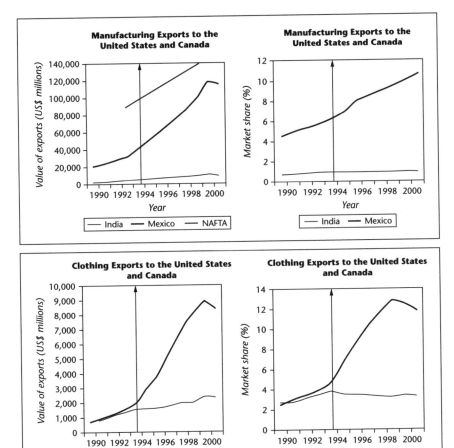

Source: United Nations Comtrade Statistics.

fundamental changes to Article XXIV that are necessary to address the trade diversion inflicted on third countries. Second, even if these changes can be effected, they will not be applied retroactively. The effects of all past regional agreements, including NAFTA and the EU-Eastern European agreements, cannot be undone through rulemaking; they will have to be addressed by eliminating the trade-diverting effects of regionalism at the source—the MFN tariff.

Agriculture

Agriculture[11] illustrates most starkly the disjunction between India's domestic policies and its external negotiating position. High tariffs for manufacturing, combined until recently with restrictions on exports of agricultural products, have led to an incentive structure that taxes rather than protects agriculture. And although manufacturing tariffs have been reduced and most export restrictions have been eliminated, manufacturing continues to be favored relative to agriculture. India's multilateral position, however, is one of defensiveness seeking the freedom to protect rather than exploiting actual and potential comparative advantage by seeking an open regime internationally.

India's average applied tariffs in agriculture are 33 percent whereas bound rates in the WTO are 94 percent, a wedge of 61 percentage points (table 13.2). In about 83 percent of agricultural tariff lines, the wedge is greater than 50 percent (table 13.4). Until the recent tariff increases, major items such as rice, wheat, pulses, and sugar were virtually fully integrated with world markets (except of course for the export quantitative restrictions) even though the bound rate was extremely high.[12] On domestic support noted in table 13.4B, the total aggregate measure of support (AMS) tends to be negative, suggesting taxation rather than protection of agriculture. On export competition, until recently Indian agricultural exporters did not receive any direct export subsidies. However, there was some support in the form of exemption of agricultural export profits from income tax and subsidies on freight and for certain floricultural and horticultural exports.

At the same time, India has significant actual and potential agricultural exports in rice, sugar, dairy products, cotton, and processed foods, and in the long run even in cereals. These exporting possibilities will be more fully realized as the discrimination against agriculture is fully eliminated.

This combination of a relatively unprotected domestic regime and potential comparative advantage means that India has a real interest in seeking to eliminate protection in international agricultural markets. India's sugar and dairy exporters have already expressed a serious interest in reducing barriers to their exports. As in manufacturing, India also suffers from the preferences granted to competing suppliers in sectors such as sugar. It therefore has a real interest in reducing agricultural tariffs as well.

And yet, India's position is defensive, continuing to focus on the freedom to safeguard food security.[13] The country should seriously consider aligning itself with the Cairns group of agricultural exporters consistent with an overall strategy of forming coalitions based on a liberalizing ideology. In this regard, many of the specific proposals presented in Gulati (1999), including the elimination of export subsidies, elimination of tariff quotas, moving from aggregate AMS to product-specific commitments, and disciplining blue box measures,[14] merit consideration.

TABLE 13.4 Indicators of Indian Agricultural Trade

A. Difference in Uruguay Round Final Bound Rates and MFN Tariff Rates, Number of Lines by Different Range Groups

Range (UR-TR)	Number of Lines[a]
UR-TR ≥ 75	401
50 ≤ UR-TR < 75	155
25 ≤ UR-TR < 50	29
10 ≤ UR-TR < 25	39
0 ≤ UR-TR < 10	41
UR-TR < 0	8
Total	673

TR = MFN tariff rate as announced in the Government of India Budget 1999/00.
UR = Uruguay Round final bound rates.

a. Tariff Lines at six-digit Harmonized Commodity Description and Coding System (HS) or subgroups of six-digit HS including only agricultural products.

B. Aggregate Measure of Support to Indian Agriculture (Selected Crops)

Year	Product Specific Support (as % of Value of Agricultural Output)	Nonproduct Specific Support (as % of Value of Agricultural Output)	Total AMS (as % of Value of Agricultural Output)
1986	−34.29	2.25	−32.04
1987	−32.08	3.2	−28.88
1988	−35.54	3.32	−32.22
1989	−36.97	3.39	−33.58
1990	−31.78	3.36	−28.42
1991	−62.23	3.6	−58.63
1992	−69.31	3.46	−65.85
1993	−54.75	3.14	−51.61
1994	−43.27	3.4	−39.87
1995	−44.09	3.9	−40.19
1996	−45.84	3.62	−42.22
1997	−32.16	4.12	−28.04
1998	−41.89	3.49	−38.4

Source: Gulati 1999.

Intellectual Property[15]

The main issues in TRIPS are using TRIPS as a device for ensuring partner country compliance; developing domestic policies and institutions to offset some of the more egregious effects of TRIPS[16] and harness the benefits of intellectual property (IP) protection in other areas; and developing mechanisms for national and international protection for IP produced in India.[17]

TRIPS as an Enforcement Device   How can the commitment by industrial countries to remove all the MFA textile quotas ("walk off the cliff") on January 1, 2005, be enforced? The answer seems to be that if the industrial countries renege on their commitment in textiles, developing countries should withdraw or threaten to withdraw their TRIPS obligations. In principle, cross-retaliation in TRIPS could be a weapon for developing countries, but the peculiarities of IP make it more difficult than in other areas.[18] In a recent proposal (Subramanian and Watal [2000] and Chapter 8 in this volume), it is argued that such cross-retaliation, if designed with care, can be feasible, effective, and probably legal.

The essence of the proposal is that India should alter its IP legislation to specify that the Indian executive retains the right to revoke some of the IP rights of foreign patent owners in the event that partner countries fail to comply with commitments that affect India's market access. Specifying that this revocation would only be pursuant to a WTO authorization to retaliate would preserve its WTO legality. Several options present themselves in terms of the form and timing of the revocation. However, one question that needs to be considered is whether current rules that allow retaliation across sectors only as a final resort circumscribe the ability of countries to use such retaliation effectively. India should be able to argue that retaliation within goods for noncompliance by partners in goods is not "practicable." Retaliation in TRIPS has the attractive property that, if implemented, it would be welfare enhancing and therefore credible and practicable. The ability to use TRIPS as a retaliation device would also address broader concerns about the asymmetry of the WTO dispute-settlement process and the lack of retaliatory power for developing countries.[19]

Developing Domestic Policies and Institutions   The two most important policy instruments available to India to mitigate some of the effects of the high levels of patent protection are compulsory licensing and competition policies. India therefore needs both to implement its new competition policy (see Chapter 9 in this volume) and to develop the capability to use compulsory licensing effectively. The flexibility afforded by compulsory licensing comes in two forms. First, countries are virtually unrestricted in the circumstances under which they can grant compulsory licenses.[20] Second, although a number of conditions need to be fulfilled when these licenses are granted, it is possible for national authorities to meet those conditions and yet dilute the monopolistic impact of the proprietary protection granted in the first place (Watal 2000).

The advantages of deploying competition policy are twofold. First, there is some latitude in determining the optimal degree of protection that balances the need to foster innovation while ensuring technological diffusion and consumer protection. For example, what constitutes abusive pricing is a question that will admit a wide variety of answers.

The second advantage follows from the language of the TRIPS agreement. There is even greater flexibility in the use of compulsory licenses—in two key respects—when they are granted to remedy anticompetitive practices,[21] which could be harnessed usefully by India.

A really crucial public policy issue that arises in relation to use of new technologies (biotechnology, including genetic modification) is how to harness their benefits while minimizing the attendant risks to consumer safety, biodiversity, health, and the environment. In India, as in other countries, opposition to the use of these technologies can be vocal and sometimes extreme. But if these concerns are to be addressed, there must be a domestic regulatory body and process that makes informed and transparent public policy choices and commands public trust. Existing institutions need to be strengthened along the lines of the Food and Drug Administration (FDA) in the United States.

Indian Intellectual Property: Genetic Resources, Indigenous Knowledge, and Geographical Indications   India and other developing countries have made sensible proposals seeking greater protection for "intellectual property" generated in these countries in the form of indigenous knowledge and geographical indications.[22] But a challenging agenda of research and policy lies ahead. How extensive are genetic resources and indigenous knowledge and to what uses can they be put? How important is the potential economic value of these resources? And, finally, how should a proprietary right be created that is enforceable internationally, and that rewards agents, including traditional communities, for preserving and creating such resources and knowledge? Similar questions arise in relation to geographical indications. How can names in the public domain be restored to proprietary protection? In these areas a credible international negotiating position can be built if such systems of protection are instituted within India and shown to be workable.

In relation to the new technologies, India's involuntary response seems to be to favor low levels of protection—for plant varieties and biotechnological inventions. But this is not a position that is based on underlying research. A case could be made that stronger proprietary protection in these areas could generate some dynamic benefits for India either in the form of research *by* Indians, *in* India, or *on* products and technologies of value to India. Some research on agriculture in India (Pray and Basant 2001, and Pray and Ramaswami 2001) suggests that these dynamic benefits could be significant. More research to underpin informed policy positions is warranted.

Antidumping

The use of antidumping (AD) actions has spread significantly from the five original industrial country users (Australia, Canada, the EU, New Zealand, and the United States) to developing countries, including India. In the period 1991–94, India initiated only 15 AD cases, compared with 226 initiated by the United States. In the period 1999–02, the number of initiations in India had increased 14-fold to 206 cases, the largest number by any country (see table 13.5).

TABLE 13.5   Antidumping Initiations by Economy Taking Action

Economy	Number of Antidumping Initiations			Index of Antidumping Initiations (1995–98) Per Dollar of Imports, USA = 100[a]
	1991–94	1995–98	1999–02	
Industrial economies				
Australia	213	77	65	1,096
Canada	84	39	68	199
European Union	135	122	134	210
United States	226	94	192	100
All industrial economies	678	353	489	74
Developing economies				
Argentina	59	72	105	2,627
Brazil	59	54	46	871
India	15	78	206	1,875
Korea, Rep. of	14	34	13	204
Mexico	127	31	30	275
South Africa	16	113	44	2,324
All developing economies	394	509	612	313

a. Based on numbers of antidumping initiations from 1995 to 1998 and values of merchandise imports for 1996. Numbers for other countries are normalized with those of the United States.

Source: WTO Secretariat, Rules Division; Anti-Dumping Measures Database.

TABLE 13.6 Antidumping Initiations by Exporting Economy

Economy	Number of Antidumping Initiations			Index of Antidumping Initiations (1995–98) Per Dollar of Exports, US = 100[a]
	1991–94	1995–98	1999–02	
Industrial economies				
France	26	8	13	34
Germany	35	30	28	70
Italy	16	16	14	77
Japan	32	23	46	67
United Kingdom	20	16	18	74
United States	70	48	42	100
Developing economies				
Brazil	50	23	38	585
China	115	94	154	751
India	24	21	43	779
Korea, Rep. of	50	40	81	385
Taiwan, China	31	30		323
Thailand	26	21	50	451

a. Numbers for other countries are normalized with those of the United States.

Source: WTO Secretariat, Rules Division; Anti-Dumping Measures Database.

Concurrently, India is a major victim of AD actions—in fact, one of the worst hit if measured in terms of AD actions per dollar of exports (table 13.6). Whereas the loss associated with the latter resonates easily with policymakers and the public, the domestic use of AD also represents a major threat.

The only justifiable use of AD—to correct predatory price behavior by foreigners—requires exporters to have market power. This is implausible in the Indian context because in a number of AD actions there were imports from 20 or more countries. In those cases where suppliers were few, discipline was present in the form of rival domestic firms (see World Bank 2000).

Given the fact that the cost of protection increases at an increasing rate, AD action by India is worse in its impact than elsewhere because it is levied on top of tariffs that are high and certainly higher than for other AD users. AD could turn out to be the nocturnal Penelope: undoing the liberalization unleashed by the tariff reductions. Furthermore, the experience in other countries has been that AD actions are typically taken against the most efficient suppliers. This in turn signals other exporters to raise prices, thereby inflicting terms-of-trade losses.

The serious costs of AD to India both as victim and as perpetrator mean that it should push strongly for the reform of AD provisions. The most intellectually coherent approach would be to fold AD into competition law provisions on predation that would provide the appropriate safeguards against protectionist use of AD. Alternatively, AD laws should be required to incorporate buyer and consumer interests and provide meaningful representation for such interests in AD proceedings. India's proposals have focused on specific provisions and have amounted to tinkering at the margin rather than eradicating the menace altogether.

Services[23]

As already mentioned, India's posture in international trade negotiations has been surprisingly defensive despite the significant autonomous reforms of recent years and the growing stake in more open markets abroad. The main reasons have been the desire to retain discretion in the design of domestic reform, and pessimism about whether multilateral trade negotiations can deliver improved access in areas of export interest. The most important initiatives undoubtedly need to be taken at the domestic level, but there remains scope for constructive use of the multilateral trading system both in realizing credible domestic liberalization and in securing market access abroad.

India's Uruguay Round (1993–94) commitments on services were conservative, reflecting not even the limited openness that prevailed then and quite far from the liberalization that has taken place in recent years. The government will need to decide whether to offer to bind the current regime and, more important, whether to liberalize further either unilaterally or as part of the Doha negotiations. The challenge is to ensure that these decisions reflect good economic policy rather than the dictates of political economy or negotiating pressure. It is useful, therefore, to recall what we have learned about services trade liberalization:

- There are substantial gains both from successful domestic liberalization, especially in key infrastructure services like telecommunications, transport, and financial services, and from improved access to foreign markets.
- Successful domestic liberalization requires:
  - Emphasis on competition more than a change of ownership
  - Credibility of policy and liberalization programs
  - Domestic regulations to remedy market failure and pursue legitimate social goals efficiently.
- Effective market access requires:
  - Elimination of explicit restrictions
  - Disciplines on implicit regulatory barriers.

Priorities for Domestic Reform   In the past, the untrammelled freedom to choose policy in services led to restrictive policy choices. In each of the three key infrastructure sectors—transport, telecommunications, and financial services—there was a reluctance to introduce meaningful competition through unimpeded entry. Limited liberalization to foreign participation was grudgingly allowed with limitations on both equity and numbers, thus perpetuating imperfectly competitive structures. There were significant policy reversals, for example, in power and telecommunications, with resultant loss to policy credibility. Moreover, the multilateral route was not used to any significant extent to liberalize or to precommit to future liberalization.

In the last few years there have seen significant changes in policy. It is fortunate that in basic telecommunications a complex policy of dividing the country into distinct duopolistic markets for fixed telephony has been abandoned. The Telecommunications Policy of 1999 announced the elimination of all restrictions on entry in the local, domestic long-distance (since August 2000), and international segments (since April 2002) (see Chapter 5 of this volume). The liberalization has resulted in a significant reduction in prices, although they are still high even compared with those of other developing countries (see figure 13.4).

FIGURE 13.4   Comparison of International Long-Distance Tariffs (Telecom) for Selected Asian Countries, 2002

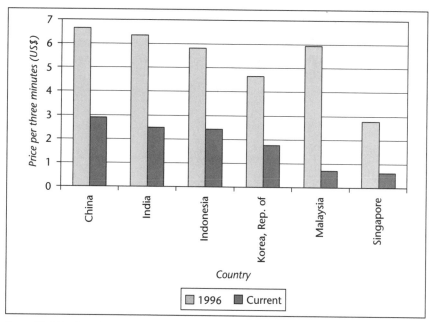

Source: World Bank Trade in Services Database.

The one remaining restriction is on foreign ownership, which is still limited in basic telecommunications to a maximum of 49 percent.

There has also been liberalization in maritime transport services. There is now no restriction on foreign investment in either shipping or ports. The pretense of adhering to the restrictive United Nations Conference on Trade and Development (UNCTAD) liner code for cargo sharing has been abandoned, even though shippers are still obliged to use domestic flagged vessels if they charge internationally competitive prices. The air transport regime for passenger transportation is, however, far less liberal than that for freight. Although there are no restrictions on foreign direct investment (FDI) in the latter segment, FDI in the former is limited to 40 percent and investment by foreign airlines is prohibited! Whereas the regime for cross-border supply of freight services is comparatively open, the passenger segment is carved up into cosy duopolistic arrangements under various bilateral air service agreements, as in most other countries. It remains to be seen whether these recent policy developments will offset the transport cost disadvantage faced by Indian exporters, for example, of textiles. As figure 13.5 shows, this disadvantage relative to competitors in Asia ranged from 30 to 40 percent.

The picture in financial services is more uneven. Recent liberalization of insurance services eliminated all restrictions on new entry but restricted foreign ownership to 26 percent. In banking, branches of foreign banks are still subject to quantitative restrictions but in the recent 2003–04 budget, the limit on foreign

FIGURE 13.5 Estimated Transport Cost Margins for Exports of Textiles to the United States, Using Singapore as a Benchmark, 2000

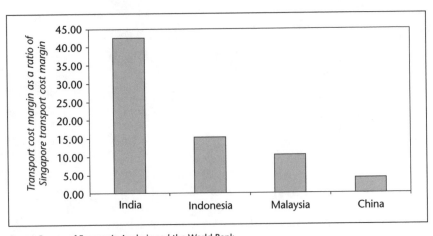

Source: Bureau of Economic Analysis and the World Bank.

ownership of domestic banks was raised from 49 percent to 74 percent. Furthermore, the voting rights restriction for any person holding shares of a banking company to a maximum of 10 percent is apparently going to be removed by a suitable amendment of the Banking Regulation Act of 1949.

In each of these key services areas, the elimination of restrictions has been accompanied by a strengthening of regulation. The Telecommunications Regulatory Authority of India, formed in 1997, today implements all the provisions of the WTO's Reference Paper on regulatory principles for telecommunications, even though India has not incorporated some in its schedule—such as the provision of interconnection under nondiscriminatory terms and conditions and the cost-based setting of rates. New regulators for ports are already in place and in a position to implement the requirements of the WTO's model schedule on nondiscriminatory access to essential port services. The Securities and Exchange Board of India already implements many of the rules on transparency proposed by the United States in the current round of services negotiations—such as consultation with stakeholders prior to the development of new regulations. The new Insurance Development and Regulatory Authority, established in 2000, is arguably in a position to do the same, as is the Reserve Bank of India, which regulates banking services.

In sum, India's domestic policy regime in services has come a long way from past protectionism.[24] Even though some restrictions persist—notably on foreign ownership in financial and telecommunications services—India is now in a position to take a far more aggressive position in services negotiations to deal with foreign barriers to its exports. Restrictions on the international movement of its service providers severely impede India's exports of services. Greater freedom of temporary movement—notionally incorporated in the WTO's services agreement but still highly restricted—would enable India and other developing countries to export not only professional services but also the labor component of construction, distribution, transport, and a range of other services.[25] That India has a strong comparative advantage in some of the highly skilled and labor-intensive sectors is beyond doubt and table 13.7 emphasizes this point in the case of software services. India also has a growing stake in cross-border exports of a variety of services, which face few restrictions today but over which hangs the Damocletian sword of regulatory impediments, like privacy legislation in the EU, and other forms of creeping protectionism, such as recent restrictions on outsourcing work on state government contracts in the United States. We consider now how India can address these impediments in the WTO context.

Securing Market Access: Natural Persons There is no doubt that the Uruguay Round outcome in services was unbalanced. The much-touted tradeoff between modes of delivery simply did not take place. Although antipathy to commitments

TABLE 13.7   Cross-Country Comparisons of Costs of Software Services

Country	Cost Per Line of Code (US$)		Average Salary of Programmer (US$)	
	Development	Support	Development	Support
Australia	n.a.	n.a.	34,940	30,644
Austria	n.a.	n.a.	33,000	33,000
Brazil	n.a.	n.a.	20,032	20,032
Canada	10	0.6	35,156	33,846
China	n.a.	n.a.	28,266	16,366
Colombia	n.a.	n.a.	n.a.	16,000
Denmark	19	1.1	n.a.	n.a.
England	11	0.7	38,785	38,179
Estonia	n.a.	n.a.	12,000	8,000
France	13	0.8	36,750	41,250
Germany	22	1.3	42,058	34,848
Greece	6	0.4	n.a.	n.a.
India	5	0.3	3,638	4,316
Ireland	10	0.6	n.a.	n.a.
Israel	11	0.6	n.a.	n.a.
Italy	10	0.6	17,655	17,655
Japan	21	1.2	n.a.	n.a.
Mexico	n.a.	n.a.	10,843	13,292
Netherlands	n.a.	n.a.	33,994	47,069
Scotland	n.a.	n.a.	24,842	n.a.
Switzerland	27	1.6	48,869	48,869
United States	18	1.1	46,550	43,395

Note: Data refer to 1996–98 averages.

Source: Adapted from Rubin (1999).

on labor mobility in partner countries was a major contributing factor, an unwillingness on the part of India to open its domestic services markets made its demands for labor mobility difficult to sustain. With India opening its markets, that bargaining dynamic can change and the prospects for serious intermodal tradeoffs—obtaining labor movement in return for allowing increased commercial presence for foreign service providers—must be greater now. Also, severe shortages of skilled labor in the United States and elsewhere and the powerful constituency of high-technology companies lobbying for relaxation of visa limits make this a propitious time to put labor mobility squarely on the negotiating agenda.[26]

India's past defensive position on services liberalization impeded the possibility of credibly advancing India's labor-related services through intermodal trade-offs. More specifically, the resistance to the use of horizontal formulas in negotiations and the insistence on a request-and-offer approach may be ill advised. Mattoo and Olarreaga (2000) have elaborated a specific proposal, based on the use of formulas, which can serve to extract meaningful commitments on the movement of individual service suppliers from trading partners.

In essence this proposal would require a country to provide increased "foreign labour content entitlements" to their domestic firms in relation to the country's increased exports of services.[27] The proposal offers several advantages. First, it is internationally symmetric. All countries would be obliged to create such entitlements, although how much they are used would be determined by sound economic considerations of modal comparative advantage. The entitlements would be international rather than bilateral. Second, the proposal is based on a balance of concessions, an appealing principle in trade negotiations. Exporters of labor services would receive benefits commensurate with efforts to open up their domestic services markets.

Electronic Commerce

WTO members have decided that electronic delivery of products will continue to be free from customs duties. For the moment this commitment is temporary and political, but there are proposals to make it durable and legally binding. Two aspects of the commitment are notable. First, only electronic transmissions are covered; goods ordered through electronic means but imported through normal channels are explicitly excluded. Second, the standstill/prohibition applies only to customs duties; there is no mention of other forms of restrictions.

It is fortunate that most electronic commerce is already free of barriers (except those created by differences in standards), and so the objective is really to bind this existing openness to preclude the introduction of new barriers. But is duty-free electronic commerce the appropriate route?

India was initially opposed to the decision on duty-free treatment for electronic commerce[28] because of concern that it would hurt tariff revenue. More recently, however, there has been a change in position. Perhaps thanks to the growing importance of software exports, India has now joined the many countries that support the existing political decision to make duty-free treatment for electronic commerce legally binding. We would argue that the initial inhibitions and the current enthusiasm are both misplaced and do not further India's real commercial interests.

The initial inhibitions were founded on fears of revenue loss. Mattoo and Schuknecht (2000) estimated the tariff revenue that countries collected from these products.[29] Even if all delivery of digitizable media products moved online—an unlikely prospect—the revenue loss would be minimal. India would lose 0.4 percent of tariff revenue and 0.1 percent of total revenue.

The current enthusiasm is equally misplaced because the value of liberating e-commerce from duties is either superfluous or virtually devoid of value. Because the bulk of such commerce concerns services, the relevant regime is that established by the General Agreement on Trade in Services (GATS) regime on cross-border trade. This agreement allows countries to decide whether to commit to market access (i.e., not to impose quotas), and to national treatment (i.e., not to discriminate in any way against foreign services and suppliers). If a country has already made such a commitment, then any further promise not to impose duties is superfluous because customs duties inherently discriminate against foreign services. If a country has not made such a commitment, then the promise not to impose customs duties is worth little, because a country remains free to impede access through discriminatory internal taxation—which has been carefully excluded from the scope of the decision. Worse, the prohibition of such duties may induce recourse to quotas, which ironically are permissible in spite of being economically inferior instruments.

Hence, the focus on duty-free treatment is misplaced. The objective for countries like India should rather be to push trading partners into making deeper and wider commitments under the GATS on cross-border trade regarding market access (which would preclude quantitative restrictions) and national treatment (which would preclude all forms of discriminatory taxation).

Table 13.8 summarizes the current state of commitments on cross-border supply in some of the areas in which developing countries have an export interest. Of the total WTO membership of more than 130, only 56 and 54 members, respectively, have made commitments in software implementation and data processing; and only about half of these commitments guarantee unrestricted market access, and a similar proportion guarantee unqualified national treatment. In all professional services there are commitments from 74 members, but less than one-fifth ensure unrestricted market access and national treatment, respectively. There clearly remains considerable scope for widening and deepening commitments.

Government Procurement

There are many good reasons to liberalize government procurement. Some benefits are analogous to those arising from the liberalization of trade, but to these must be added the budgetary benefits of efficient procurement and significant

TABLE 13.8   GATS Commitments on Modes 1 and 2 in Selected Service Sectors

Sector/Subsector	Number of Countries	Market Access Cross-Border Supply (%) Full	Part	No	National Treatment Cross-Border Supply (%) Full	Part	No
Professional services	74	19	17	64	14	10	76
Computer and related services							
Consultancy service related to the installation of computer hardware	51	57	20	24	51	22	27
Software implementation	56	54	27	20	48	29	23
Data processing	54	54	26	20	46	31	22

Note: Full = full commitment; part = partial commitment; no = no commitment.
Percentage may not add up to 100 due to rounding.
Source: Compiled by authors.

reductions in rent-seeking, which is rampant in procurement. Thus both the consumer and the taxpayer will benefit. But WTO experience shows that most industrial and developing countries are reluctant to immediately accept full liberalization of procurement.

In Chapter 10 of this volume, Srivastava estimates for India that the total value of purchases by the central and state governments and public enterprises, which in principle could be subject to international government procurement rules, varies between 3.5 and 5.9 percent of gross domestic product (GDP). For certain procurement contracts, a price preference of 15 percent is given to indigenous equipment suppliers, requiring that at least 20 percent value must be added in India. In the shipping sector, price preferences up to 30 percent apply to Indian bidders on procurement contracts. If more efficient procurement practices can be implemented domestically, Srivastava calculates that the total savings could be as much as 1.8 percent of GDP or about US$8 billion. Even if only a fraction of the estimated savings is realized, the gain could be substantial.

It is clear once again that India has exercised the freedom to choose in ways that are probably very costly for consumers and taxpayers. Even if it had chosen wisely, it is reasonable to ask whether a multilateral agreement can add to national legislation that often contains similar provisions to mitigate agency problems. One of the biggest problems in procurement is that of moral hazard on the part of the procurer. For instance, a recent survey conducted by the Confederation of

Indian Industries shows that procurement contracts frequently involve corruption. The significant benefit of a multilateral agreement is in helping to overcome national agency problems in procurement by creating mechanisms for reciprocal international monitoring supported by multilateral enforcement. It achieves this by shifting the legal scope for monitoring from dispersed taxpayers, who may have little interest in monitoring individual procurement decisions, to the bidders for contracts, who have a significant stake.

Two elements of a possible multilateral agreement are crucial in this context. First, the agency problem is mitigated by creating obligations on the procurer to be transparent. Second, foreign suppliers are given the opportunity to challenge the decisions of the procurer before national courts or independent and impartial review bodies. As a starting point, it would seem both desirable and feasible for India to be open to commitments on increased transparency and strengthened enforcement.[30] This is in fact the raison d'être of the Working Group on Transparency in Government Procurement.

In addition to improved domestic policy, government procurement offers the potential for making negotiating linkages. Foreign suppliers can only effectively contest the market for government procurement if they are not unduly handicapped by restrictive trade measures. Hence, the creation of genuine international competition for procurement contracts depends crucially on the liberalization of trade. It would, therefore, be natural for developing countries to make their willingness to accept disciplines on government procurement dependent on future negotiations on market access for goods and under the GATS on measures affecting trade in services.

For instance, one of the most important service sectors in the context of government procurement is construction. Yet in the GATS, members have usually not bound themselves to grant market access to the supply of construction services through the presence of natural persons, except for certain limited categories of intracorporate transferees. The assurance that workers can be temporarily moved to construction sites would greatly increase the benefit of nondiscriminatory government procurement for developing countries. The same applies to procurement of other services, such as software and transport.

Standards and Related Domestic Regulations

Effective market access for both goods and services requires the elimination not only of explicit restrictions, but also of implicit barriers created by standards and other domestic regulations. In goods, environmental standards (for shrimp) and safety standards (for certain types of apparel) have affected Indian exports.

In services, trade-restrictive effects have arisen from a variety of qualification and licensing requirements in professional and many other services.[31]

There are in principle three international routes to dealing with such barriers: harmonization of national regulations (leading possibly to the creation of international standards); mutual recognition; and strengthening multilateral disciplines on national standards. These routes need to be complemented by an upgrade in domestic standards.

Harmonization   In both goods and services, where countries have varying preferences for quality, including in relation to safety and the environment, harmonization is probably not desirable (see Bhagwati and Hudec 1996). In the case of services, the difficulty of harmonization is revealed by the absence of widely accepted international standards. Where such standards exist, as in banking or maritime transport, meeting them is seen as a first step toward acceptability, rather than as a sufficient condition for market access.

Mutual Recognition Agreements   India's concern about mutual recognition agreements (MRAs) is justified because the agreements are like sector-specific preferential arrangements. If regulatory barriers are prohibitively high (i.e., if you start from autarky), then recognition can only be trade creating. But if they are not, then selective recognition can have discriminatory effects and lead to trade diversion away from those who are left out of MRAs. India's attempt to address the problem by requiring that developing countries be allowed to join MRAs, however, is not tenable and ignores a basic fact: MRAs are voluntary; they cannot be *made* to happen. A multilateral agreement cannot oblige countries to conclude MRAs—just as any provision such as GATS Article V or GATT Article XXIV cannot make regional integration happen.

So what is to be done? Multilateral disciplines must be used to ensure that MRAs do not become a means of discrimination and exclusion. These disciplines operate at two levels: the general rules on preferential arrangements (GATT Article XXIV for goods and GATS Article V) and the specific rules for MRAs (in the Agreement on Technical Barriers to Trade for goods and GATS Article VII). Both sets of rules need to be strengthened and enforced. It would seem that Article XXIV, which disallows discrimination between countries in regard to domestic measures (including standards and regulation), would not allow MRAs to be justified as elements of integration agreements. However, the Agreement on Technical Barriers to Trade, which encourages the conclusion of MRAs, should not be interpreted as permitting discrimination through MRAs. A clarification of this point is essential.

In services, Article V on integration agreements does not explicitly preclude MRAs, and several countries have chosen to publicize their MRAs under this provision. However, GATS Article VII, dealing specifically with recognition, strikes a delicate balance by allowing such agreements, provided they are not used as a means of discrimination and third countries have the opportunity to accede or demonstrate equivalence. It should be clarified that this provision, with its desirable nondiscriminatory and open-ended nature, overrides GATS Article V as far as MRAs are concerned.

Multilateral Disciplines Based on the "Necessity" Test   In our view, the most important strategy for addressing barriers is to strengthen multilateral disciplines on standards per se. The trade-inhibiting effect of the entire class of domestic regulations can be disciplined by complementing the national treatment obligation with a generalization of the so-called necessity test. This test essentially leaves governments free to deal with economic and social problems, provided that any measures taken are not more trade restrictive than necessary to achieve the relevant objective.

This test is already part of the Uruguay Round Agreement for goods and the recently established disciplines in the accountancy sector. It would seem desirable to use the test to create a presumption in favor of an economically efficient choice of policy in remedying market failure and in pursuing noneconomic objectives.[32] For instance, in the case of professionals like doctors, a requirement to requalify would be judged unnecessary because the basic problem—inadequate information about whether they possess the required skills—could be remedied by a less burdensome test of competence.

This test could also be applied to situations in which a country is contemplating trade-restrictive measures on the grounds that environmental or labor standards in a partner country are too low. The necessity test would not seek to deny a country's right to be concerned about environmental and labor problems in other countries, but would subject the instruments it chooses to critical scrutiny. The following questions would be posed—are trade restrictions the best instrument to address the relevant problem, and would alternatives to the trade restriction, say, compensation or international negotiation, be more efficient in attaining the country's objectives?

Upgrading of Domestic Standards   Finally, India must upgrade its standards and related institutions consistent with domestic preferences for quality. This would strengthen the case for obtaining foreign recognition and would allow foreign technical barriers to be challenged credibly. For instance, the poor standards of a few professional colleges in the country and their willingness to award certificates without adequate examinations penalize all members of the profession seeking to work abroad by legitimizing the imposition of elaborate requalification requirements.

Competition Policy

Following decades-long reliance on the Monopolies and Restrictive Trade Practices Act, India recently enacted a new competition law (see Bhattarchjea, Chapter 9 in this volume). This law could be used to further efficiency and welfare in a number of areas. For example, competition policy, coupled with compulsory licensing, offers one avenue for mitigating some of the most egregious effects of the TRIPS agreement. Competition policy would also need to address the concentration of production in several sectors sometimes associated with the entry of foreign investors. Domestically, the challenge for India will be to build the institutional capacity to implement the complex provisions of the law. Furthermore, there is always a large and irreducible discretionary component in competition law, which needs to be exercised in a manner that promotes efficiency rather than arbitrariness and the favoring of vested interests.

In the light of these developments, should India embrace efforts to have multilateral disciplines on competition policies? A negative response could be based on the fear that multilateral disciplines will constrain the implementation of India's own competition policy or on the view that multilateralism can add little to national efforts. On the first point, it should be noted that any future rules are likely to be very general and probably not very ambitious. Competition policy standards, practices, and institutions are divergent enough between industrial countries to militate against very detailed and specific multilateral rulemaking.

On the second point, there are a number of cases where multilateral engagement on competition policy can bring about outcomes that could benefit India. Reform of antidumping to bring it within the fold of competition policy is one case in point, but the prospects of this happening in the near future are dim, given the opposition of the United States and the EU. The most coherent multilateral case for a competition policy rests on the possibility of negative spillovers across markets that need cooperation to ensure an outcome that maximizes global welfare. Several examples of potential interest to India can be found. In the shipping market, international cartelization may be inflicting terms-of-trade losses on India. Excessively high levels of intellectual property protection can inhibit the transfer of technology. Foreign export cartels may charge excessively high prices. In all of these cases, although domestic competition policy could attempt to redress the anticompetitive impact, redress may be relatively ineffective because of jurisdictional problems or because remedial measures (e.g., refusing domestic market access to foreign owners of intellectual property rights or foreign suppliers of essential products access) may not be credible. Enforcement can be more effective when taken at the source, involving the cooperation of partner countries.

On balance it would seem that the most substantial gains for India would arise from effectively implementing its own competition policy. Multilateral rules on competition policy are likely to provide net benefits. Even though these benefits may not be large, because the prospects of addressing the proliferation of antidumping are slim, India may wish to consider adopting a cautiously open position toward multilateral rules on competition policy.

Investment

The strongest analytical case for multilateral rules on FDI stems from the proliferation of investment incentives that creates policy-induced distortions in FDI flows without augmenting their aggregate size. In view of the superior ability of richer countries to grant such incentives, multilateral rulemaking on investment could be unambiguously beneficial for developing countries such as India. Given the widespread use of these incentives by industrial countries (not just at federal but also at subfederal levels), the prospects for disciplining them are likely to be slim.

Thus if multilateral discipline on investment incentives is ruled out, can a case still be made for a multilateral agreement on investment? It generally would be acknowledged that clear benefits derive from a liberal domestic regime for FDI. In the case of India, despite considerable and ongoing liberalization, FDI continues to be regulated in an ad hoc manner, thus imposing serious costs (see Das, Chapter 7 in this volume). The issue is whether multilateral rules on investment are necessary and desirable or whether FDI regimes should be determined unilaterally. Even strong advocates for multilateral disciplines on tariffs tend to be less enthusiastic about such disciplines on FDI.

It is puzzling why the case for multilateral rules on FDI is different from that for conventional trade policy or for trade in services that, after all, involves opening domestic markets to FDI. Theoretically, should countries have greater flexibility in designing an FDI regime for cars and electronics than for banks and telecommunications? If anything, the need for regulation, which is so intrinsic to services and which qualifies to some extent the nature and pace of opening up to FDI, is not as strong in the case of FDI in goods.

The arguments in favor of multilateral engagement made above—facilitating domestic reform and providing a means of precommitment to good domestic policies—seem to be no less relevant to FDI in goods than to conventional trade policy. Moreover, under the new competition policy India, like all other countries, can prevent the acquisition and abuse of market power by, and regulate other anticompetitive practices of, foreign (and domestic) firms. The interesting questions then are whether there is need for additional discretion to regulate FDI and whether this will be unduly circumscribed by multilateral rules. One example would seem to be measures designed to ensure the transfer of technology and the training of local workers.[33] There is undoubtedly a need for more research on whether other safeguards should be built into an investment agreement to preserve the freedom to pursue national objectives. But again blanket opposition to any investment agreement is not easy to comprehend.

Concrete Proposals

We now present a set of concrete proposals that India could consider in the ongoing Doha trade negotiations. These are summarized in table 13.9.

- *Industrial tariffs:* It is in India's interest to reduce its bound and actual tariffs and to seek to reduce tariffs in industrial countries, especially in textiles, clothing, and footwear. The latter is particularly urgent in view of the large trade-diversion costs imposed on India consequent to preferential arrangements such as NAFTA. Reforms to Article XXIV, even if feasible, will not compensate for the trade diversion from existing preferential agreements.
- *Agricultural reform:* Given India's actual and potential comparative advantage in agriculture, and the policy regime, which for the most part taxes rather than protects the sector, there is good reason for a change in India's negotiating position. Defensiveness could cede to active advocacy of global free trade in agriculture. India could even consider joining the Cairns group in supporting full liberalization of international agricultural markets.
- *Services:* Although the most serious challenges are domestic (enhancing domestic competition and improving the regulatory framework), India should be open to multilateral disciplines on services liberalization. This openness could serve as the basis for creating credible negotiating linkages through a formula approach, trading domestic liberalization for increased mobility of individual service providers. At the same time, India should press for strengthened multilateral disciplines on domestic regulations under the GATS to address implicit barriers posed by technical regulations, qualification, and licensing requirements.
- *Electronic commerce:* While supporting the current limited initiatives to liberalize ecommerce, India should push actively for commitments under the GATS on cross-border services trade to secure market access (by prohibiting quantitative restrictions) and to preclude all forms of discrimination (by guaranteeing

TABLE 13.9   Current and Recommended Negotiating and Domestic Policy Positions for India

Issue	Current position	Recommended Strategy
Industrial tariffs	Reluctant but willing to accept negotiations	Reduce own bound and actual tariffs and seek to reduce tariffs in other countries, especially in textiles, clothing, and footwear.
Agriculture	Seeking the flexibility to protect domestic agriculture while pushing for liberalization abroad	End policies that discriminate against agriculture. Push for liberalization on a global basis and consider joining Cairns group.
Services	Defensive position in relation to opening domestic services markets, while pushing for increased mobility for individual service suppliers	Further domestic liberalization, emphasizing competition more than a change of ownership, and greater use of GATS to precommit to future liberalization. Create intermodal negotiating linkages to enhance access for individual service suppliers. Strengthen domestic regulations and push for stronger multilateral disciplines on regulatory barriers to trade.
Electronic commerce	Initially opposed but now willing to support decision not to impose customs duties	Current decision has little meaning because quotas and discriminatory internal taxation are still permitted in many cases. Therefore, widen and deepen scope of cross-border supply commitments under GATS on market access (prohibiting quotas) and national treatment (prohibiting discriminatory taxation) to ensure current openness continues in areas of export interest such as software and database services.
TRIPS	Seeking general provisions on transfer of technology and increased protection for traditional knowledge and bioresources	Change IP legislation to ensure that TRIPS benefits can be withdrawn in the event of noncompliance by partners with commitments that affect India's exports. Institute workable systems for protecting traditional knowledge domestically to seek their replication internationally. Use new competition policy and judicious use of compulsory licensing to mitigate the egregious effects of the TRIPS agreement.
Preferential agreements	In favor of strengthening rules	Argue for inclusion of compensation provision for third countries adversely affected by trade diversion.

TABLE 13.9 *(Continued)*

Issue	Current position	Recommended Strategy
Competition policy	Opposed	Strengthen implementation of new competition law and be open to the development of meaningful multilateral disciplines, which ideally would also cover antidumping.
Standards	Pushing for inclusion in MRAs Opposed to labor standards	Strengthen disciplines on MRAs to ensure that they are nondiscriminatory. Push for multilateral disciplines on domestic regulations in goods and services based on the necessity test. Improve domestic standards. On labor standards, be proactive in the ILO while resisting attempts to bring the issue into the WTO.
Government procurement	Opposed	Be open to creation of multilateral disciplines, but link them to the elimination of barriers to trade in goods and services so that foreign procurement contracts can be contested in areas of comparative advantage, such as labor services.
Investment	Opposed	Be willing to discuss multilateral disciplines, but examine case for preserving discretion beyond that provided by strengthened competition policy.
Antidumping	Seeking to limit scope for foreign action	Curtail domestic use of antidumping. Argue for drastic reform of multilateral antidumping rules to eliminate current protectionist use, ideally by subjecting them to competition policy.

national treatment). Again, India should support strengthened disciplines on regulatory barriers to services trade.

- *TRIPS:* India should change its intellectual property legislation to ensure that TRIPS benefits can be withdrawn in the event of noncompliance by partners with commitments that affect India's exports. Simultaneously, it should seek to clarify WTO dispute-settlement procedures to prevent the within-sector retaliation rule from becoming an obstacle to such action. Domestically it should institute workable systems for protecting intellectual property in order credibly to seek their replication internationally. The new competition policy, combined with judicious use of compulsory licensing, can help mitigate the most egregious effects of the TRIPS agreement.

- *Preferential agreements:* The real problem with GATT Article XXIV and GATS Article V is the lack of compensation for third parties adversely affected by trade diversion. Such compensation should be incorporated into the rules. Furthermore, there should be a clear reaffirmation that MRAs cannot be used as a means of discrimination.
- *Competition policy:* India should ensure effective implementation of its new competition law and be open to discussing multilateral disciplines on competition policy. These disciplines should include outlawing practices that involve negative international spillovers, such as export cartels (as in shipping), and bringing antidumping within the ambit of competition policy.
- *Standards:* India should ensure that MRAs are not used as a means of discrimination. To this end, the Agreement on Technical Barriers to Trade would need to be clarified, as would the relationship between GATS Articles V and VII to establish the primacy of the latter. At the same time, it should push for multilateral disciplines on domestic regulations in goods and services based on the necessity test. On labor standards, India should be proactive in the International Labour Organisation (ILO) to ensure universal adherence to the basic ILO conventions while resisting attempts to bring the issue into the WTO.
- *Government procurement:* Given the potential gains from more efficient and transparent government procurement, India should be willing to undertake multilateral disciplines on government procurement. At the same time it should seek to create natural linkages with the elimination of barriers to trade in goods and services so that it can meaningfully contest foreign procurement contracts in areas of its comparative advantage, such as labor services.
- *Investment:* Liberalization of India's FDI regulations will continue to yield substantial benefits. The new domestic competition law can regulate anticompetitive behavior of foreign (and domestic) firms. Subject to preserving the discretion necessary to regulate FDI consistent with desirable domestic objectives (e.g., facilitating transfer of technology), India could be open to considering multilateral rules on investment.

Conclusion

Trade can be an engine for growth. In the past this engine has sputtered, owing to India's policies rather than its geography. The challenges ahead for India now lie in implementing sound domestic policies that increase competition in, and improve the contestability of, domestic markets. These challenges are, above all, domestic.

However, active multilateral engagement can be incrementally helpful in facilitating domestic reform and gaining access for India's exports of goods and labor services.

The value of such engagement might be limited if prospects for securing increased market access seem dim. Such negotiating pessimism is not without basis, but the launch of a new round of negotiations at Doha marks an improvement over the fiasco at Seattle. In any case, this pessimism needs to be credibly tested by a willingness on India's part to open its markets in return for improved access. Success in this regard is not ensured, but its chances can be improved if India aligns itself with countries that coalesce on a shared premise of sound open policies. Liberalization-based coalitions (which can differ across issues) can be an effective force for reform internationally with beneficial internal consequences. The success of developing countries such as India in resisting demands for the inclusion of backdoor protectionism at the Seattle and Doha Ministerial Conferences is testimony to this possibility. In the long run, the power of good arguments buttressed by India's growing economic weight should not be underestimated.

Endnotes

1. The other prong was to seek preferential access for one's own exports in industrial country markets.
2. Of course this suited the protectionist interests in industrial countries because it allowed them to procrastinate on liberalizing the two sectors in which developing countries had intrinsic comparative advantage—agriculture and textiles.
3. This is an oversimplification because in some sectors, such as textiles and clothing, arguably there will be increased access.
4. The Indian experience with TRIPS illustrates this point. The fact of the considerable domestic opposition to higher patent protection prompted trading partners to realize that without offsetting compensation it would be extremely difficult for India to accede to their TRIPS demands.
5. There are several other examples of benefits from binding international rules. For instance, WTO rulings will lead to the elimination of quotas that India has long and inappropriately maintained for balance-of-payments reasons. Even though India's commitments to phase out local content requirements under the TRIMs agreement have not prevented the recent re-imposition of such requirements in the automobile sector, they could be challenged by partner countries.
6. The recent initiatives in the South Asian region are an exception to India's general preference for multilateralism.
7. Some of the information in the following subsections is drawn from WTO (1993, 1999).
8. See Hertel and Martin (2001) and Chapter 2 of this volume for a quantification of the benefits accruing from further global liberalization of manufacturing tariffs.
9. In the 2003/04 budget, the unweighted average customs duty declined to 26.8 percent. Allowing for the approximate average incidence of the special additional duty, the average unweighted protective rate is now about 32.7 percent.
10. Although this measure was intended to rectify negative protection by imposing a tax on imported goods whose domestic counterparts already faced a 4 percent sales duty, the manner in which the tax was levied afforded some extra protection to domestically produced goods.
11. This section draws heavily on Gulati (1999).
12. However, state-trading enterprises continue to influence trade in agricultural products.

13. As Gulati (1999) argued, food security concerns can be adequately addressed through policies other than domestic trade protection.

14. Direct payments under production-limiting programs are provided in accordance with the provisions of Article 6.5 of the Agreement on Agriculture.

15. This section draws heavily on Subramanian (1999) and Chapter 8 of this volume.

16. The Uruguay Round TRIPS agreement did impose costs on India, particularly in the pharmaceutical sector (see Subramanian 1995), which are likely to be felt in the early part of the 21st century.

17. There are a number of issues that have generated well-entrenched and occasionally extreme positions, such as compulsory licensing for nonworking, parallel imports, transfer of technology, and restrictive business practices. These issues, however, are either not seriously important or are misguided (see Subramanian [1999] for a fuller discussion). They should be spared negotiating effort and time.

18. To see why, it is important to recall that IPRs are private rights conferred through domestic legislation. Whereas it is easy to raise tariffs in retaliation, to withdraw private rights granted through domestic legislation would be very difficult, perhaps even unconstitutional in many legal systems. Furthermore, withdrawing rights would be of little value unless alternative sources of production for the patented product can be found.

19. It is notable that Ecuador has taken similar steps in retaliating against the European Union for its failure to remedy the WTO inconsistencies in its banana import regime.

20. The only grounds on which compulsory licenses cannot be granted is nonworking of the patent locally.

21. When compulsory licenses are used to remedy anticompetitive practices, the TRIPS agreement provides that (a) no case needs to be made that the patentee was unwilling to license the patent on reasonable commercial terms as a precondition for granting the compulsory license; and (b) the principle that remuneration for the compulsory license should be "adequate" need not be respected.

22. On geographical indications, it might be sensible for India to form an alliance with the EU, which is a major demandeur in this area.

23. Services trade will refer in our discussion not only to cross-border delivery, as in the case of goods, but also to supply through the establishment of firms and the movement of individuals.

24. There remains a need to improve policies to help poor people obtain access to essential services in liberalized markets. India has taken important steps in telecommunications, but much more needs to be done in other sectors like education, health, and transport. Such action is not only socially desirable but also necessary to make liberalization politically feasible.

25. Such temporary movement offers arguably the neatest solution to the dilemma of how best to manage international migration, enabling gains to be realized from trade while averting social and political costs in host countries and brain drain from poor countries. Recent research finds that if OECD countries were to allow temporary access to foreign service providers equal to just 3 percent of their labor force, the global gains would be over US$150 billion—more than the gains from the complete liberalization of all trade in goods.

26. The notions of the United States as the unrivaled center of technology and the role of technological progress in motoring the 1990s U.S. economic expansion resonate very deeply with the U.S. public. They may be loathe to countenance any obstacles to this march of progress, even if it involves greater imports of labor-related services.

27. In a way Bill Gates' recent testimony before the U.S. Congress arguing for the need to allow more software engineers to enter the country so as to maintain international competitiveness is not far removed from the suggested scheme.

28. In principle all types of products can be advertised and purchased over electronic networks. But the scope of the WTO decision not to impose duties is more limited. It requires that a final product be presented as digitalized information and transmitted electronically, typically over the Internet. The bulk of the products that can be supplied in this manner are services, financial, legal, customized software, and so forth. Some information and entertainment products typically characterized as

goods, such as books, standardized software, music, and videos, embody digitalized information that also can be supplied electronically over the Internet.

29. Services are not subject to customs duties as far as we know. So we need concern ourselves only with the fiscal implications if international trade in digitizable products currently classified as goods shifts to the Internet, and if no tariffs are levied on such products. The estimates are reasonably reliable for the most important categories where trade and tariff data were available for the most important countries. A few data problems persist as volume data for some products facing specific tariffs were not available, sometimes the tariff rate was not provided, and applied tariff rates for some of the smaller countries were not available.

30. It also has been suggested that countries could continue to maintain preference margins, but agree to bind them and make them subject to unilateral or negotiated reductions in a manner analogous to tariffs.

31. The requirement of registration with, or membership in, professional organizations can also constitute an obstacle for a person wishing to provide the service on a temporary basis. For instance, in the United States requirements to practice medicine for foreign-qualified doctors vary from state to state. Candidates also must pass the qualifying examination of the Educational Commission for Foreign Medical Graduates, and then undergo a period of graduate medical education at a hospital in the United States.

32. This argument is developed in Mattoo and Subramanian (1998).

33. It is relevant that India has reserved the right to impose these requirements on foreign investment under the GATS, on which any investment agreement is likely to be modeled.

References

The word "processed" describes informally produced works that may not be available commonly through libraries.

Bhagwati, J., and Robert Hudec, eds. 1996. *Fair Trade and Harmonization: Prerequisites for Free Trade?* Cambridge, Mass.: MIT Press.

Gulati, Ashok. 1999. "Agriculture and the New Trade Agenda in the WTO 2000 Negotiations: Interests and Options for India." Delhi: Institute for Economic Growth. Processed.

Hertel, T. W., and W. Martin. 2001. "Liberalizing Agriculture and Manufactures in a Millenium Round: Implications for Developing Countries." In Bernard Hoekman and W. Martin, eds., *Developing Countries and the WTO*. Oxford, U.K.: Blackwell.

Mattoo, Aaditya, and M. Olarreaga. 2000. "Liberalizing Mode 4 under the GATS: A Proposed Solution." Policy Research Working Paper 2373. World Bank, Policy Research Department, Washington, D.C.

Mattoo, Aaditya, and L. Schuknecht. 2000. "Trade Policies for Electronic Commerce." Policy Research Working Paper 2380. World Bank, Policy Research Department, Washington, D.C.

Mattoo, Aaditya, and A. Subramanian. 1998. "Regulatory Autonomy and Multilateral Disciplines: The Dilemma and a Possible Resolution." *Journal of International Economic Law* 1: 303–22.

Pray, C. E., and R. Basant. 2001. "Agricultural Research and Technology Transfer by the Private Sector in India." Indian Institute of Management Working Paper 99-06-03. June. Ahmedabad, India. Processed.

Pray, C. E., and B. Ramaswami. 2001. "Technology, IPRs and Reform Options: Case Study of the Seed Industry with Implications for Other Input Industries." Paper presented at the NCAER-IE6. Processed.

Rubin, Howard. 1999. "Global Software Economics." New York: Hunter College, Department of Computer Science, and Rubin Systems Inc.

Subramanian, Arvind. 1995. "The Impact of TRIPS on Asian Developing Countries: An Analytic View." In Arvind Panagariya, ed., *The Uruguay Round and Asian Developing Countries*. Cambridge, U.K.: Cambridge University Press.

————. 1999. "TRIPS and Developing Countries: The Seattle Round and Beyond." Paper presented at the Conference on Developing Countries and the New Multilateral Round of Trade Negotiations, November 5–6, Harvard University.

Subramanian, Arvind, and Jayshree Watal. 2000. "TRIPS as an Enforcement Device in the WTO for Developing Countries." *Journal of International Economic Law* 3(3): 403–16.

Watal, Jayshree. 2000. *Intellectual Property Rights in the World Trade Organization: The Way Forward for Developing Countries.* Oxford, U.K.: Oxford University Press.

World Bank. 2000. *Policies to Reduce Poverty and Accelerate Sustainable Development,* Report 19471-IN. Washington, D.C.

WTO (World Trade Organization). 1993. *Trade Policy Review of India 1993.* Geneva.

————. 1999. *Trade Policy Review of India 1999.* Geneva.

CONTRIBUTORS

Pradeep Agrawal is professor of economics and holds the Reserve Bank of India Chair Unit at the Institute of Economic Growth in New Delhi.

Anjali Bhardwaj is a senior program officer with Winrock International in New Delhi.

Aditya Bhattacharjea teaches industrial organization and international economics at the Delhi School of Economics, University of Delhi.

Drusilla K. Brown is associate professor of economics at Tufts University, Medford, Massachusetts.

Rajesh Chadha is reader (associate professor) in the department of economics, Hindu College, University of Delhi, and honorary adviser (chief economist) at the National Council of Applied Economic Research, New Delhi.

Satya P. Das is professor of economics, Indian Statistical Institute.

Alan V. Deardorff is John W. Sweetland professor of international economics and professor of economics and public policy at the University of Michigan.

Veena Jha is the project coordinator for UNCTAD in New Delhi, affiliated with the International Trade Division of UNCTAD in Geneva.

Rajat Kathuria is professor of economics at the International Management Institute, New Delhi, and a consultant with the Telecom Regulatory Authority of India.

Sanjay Kathuria is currently a senior economist in the Caribbean Country Management Unit of the World Bank in Washington, D.C.

Will J. Martin is a lead economist in the Development Research Group of the World Bank in Washington, D.C.

Aaditya Mattoo is lead economist in the Development Research Group of the World Bank in Washington, D.C.

Mohammed Saqib is a fellow with the Rajiv Gandhi Institute for Contemporary Studies, Rajiv Gandhi Foundation, New Delhi.

Harsha Vardhana Singh is secretary and principal adviser for the Telecom Regulatory Authority of India.

Anita Soni is head of the treasury management and budget division of Bharat Sanchar Nigam Limited, New Delhi.

Vivek Srivastava heads the India Country Team of the World Bank's Water and Sanitation Program-South Asia, Washington, D.C.

Robert M. Stern is professor of economics and public policy (emeritus) at the University of Michigan, Ann Arbor.

Arvind Subramanian is an advisor in the Research Department of the International Monetary Fund in Washington, D.C.

INDEX

Note: f indicates figures, t indicates tables and n indicates notes.